United States v. Apple

United States v. Apple

COMPETITION IN AMERICA

CHRIS SAGERS

Harvard University Press

Cambridge, Massachusetts · London, England

2019

Library of Congress Cataloging-in-Publication Data

Names: Sagers, Christopher L., 1970– author.
Title: United States v. Apple : competition in America / Chris Sagers.
Description: Cambridge, Massachusetts : Harvard University Press, 2019. |
Includes bibliographical references and index.
Identifiers: LCCN 2019010761 | ISBN 9780674972216 (alk. paper)
Subjects: LCSH: Price fixing—United States. | Restraint of trade—United States. |
Antitrust law—United States. | Publishers and publishing—United States.
Classification: LCC KF1627 .S242 2019 | DDC 343.7307/25—dc23
LC record available at https://lccn.loc.gov/2019010761

Dedication

I realized on a trip home in July of 2016 that this book is for my dad. Books mattered so much to him that as a boy, he once told me, he lost some of his sight reading by kerosene lamp. It was for him in part as one more attempt to confront his lifelong pain at having had to quit his schooling at age twelve. That was a thing that happened in Iowa childhoods in those days, so that kids could start working. It's for how hard it always was to convince him that that circumstance said no more about him than outward signs say about the large number of abject morons afoot who've managed to secure elite degrees. But it is also for him because, beginning with the power it had when he first told me as a young man that he liked my writing, I keep realizing in how many different, small ways he made me who I am. In that respect he is like the clouds in Iowa. I never gave them much thought until I'd lived away for many years, despite the great and quiet size of the skies in flat lands.

Amazon was using e-book discounting to destroy bookselling. . . . The irony bites hard. . . . This would be tragic for all of us who value books, and the culture they support.

—*Scott Turow, President, Authors Guild, March 9, 2012*

[Amazon's eBook pricing policy was] impervious, of course, to the . . . overall welfare of the industries in which it [was] operating. . . . The book publishing industry was and is one of delicate balances and cross-supports. It has a cultural role in a civilised society, and a sublime one. New, potentially important and perhaps great authors need to be found. They need to be nurtured.

—*Tim Waterstone, Founder, Waterstones Booksellers, April 6, 2012*

I say to you that the VCR is to the American film producer . . . as the Boston Strangler is to the woman home alone.

—*Jack Valenti, President, Motion Picture Association of America, April 12, 1982*

[If player pianos are permitted to exist, then] a condition is almost sure to arise where all incentive to further creative work is lacking and compositions will no longer flow from [composers'] pens.

—*John Philip Sousa, 1906*

Contents

Introduction: A Case Bigger Than It Seemed   1

PART I. POLICY AS PROLOGUE

1. The Great Generalization   17

2. In the First Ships: Competition as a Concept
   and Its Special Role in American History   28

3. And Yet, Uncertainty:
   The Long Shadows of the American *Methodenstreit*   43

4. Uncertainty of Another Kind:
   Coping with Capitalism through
   Association and Self-Help   55

5. Tensions of the Latter Day and Some
   Unexpected Skepticism   63

6. Competition as a Living Policy, circa 2019   69

PART II. THE EBOOKS CASE

7. The Old Business of Books   77

8. Bookselling and the Birth of Amazon   97

9. Publishers, Booksellers, and the
   Oldest Problem in the World   105

10. Price-Fixing in Books   121

11. Content and the Digital Transition in Historical Context   128

12. The Promise and Threat of Electronic Books   140

13. How Electronic Books Came to Be,
    and What It Would Mean for the *Apple* Case   150

14. Google Books   164

15. The Kindle   171

16. The eBooks Conspiracy   180

PART III. COMPETITION AND ITS MANY REGRETS

17. The Long Agony of Antitrust   205

18. So Are Books, After All, Special? Is Anything?   213

19. The Virtues of Vertical and Entry for Its Own Sake   220

20. Amazon   228

21. The Threat to Writers and the Threat to Cultural Values   247

22. The Creeping Profusion of Externalities   253

Conclusion: Real Ironies   261

Notes   267
Acknowledgments   315
Index   319

United States v. Apple

Introduction

A Case Bigger Than It Seemed

THE DANIEL PATRICK MOYNIHAN United States Courthouse is a mostly unadorned granite tower in lower Manhattan. It is short as big-city buildings go, but it seems taller and more imposing among the low-slung judiciary buildings of Foley Square. An important federal trial unfolded within one of its ornate courtrooms during the very hot July of 2013, which brought to a head several long-simmering tensions, impacting three separate industries, and by some accounts, reshaping the future of the written word. But from outward appearances, *United States v. Apple* should have been mundane as antitrust cases go. The Department of Justice charged the Apple computer corporation and several publishing houses with fixing the prices of electronic books, or "eBooks," in violation of federal antitrust laws.[1] It was plainly enough a big case in some respects, because Apple was one of the world's largest and most admired companies, and because the figure of the company's legendary founder, recently deceased, loomed over it. Before this death, Steve Jobs had made several damaging statements that had gotten much attention in the press and would later prove important to the government's case. The publisher defendants, too, added their drama. Each of them was a subsidiary of one of the massive conglomerates that dominate the world's media, and by the time of the trial their conspiracy affected the vast majority of general-interest publishing in English. Their executives piled up a trove of exceptionally damaging, embarrassing evidence through clandestine meetings in extremely swank restaurants, frenzied, secret communications, and telling efforts to cover their own tracks.

Apple, strictly speaking, was just a price-fixing case, with straightforward facts and legal issues. Of the eight or nine hundred antitrust cases filed each year, most of them are price-fixing cases, because price-fixing is taken as an important and serious violation. It is also the simplest antitrust claim to prove. Price-fixing is subject to a special rule in antitrust called "per se liability," and it is the plaintiff's surest route to victory. These cases usually have simple facts and straightforward legal issues, and most of them look more or less like *Apple.* Even the harshest critics of the aggressive bookseller Amazon—against which the *Apple* defendants claimed they needed their conspiracy to survive—admitted that the conduct challenged in the case was in "blatant disregard" of the law.[2] As the country's foremost antitrust authority said a few days after the complaint was filed, if Apple did engage in the conduct the government alleged, "then I don't think it has a defense."[3]

And yet, in so many ways, *United States v. Apple* would prove unusual, and much more philosophically significant than its circumstances suggested. It was not because the defendants were big companies or had celebrity CEOs. It was not because the case involved new-economy technology, or because it involved a seemingly special product— books—or even because it involved a substantial, perhaps industry-shaping technological transition. Those were all significant matters in their own way, but antitrust cases often involve sectoral change and the potential for lost jobs and investments. What was remarkable about the case—remarkable enough to justify writing this book—was the public's reaction.

On Wednesday, July 10, after the close of a three-week trial, a well-regarded federal judge named Denise Cote issued her final judgment in the matter. It was surprising that the case had even made it that far—that it went through a full trial and called for Judge Cote's final judgment.

Almost all antitrust cases are dismissed or settle, even more often than other federal lawsuits. In that regard, the material nature of the Moynihan Courthouse and the many federal buildings like it—large, capacious, often lavishly appointed facilities—says something about our legal system and especially our faltering, little-used system of antitrust rules. These extravagant buildings contain hundreds of courtrooms richly appointed at taxpayers' expense, but they mostly sit empty, waiting for people to use them.[4] In the *Apple* case, all five of Apple's codefendants settled before trial. Exactly why Apple stuck it out so long will probably always remain between the company and its lawyers, but there were plenty of reasons to expect it to settle as quickly as the other defendants did.

To a degree unusual even in high-stakes federal litigation, the press and an active blogosphere hung on the trial at every step. Although Judge Cote was well known in New York legal circles, she had mostly escaped popular attention during her long career. During the *Apple* trial, she became the focus of a media debate that at times bordered on hysteria. Her personal integrity was frequently attacked, and critics occasionally went so far as to describe her as bizarre or perhaps mentally ill.

But in person, Judge Cote is like the federal building where she works. She is physically small and speaks with quiet calm, but in the surroundings of her courtroom she is a force. After her long, elaborate, and unflinching opinion became public and was affirmed, it was clear at least that she understood the law rather better than her detractors did. Most of them non-lawyers, for what that may be worth, they denied her competence and sometimes her integrity, but their confidence of their own vindication on appeal proved quite mistaken.

On that hot July morning, Judge Cote announced an unmitigated victory for the government. The outcome was anticlimactic for some, especially in the bar of specialist antitrust attorneys, since the government's case was strong. In her long, final opinion Judge Cote wrote no fewer than five separate times that the evidence against Apple was "overwhelming," and most impartial experts had agreed that if the government could prove the facts alleged then it couldn't lose. It was widely predicted that Apple would face antitrust law's harshest rule, the rule of per se illegality, and indeed, it did face that rule in Judge Cote's final analysis, so it lost. But for thousands of others, and by all appearances for Apple and its legal team, the decision was a shock, and an injustice.

Virtually no one, including those who follow antitrust and markets closely, knew much about the case until the day the government filed its complaint and it became an instant sensation. A few details had previously trickled out of the government's nonpublic investigation and from a concurrent private suit filed in August 2011, but only publishing insiders paid much attention.[5] No one was prepared for the complaint's detailed disclosures of disregard for legal rules we expect corporate executives to understand. When it was made public, its thirty-six fact-studded pages were the subject of days of breathless debate across the internet and popular media.

Something else emerged soon after the case became public, and the quiet puzzle it revealed was the inspiration for this book. It became clear that while the case seemed easy to most antitrust lawyers, much of the public found it very troubling indeed. The case was surrounded by controversy from the beginning, and the defendants found supporters across the political spectrum. The government's decision to sue was condemned by a Democratic and ordinarily pro-enforcement member of the Senate Antitrust Subcommittee, by newspapers as editorially divergent as the *New York Times* and the *Wall Street Journal*, and by scores of journalists and commentators.[6] Many on the left of American opinion saw not a selfish conspiracy against the public interest but the last stand of a crucial and embattled social institution, the last defense of the trade publishing industry against the monopolist retailer Amazon. For them, the case embodied the jeopardy that threatens those things that are good in society and culture during this new Gilded Age of rapacious capitalism. Many on the right found the case frustrating, too, but for different reasons. For them, it was a government intrusion that would wrongheadedly upend private self-ordering meant to correct problems that prevented a market from working well. In line with a surprisingly common gesture in conservative economic thinking, they thought the *Apple* agreement was needed because some flaw in the market itself would frustrate Apple's entry into eBook distribution. Society would be the loser, denied Apple's contributions to innovation and quality in the longer term.

Some strange bedfellows emerged. The true aim of the bitterest critics on the left was aggressive government intervention in the economy on stridently populist grounds. But they described the case in terms essentially identical to those of the one judge in the lawsuit who doubted the government's case—a genteel, very conservative Republican who had spent much of his career defending big corporations at one of the world's leading law firms. Many others spoke of the case in unprecedented terms. Perhaps most surprising was a certain subset of big-firm antitrust defense lawyers who in discussion panels, op-eds, and talk shows argued at length that the government case was misguided and counterproductive. Typically, these women and men are confident that virtually no conduct violates antitrust and that the size of even of the biggest firms is irrelevant. But they talked about the *Apple* case like they were Louis Brandeis. Amazon was the danger, they said, because of its size and its low prices. That *this* group would claim to fear a firm just because it was large, and especially because it *charged low prices,* was mind-boggling. Meanwhile, traditionally more hawkish antitrust watchers who had been beating the drum for more aggressive antitrust during the long season of its neglect—people like me—wound up in the awkward position of talking about the case like Robert Bork. We found ourselves arguing that Amazon had done nothing more than compete on price and quality, and that if price-competitive vigor squeezed out some publishers or booksellers, that was simply the will of the market.

On some level, the confusions and animosities that surrounded the *Apple* case reflected the presence of an elephant in the room: the online retailer Amazon. That firm and a handful of other technology titans have become elephants in many other rooms, too. Their power not only over individuals' pocketbooks but also over the fates of workers, small business, and cultural institutions has lately put them at the forefront of domestic politics, and that has helped to rekindle popular interest in antitrust. As they have grown, an improbable range of observers have come to believe that America might have a "monopoly problem" after all. For the first time in seventy years, that problem became a talking point for presidential candidates, their think-tank support staff, and briefly even the Republican presidential platform committee. It became a focus during the later days of the Obama White House, and it has played a prominent if erratic role in the Trump domestic agenda.[7] It has also played a small role in the growing American fractiousness. The frustration among some new antitrust activists that American law has proved useless against firms such as Amazon—and indeed that our government perversely sued the wrong parties in *Apple,* as if to deliberately help Amazon get even bigger—reflects in microcosm the worsening divisions in progressive politics.[8] To activists on the left, establishment Democrats' antitrust views were just as confused, coopted, or intimidated by conservative economics as the rest of American policy had been since the 1970s. Those divisions were bad enough during the poisonous presidential primaries of 2016, but since then they have only gotten worse.

Therein lies one of the most important reasons to study the *Apple* case. Much of the agitation in antitrust has dwelt in moral polemics, but in fact there are no heroes or villains in this kind of story, or there need not be. When we conceptualize stories of competition policy as morality plays we sometimes get cases seriously wrong. When we try to figure out competition problems by asking who is the bad guy, or which party is the big guy and which is the little guy, we often discover only after the passage of time that we'd diagnosed things quite incorrectly, to our lasting regret. The danger is not the risk of inadvertently chilling business conduct, a hobbyhorse of conservative antitrust that seems overstated and lacks empirical support. Rather, it is in jeopardizing the interests of those that antitrust is most meant to protect. To critics of the *Apple* case, the government perversely persecuted parties that were only trying to protect themselves from a monopoly that itself should have been the antitrust defendant. The most poignant victim was the littlest of little guys, the working author, whose livelihood would be squeezed to nothing to satisfy Amazon's greed.

While that vision played very well to the lay public and served the polemical needs of some activists, it could not have been more desperately wrong. The actual victims of Amazon's aggression were large corporations, grown massive themselves by a dormant antitrust policy that allowed them to merge and combine dozens or hundreds of times, which were working together as a well-coordinated oligopoly. Their conduct, as shown in an extensive evidentiary record, had no plausible effect other than taking a few hundred million dollars from the reading public and giving it to their shareholders. Moreover, they were hardly the guardians of high culture they were made out to be. For several decades they had focused on crass sensationalism and whatever else they could sell most profitably. Likewise, in no sense did they design their conspiracy to benefit authors. Why would they? On the contrary, making books more expensive has the same consequence as charging more for any other good that obeys the law of supply and demand: fewer books are sold, fewer new ones are signed for publication, and fewer new, unknown authors find their audiences. No oligopoly consolidates its power for the purpose of giving more money to its *suppliers*, a group with whom it is financially adversary.

There were larger reasons not to idealize the publishers or their conspiracy. In addition to raising book prices, the *Apple* conspiracy and other efforts to obstruct the digital distribution of text may have forestalled advancements of real value to society, even as the publishers persuaded the reading public that it was all done in their service. The decades-long coming of digitization made it possible that every single page of the roughly 130 million extant books, comprising some large portion of the entire store of human knowledge, might be digitized and costlessly shared anywhere in the world. The same could be done with all magazines, newspapers, journal articles, public documents, legal texts, ephemera, and so on. Moreover, every letter of it could be *searched*, by the super-computers now in our everyday grasp. By the turn of this century, that essentially magical vision was not conjectural. It was already in our hands, fully within technological feasibility, and various firms were already spending hundreds of millions of dollars on the project. It could have been (and might someday be) among the great humanitarian gains in modern history. But the legal and illegal conduct of various publishing firms and authors' groups has so far kept it out of reach, for no reason except the short-term pecuniary interest of a small number of people.

In this, the story of eBooks is in keeping with a theme in the history of technology. As much as anything, the visionaries of technological history have longed for revolution in economies and societies. From the 1930s hotbed of avant-garde letters in which Bob Brown created his extraordinary "Reading Machine" to the hot Fourth of July night in 1971 when Michael Hart distributed the world's first true eBook—a copy of the Declaration of Independence, no less, typed into a computer and posted on the cutting-edge ARPANET—to the morning forty years later when Judge Cote released her decision in *Apple,* the electronic distribution of information has been envisioned as a project in human emancipation. But it has also remained a struggle against vested interest.

There is no need to paint Amazon as any kind of hero and I have no inclination to do so. Amazon is big and dangerous in its own right, and increasingly so, to the point that it and the other major online platform companies may present some of the most significant antitrust problems in contemporary history. It seems likely that one or more of them are heading toward substantial antitrust trouble of their own. But that just proves the point that nothing is gained from turning the mundane effort of competition policy into a saga of moral right and wrong. No matter how naturally we see competition disputes in terms of moral narratives, they actually represent only the unfolding logic of a social process.

The fact that critics have so often found antitrust contradictory or confusing reflects the misunderstanding that the "efficiency" goal at its heart is at best some homely measure of businesspeoples' dollars and cents, and at worst the mechanistic and dehumanizing evil of Max Weber's "iron cage" or Frederick Taylor's optimized factories. It is not. The allocational efficiency that antitrust aims to improve by protecting markets from private abuses is the social allocation of *all* values. The real reason to favor antitrust enforcement is its protection of the values that are often championed by the Left. At its best, antitrust uses the power of markets to undo private power and to protect the weak.

Failure to see that is why antitrust has often seemed alienating and contradictory to those who ought to embrace it most. It has often seemed to be a conservative policy, and indeed, one of the oldest criticisms in the law's history has been that it shelters business interests by giving the appearance of vigilance without actually doing anything. A movement remarkably similar to the one brewing now, which was more or less led by Ralph Nader and fueled by the same reaction to centrist Democrats and their perceived compromises, achieved substantial public relations successes during the 1970s. But in terms of lasting policy achievements, it was a dramatic failure.[9] Prior efforts too were stoked by frustration with centrist inaction or the perception of enforcement aimed at the wrong parties. They were fraught with the same hot political enthusiasms, radically differing explanations of unfolding events, and confusion.

The common ground discovered by critics on the left and right in the *Apple* case is part of a much larger history that goes to who Americans are as a people and how we have chosen to accommodate our circumstances. It is the story of a people who are said to value free enterprise, but who in fact have very complicated and ill-examined commitments, and it helps explain why antitrust has been such a troubled and frustrated policy. Namely, what united the critics was their shared confidence that markets alone could not be trusted to reach a good outcome. Their shared instincts reflected not just some peculiarity of the *Apple* case itself. All of the arguments they raised, that this purportedly novel and unusual case was special and required special legal treatment, came from the same short menu of arguments that all kinds of antitrust defendants have made about all kinds of industries, throughout the law's long history. There has never been an antitrust defendant that didn't think its market was special, nor any shortage of observers among the public to sympathize and agree. As a result, the public policy of competition as a means to social values, a policy we've had in Anglo-American government in some form for at least six hundred years, has been fraught and uncertain throughout its long life.

Given that range of popular doubt and disagreement, one might be surprised by a commitment that is baked deeply into our antitrust itself. The law as it is written applies broadly, generally, and without much qualification for defendants who claim they need special clemency. That implies a deeper generalization yet. For its truth, the commitment to broadly generalized antitrust without special clemencies depends on a very fundamental claim of empirical social science. By applying its relatively simple rules so broadly across all markets, American antitrust implies that markets are mostly the same. They need more or less the same price competition, and the same sort of legal enforcement to keep it vigorous. They don't differ as much in their practical performance as we frequently believe, at least not in any way relevant to the goals of antitrust.

Most of this book is devoted to asking whether that totalizing vision and the striking empirical claim it implies deserve our support. Whether they do or not, in any case, the failure of most Americans to support them most of the time explains why American antitrust has mostly not worked very well.

These deep tensions make *Apple* an extremely useful study. That this fairly ordinary case went to the heart of such issues betrays a political dilemma involved in having any competition policy at all. A case in which the plaintiff *won* may not seem like strong evidence that antitrust is failing, but indeed it is ideal. *Apple* has much in common with a number of important historical cases in which a strong theory of legal liability lacked popular support.[10] Moreover, because it involved innovative technology, and a changing marketplace in which a wholly separate firm (nonparty Amazon) had gained a large market share, *Apple* features a range of issues that trigger fear of simple rules and dangerous competition. At stake were change, business failure, lost jobs and lost revenue, and confusion of the interests of competitors with the interests of competition.

Apple is ideal also because it encapsulates a timely policy problem: transition from an older technology to a newer one. Times of change often test our faith in competitive markets. But technological transitions, such as the rise of digital distribution, are not new; they are as old as capitalism. The uncertainty and risk of loss that surround the digital revolution, like those that have surrounded other technological transitions, are not problems unique to change, or special incidents of the much-abused concept of "disruption." They are just instances of the pain and dislocation that is inherent in all working competition. This is a poignant observation for me at this particular moment, as market changes have forced my employer and other law schools to face existential challenges of their own.

One benefit of *Apple* as a study is that it is so visceral and present, and we are each personally involved in the issues it raised. But our personal entanglements can frustrate how we understand it. For that reason, much of this book is historical in nature. Similar stories have played out concerning many other industries and technologies, and now that we are at a historical remove and have lost our immediate emotional connection to the issues they involved, they can help to clarify policy.

A key problem in a work such as this is that it poses questions that no one can presently answer with empirical rigor. That is not because nobody has tried, or because people wouldn't like to. Specifically, we can't say for sure what the actual effects of competition enforcement are, with satisfyingly empirical proof. Special, unusually difficult problems frustrate empirical study of antitrust, and for the most part, it just hasn't been done. First, studying its net effects poses a counterfactual problem. In order to say whether enforcement in the United States has been net beneficial during any given period, it is necessary to ask how US markets would have performed without antitrust during that same period—a state of affairs that did not exist. Comparative study might help, but it is frustrated by widely varying legal rules, enforcement priorities, and economic conditions.[11] Further, even a successful antitrust policy will tend to operate at the margin. While its effects might be quite significant in and of themselves, they often constitute small efficiency increases by comparison to the other variables affecting an industry, and can be overwhelmed by them.[12] There is strong evidence in a few areas that particular kinds of conduct are harmful.[13] However, there is little systematic measurement of the overall costs and benefits of the policy itself.[14] The global assessments that exist are either inconclusive or hotly controversial.[15]

Likewise, given the nature of the *Apple* case, one special economic problem will pop up often, and it, too, poses questions for which at the moment we have no hard answers. The case involved technological innovation, and occasionally it raised questions about when innovation is good and whether more competition or less optimizes it. Those questions have been the subject of empirical and theoretical literatures in economics and management that are both vast and almost wholly inconclusive.[16]

So instead, the arguments here are the kind that through much of our policy, and especially broadly overarching ones like antitrust, they must remain. Because they present themselves as more or less empirical problems that we cannot answer with certainty, they remain in their essence political.[17] The only methodology in this book is a rhetorical one familiar to lawyers, of showing that the purportedly special, distinguishing characteristics of a given case have occurred before, in differing circumstances and time periods. The pain and fear in the book industry in the mid-2000s were real, and to some degree each of us was bound up in them along with the men and women who faced them personally. But the same apprehensions have featured in similar situations, and once we can look at them from some distance, they seem more clear. For example, we do not now fear the introduction of videocassette players or player pianos. We also feel comfortable with steam power, mechanized ocean shipping, and variety retail stores with self-service shelf displays, all of which, during their day, were seen as calamities and proof that capitalism must be constrained. This book argues that that instinct can be generalized. The stresses and fears that made *Apple* seem like such a special case were actually just incidents of markets in their ordinary operation, or at the very least, they were very common. If that argument persuasively shows that *Apple* involved nothing more than a set of garden-variety, anticompetitive trade restraints unjustified by any special complexity, then it supports the view that markets are largely similar for purposes relevant to antitrust, and that circumstances that demand its relaxation are rare.

But if only making a competition policy work were so simple. The losses and setbacks may be ordinary, but they are real and the pain they cause is serious. They must to some degree be blamed for the law's persistent disappointments. Thurman Arnold, the most celebrated and influential enforcement chief in the law's history, said, "Antitrust law enforcement under any plan depends on the public attitude."[18] If he was right about that, then finding more popular legitimacy for it seems key, and accomplishing that calls for more than just telling people they are wrong.

Moreover, there are some genuine problems in the doctrinal law of antitrust itself that require correction. One of them is the focus of special attention in this book—the need to reinvigorate our law against single-firm "monopolization," Sherman Act section 2. Without a viable monopolization rule—ours is almost completely dead—there was just no satisfying answer to the *Apple* critics' complaints that however bad price-fixing is, Amazon seems dangerous, too. Without a monopolization law, an economy will be prone to individual firms accumulating power that can be exercised unilaterally, leaving buyers and suppliers no resort to protect themselves other than some collective self-help. We see this in our economy now, not only in the secret self-help remedy of firms such the *Apple* defendants, but also in efforts by doctors to negotiate collectively with insurers, in attempts by the news industry to negotiate collectively with the online media platforms over ad revenue, and in mergers of firms at one level of distribution to empower them in negotiation with powerful firms at other levels. This is a terrible outcome. Its long-term result is a series of bilateral monopolies whose only interest is to haggle over which of two monopolists gets more of the money they squeeze out of consumers' wallets. Still, that is no good reason to give up on competition as a policy, or to decide that markets are the problem. It is a reason to fix the law and enforce it for real.

Instead of telling the people that losses caused by markets are irrelevant, or denying that the law to preserve them is imperfect, an appeal to popular consensus might focus on the good that markets do while fully acknowledging their weaknesses and addressing them as equally important problems of a competition policy. The additional components that a sustainable and humanly decent competition policy could adopt to confront them might include progressive fiscal and social safety net policies. What they should look like is a topic for someone else's book and beyond my competence, but they should be understood as necessary components of any "competition" policy that aims to be both effective and democratically sustainable. We must recognize, too, that long-term sustainability requires that a competition law prosecute not only low-hanging fruit such as the publishers' conspiracy in *Apple*. It must also constrain other accumulations of power, and therefore must have vigorous monopolization and merger programs along with its prohibition of conspiracies. Those things are difficult and problematic, but without them, there is reason to doubt whether we should have competition policy at all.

Such an approach would highlight that many popular misgivings about individual antitrust cases are driven by fears of the wrong thing. They are fears of price competition and the legal rules meant to keep it rigorous, and so they presume that problems caused by competition will be fixed by making competition stop. But instead, we should let competition do what it does well, and solve the real and serious problems that remain with policies that will actually address them and not make them worse.

PART I

POLICY AS PROLOGUE

1

The Great Generalization

I always say the chief end of a man is to form general propositions—
[and] no general proposition is worth a damn.

—Letter from Oliver Wendell Holmes Jr. to Frederick Pollock (1919)

A PROBLEM HID at the heart of the *Apple* case, and it hides in other laws as well. In competition policy it is uncommonly acute, and it runs throughout the history of American antitrust as its most fundamental theme. The problem is the struggle between the general and the specific.

Laws must mediate the tension between generalized rules and case-by-case idiosyncrasies, and this problem goes to the core of having laws at all. Indeed, the problem is not limited to law. It is pervasive in other kinds of intellectual efforts, particularly the social sciences, a fact that itself is interesting and important to this story. The problem of generalization has been as difficult and politically divisive in social science as in law, hinting at a tantalizing, significant relationship between the two fields and their roles in society. To many people, generalization about social phenomena in either the social sciences or the law seems to have bad ideological effects. It seems to favor status quo social order, to disregard ad hoc peculiarities that deserve our shared concern, and to dehumanize individuals. Those critics believe that we reach real understanding and achieve justice only by examining the details of particular cases. On the other side are those who believe that slivering the world into its infinite detail impedes useful knowledge, because it is from generalization that we find explanatory power.

And so it is with competition policy. A central ideological conflict in antitrust has been whether particular markets are special and require detailed judgments about their local features or they can safely be generalized and regulated with abstract rules. Thus, the central political tension in *Apple* was whether books and the institutions that make them are "special" or instead are like other commercial commodities that can be left to compete in markets kept healthy by antitrust. The human need for abstraction is real, it seems, in law, the social sciences, and no doubt in other affairs. But it is also very problematic.

Fundamentally, laws need some comparatively simple rules for knowing what is legal and what is not. Simplicity is needed for several reasons, but one is key here: without some degree of simplicity, policy becomes unmanageable for both the government and the people it regulates. As more factual or legal complexity is entertained in litigation, trials become more lengthy, expensive, and uncertain, so the line must be drawn somewhere. But simplicity implies generalization. To preserve simplicity, a rule denies that the situations to which it applies differ very much, in ways relevant to the rule. That generates some opposing problems, including overly rigid application of a rule where it should permit an exception in order to protect values important to society. In *Apple,* for example, many thought that if the law insisted on unrestrained price competition without permitting some arrangement to protect authors and publishers from Amazon's price-cutting power, it would imperil the writing of literature and the independent terrestrial bookstores that people value. But when a rule deviates from generality to accommodate those other values, it introduces complexity, uncertainty, and difficulty in application. Accordingly, the law will sometimes get cases wrong. A legal rule—a generalization—will be applied to facts that the rule doesn't handle well.

First-year law students are often confronted with a battery of questions to test the many puzzles that thereby arise. They are sometimes asked whether a law against "drawing blood in the streets" should apply to a doctor performing emergency surgery, or whether a death penalty for prison breakers should apply when the prison is on fire.[1] They may be asked about a hypothetical ordinance requiring "dogs" to be leashed.[2] It seems obvious that such a rule would not apply to cats but less obvious whether it applies to wolves, and harder still, whether by omission the law-making body inadvertently permitted unleashed tigers. In another famous example, a legal philosopher set off an epochal debate by posing what has been called "the most famous hypothetical in the common law world."[3] "[Imagine that a] legal rule forbids you to take a vehicle into the public park. Plainly this forbids an automobile, but what about bicycles, roller skates, toy automobiles? What about airplanes? Are these, as we say, to be called "vehicles" for the purpose of the rule or not?"[4] That philosopher, the English scholar H. L. A. Hart, considered these questions easy. He noted that most legal cases are in the "core" of a legal rule, and only in some "penumbral" range of its applicability do questions get hard. Hart's hypothetical drew an equally famous reply from the American philosopher Lon Fuller, who asked whether a World War II service truck set up in the park as a memorial would violate the law. He had an interesting point. Nothing inhering or immanent in the nature of the vehicle would obviously put it outside the meaning of the ordinance. What would put it outside the ordinance—the purpose for which the ordinance was adopted—did not appear in the text of the provision itself.[5] That introduces a different set of deeply fraught political or philosophical problems. In any case, even Fuller's single counterexample would become a bone of contention.[6] Over the years, philosophers have asked whether Hart's rule would cover an ambulance, a baby stroller, a wheelchair, an ice cream truck, a bicycle, a *police* bicycle, and other things.[7] The example's deceptive triviality conceals deep problems in the transmission of policy choices from lawmakers to the enforcement authorities, the tribunals where rules are applied to specific situations, and also the public, who are entitled to understand the rules they must follow. The problem is generalization and its inevitable tendency to oversimplify problems that are inherently complex.

One common reaction is that this is an issue of legislative incaution, of failure to foresee likely problems, which could be solved by writing more specific rules. But it is not that simple. Consider the US Internal Revenue Code. The statute itself consists of a few thousand pages of very complex and precise text, and it is made yet more specific by several thousand additional pages of interpretive regulations issued by the Treasury Department. All of that has been generated to implement a policy that in principle is not complicated: most people should give a share of their income for the public use. And yet, even with the Talmudic midrash of specificity we've developed to give it life, there is still extensive, routine litigation over what the Code actually says.

What these examples illustrate is not merely a problem of insufficient specificity but a fundamental mismatch, which is apparently not correctable, between the language in which legal rules must be expressed and the disputes to which they apply. Actually, it is not even fair to blame language. The problem with law and generalization at its most basic is that human *concepts*, however expressed, cannot be made to fit hand-in-glove with the facts to which they must apply. We are hamstrung by our inability to construct rules that will correctly match even our most basically agreed-upon values to the situations that arise over time.

For this reason, and other reasons as well, in the making of our laws we compromise. We deploy proxies for truth because actual truth is not within reach. To the many other compromises we routinely employ in making and applying law—including presumptions, legal fictions, burdens of proof, and the entire law of evidence—we add this compromise of legal generalization. We deploy them all knowing that they will leave the law imperfect because after all, life must go on, and we have no better choice.

And so it is with antitrust. It seems clear that some anticompetitive activities ought to be legally prohibited because they are obviously within the lawmaker's intent and they obviously cause harm. In Hart's phrase, they are "in the core." But just as in law school exercises of shedding blood in the streets or walking one's dog on a leash, it is easy to modulate seemingly straightforward hypothetical facts to generate antitrust scenarios that aren't so clear-cut. One case usually considered to be simple is the most basic antitrust violation, horizontal price-fixing. Price-fixing is an agreement by direct competitors to set a minimum price in order to end competition among them. Since the early twentieth century, no serious observer has disagreed that it should be illegal. In the United States price-fixing is one of the few kinds of conduct still subject to the per se rule of automatic liability, and essentially the only violation now prosecuted criminally. But even that seemingly "core" example is deceptive. The problem is to say how we should apply the rule when on its surface the challenged conduct looks like price-fixing, but it is not some unapologetic, antisocial conspiracy hatched in cigar smoke behind closed doors. It is harder to know how to apply the rigid generalization of the per se rule against price fixing when there seem to be distinguishing facts, or the case seems somehow special. For example, it is not obvious what should be done when workers get together and say they won't work for their employer unless wages go up. Collective bargaining is permitted, and many consider it an important tool to preserve basic human values, but on one plausible reading of the original Sherman law it was price-fixing. Whether collective bargaining should be illegal was very uncertain when the law was young, and working out its still-controversial limits required several legislative interventions and dozens of judicial opinions over the course of the twentieth century.[8] As another example, the National Collegiate Athletic Association (NCAA) regulates the activities of its member schools, who sell their sports products and in various other respects compete in the marketplace as well as on the field of play. Many defend the NCAA rules as preserving embattled values of amateurism and sportsmanship and protecting a parity of skill among teams that keeps the competition lively.[9] But many others point out that Division 1 men's football and basketball together generate billions of dollars per year and NCAA rules deny the players themselves all but a meager share of it. Those rules in any other industry could well land people in prison. So while many sincerely believe in the need for some regulation of amateur sports, others have called the NCAA "the best monopoly in America," a "cynical hoax," and a machine designed to "transfer[] wealth from poor ghetto residents to rich colleges."[10] These are not isolated or idiosyncratic exceptions; there are many cases in which the rule against price-fixing, purportedly the simplest of all antitrust rules, is hard to apply. Facts routinely seem distinguishing or special. Trade associations of learned professionals such as architects and pharmacists often set up ethical rules that may limit price competition. Do rules like that just pad the members' own wallets, or do they root out quacks and scam artists?[11] Likewise, doctors' groups in recent years have sought to bargain collectively with health insurers. One player in that bilateral equation may or may not be an anticompetitive bad guy, but it's hard to know which is which or what to do about it.[12] Our beleaguered news industry wants to protect its flagging business with legal permission to bargain collectively over ad revenue with the big online ad platforms such as Facebook and Google.[13] Their case may seem sympathetic, given the apparently lopsided bargaining power of the platforms and the special role of the news in culture and politics. But would the news organizations use their new revenues to invest in content or do other good things, or would they just pass the gains on to their shareholders? It doesn't seem that they have any more reason to reinvest now than they did under another statutory exemption they secured in 1970, a law widely considered to have failed outright.[14] And finally, what about consumers themselves? At times people have boycotted monopoly manufacturers or retailers to demand lower prices, but that at least nominally entails a horizontal price conspiracy. Would it not be poignantly ironic if it were illegal?

On some level, much of this tension came to a head in one of the first and most famous of all antitrust cases, the 1890s price-fixing case *United States v. Addyston Pipe & Steel Co.*[15] By no means did it settle the question—many of the same uncertainties have lingered ever since—but the way *Addyston Pipe* resolved it had important consequences for the law and for latter-day stories such as *Apple*.

The most important opinion in *Addyston Pipe*, which would shape the subsequent law perhaps as much as any other case in antitrust history, was written by Judge William Howard Taft, who later served as both president of the United States (1909–1913) and chief justice (1921–1930). He was also a Yale law professor and an early scholar of the federal Sherman Act. At the time he wrote his opinion in *Addyston Pipe*, he had been appointed to the intermediate federal appellate court for the Sixth Circuit. The case was his opportunity to explore some of the deepest themes in the new law and stake out early guidelines in interpreting its laconic language.

The case dealt with manufacturers of cast iron pipes who had set up a price-fixing conspiracy. Their arrangement covered much of the United States, and among them they controlled a substantial chunk of the country's pipe-producing capacity. They made no attempt to justify their actions except to say that they wanted protection from price competition, which under the circumstances of their industry, they said, would be "ruinous." At the time, such arguments were understandable. When the Sherman Act was adopted in 1890, no one knew what its nebulous words really meant. When *Addyston Pipe* was heard in the late 1890s, the courts had not yet clarified the per se rule against price-fixing, and that rule's details would not fully be resolved until some decades later.[16] Moreover, while the defendants' product was ordinary and technologically mundane, they deployed the prevailing economic reasoning that even very simple products could have cost or technological peculiarities making them unfit for regular competition.[17] That is, a growing consensus among the American elite, developed during the wrenching and unexpected dislocations of the Industrial Revolution, was that competition had become "ruinous" or "destructive."[18] And so—rather like the *Apple* defendants did, but in different terms—the *Addyston Pipe* conspirators argued that something special about their market required legal clemency.

Judge Taft was unmoved. In effect, he'd been asked to decide whether the actual prices the defendants had charged were "reasonable" or appropriate in light of their need to protect themselves from ruinous competition. He declined, both because it would be an infeasible and capricious exercise and because, in his view, the law's generalization against trade restraints did not permit it.

In some of the most famous words in all of antitrust law, he wrote that inquiring "how much restraint of competition is in the public interest, and how much is not," would be to "set sail on a sea of doubt." "So shifting, vague, and indeterminate a standard," he said, would be "a manifest danger in the administration of justice."[19] While he did offer some reasons to doubt that the defendants' restraints were "reasonable" or that competition would be ruinous without them, more importantly he said that none of that mattered. The court held that a horizontal price cartel is illegal no matter how "reasonable the prices they fixed, however great the competition they had to encounter, and however great the necessity for curbing themselves by joint agreement from committing financial suicide by ill-advised competition."[20] It didn't matter that the "restraint . . . was only partial," that it "did not cover the United States," or that it created no "complete monopoly" because "it was tempered by the fear of competition" from third parties.[21] Taft explicitly rejected emerging state law decisions of the day that permitted such defenses, which much of popular opinion of the day might have found reasonable as accommodations to destructive competition.[22]

In other words, Judge Taft dealt with problems so basic to the having of a competition law that they arose in its earliest years by adopting a broad and simplifying generalization. That set the stage for many further iterations of the same gesture throughout the law's history. It implied faith in both the model of healthy competition and its generalizability across markets, since Judge Taft adopted it at the risk of the defendants' ruin. Of course, if the defendants' businesses failed because they couldn't compete, that might be fine as a matter of public policy. A most basic claim of our economics is that if a firm can't survive under the pressure of ordinary competition, then it *should* fail. But that is a good policy only if most markets are mostly the same and they work the way economic theory says. If those assumptions were wrong they would cost the defendants their existence and society would be the less for it.

Over time, the commitment to generalization—and its implicit claim that markets in relevant respects are the same—has become so broad that defendants essentially cannot defeat it, at least not by attacking it head on. As Justice John Paul Stevens wrote in a leading opinion: "The assumption that competition is the best method of allocating resources in a free market recognizes that all elements of a bargain—quality, service, safety, and durability—and not just the immediate cost, are favorably affected by the free opportunity to select among alternative offers."[23] Likewise, conduct challenged in antitrust "is not saved because, on some ultimate reckoning of social or economic debits and credits, it may be deemed beneficial. A value choice of such magnitude is beyond the ordinary limits of judicial competence, and in any event has been made for us already, by Congress when it enacted [the antitrust laws]."[24] Accordingly, "Whatever may be [the] peculiar problems and characteristics" of any given market, the Sherman Act "establishes one uniform rule applicable to all industries alike."[25] It is no defense to argue that the challenged conduct was necessary because under the particular circumstances, unbridled competition would produce bad results. Empirically that may well be, and

Congress has in fact been convinced of it in some particular circumstances. But otherwise, it is not a problem the courts will entertain.

Perhaps many courts indulge this conceit as a "legal fiction"—a factual assumption we make because it is useful in deciding legal cases, even though we don't know it is true or we know it is false. In applying the antitrust presumption of generality, courts often acknowledge in principle that some market might be special and in need of antitrust clemency, but then they uniformly hold that arguments to that effect must be made to Congress. But the strength of their words implies that judges by and large believe in the empirical sameness of markets quite personally and subjectively. However much they differ over *how* the specific substantive rules should apply in any given case, courts agree that antitrust almost always *should apply,* and that purportedly special features of any given market rarely or never require special results.

So have they got it right? That question cannot be answered concretely, and even addressing it rhetorically will take up the rest of this book. But some general thoughts first will help. One reason generalization seems a mistake in some cases is that competition generates painful outcomes. When firms vigorously compete to steal each other's customers through lower prices or better products, some of them will fail. Investments and livelihoods are lost. Well-loved products or institutions, or even traditional ways of doing things, can fail too. The losses sometimes seem very serious and sociologically complex, as when change in an industry causes substantial, lasting unemployment or increases the number of people who will be employees rather than independent entrepreneurs. But however controversial or problematic it might be, by broadly generalizing antitrust the courts merely recognize that choosing markets as our regulatory convention means making peace with the following fact:

Markets in their ordinary operation are machines for producing pain.

Another reason generalization may seem mistaken is that it requires us to believe that markets can in fact sort everything out, that they can spontaneously create all of the institutions and procedures that businesses need to get their work done. In adopting a law against trade restraints we substantially interfere in arrangements that private parties claim they need in order to set up those institutions and procedures for themselves. When government steps in to hold such an arrangement illegal, critics almost always say that the arrangement was adopted to provide some desirable thing the market itself could not provide.

These various popular doubts tend to generate one or the other of two criticisms of markets and competition policy: that the market in a given case generates pain, and that in a given case it cannot supply something automatically. Those criticisms may not seem to have much in common, but in fact they do. They both depend on skepticism that markets can do what they are supposed to do automatically, without intervention by either government or private agreements. They both oppose the seemingly naive and ideological faith conveyed in Justice Stevens's platitudes. Namely, they both boil down simply to the same doubt that markets left alone can always produce the right mix of quality, safety, variety, and so on. Moreover, these apparently different criticisms not only share skepticism of market fundamentalism, they also cite the same mechanism by which the markets allegedly fail. No matter how different the language in which the criticisms are expressed and how dissimilar the politics of the critics, the two arguments depend on the same inner logic to show that competition causes harm. They both imply that *price competition*—the very mechanism by which antitrust and the economic theory it incorporates expect markets to do the basic task of allocating resources—sometimes destroys things that society actually wants and would arrange for if only price competition didn't make it infeasible. For example, engineers might propose bridge designs that cut corners and endanger safety because it would help them undercut their competitors in price, so in the interest of the public good, maybe the law should permit them to limit price competition when they make bids to local authorities. Retailers might not be able to provide high-quality showrooms with well-trained sales staff, even though consumers need those services in order to make proper decisions when buying certain products, because they cannot fund those expensive services and meet the price competition of discount stores and online retailers. So perhaps the law should permit manufacturers to fix their own retail prices, and prohibit price-gouging discounters. And indeed, book publishers and sellers might not be able to provide artistic works that society values, or Apple might not be able to enter the market with its innovative, higher-quality e-reader. Critics said that the costs of doing those things couldn't be recouped because of price competition—that is, that Amazon's retail prices were too low.

In other words, the inner logic of common criticisms in antitrust cases is really the same. They mostly imply the following important, shared proposition:

Some markets are special, because sometimes low prices are destructive.

Some very hard questions remain, and they tend to resolve themselves to problems that are inherently empirical and probably cannot be feasibly tested. In the end, we will have to leave some of them unanswered. But this book's in-depth consideration of *Apple* is aimed at addressing them, and it may answer some of them better than one would expect.

2

In the First Ships

Competition as a Concept and Its Special Role
in American History

On the shoals of roast beef and apple pie, socialist utopias founder.

—Werner Sombart, *Why Is There No Socialism in the United States?*

FOR BETTER OR WORSE, since sometime in the mid-nineteenth century Americans have had a faith in private markets that is perhaps unique in the world. We have defined ourselves as a pragmatic people governed first by enterprise and experiment and only more distantly by ideas. It has seemed congenial to privilege economic individualism and private property at least as instrumental tools toward other goals, and we have usually left private initiative alone, more or less. Accordingly, by comparison to other nations, America has never had radical traditions on either the left or right. Instead, we have had broad agreement on a set of background political commitments. Our conflicts have been more psychic than material, and they take place within recognizably shared bounds. Early on, we found it fitting to import economic theory as it emerged from Europe, and later we took over as the world leader in its development. Even more so than the nineteenth-century British economists who gave the theory its modern life, we absorbed it with zeal, occasionally to a literally religious degree. As a consequence, since at least the age of Andrew Jackson, we have mostly agreed that leaving markets broad freedom for private initiative suits our consensus.[1]

Or at least it is commonly so said. In fairness, arguments that American history is a history of "consensus" have divided American historians rather tensely.[2] Radical movements have existed in America and have scored meaningful victories—including, depending on who tells the story, the Sherman Act—and their failures may have resulted from suppression as much as lack of popular support.[3] Indeed, the dominant paradigm among American historians prior to World War II stressed conflict rather than consensus, among factions, sections, and classes. Critics of the consensus revisionism that followed allege that it was in itself an ideological power play.[4] Historians fighting over the issue generated a fruitful, critical dialogue and much new insight. But the idea that there was one politics in America, or even two or three, came to seem irreducibly subjective and sterile, requiring a metaphysics of what it even means that the people believed something.[5] The reality was more complex than either the consensus model or its alternatives acknowledged. Today, accordingly, most historians view consensus claims as incautious, at least in any strong form.

But whatever may be the case, the history of the United States is concretely different from that of other nations. Unlike much of the world, America lacked a feudal tradition.[6] It began with less class striation, and it began with a rapidly expanding frontier and centuries of seemingly unlimited resources. Even after the final close of the frontier, Americans enjoyed comparatively high living standards. Since its founding, and interrupted only by the Civil War, America has had a long history of peaceful transitions of power under one constitution, making it the world's longest-lasting and most stable democracy. Neither avowedly socialist nor far-right parties have ever held meaningful power. The European experience is very different. Radical parties have held significant power in Europe at various times. Among other things, socialist governments nationalized some production during the peacetime twentieth century. The United States has never done that. In fact, the United States was virtually alone in the Western world in preserving its traditional liberalism after World War I, whose fallout drove other nations to radical extremes.[7] At the very least, it is true that the United States has faced a narrower range of cultural and political experience than Europe.

None of this has to be a celebration in order to be true. That a given view may have been more widely or longer held than others is not an argument that it is good or enjoys some privilege. It likewise may not be that illuminating for modern politics, because the circumstances in which this history unfolded have changed so much. It is not a defense of modern policy arguments that Americans in times past had any particular political economy. The strictly individualist, small-government political economy that first took hold during the early nineteenth century and the accompanying emphasis on negative rights and formal equality were not simply a premonition of modern conservatism. They were part of the transition of a society quickly disposing of the mercantilist economics that had dominated European and American thought. They were a rejection—by farmers, small producers, and the disadvantaged—of government-granted monopoly and privilege for the rich. They could not have taken as their hero anything like "big business" because no such thing existed in America until late in the century. As Hovenkamp says, to be a free marketeer during much of the nineteenth century was not to be right-wing, it was to be left.[8]

So what is the current state of American economic thought, and what does popular reception of the *Apple* case suggest about it? More importantly, what does it mean for the feasibility of American competition policy? This book poses some hard questions about the consensus model. For one thing, to whatever extent our embrace of liberal capitalism means favoring unfettered markets, we have betrayed that faith in drastic terms several times, including under the National Industrial Recovery Act (1933–1935) and with the rate-and-entry regulation imposed on infrastructure markets during the Progressive Era. We have frequently found ourselves doubting competition and markets when the losses of price-competitive vigor in specific cases test our resolve. In other words, over and over throughout the history of our competition policy, we have found ourselves in the same shoes we wore during debate over *United States v. Apple.*

It is interesting that a people purportedly devoted to liberal capitalism would be conflicted about its basic ideas, but that conflict in itself does not disprove consensus history or establish any economic philosophy. All kinds of doubts and regrets can be consistent with a strong commitment to markets and competition because "competition" has meant different things at different times. Moreover, as economic theory has grown complex, one can argue in principle that essentially any conduct is either procompetitive or anticompetitive. But the lack of commitment can sometimes be surprising, and it calls into question how unified our history has really been. And, significantly, it calls into question whether a competition policy can work in a society that is so ambivalent, however often we claim antitrust as part of a proud inheritance. Economic theory and the competition law it informs are not always the comfortable fit for rugged individualism that we take them to be. Even basic economic theory tends to generate prescriptive interventions in tension with our purported individualism. But fundamentally, the most interesting tension at play and the most profound lesson of the *Apple* case is that markets are hard to watch in their ordinary operation. That is the reason that for so long we have doubted, equivocated, and sought exceptions or qualifications for the political economy said to be so fundamental to America.

The economic theory that would later inform antitrust has a long, colorful history. Since classical antiquity, it has occurred to people in Western societies and elsewhere that something systematic characterizes the trading of goods and services. Exchange is not random, and even when left to operate purely through uncoordinated individual transactions, it is not chaotic.[9] Developing the theory took a very long time. While writings unmistakably "economic" in some broad sense date as far back as ancient Greece, the first few thousand years of the history of economic thought were marked by confusion and misdiagnosis. Markets *existed,* of course, from at least the time of classical Athens and its Near Eastern peers, and important contemporary writers remarked on their workings. Scholastic theologians worked out a fairly elaborate theory on the subject. In the 1260s Thomas Aquinas and his followers described market price as the "just" price, worked out a theory of value based on scarcity and demand, and began to explain monopoly and anticompetitive conduct.[10] But a genuinely economic theory would have to wait for the great conceptual achievement of disentangling the institutions we think of as the "market" or the "economy" from all the other social institutions through which they flow—the family, religion, law, and society. The full realization of that distinction occurred no earlier than about the early eighteenth century.[11] Before then, great thinkers struggled to explain basic economic facts, as in the famous paradox of water and diamonds.[12] The English historian William Letwin, who also happened to be a distinguished student of American antitrust law, locates the beginnings of truly modern economics in late seventeenth-century England.[13]

This theoretical tradition would assume a large part of America's political inheritance from Europe. As Dorothy Ross says, social science itself "belonged to the broad stream of social and political thought that was antecedent and tributary to liberalism." It reflected an increasingly humanist vision of history, not as the static iteration of events according to already perfected divine purpose, but as an unfolding process whose logic reflects human agency and values, and takes as given the possibility and primacy of progress.[14]

It was not the unelected federal courts that imposed this tradition on us in their interpretation of antitrust law, or even the Congress that adopted the Sherman Act in 1890. Through several different channels, the colonists brought England's emerging economic theory and its characteristically liberal political philosophy with them across the Atlantic, as part of their own culture. As the historian Carl Degler put it in a famous book, they brought it here "in the first ships."[15]

They did so without any deliberation or moment of conscious consensus, in part because our legal system was a uniquely important vehicle for this tradition. These values were already embodied in the English common law imposed in America as the law of the colonies and preserved as a part of our own law after the American Revolution. Certain important competition rules of English law were known to American lawyers in the colonial period. For example, one of the oldest rules in the common law of property is that of "alienability," under which courts refused to enforce limits imposed by sellers on resales of property after sale. In the rule's distant origins, the courts stuck down restraints on alienation not to defend free markets but to soften the harsh effects of primogeniture and the feudal land-law hierarchy.[16] But it came to be a core assumption among common lawyers that restraints on alienation were prohibited for the sake of competitive markets.[17] Later, by the turn of the fifteenth century, the English courts were holding certain kinds of contracts illegal for limiting competition.[18] In cases that would make up a body of law well known to American lawyers against "restraints of trade," judges explained competition rationales in increasingly modern terms.[19] Common law courts in England and the United States also began in the late eighteenth and early nineteenth centuries to develop the view that competitive injuries would no longer be compensable. That is, they no longer allowed recoveries in tort for mere losses of sales or profits to another who sold better or cheaper products.[20]

What we think of as "economics" proper—the synthesis of classical theory by eighteenth-century British academics—made its way to America quickly and was incorporated very deeply during the first decades of the nineteenth century. Members of the founding generation knew the work of Adam Smith specifically, and his early reception in America was unusually enthusiastic. Copies of *The Wealth of Nations* were imported as soon as it was published, and it appeared in American reprint editions as early as 1789.[21] In 1790 Thomas Jefferson proclaimed it "the best book extant" on political economy, and other Founders cited it as authority. Influential sermons and popular debate of the day often referenced it, perhaps because Smith explicitly urged Britain to give the colonies their freedom. Along with the writings of other influential Scottish thinkers including David Hume, Francis Hutcheson, and James Steuart, Smith's work made up a large part of the Founders' reception of the Scottish Enlightenment. American economic theory was not yet fully modern in its details, no more so than the English theory on which it was based. The American intellectual elite of the founding era was mercantilist in monetary matters and international trade, and in general, at least until the 1830s, American economic opinion remained a fairly indiscriminate mix of ideas drawn from various sources. But in its rhetoric and its spirit, and its basic impressionistic commitment to private enterprise, the American political economy was recognizably modern and theoretical.[22]

So what is the state of this theory today? To be clear, the basic concept of "competition" has had many different meanings over time, both in the vernacular and in economic theory. It has often been thought of as simply a numerosity of firms—that is, that a market with many sellers of a thing is more competitive than one that has few. It is also sometimes thought of just as firms working hard, as when they invest heavily in marketing, research, litigating over their intellectual property rights, and so on. That is what many businesspeople have in mind when they say that their markets are "competitive." But it is important to understand that current economic theory and antitrust define competition very narrowly and precisely and consider only that precisely defined competition to be relevant. In this definition, competition is the effort among sellers to win the business of the same consumers either by selling a better product than the others or by selling the same product more cheaply. That is to say, competition means *price* competition. (To be clear, what is meant by "price" is *quality-adjusted price*. That is, one can compete on price by selling either an identical product at a lower price or a better product at the same or even higher price.) In antitrust, price competition is often known as "competition on the merits"—the hunt for advantage not by conspiring with competitors, or trying to exclude them, or acquiring them, but by giving purchasers a better deal. The Supreme Court has long held that price competition is the competition relevant to antitrust law. As it wrote in a seminal case many decades ago, "Price and competition are so intimately entwined that any discussion of theory must treat them as one."[23]

This fact is central to the argument of this book. Quality-adjusted price is the sole mechanism by which markets are thought to do the things that make them good regulators, by which they allocate resources and generate efficiency. And indeed, although competition has at times meant different things, especially in nontechnical discussion, Americans have by and large believed specifically in price competition, at least in loose terms. It has been taken for granted in our rough consensus that the power to raise prices for lack of competitive discipline is a social harm, and something we should control with public policy. We further take it for granted that the harm isn't just a moral wrong of taking more from individual buyers than seems fair. We believe that selling things for prices set by markets, not by either governments or monopolists, tends to make the workings of production, distribution, and the allocation of resources turn out better. By and large, even if many of us believe in it less in the calculating precision of economists and more as a loose rule of thumb, we believe in the invisible hand.

For that reason, it is surprising how often we doubt competition and believe that its failures are caused by price itself. As we've already seen and will explore in more detail, diverse critics' doubts about competition and antitrust enforcement meant to keep it vigorous often stem from the same concern: the fear that low prices themselves will keep markets from generating goods or values that society needs.

So how, according to the theory, does price do all this work? As one might guess, the theory is complex, and as it is deployed by economists and (sometimes) by courts in antitrust cases, it is mathematical. But to grasp how economic theory currently informs our antitrust law, we can actually get by well with a summary like the following.

Over time, antitrust has come to embody a policy that holds that, as much as possible, markets should be free of either government or private restraints. Economists believe that markets' ability to self-regulate works best when certain conditions apply, and the policy underlying antitrust is to make the American marketplace resemble those ideal market conditions as much as possible. Although the conditions are not fully attainable in reality, it is useful for theoretical purposes to hypothesize a world in which they are perfectly realized. The conditions are: (1) the absence of entry barriers, (2) perfect information for all buyers and sellers, with regard to cost, price, and all alternative products or services, (3) fungibility of products or services in the market, and (4) zero transaction costs.

Self-regulating markets under these ideal conditions are thought to be superior to government regulation of production, because they optimize resource allocation. They do this because perfect competition demands the lowest possible prices for products. As soon as a seller raises its price above the bare minimum needed to cover costs, other competitors will be able to steal that seller's business. Because new entry will continue until the good or service is sold at the lowest possible price, the long-run equilibrium price in perfect competition is exactly equal to the cost of production (a part of which is a competitive return on investment for those who invested in the business).[24] This means that all producers in a perfectly competitive market will earn zero economic profit. Moreover, competition will continually push down the cost of production, using the cheapest means that is technologically feasible at a given time, because every producer has an incentive to improve its own productive efficiency. If they can lower their costs in ways that other sellers can't match, then they can either earn some economic profit at the prevailing price or steal competitors' business by charging lower prices. This competitive process therefore both reduces price and cost to the lowest possible level and devotes the least possible amount of society's wealth to any particular productive endeavor, leaving more for all other endeavors.

In reality, not only are the ideal conditions not perfectly attainable, but to the extent are attained in a particular case, they are not always self-preserving. They can be impaired in several ways, either by naturally occurring failures in particular markets or by the intentional acts of persons or governments. A partial list of possible impairments includes: (1) entry barriers such as very high start-up costs, regulatory barriers, license requirements, or control by one seller of facilities essential to effective competition; (2) informational dysfunctions such as information costs, fraud, and asymmetries that might exist, for example, between manufacturers and retail consumers or between trained professionals and their clients; and (3) product differentiation and imperfect substitutes that frustrate fungibility.

A basic fact is that competitors are hostile to free competition. It drives down their prices and, other things being equal, their profits. Therefore, they have a strong incentive to abuse markets, and they will take steps to create market impediments whenever it will make them more profitable. A second basic fact is that because the ideal conditions are neither fully attainable nor always self-preserving, it is possible that in a particular market healthy competition may not prevail, and one producer or a group of producers will acquire some market power. Market power is the ability of a seller to raise its prices without losing its business, which theoretically a seller without market power should be unable to do. A third basic fact is that for a seller with market power, it is almost always more profitable to raise its price above the competitive price, even though that seller will sell fewer units. This is true only up to the point called the monopoly price. Any increase in price above that point will begin to reduce the monopoly seller's profits. That happens because of the relationship between price, demand, and per-unit cost of production at different levels of total output. In any case, this third basic fact provides the motive for competitors' hostility to competition.

A final basic fact is that the model of perfect competition does not take into account one very important need of real-world markets: the institutional arrangements necessary to make them exist. It is sometimes necessary for governments or private persons to provide these institutional arrangements, which may include buildings, infrastructures, laws, agreements, means of communication, and other things needed for particular transactions to occur. For example, markets may not work in the way described here unless there is an existing government that can protect property rights.

After first arriving with the colonists, competition rhetoric eventually bled its way through most of American law, even before the Sherman Act federalized it in its most explicit form in 1890. That process was not simple or straightforward, and it has resulted in a large collection of ideas that often are confused and contradictory, reflecting in part the many different things that "competition" can mean, Americans' continuing ambivalence, and sometimes the duplicity or mistakes of politicians. But the important point is not about a theoretically coherent model in the law, or anything about the law itself, but about Americans as a people. The extraordinary diffusion of competition ideals throughout American law reveals a people devoted to some conception of competition, however confused its details. Reaction to *United States v. Apple,* however, seemed to reflect a great ambivalence to competition or rough rivalry, or at least about what competition should mean.

In addition to the antitrust laws and many other rules that serve "competitive" values in the sense of price rivalry, American law has used the terms and rhetoric of competition in all kinds of other ways. They play a significant and not merely metaphorical role, for example, in our constitutional policy of free speech. Among the most famous and durable images in First Amendment law was Justice Holmes's "marketplace of ideas."

He used the phrase in dissent from prosecution of five immigrant anarchists for their political statements, and explained it in competitive terms: "The best test of truth," he said—and the one adopted in our First Amendment—"is the power of the thought to get itself accepted in the competition of the market."[25] Similar reasoning drove a later antitrust decision with First Amendment overtones. The Supreme Court held that antitrust law should apply to a scheme set up by several news organizations, despite their special First Amendment status, because more competition in news would serve First Amendment values. Justice Hugo Black wrote that "the First Amendment . . . rests on the assumption that the widest possible dissemination of information from diverse and antagonistic sources is essential to the welfare of the public, that a free press is a condition of a free society. Surely a command that the government itself shall not impede the free flow of ideas does not afford non-governmental combinations a refuge if they impose restraints upon that constitutionally guaranteed freedom."[26]

At times, the courts have gone even further. During the remarkable and controversial period between the 1880s and the Great Depression, much of American constitutional law was overtaken by a rigorous and simple theory that was to some degree a theory of competition. With the adoption after the Civil War of the Fourteenth Amendment, with its promise of "due process of law" for deprivations of "life, liberty, or property," some judges took the opportunity to confront that era's rising popular agitation for economic regulation. Using their new power to require "due process," the courts constitutionalized a strong protection for "freedom of contract," which broadly prohibited regulation of economic activity. For example, some laws controlling wages and working conditions were thrown out to protect the freedom of both workers and bosses to bargain for themselves. The courts said that the inequality of their power to bargain was not a proper concern. By the time the doctrine was finally thrown out in the 1930s, it had been used to reject dozens of laws, many of them regulatory interventions that addressed the crisis of industrialization.[27]

Various policies have sought simply to preserve a numerosity of firms in order to achieve specific goals. They commonly purport to serve competition values, even when their specific goals do not seem literally "economic" in narrow terms. That was prominently the case in American banking law, which for nearly a century formally limited the size of banking entities and the lines of business in which they could engage. The goal was economic, in the sense that a numerosity of firms might diminish systemic financial risk. But it was probably noneconomic too, because concentrations of capital and the political favoritism that banks enjoyed were matters of political concern. A similar policy long prevailed in communications law. The Federal Communications Commission throughout most of its history imposed a set of ownership rules on newspapers and radio and television stations, on the theory that preserving a numerosity of firms would preserve intellectual diversity.[28]

And indeed, politicians and businesspeople have often used competition not as an actual policy tool but for its rhetorical appeal alone. It has historically played well on Capitol Hill to sell any policy as a "competition" or "competitiveness" policy, even when it is obvious that the "competition" in question will solve no problems, because policymakers can't think of anything else to do or can't muster the political will for a different approach. Following the several financial crises of the 2000s, Congress felt pressured to take action on the so-called credit rating agencies. Those firms, which dominate the assessment of corporate creditworthiness, were widely blamed for failing to predict or even helping cause the crises. Congress's only response was to authorize the Securities and Exchange Commission to license more new credit rating firms, to encourage entry.[29] But there had been plenty of entry, over many years, which did nothing to improve performance and which almost always ended in insolvency or acquisition by one of the industry's dominant firms.[30]

Sometimes, alas, politicians just lie. They claim to serve competition values with policies that they know have nothing to do with it, like the America COMPETES Act.[31] Despite its title, the law had no connection to competition or efficiency; it was just a pork-laden spending bill, lobbied for by corporate recipients predominantly located in its cosponsors' home states.[32]

As for antitrust, the long heritage of economic theory has always been part of it. It is sometimes said that at one time antitrust was not "economic," in that it served goals such as protection of small business, individual rights, and the undue political power of large businesses. In particular, the leaders of the conservative antitrust revolution of the 1970s often take credit for having *made* antitrust "economic."[33] But that is misleading. The Supreme Court from the beginning described the law's purpose as economic, and stated its goals in terms that at least superficially sound quite modern. In all of it, the courts expressed awareness of natural, autonomous social processes and their tendency to generate social benefit, and were aware of Congress's choice to privilege them over public or private regulation. As the Court wrote in its very first opinion under the new Sherman Act, the law was directed at restraints that "deprive the public of the advantages which flow from free competition."[34] Since the beginning there has been the conception that "free competition" automatically generates "public advantages," and that Congress meant to establish it as the preferred means to achieve them. The only thing that has changed is Americans' conceptions of what "competition" specifically means, and how best to ensure it.

As it now stands, the law is voluminous and complex and bears the scars of many long battles. Most agree that the rules we've got exist primarily to put into effect some theoretical vision of vigorous competition, and most agree that it is the modern vision of price competition laid out a bit ago. Though technically the law arises from just a few old, short, and simply worded lines of statutory code, it now exists as many thousands of judicial opinions written over more than a century, supplemented by several dozen more recent statutes that modify or clarify the original ones, and yet more judicial caselaw interpreting them. And yet, for all that, the law as it now exists can be summed up without much difficulty, just as we did with the underlying economic theory, in a comparatively simple set of ideas.

First of all, most fundamentally, a basic statement of the law might read something like this: it is the policy of the United States that private persons may not take actions to interfere improperly in the functioning of competitive markets. This policy is given effect by a body of law that mainly consists of only three rules. The way the law serves the stated policy—the way it prevents actions that interfere with healthy competition—is by prohibiting three broad classes of conduct in which businesspersons might engage. Section 1 of the Sherman Act prohibits "contract[s], combination[s] . . . or conspirac[ies]" by which they might seek to "restrain[] . . . trade." This means roughly that persons engaged in business cannot agree among themselves to do things to injure their markets. They might do that by agreeing a minimum price at which they will sell some good, or dividing geographical markets in which they will not compete with one another, or making similar kinds of agreements. Sherman Act section 2 prohibits "monopolization," making it illegal for any one large business to try to exclude all or most of its competitors from the marketplace. Finally, Clayton Act section 7 prohibits "acquisitions" by one firm of the assets or control of another firm, where the acquisition would "substantially . . . lessen competition, or . . . tend to create a monopoly."

Importantly, none of these rules flatly prohibits all "conspiracies in restraint of trade," or all "monopolies," or all acquisitions. They prohibit only those that are "unreasonable." While that has meant different things at different times, at present it is accurate to say that conduct is unreasonable when it sufficiently impairs the ideal conditions of competition such that price will go up, output will go down, or quality will be impeded.

One specific kind of rule is missing from this list, for good or ill: the no-fault monopoly rule. The United States has almost never made the mere size of a business illegal in itself, even when its size persuasively implies market power. That is one reason the government has not yet taken antitrust action against Amazon.

There have been a few exceptions over time, beginning with a "gentlemen's agreement" among state legislatures of the later nineteenth century, under which they maintained state incorporation laws that limited the size and powers of corporations. When that agreement broke down, there were many attempts to reestablish it by federalizing corporate law, but they were unsuccessful.[35] Likewise, some states at times attempted to limit chain stores with special taxes, and Congress during the Depression imposed a corporate income tax graduated by gross revenue, which was in effect a tax on size.[36] But the only really meaningful no-fault monopoly law ever adopted in the United States was a sector-specific one that was in force only briefly. The Public Utility Holding Company Act of 1935 was used to break up some big firms thought to have contributed to the Depression.[37] When the government's reorganization work was finished under that law, after a few years, it was allowed to lapse.[38]

The closest thing we have had to a generally applicable no-fault monopoly rule is Clayton Act section 7, a law against anticompetitive mergers and acquisitions. It can be used to stop deals for no more reason than that they increase the likelihood of anticompetitive conduct in the future, even when there is no evidence of any such conduct in the past. But it is a limited tool because it applies only to acquisitions, and it has been difficult to use because of its prospective nature. It is of no use at all against a firm that has simply gotten very big.

Whether or not we *should* have some general no-fault monopoly rule is a different question, and it has been seriously debated at times. Following a period of concentration perceived as undesirable during the 1950s and 1960s, and the enforcement agencies' apparent failure to act against it, public support grew for some affirmative deconcentration measure. The effort culminated in a 1969 study commissioned by President Johnson and led by University of Chicago Law School dean Phil C. Neal. The Neal Commission recommended the adoption of a no-fault deconcentration statute and the (ultimately unsuccessful) introduction of deconcentration and no-fault monopoly bills in Congress during the 1970s.[39] But no such law ever came to be.

3

And Yet, Uncertainty

The Long Shadows of the American *Methodenstreit*

AMERICAN AMBIVALENCE OVER COMPETITION as a public policy has old antecedents, and on some level no doubt they predate the American people. As long as there has been capitalism, competition in operation has been confusing and often painful. But certain themes that dominate this book began to appear in their modern form during the American Industrial Revolution. That period, the "formative birth-time of [our] basic institutions," saw change and social stress but also an American intellectual renaissance. What was strikingly new about it, and what American culture and policy have struggled with ever since, was a tension between a long-held economic philosophy and the new problems it had produced and was unable to solve. The vision that had predominated for generations, of automatic social processes that optimize themselves by way of free markets and limited government, had seemed plausible to a nation of farmers and small businesses. But with the changes that followed the Civil War, Americans had to reconcile that understanding with the rise of massive firms with threatening power, and a series of severe market downturns. The liberal individualism that had been well served by free markets was now threatened by them, by both the disparities in power they had produced and by apparently calamitous risks to economic well-being. Intellectuals and people of public affairs were concerned to avoid the ugliness and suffering of the British Industrial Revolution, which had played out at the beginning of the century.[1]

Even before things really began to change, and as if the trauma of the Civil War hadn't been enough, difficulties had persisted for many years in the economies of the North Atlantic. Several financial panics and depressions struck between 1870 and 1907. In fact, the period between 1873 and the mid-1890s was so severe that in its day it was known as the "Great Depression." Then, in about 1895, a large wave of mergers began that is still known today as the Great Merger Movement. Thousands of firms were swallowed up into new corporate megaliths that came to dominate whole industries. In only ten years it resulted in the largest consolidation of business in history. Probably more than any other single development, it drove a growing sense that open competition no longer worked. Labor conflict was rising and sometimes brutally violent, and at least among business leaders, a natural explanation for the day's economic difficulties was the decreasing productivity of labor and its purportedly increasing share of the cost of doing business. Meanwhile, a once mainly rural people coped with urbanization that resulted from both domestic movement from the countryside and immigration.[2]

It was also a time of fervent theoretical advancement and controversy among economists in Europe and America that was to some degree unrelated to real-world events. The new "marginalist" economics approaching synthesis in Europe would eventually work a revolution in the theory and solve difficult puzzles that had eluded economists for centuries. But during its first decades, it exacerbated already brewing professional disagreements and drove what would be lasting, defining criticisms of markets and market capitalism. Even as marginalism spread, other important movements were pushing in essentially the opposite direction. That occurred particularly in the then-dominant academic establishment in Germany and among a generation of American economists who took their graduate training there, who came to be known as the institutionalists. The basically methodological dispute dividing them from marginalists echoed an older and much deeper drama in Western thought, originating at least as early as romantic reaction to the manic system-building of the Enlightenment.

Marginalism posed another problem as well. During its development, marginalism's progenitors closely analyzed the costs of doing business and came to fear that the very high fixed costs characteristic of manufacturing and infrastructure firms in the newly industrial economy might be too difficult to recoup under vigorous competition. That lent itself to a strong criticism of markets under industrial conditions: that competition itself had become "destructive" of businesses trying to operate within it. Particularly against the unfolding calamity of the Industrial Revolution, it gave academic credibility to what was already a long-standing preference in American business for private self-help though industry cooperation and cartel.[3]

So, during the Industrial Revolution, American society was primed to rethink its political philosophy entirely. It is difficult to untangle the profusion of ideas developing during that time, the complexity of real-world change, and the many, varying syntheses of the period that American historians have put forward. But a few themes emerge that are key to this book and will help explain *Apple*. As it turns out, Americans did *not* rethink their philosophy on any broad basis. They did something else instead, and it was extremely interesting.

In a masterful analysis, the historian Gary Gerstle argued that during this period American society began a complex of compromises needed to preserve an individualist ideology in the face of the Industrial Revolution.[4] Compromise was required not merely between competing groups. Society itself compromised with its own internal conflicts, allowing them to persist, submerged, so that everyday life could go on. It was a period of transformational intellectual change, characterized by fluidity of alignments and alliances—not only changing alignments among groups, and changing membership within them, but individuals' changing allegiances to ideas. In this environment the collapse of formerly dear political values rendered uncertain the future of political alignments and made social experimentation possible. The many social movements of the day and their sometimes utopian programs to better the human condition could be understood as a fragmentation of classical liberalism. As divergences from the comparatively homogeneous, shared liberal politics of the nineteenth century, these movements began with a sense that the traditional vision had failed to cope with the unanticipated complexities of newly industrial society. According to Gerstle, the challenge for liberalism at the turn of the twentieth century was to grapple with the reality that liberal policies had failed to produce promised results: "Free enterprise became corporate monopoly, . . . freeing the slaves produced a caste system in the South, [and] America's free social and political environment failed to dissolve 'coagulated' ethnic attachments."[5] This uncertainty prompted flirtations with technocracy and collectivism among actors all along the political spectrum, in organized labor, in the flourishing Taylorist and standard-setting movements, and in the emancipatory aspirations of the developing social sciences.[6] Among other things, it drove an interest in experimenting with state-centered social planning. Gerstle goes so far as to say that "American liberalism" as it would come to be during this period "is in part traceable to its role as a surrogate socialism."[7] Indeed, the National Industrial Recovery Act in 1933, a crowning achievement of the period, was in many ways a flirtation with corporate fascism; one of its brightest lights was an outspoken admirer of Mussolini.[8] But all these desires ran up against the old and powerful theme of individualism. The still-lingering conflicts among them were at work in *Apple* and they are at the heart of this book.

Most importantly, the legacy of this era was not just a transition to some new consensus. When we arrived at the "corporate liberalism" or "organizational synthesis" now commonly portrayed in American history writing, we had not simply chosen a new norm to replace an old one with which it conflicted.[9] Instead, conflicts were cabined and submerged, persisting out of sight. In large part by reconceiving large organizations as "individuals" and by denying that class exists, a strong individualism could endure in America in the face of social and economic changes that severely imperiled individual freedom. At the same time, we adopted values and policies—a preference for allocational efficiency, for example— that make sense in a corporate order with a collectivist, interventionist state but are not easily reconciled with individualism.

The tensions left unresolved by this great compromise seriously complicate the operation of a competition law. For a people trying to preserve traditional individualism while watching mass market capitalism work its often ugly way through unconstrained markets, the compromise looks something like the following. On the one hand, most of the time, most of us view markets and enterprise as good or at least tolerable, and an ordinary part of our political tradition. On the other hand, because their workings and the laws meant to keep them vigorous sometimes jeopardize things we hold dear, we resort to an intellectual escape hatch. To repeat an idea introduced earlier, we hold that *some markets are special because sometimes competition itself is destructive.* And as we saw earlier, the reason that markets seem special and competition seems destructive is usually the same. The problem is thought to be price itself, because it can be driven so low that participants in the market won't be able to provide things that society needs. If prices are too low in these hypothesized cases, they have bad consequences.

The difficulty is that we have no useful or shared means for deciding *which* markets are special. In fact, we differ on that question enough that there will typically be someone prepared to criticize any antitrust action against any defendant. I argue that this long-standing, tense compromise resurfaced in the twenty-first century *Apple* debate, albeit in modern terms that would have been unfamiliar in the Gilded Age.

The roots of the tension are old, in both Europe and America. Taking events out of order, it is useful to begin by considering one of the most important. In economic theory, marginalism, or "neoclassicism," was a theoretical innovation that began in the 1870s. It plays an outsized role in this story, both because its rise drove so much controversy and confusion and because it is now so woven into antitrust and basic economic theory.

At first, marginalism was largely ignored, in part because it was the work of outsiders to academic economics, but also because it was substantially more difficult to understand than what had preceded it. It was in some broad sense the same economics that had come before it, but it was based on a new, more elaborate, and rigorously mathematical means to explain human decision making. Initially, the less mathematically sophisticated scholars who mostly made up establishment economics couldn't grasp it. But when mainstream economists did begin to digest this new work it became a watershed, and it would remake all of economic theory during the first decades of the twentieth century.[10]

Marginalism was first synthesized in a remarkable, coincidental turn of events. Because the theory is difficult and counterintuitive, it is not the sort of thing that might naturally occur to people, like ideas that are obvious. Yet it was developed independently, apparently by chance, in three separate countries and three different languages. The coincidence brings to mind the large number of technological innovations that have been made simultaneously by different people working independently, or the simultaneous discovery of calculus by Isaac Newton and Gottfried Liebniz. While each of the three economists built on work that had come before them—so their books were not entirely bolts from the blue—the singular improbability of it happening at the same time gives it some ring of discovery rather than ideology. In any case, the books that these men wrote went mostly unnoticed for some time, and to the extent they were noticed, they were attacked as heretical.[11]

Marginalism begins with a simple assumption that also played a role in classical economics and utilitarianism: market participants serve their own interests and try to improve their own satisfactions. As their central contribution, the marginalists formalized this intuition mathematically and then built it into a framework by which to explain whole markets.

Economists usually describe the satisfaction consumers get from consuming things as "utility" or "welfare." The new marginalist model built on an idea that people choose how much to consume of each of the things they like by apportioning their satisfactions among them all, equilibrating the net benefits they get from them. They essentially figure out a list of goods and services to buy that gives them the most overall satisfaction, taking into account how much it all costs. In mathematical terms, doing this—balancing the overall net benefits of some set of purchases—is known as balancing *at the margin*. For these reasons, the basic argument by which marginalists attempted to explain markets was based on market participants' "marginal utility."

Part of the reason for the theory's quick rise to dominance, once the establishment began to understand it, was its elegant solution of a number of old theoretical problems. Perhaps most striking was the maneuver by which it solved the dilemma of value. For centuries thinkers had struggled to explain why some very important things are cheap and some gratuitous luxuries are expensive (as in the famous paradox of water and diamonds). Marginalism explains the problem easily. Starting with the assumption that people maximize their own satisfactions, it adds an insight that superficially seems obvious but in rigorous application becomes penetrating. The satisfaction a person gets from having some thing will decrease as they consume more and more of the thing. At some point, the value of having another unit of it will be less appealing than consuming other things, even if the person values the original good very highly. So, the fact that water is comparatively cheap is not at odds with the fact that humans value it highly, because water is also comparatively abundant. In developed societies most people have easy access to much more clean water than they could personally consume. By contrast, diamonds are very rare, so to consume even one of them, the people who want them will compete with one another in what they are willing to pay, pushing up the price. Were the quantities reversed, the outcomes would be different. If diamonds were as common as water, people might still think they are pretty and might still make jewelry out of them, but they also would probably pick them up for free off the ground. If water were very rare, in an otherwise prosperous society, it would be provided at extremely high prices.

This insight, built on the phenomenon of "decreasing marginal utility," was critically important. For one thing, as a description of markets, it actually worked. The working theory of value for most economists during the nineteenth century had remained the "labor theory of value," according to which a thing was valued by how much labor was required to produce it. That theory could explain a lot of observed behavior, but it also had obvious shortcomings. In particular, some things might not sell for much even though they are laborious to make, and many things were more expensive than their labor cost could explain.

Marginalist utility theory did much more than just solve the problem of value. It was the tool for explaining how whole economies worked. One problem in an economy is that producers of things must decide what and how much to produce. According to the theory, producers are like consumers in that they too maximize their own satisfactions. In money economies they experience their satisfaction in profit, measured as the amount of revenue they take in minus all the costs of earning it. Whereas consumers consume some given thing until the utility of consuming one

more unit is outweighed by the utility of having something else, a producer produces a thing until producing one more unit of it would not yield
more total profit. A producer can make more profit by selling more, as
long as consumers are available to pay more for the additional output than
it cost to make. But the more of the thing that producers make—and the
more abundant it therefore becomes—the less that consumers will be
willing to spend for it, because their marginal utility will decrease as the
supply of the thing increases. Something almost magical then happens at
a certain point, and it happens automatically. Except in unusual circumstances, there will be a quantity of output such that the very last unit costs
the same that the very last consumer is willing to pay for it. Beyond that
point, producers won't put any more resources into making the thing, and
remaining resources can be turned to making other things. Thus, as-
suming that this theory actually explains the working of the real world,
markets can automatically solve a truly vast set of administrative problems simultaneously, apparently to the best satisfaction of all. Although
it can be a little complex to explain, it turns out not to be magical at all.
Once one understands the basic argument, it is strikingly clear common
sense.

But in any case, for whatever inner elegance it might have had and however well or not it explained actual experience, marginalism also contributed to certain divisive, ongoing ideological differences. While on
many levels marginalism was its own special event in the history of economics, it arose within the context of long-standing disputes. Those tensions had long simmered, but in various ways margnalism worsened them.
For many critics, the very method of deductive generalization was a
problem, and had been throughout the nineteenth century at least. Its tendency was to deny the relevance of case-specific characteristics that
seemed to humanize particular cases or call for softening the harshness
of market outcomes. In marginalist form the problem was worse than ever,
as the newly central emphasis it placed on individual willingness to pay
seemed so deliberately to privilege the interests of business and the
wealthy. Indeed, whole social aggregates, including social classes, ethnic-
ities, religions, and the like, were made irrelevant, because everything
depended on selfish individual action. Marginalism seemed to exclude
some aggregates in particular, such as class, that for a long time had been

of such concern to the Left. For more conservative critics, the impact of marginalism was rather different. Again, there had long been concern within industry and the capitalist class that price competition itself could be a social problem. Too much competition, it was thought, would spell ruin for all concerned. There had also long been some degree of private self-help to prevent it, by way of industry cooperation. Marginalism introduced new ideas that seemed to corroborate the need for private cooperation. Specifically, in its early attempts to understand the motives of producers, marginalism carefully examined the costs that producers bore at different levels of output. That examination produced a sobering discovery that in industries requiring large initial capital outlays—which possibly included many sectors of the Industrial Revolution—unrestrained price competition could keep firms from covering their own costs. In this way, the marginalism of the day gave rise to the "ruinous" or "destructive" competition reasoning raised by defendants in *Addyston Pipe*. Although Judge Taft rejected the argument in that case, to much of the public, and for many years thereafter, marginalism supplied what seemed like a theoretically respectable justification for collaboration and cartel.

The origins of much leftward critique of capitalism lie in what is really a difference over methodology. Even well before marginalism, the dominant mainstream approach in Britain and America had been deductive generalization. For the most part, the more abstract and general the theory could be made, the better it seemed to be, because with generality comes explanatory power. But that approach has consistently been opposed by those who demand inductive reasoning from empirical evidence, individualized study of discrete cases for their special circumstances, and insight from history, ethics, sociology, and kindred study.[12]

To those critics, the world seems complex and abstraction simplifies. The generalization common in economics has tended to minimize the role of nonmarket institutions and cultural traditions in explanations of social order. Given the messy complexity of real-world subject matter, that stance can seem naive and intuitively implausible. As we saw earlier, this problem in social science parallels a problem in law and public policy. Laws must find expression through the intermediary of human concepts, which can never perfectly fit the real-world situations to which they must apply. Ultimately, we seem unable to match even our most basic policy commitments to specific circumstances. Likewise, social theory apparently cannot avoid the tension between the explanatory power and the dehumanizing simplifications of generality. Abstraction is a problem, but humans to some degree seem inescapably to do it.

More to the point, abstraction has driven the persistent apprehension that orthodox economics is inherently conservative, such that generalizing away case-specific distinctions seems morally objectionable. That criticism is understandable, at least on a human level, and it probably does have real-world policy implications. As a description of social phenomena, economic theory has seemed somehow wrong in its amoral bloodlessness, its dehumanizing theoretical generality, and its denial of essential attributes of human nature other than self-interest.[13]

To its critics, marginalism seems to make all these problems worse. Its reduction of the individual is so severe that actual individuals are literally irrelevant; only the *average* behavior of large groups matters.[14] A deeper problem is that marginalism's new measure of value is strictly subjective and amoral. A thing is said to have value only to the extent that a person derives satisfaction from having it. As far as marginalist theory is concerned, the cost of the inputs used to make a thing, or the value of the labor it requires, is irrelevant. Accordingly, marginalism seemed to deny the possibility that things could have value to society even if they were not valued in the grimy precincts of venal commerce. By allocating resources only according to selfish personal satisfactions, it seemed to imperil things many of us value very much. Art works, for example, or expenditures for public safety or pollution reduction, or quaint neighborhoods or small-entrepreneur lifestyles, are all important only to the degree that someone is willing to pay for them. It further seemed to imply a model of the individual as a narrow-mindedly acquisitive sociopath whose only motives are selfish—a model at odds with both our ideals and our common experience. It seemed unable to explain altruism or other "noneconomic" motivations, or to acknowledge that they could help explain economies. And a key problem arose with the realization that, like all other goods in marginalist theory, money also has a decreasing marginal utility. To a person with little money, every dollar is comparatively precious, whereas we imagine fat-cat industrialists using dollar bills to light their cigars. This has a crucial political consequence. In the marginalist model we take it as natural or automatic, and therefore in some sense "correct," that resources will be allocated to uses people value most highly. But we do *not* directly measure the satisfaction a person actually gets from the thing. Because there is no other way to compare objectively the value that two people put on some thing, the only question we ask is how much each of them would be willing to pay for it. But the rich, who have more dollars and therefore value each individual one of them less, will be willing to pay more for a thing than a poorer person, even if the poor person derives more satisfaction from it. Accordingly, the marginalist model of markets cannot account for, and in effect does not care about, inequality of wealth. It systematically privileges the wants of the rich.

One actually can counter each of these points, so that their lesson need not be so inherently ideological. But from a certain perspective they obviously contribute to the sense that the marginalists' real motive was to justify plutocracy and greed.

The tension between abstraction and inductive case-specifics had persisted for a long time in Europe. On some level, it originated in the romantic reaction of the nineteenth century, a revolt against the stridently abstracted system-building of the Enlightenment.[15] During the century it would manifest in one way or another in all departments of social thought. It was a significant problem, for example, for scholars and historians of law, pitting the influential analytical jurisprudence of the British scholar John Austin against a newer historical approach that arose in, above all, the extraordinary new synthesis by his countryman Henry Sumner Maine. It also played its role in reaction to British utilitarianism, which was attacked for its effort to solve inherently moral problems through abstract and a priori logic.[16]

In economics proper, the romantic reaction found its first and most important home in the German Historical School. The Historicists stressed that economics must base itself not only in abstraction, but also in study of history and case-specific detail. It was itself the focus of a methodological dispute in Germany and Austria so significant that it has its own name—the *Methodenstreit.*

German historical economics heavily influenced American thought. Because the German university system maintained intellectual dominance in the West during the nineteenth century, many young Americans went to Germany to do their graduate training, and the Historicists trained a whole generation of American economists during the 1870s and 1880s.[17] That generation would cast long shadows, as a group of the brightest of them founded the American Economic Association in 1885, as well as what would become one of the profession's most influential journals, the AEA's *American Economic Review.*[18] The Historicist influence still persists in the United States in various ways. It flourished early in the twentieth century in an economic school known as institutionalism, with influential exponents in the famous iconoclast Thorstein Veblen, the economists John Commons and Wesley Mitchell, and the legendary study by Berle and Means called *The Modern Corporation and Private Property.*[19] The American school of legal thought known as legal realism was in some sense a wing of institutionalist economics. As those early efforts faded, their motivations persisted, and others kept up the hostility to orthodox economics as an ideological coup masquerading as honest science. Those motivations flourished in legal academia, where they were explicitly at the heart of critical legal studies and other efforts that spanned several decades. Obviously, work critical of economics as ideology also extends well beyond economics and legal academia. Substantial movements throughout the twentieth century attacked orthodox economics on various grounds. Among the most important criticisms have been sophisticated attacks on marginalism's assumption of human rationality, as in Herbert Simon's Carnegie School movement and recent work in behavioral economics. All of these movements stressed, in one way or another, a methodological empiricism that was deliberately antitheoretical.[20]

4

Uncertainty of Another Kind

Coping with Capitalism through Association and Self-Help

A DIFFERENT TREND with roots deep in American history emerged during the late nineteenth century, and it too would live on as a component of the submerged, fraught compromise of modern liberalism. For a long time, businesses had sought to moderate rough competition through collective self-help. Cartels and other trade-restraining arrangements had been common in the United States since at least the mid-nineteenth century. That in itself is unsurprising—the pressure of competition inherently invites competitors to seek comfort from each other—but these arrangements also found echoes in the American tradition of solving problems through private association. That habit was already present, and it grew within the context of an old tradition, but it was exacerbated by the rise of marginalism. In the careful consideration of producers' costs made necessary by marginalism, it became clear that under some circumstances, where initial capital outlays were large, competitors facing vigorous price challenge might be unable to cover their costs. And because it was thought that high fixed-cost situations of that nature might be increasingly common in the new markets of the Industrial Revolution, many came to fear that competition itself had become "destructive."[1] As it evolved over the first few decades of the twentieth century, this view would drive some of the most spectacular policy misadventures of our history.

Americans have long sought to solve problems through private collaborations. Defense of the private sphere against central control predates even our individualism. In an important, meticulous analysis, Barry Alan Shain showed that prior to about 1790, the driving political ideal of most Americans was a strong preference for the "private," but not to preserve some individual liberty or self-realization. It was rather a strong localism, preoccupied with the autonomy of local church and local community. "Liberty" to the typical American of the eighteenth century did not mean liberty to do whatever one pleased. It meant liberty to choose the community of one's preference, and then be obedient to it. Deep in our history was a commitment to private *association*. It was later, around the time of ratification of the Constitution, and to some degree as a matter privileged by the elites of the founding generation, that individualism overshadowed the associationalist folk culture of the colonies.[2]

To be clear, though, devotion to private association survived the rise of individualism at the turn of the nineteenth century, even the radical individualism of Jacksonian times. De Tocqueville famously wrote in the 1830s, "Americans of all ages, all stations in life, and all types of disposition are forever forming associations. . . . In every case, at the head of any new undertaking, where in France you would find the government or in England some territorial magnate, in the United States you are sure to find an association."[3]

As in other sectors, association played a significant role in business affairs.[4] Businesspeople have always collaborated, as long as there has been capitalism, and the incentive to do so is innate to anyone facing competition. But what is noteworthy is that they rationalized it, even in the face of well-established social opprobrium. Price-fixing had been famously described as antisocial in *The Wealth of Nations,* and under some circumstances it was illegal as a common law restraint of trade in both Britain and America.[5] Yet businesspeople in every part of the economy formed cartels and other trade restraints throughout the century. By midcentury, some cartels, particularly in the railroads and ocean shipping, had become large and elaborate. It was done mostly in the open, and justified as civic-minded self-regulation of the markets that was necessary for the greater good.[6]

That activity was not yet justified by the explicit destructive competition reasoning that would dominate later, following the rise of marginalism. Although some such reasoning did exist—including among American publishers, as it happens, in the custom of "trade courtesy" they devised around midcentury to combat unlicensed piracy—there was not yet much rigorous theory that competition itself was dangerous. But that is not to say there was none, and indeed there were even connections made between destructive competition and the need to prevent it through specific interventions. As early as 1851 the American economist Henry Charles Carey laid out an elaborate theoretical formulation that prefigured the objection to classical orthodoxy that associationalists would raise in the early twentieth century. Carey was the son of the great American publisher Matthew Carey, who had begun the famous Philadelphia publishing house Carey & Lea with the backing of Ben Franklin and the Marquis de Lafayette. Henry joined his father in that business. The two of them also were among the best known American economists of the day, and they both wrote leading treatises. Late in life, Henry served as economic advisor to Abraham Lincoln, and his work was known and commented on by Karl Marx.[7] Among Carey's contributions was exegesis of the so-called American system in international trade, a program introduced by Lincoln's mentor, Senator Henry Clay. While Carey professed that "of the advantage of perfect freedom of trade, theoretically considered, there can be no doubt," his philosophy consisted of a savage critique of vigorous competition itself within young nations such as America. The "universal discord" of competition produced disagreeable macroeconomic consequences, as well as domestic social strife and literal war.[8]

When unsettling social and industrial changes began after the Civil War, it was natural that Americans would respond with a frenetic season of private association. Befitting a time of transition, bouts of coalition building and organizational fluidity appeared in sectors all through society. In business there was a great deal of cartel activity. Interestingly, American book publishing not only observed the "trade courtesy" custom but also established one of the largest horizontal cartels in the industry's history. It was also during this period that the major institutions of American law reform were established, including the American Law Institute and the National Conference of Commissioners on Uniform State Laws, and among their key goals was to use their influence to rationalize a newly national economy. Similar goals drove the exploding movement to set technological standards. Although today there are tens or hundreds of thousands of standard setting organizations active in the United States, the twenty or so that produce most of our current standards came into being around the turn of twentieth century.[9] They addressed familiar concerns of the Industrial Revolution—including protection for labor and consumers and the growing need for product interoperability—and their proponents saw standardization as a large-scale social movement.[10] Likewise, it is only too telling that it was a predominantly private coalition of business, labor and community leaders who convened influential conferences in the early twentieth century to consider the problem of monopoly itself. Associated with the National Civic Federation, conferences of 1899 and 1907 generated the proposals that would eventually become the Clayton Act and the Federal Trade Commission Act.[11]

The boost that the emerging marginalism would lend to this associationalism was the most interesting development of all. Economists of the turn of the century struggled to explain the repeated depressions, pervasive unemployment, and concentration to oligopoly or monopoly, given that classical theory anticipated more desirable outcomes. A predominant explanation was destructive competition, which held that where fixed costs were high, as they were thought to be in the many capital-intensive industries of the day, open competition would produce rate war, leading to either monopoly or the destruction of all competitors. In marginalism's search to understand the producer behavior, the theory had to encompass the problem of costs. In particular, it had to carefully analyze *marginal* costs, because it predicted that in perfect competition, producers would continue expanding output until price just covered the additional cost of producing that last item. But that posed a big problem. Strictly speaking, in the short run, a price equal to marginal cost will not cover fixed costs—that is, those costs that must be expended in order to enter the business, and that don't vary with the number of units sold. That seemed like an especially serious problem where fixed costs were large, because once two firms both committed to very large fixed outlays, they might find themselves desperate to cover it, even though marginal cost would be much lower than the average cost of the business overall. The result could be persistent price war, followed by bankruptcy of all players except for the winner, who would enjoy monopoly for some period until new entry attracted by monopoly profits triggered a new price war.

Nowadays we are not much bothered by this problem. While economists recognize that price war is possible, businesspeople and their financiers do not actually enter markets blindly without considering longer-term consequences, especially where large initial outlays are required. Thus, it is taken for granted that even industries with large fixed costs are rarely "destructive," and firms in virtually all industries actually earn at least some cushion over their marginal cost.[12]

But in its day, the argument led an expanding academic consensus that competition in general might no longer work. Moreover, it was widely agreed that the only variable within the control of business managers was output. It was thought that a chief problem was the rising cost of labor, but that labor's power was also growing and was beyond the control of the capital class. It was natural to a people already given to association that the businessman's only hope for survival would be either consolidation or horizontal output constraints. Thus, by the turn of the century, the rhetoric of the benevolent cartel was second nature in business.

Associationalism and destructive competition theory drove several remarkable policy developments in the early twentieth century, and to varying degrees they displaced antitrust and competition as public policy. First was the movement during the Progressive Era and the New Deal years to regulate several specific industries thought to be ill-suited for unrestrained competition. The "regulation" typical of these programs was quite different from the laws we now commonly call "regulation." The term now generally refers to any law that controls individual or business behavior, but few laws today actually control the terms of competition itself. Economic regulatory programs of the early twentieth century did that extensively. Typically, these programs would establish regulatory agencies that had the power to decide who could participate in a given market; to determine the nature of the products and prices; and sometimes even to decide whether a seller was permitted to exit the market. This sort of approach was applied mainly to heavy infrastructure industries such as transportation, communications, and utilities, and to industries seen as especially important to the public and at risk from unrestrained competition, such as banking, securities, insurance, and health care. Rate-and-entry regulation became controversial, as first a body of economic theory and then substantial empirical evidence showed that it mostly caused prices to go up, and it was not needed to prevent any particular economic dysfunction. Beginning with major efforts in the 1970s, much of this apparatus was repealed during a period now known as "deregulation." Some of it remains, such as municipal taxi regulation and hospital certificate-of-need laws, but even those have often been limited and tailored to permit as much competition as possible.[13]

More extraordinary was a second policy reaction to destructive competition. It was then that business sector associationalism reached its peak, under the commerce secretariat and presidency of Herbert Hoover, in the Federal Trade Commission during its first few decades, and culminating in its most spectacular form in the adoption of the National Industrial Recovery Act in 1933.[14]

As the twentieth century began, from within associationalism there emerged those who hated competition with a new fervor and believed that ending it entirely was needed for domestic stability. They began with arguments similar to those of Henry Carey fifty years earlier, but expanded them into a thorough-going rejection of competition altogether. Ultimately they called for nothing less than a reorganization of society under benevolent business organizations.

One such argument, famous in its day but now largely forgotten, was the work of a Chicago attorney Arthur Jerome Eddy. He wrote in *The New Competition* (1912) that "competition in the world of labor, trade, and industry . . . is as disastrous to the material advancement of the community as war, and disastrous in very much the same manner—in appalling waste of time, effort, money, and life."[15] There were many others who felt the same way, and business associationalism grew to become a national movement, openly engaged by leaders in business. One of the founders of U.S. Steel, Elbert Gary, arranged the famous "Gary dinners," informal gatherings of steel industry executives to coordinate business affairs, which began in 1907 and were well known to the public at that time.[16] By then, businesses had significantly cartelized the American economy in a variety of sectors.[17] Testimony surrounding the 1914 antitrust amendments included many references to destructive competition and requests for permission to fix prices.[18] The "open price associations" that many businesses formed were to varying degrees just horizontal price coordination vehicles, but they were more or less sanctioned by the Federal Trade Commission (FTC). Many of them filed their initial constitutions with the FTC and then regularly filed minutes of their meetings.[19] The FTC even sometimes made their rules mandatory through its "trade practice conference" procedure, a program inaugurated just after the agency was formed and that by the 1940s covered some two hundred separate industries.[20]

But the associationalist movement reached its true peak with the adoption in 1933 of the National Industrial Recovery Act (NIRA). The law was the cornerstone of Franklin Roosevelt's first New Deal, and it carried the hopes of Americans of all classes. But like much of New Deal policy, it was not at all Roosevelt's own idea or even his advisors'. It was part of a varied package of economic experimentation, and it owed more to the thinking of people such as Herbert Hoover, Arthur Jerome Eddy, and other associationalists. Under NIRA, Congress authorized the new National Recovery Administration (NRA) to convene conferences comprised of business, capital, and labor representatives from American industries. The participants would negotiate "codes of fair competition," which were then subject to approval by the NRA and ultimately by the president. Upon approval, they became binding federal law, enforced by criminal prosecution by the US attorneys. The NRA convened thousands of such conferences, and at length they came to regulate much of the economy. While other interests were required to be represented, and while the statute nominally set various limits on what could be agreed, the codes were dominated by business interests and largely amounted to federally enforced horizontal price cartels. So although the NIRA was at first broadly popular, it quickly fell out favor with the public. It did nothing to ease the Depression and had no evident effect except to make things more expensive.[21] Students of NIRA history have suggested that even if the Supreme Court had not held it unconstitutional in 1935, it would have been abandoned.[22]

And so, however much we may be a people of "consensus" on some abstract level, Americans have been conflicted in our basic political philosophy. Even during periods of strident individualism—such as the early twentieth century, when the Supreme Court built a radical individualism into the Constitution itself—it felt natural to groups throughout the economy to solve social problems collectively, sometimes with coercively prescriptive means. We were apprehensive of letting the markets sort those things out, as we'd be expected to do if we were the free marketeers we claim to be.

That suggests a new and interesting question that is the focus of the next chapter. If the issue is simply that we sometimes don't trust our markets, why have we so often resorted to *private* self-help, rather than turning to government? While there have been major exceptions such as the utility regulation of the Progressive Era, there are countless examples of America using private means to address needs that in other nations would be handled by a government agency. We have tax-deductible charity instead of welfare, purely private product-design and workplace-safety standards, and a central bank that is a weird amalgam of government and for-profit banks. As Gerstle says, we have used liberalism as a surrogate socialism, because for some reason we're loath to let government do the work even when we think the market can't. To some degree that probably reflects the long history of American associationalism that so impressed de Tocqueville. It has also probably reflected the desire of businesspeople to control their markets. The native associationalist habit has been very useful to business when it argues against government intervention, because private control can be very, very profitable. But it also reflects a deep and pretheoretical aversion to government that is perhaps uniquely American. Ironically, as we shall see in the next chapter, that impulse is hard to square with the belief in competition and free markets that is supposed to be our national character.

5

Tensions of the Latter Day and Some Unexpected Skepticism

IT REMAINS TO MAKE one final point about the long intellectual background preceding *United States v. Apple.* It is surprising and it is important to this book's central claim, which is that antitrust has frequently failed because Americans doubt markets extensively. What is worth a bit of extended demonstration is that this has been as true of the American Right as of the Left, even in this apparently right-leaning latter day.

Conservative antitrust has mostly been known for a near-religious faith in unrestrained competition. Modern conservatives have said that markets are so self-corrective that government should just keep out of them. In fact, critics of conservative antitrust take for granted that attacking its arguments means showing when markets are weak, not that they are systematically strong.[1] And yet conservative economics has often entailed a theoretical effort to show how flawed and defective markets might be, to demonstrate that private restraints are needed to make them work.

Fear of vigorous prices was at the heart of the destructive competition reasoning of the early twentieth century, but the fear did not die with that theory. It also drove many more recent arguments, and it is basically the inner engine driving all conservative defenses of private restraints. It has been part of many elaborate defenses of tying, bundling, most-favored-nation plans, and other common contracting practices. It was at the heart of the rather exotic "empty core" theory, once zealously pursued by some conservative economists, that claimed that certain markets cannot reach equilibrium prices.[2] It is also key to the emerging "two-sided market" theory, which recently saw the Supreme Court largely exempt credit cards from antitrust, and which some believe will have similar consequences for online platform firms.[3] Perhaps most surprising and illuminating is a point to which we will return, which is that fear of destructive prices underlies our entire edifice of intellectual property. And finally it has been part of bespoke theoretical defenses of the conduct challenged in numberless miscellaneous cases.

One particular critique in this tradition is especially important because it demonstrates the willingness across the political spectrum to doubt markets when it is rhetorically useful, and also because it happened to play an important role in the *Apple* case. Among the arguments most dear to latter-day antitrust conservatives is that "vertical" restraints are often needed to make markets work, and therefore they should usually be legal. The movement's manifestos identify it as a fundamental commitment, and its successes before the courts have been epochal. Its initial adoption by the Supreme Court in 1977 is still celebrated by some as the turning point when antitrust became "economic."[4]

Vertical relationships are between manufacturers and their distributors. Although it was not a typical vertical case, *Apple* involved vertical relationships between publishers of eBooks and their distributors, Apple and Amazon. (The economics of vertical relationships, and their special significance for the *Apple* case, are discussed later in greater detail.) Contractual restraints in vertical relationships can directly limit competition. For example, a manufacturer might require that its goods be resold at no less than some minimum retail price. That practice, commonly known as resale price maintenance (RPM), ends price competition between retailers over that manufacturer's products. There are other ways vertical restraints can limit retail competition, for example by giving individual retailers their own exclusive territories or requiring them to sell only one manufacturer's products.

Until the 1970s, antitrust was hostile to such arrangements, especially RPM. Courts had held several small vertical mergers illegal; RPM was per se illegal for most of the twentieth century; and for a brief period at midcentury, the courts held all other vertical restraints per se illegal as well. Conservative critics found this absurd, and beginning in the 1950s they generated elaborate theoretical arguments that vertical restraints solve market defects and benefit consumers.

The point at this stage in the story is not to explore the vast academic literature that followed, that purported to explain when vertical restraints were procompetitive, or to understand the complex esoterica of which it mostly consists. It is only to show the degree to which even modern antitrust conservatives—people usually taken to be free-market zealots—were willing to believe in a speculative and problematic theory of market failure when it suited their ideological impulses. A simpler explanation was that the markets in question worked just fine and the real motive for the observed conduct was profitable restraint of trade. The point instead is to analyze that central mechanism by which most critiques of competition work. They most often explain social harms as a consequence of competitive price itself.

The idea behind vertical restraints defenses is usually that there might be things that manufacturers want their distributors to do, and they might use limits on retail competition to get them to oblige. Every manufacturer cares how its products are presented and delivered to customers. However, it can be costly to sell goods in the way that manufacturers might like—providing large and well-appointed display spaces, in-store demonstrations, well-trained and unhurried sales staff, and so on. Retailers will not do it for free, and they must pass the cost on, either to consumers in higher retail prices or to the manufacturer in lower wholesale prices. But if the retailers selling that manufacturer's goods compete with each other directly, prices might dip too low to cover the cost of expensive promotional services.

Arguments of that nature had circulated for a long time, and the Supreme Court in its earliest vertical restraints cases had acknowledged and rejected them. But they took on a cogent new form after the publication in 1960 of a paper by the University of Chicago economist Lester Telser. Telser's major contribution was to explain why this all might happen, even though one would expect retailers to happily supply whatever promotional services would help sell their products. His explanation came to be known as the "free-riding" argument because it involves price-chiseling, where discount retailers take a free ride on promotional services provided by quality retailers. Imagine that some retailers provide the marketing services and others don't. Consumers might learn what they need to know by visiting a quality retailer, but then go buy the goods from a discount retailer who doesn't provide those services and therefore can charge lower prices. Eventually, quality retailers would no longer supply the services. Consumers wouldn't learn about things they might like to have, fewer goods would be sold, and everyone would be worse off.[5]

What is fairly amazing is that this purely speculative model persuaded entire generations of conservative lawyers and economists, when in fact there is so much wrong with it, and no empirical verification. First, it is a claim that competition itself is the problem. Because the discounter's prices are too low to cover the cost of quality retail services, it is the prices themselves that deprive society of something desirable. Telser himself recognized that ordinarily this shouldn't happen. Markets should work out a way to get consumers the things they want—including product information and marketing services—efficiently and without the interference of private trade restraints.[6] The circumstance he imagined as an exception to that rule contemplates a routine, systematic breakdown of the most basic tool by which all markets work—the presumption that on average, consumers rationally choose the goods they prefer. He presumes it to be so fragile that it can be defeated by the ordinary price competition of healthy markets. The point is not that such things are impossible. Most specialists agree that the free-riding theory could be correct in some cases. But believing in it, and especially believing it is likely to occur very often, is a significant departure from conservative market orthodoxy.

Accordingly, one might expect the argument to be cogent and well-substantiated, but it is not. It is riven with problems and implausibilities, and it is not borne out by real-world experience. Even in circumstances where some consumers would benefit from promotions, a variety of theoretical reasons suggest that socially harmful free-riding is rare.[7] They are corroborated by the common-sense instinct that that any reasonable mass-merchant would ordinarily consider it risky to operate as a free-rider.[8] It is therefore unsurprising that real-world instances of RPM are common for products that are unlikely to require or even benefit from brand-specific services, including boxed candy, pet foods, blue jeans, vitamins, and shampoo. Indeed, RPM has frequently occurred in markets where higher-priced and discount retailers actually provided the same promotional services.[9] Eventually, even strong defenders of vertical restraints acknowledged that free-riding cannot explain RPM in most products.[10] A few other theoretical explanations that don't require free-riding have been offered, but they all have been shown to have their own problems.[11] Most significant of all is just that if RPM has the benefits ascribed to it, then it should be observed consistently across markets and time periods with respect to the products for which it is used. But that does not occur. Its use is sporadic and idiosyncratic, and even in places where it is legal, it tends to be unstable over time.[12]

Moreover, even if free-riding and other problems do frustrate some markets, RPM is in practical terms a poor solution. There is no reason to believe that retailers are more efficient promoters than manufacturers themselves.[13] Even if they were, as even Telser recognized, manufacturers could just contract for the services explicitly.[14] Contracting should be preferable, in fact, because RPM leaves retailers with strong incentives to shirk and free-ride, pocketing the extra gains they earn from high prices.[15] And lastly, RPM only works when only some of the competing manufacturers of a given product use it.[16]

Furthermore, there is reason to think that RPM may threaten serious harm. At a minimum, even if it does achieve some socially desirable benefits, it does so at a high cost. It usually raises price, and the evidence suggests that when it was prevalent it may have cost consumers several billion dollars per year.[17] If it's a good thing for society, it must produce substantial benefits to outweigh the harm of increased price. But it probably does real good only in uncommon circumstances. In most situations, the harm it does to most consumers probably dwarfs the benefit to those few it helps.[18]

It is striking, too, that policies permitting vertical price fixing have so often been sought not by manufacturers, but by small retailers and wholesalers trying to preserve their own higher-cost existence at consumer expense. And it is surprising to see support for it from American conservatives, who usually are certain that any government policy, of any kind, is just pork-barrel politics to serve selfish private gain.

The Nobel laureate Ronald Coase, a foundational figure in the conservative Chicago School of antitrust and economics, famously mocked mid-century economists' "preoccupation" with "the monopoly problem." When such "an economist finds something . . . that he does not understand," said Coase, "he looks for a monopoly explanation."[19] That shoe has emphatically switched feet. Economists now refuse to accept even the most obviously persuasive monopoly explanations unless we disprove whatever theoretical conjectures they can dream up. For several decades, the first reaction of many conservative critics to antitrust actions has been to generate explanations to show that the underlying conduct is in fact procompetitive, in that it corrects some market defect. The effect has not been just to inject some preliminary caution. It has severely burdened government and private plaintiffs and made the law extremely difficult to enforce, without any empirical evidence of the purported costs of chilled business conduct that are thought to be averted.

If this was absurd in Coase's time, then it is absurd now, too. Though it has been rare, even the conservative movement's own members have occasionally admitted that the exercise was not scientific, or even empirically or theoretically promarket. It was just antigovernment ideology.[20]

6

Competition as a Living Policy, circa 2019

AND SO, AT THIS late date our competition policy is a very mixed patrimony. Antitrust law remains a storied inheritance of the American Industrial Revolution, and it still enjoys a certain rhetorical privilege in our politics. Judges usually discuss it less rhapsodically than they once did—the Supreme Court of an earlier day earnestly equated it with the Magna Carta and the Bill of Rights, calling it "a comprehensive charter of economic liberty"[1]—but antitrust and competition are still, in principle, held in a certain abstract reverence across the political continuum. We retain two federal agencies to enforce it, and we allocate to them substantial budgets every year. The Antitrust Section is one of the largest and most lucrative units of the American Bar Association, the preeminent association of American lawyers, and it routinely issues statements, publications, and testimony strongly supportive of vigorous antitrust.[2] And politicians of both party affiliations pay homage to antitrust. A particularly emblematic example immediately followed the election of George W. Bush, when the generally conservative representative James Sensenbrenner proposed the creation of a study commission to review the antitrust laws. Many at the time feared it would be used to limit antitrust law, given the prevailing politics and control of Capitol Hill. But one would never know it from Sensenbrenner's words. He introduced his bill by saying, "Our antitrust laws have worked well by fostering a competitive marketplace where American consumers have affordable choices. However, we shouldn't shy away from taking a look at some of these antitrust laws that have served us well over the past one hundred years to see if any changes might help ensure a competitive and innovative marketplace for the next one hundred years."[3]

Politicians have always praised antitrust law, whatever their true feelings toward it. In 1914 the political commentator Walter Lippman wrote that antitrust was widely believed to be incoherent and ineffective, but that politicians nevertheless "all say in public that it is a great piece of legislation—an 'exquisite instrument' someone called it the other day." Somewhat later, the crusading New Dealer Theodore Kreps wrote that while it was "doubtful whether during most of the period since 1890 Congress has actually . . . desired" to preserve competition, its "oratory has been 'agin monopoly.'"[4] More recently, during the long push to dismantle the rate-and-entry regulatory apparatus of the Progressive Era and New Deal years, politicians across the spectrum—even officials of the Reagan White House—felt obliged to stress that even as regulatory oversight was removed, the public interest would be protected by the return of antitrust to the regulated industries.[5]

Likewise, requests for special exception from antitrust almost always meet with hostility from both the courts and Congress, and exceptions already on the books face perennial pressure for limitation or repeal. The courts routinely stress the law's broad applicability, often in fairly majestic language.[6] They have traditionally observed a strong presumption against judge-made limits, and they purport to construe statutory exemptions narrowly.[7] In Congress, each of the many blue-ribbon antitrust study commissions established over the past several decades has urged repeal of existing exemptions and warned against new ones.[8] The Shenefield Report of 1979 contained seven full chapters comprehensively calling for their drastic limitation or repeal.[9] However controversial the doctrinal details of antitrust may be, the rare calls for its outright repeal are marginalized and ignored.

And yet, on many measures, antitrust is failing and losing whatever effectiveness it once had. While counting cases may be a crude measure of "failure," it is probably not irrelevant that enforcement by both govern-

ment and private plaintiffs has hit historic lows.[10] The drop in enforcement likely reflects the increased cost of bringing antitrust claims, which
in turn is driven by the attitudes of the federal judiciary.[11] Since about the
mid-1970s, the courts have fashioned a long series of prodefendant substantive and procedural rules. The serial repeal of several rules of per se
illegality since 1977, and new procedural rules on pleading, class litigation, arbitration, and expert testimony, have gotten a lot of attention.[12] Less
noticed but no less significant have been changes in the substantive standards governing mergers and monopolization, the apparently sub silentio
repeal of a once-strong rule making wrongdoers bear the risk of uncertain damages, and a rather bizarre chain of events by which once heavily
regulated industries have become subject to *neither* regulation *nor*
antitrust.[13]

In addition to these specific doctrinal changes, a truly remarkable turn
has been the courts' new reliance on what is essentially tort-reform rhetoric. They have cited litigation costs, the purportedly misplaced incentives of the plaintiff's bar, and the threat of nuisance settlements as reasons to limit substantive antitrust rules and access to the courthouse.[14]

Indeed, while the courts still frequently repeat rote plaudits to the importance of antitrust, they usually do so either in the breach or only with
respect to the law's scope, not when they actually reach the merits. For
example, in all the antitrust cases the Supreme Court has decided since
1992, defendants have won all but five. Three of those five were re-
sounding, 9–0 victories for plaintiffs, but they went only to the scope of
antitrust and did not reach the merits. A fourth plaintiff victory, decided
5–4, failed to reach the merits as well.[15] In the only substantive plaintiff
victory to reach the merits in nearly thirty years, *FTC v. Actavis,* the
Court split 5–3 on ideological lines and produced a strongly worded
dissent.[16] Yet most observers, outside the industry involved in that case,
viewed the conduct in question as glaringly anticompetitive and illegal.
Many believed it should be per se illegal.[17]

Growing judicial hostility may be in part political. For what it's worth,
historians and law professors already believe that there has been a conservative turn in the federal courts, and with respect to the Supreme
Court, there is increasingly sophisticated empirical corroboration of that
view.[18] But the stronger influence is an academic one. Judges must

contend with what is now a massive theoretical literature demonstrating the ways that virtually any conduct might be procompetitive.

Fundamentally, these trends reflect a shift away from a presumption in favor of enforcement, which was in place from World War II until the late 1960s or 1970s. It emphasized empirical confidence in large-numbers competition that loses more from interfirm collaboration or very large-scale production than it gains. The presumption has shifted now against enforcement, and emphasizes the risk of chilling procompetitive conduct and politically inappropriate limits on individual freedom.[19] During this long season of antitrust decay, the courts have begun to issue opinions so radical that one doubts some judges could imagine a defendant ever losing.[20]

Competition as a policy has lost esteem in other areas. In intellectual property, especially in the developing copyright law of software, the internet, and digital distribution, protection of content owners' revenues has almost completely eclipsed concern for the public interest, in both the courts and Congress.[21]

Competition also plays little role in the priorities of officials outside the antitrust agencies, in administrations of either political party. Even in this deregulatory era, when competition kept healthy by antitrust is supposed to replace government regulation, sectoral regulators frequently downplay the values of competition and seek to protect firms from it. Well-known examples include the Securities and Exchange Commission's long-running refusal to end the brokerage house price-fixing system—in which stockbrokers agreed how much they would charge their clients to execute stock trades—despite its statutory mandate to protect competition.[22] Even more remarkable was that agency's battle to secure general antitrust immunity for its regulees. That saga began in 1963, when the Supreme Court first held that conduct regulated by the Securities and Exchange Commission might nonetheless violate antitrust.[23] After that, the Commission participated in several lawsuits to secure antitrust immunity for its regulees, an effort that largely succeeded in *Credit Suisse Secs. (USA), LLC v. Billing.*[24] Often, it defended those private firms not only against private plaintiffs, but also against the Justice Department.

Gordon v. New York Stock Exchange, United States v. National Association of Securities Dealers, and *Credit Suisse* all featured the spectacle of two federal agencies taking opposite positions in the same case.[25] The Department of Agriculture has been similarly lax as competition enforcer for agricultural cooperatives. The cooperatives, which in the absence of antitrust exemption would probably constitute illegal price fixing cartels, were authorized in 1922 to act as self-regulating groups of farmers, and they operate on the theory of countervailing force to protect them from powerful agricultural intermediaries. Critics expected the Department never to use its competition enforcement power, even when it was first enacted, and that expectation proved quite accurate.[26] Meanwhile, the cooperatives have grown into large, very commercial bureaucracies, with little resemblance to the family farm.[27]

There are countless other examples. The Surface Transportation Board, the successor to the Interstate Commerce Commission, was overwhelmingly lax in its acquiescence to rail consolidation.[28] The Department of Transportation was similarly lenient during its brief career as airline merger regulator.[29] Competition values have long been disregarded by federal energy regulators and by the Federal Maritime Commission in oversight of ocean shipping, even though in both sectors, the agencies have statutory authority and mandates to protect competition values.[30]

The most revealing cases are those in which it no longer even occurs to us that competition could be any part of our policy. An example is the Dodd-Frank financial regulatory reform legislation of 2010. Systemic risk is widely associated with small-numbers, large-firm finance markets, both in the popular mind and among important commentators.[31] Breaking up those big firms or encouraging the presence of more, smaller firms in order to spread risk and decrease interconnectedness seems like a common-sense step toward systemic stability. However, the draft bill that became the Obama administration's Dodd-Frank law failed to incorporate competition as any part of any solution, and it actually contained a handful of new and potentially serious antitrust exemptions.[32] The administration actively opposed more competition-oriented tools during the congressional debate.[33]

A sustained or increasing commitment to competition enforcement exists in only one narrow area, and the exception proves the more general trend. We have vigorous antitrust only in the criminal enforcement of Sherman Act section 1, and that is because there bipartisan support for it. Naked price cartel is no one's constituency, so there is no political cost in squashing it. The Justice Department maintains an aggressive program, increasing criminal prosecutions significantly even as civil enforcement has waned, and it widely publicizes the fines and prison terms it secures.[34] Congress has also dramatically increased penalties over the past few decades.[35] But even within that area, the focus has not been the entire class of conduct subject to criminal challenge—naked, horizontal price or output restraints—but only certain segments within it. For considerable periods in recent history, criminal prosecutions have disproportionately focused on small businesses in a limited range of sectors. In particular, there was a significant stretch during which prosecution targeted mainly bid-rigging in state government procurement and construction contracts.[36] Perhaps due to this selective prosecution, as well as the exceptional profitability of price-fixing in some sectors, the evidence is that it remains quite common.[37]

The result of these trends is that antitrust enforcement has become more rare, the cost and difficulty of bringing it ensures that cases are brought mainly against the nakedest horizontal collusion and the largest horizontal mergers, and many courts now receive even those cases with skepticism. And finally—although many would disagree that this has any causal relation to declining antitrust enforcement—it is empirically demonstrable that there have been substantial increases in concentration in many individual sectors.[38]

PART II

THE ᴇBOOKS CASE

7

The Old Business of Books

From then on, [after taking Random House public in 1959,] we were publishing with one eye and watching our stock with the other.

—Bennett Cerf, *At Random: The Reminiscences of Bennett Cerf*

WHEN AMAZON INTRODUCED the Kindle eBook reader in late 2007, to a hopefulness among publishers that would turn quickly to outrage and fear, it accomplished something at which others had failed several times and many had thought not feasible. It created a commercially viable eBooks sector. This occurred during an important point in the history of the book industry, as publishers struggled with certain heavy pressures and faced potentially significant transitions on more than one front. During the *Apple* suit, in their litigation strategy and public comments, and in the views of those who supported them, the publishers portrayed a desperation that was no doubt quite sincere. They foresaw losses not only to the publishing firms themselves, but to deeper cultural values and to literature itself.

That theme is a very old one. The premise that there is "a tension between books as instruments of culture and books as products in a profit-making business" is uncritically taken for granted, even in works of serious social science.[1] In fact, the notion that it is dangerous to expose books to open competition has supported special policy treatment for a century or more in many countries, especially in Europe. National culture ministers and whole bureaus of nongovernmental organizations have as major portfolio items the defense of such policies, and in addition to granting tax concessions and subsidies, many governments have protected publishers by authorizing them to fix retail prices, or have even directly fixed book prices by law. In this respect, books have been a major exception to many countries' legal norms. In Europe, for example, retail price-fixing of most products is mostly banned outright, but with respect to books it is widely permitted.[2] Although US law has never been so solicitous of publishing, it was the same ancient concern for cultural values and publishers' role in safeguarding them that made *Apple* such a difficult case for so many people.

But there is more to this story, and it cannot be understood without some historical context. On the one hand, there is no doubt that publishers were coping with change and new challenges. They were under pressure from revenues that had been flat or falling for years, as well as the growth in the bargaining leverage of their distributors, including the mall stores B. Dalton and Waldenbooks, which came to prominence in the 1980s, the chain superstores Borders and Barnes & Noble in the 1990s, and Amazon in the 2000s.

But on the other hand, one must be somewhat wary of publishing executives' own fears of the competition they faced and the gravity of their crisis. In the words of the legendary Simon & Schuster editor Michael Korda, "I've been in publishing for nearly forty years, and in that time people have always behaved as if the sky were about to fall. The sky was about to fall because of television. The sky was about to fall because of discounting books. The sky was about to fall because of conglomerates. The sky was about to fall because of agents. The sky hasn't fallen."[3] Moreover, a major problem in judging the publishers' recent history is that it is hard to know how much their challenges had to do with outside actors, or with any change in business or technology, or with anything else outside their own control. Their problems were at least partly self-inflicted, the result of a long course of debt-fueled mergers and acquisitions and a history of conglomerate diversification that tended to confuse a traditional business model that once drove stable profitability. Those same changes and the strategic goals that drove them also deeply complicated the publishers' claims to cultural stewardship. By 2007, the cultural legacies of the small, arts-minded firms that each of the *Apple* defendants had once been amounted to not much more than the names that their long-departed founders had given them.

This chapter and the next few will examine these themes in their historical richness, and the story begins a long time ago.

For a long time, the business of books has been conceived as two separate businesses: publishing, which means selecting works, preparing them as manuscripts, and binding them in physical form; and the distribution and retailing that gets the books to the reading public. The two functions have sometimes been integrated in the same firm, particularly during the first century or so of publishing in America. Ben Franklin, for example, was both America's first real publisher and Philadelphia's largest bookseller.[4] Prior to the Civil War most American publishers also maintained bookstores or some other means of distribution.[5] But since that time, the two jobs have mostly been done by separate firms, and the two resulting businesses have a long history of tension and conflict. That part of the story and the important lesson it holds for this book—that there is nothing really new about the story of the *Apple* controversy—contain some theoretical complexities that will be discussed in later chapters. This chapter examines how the publishers came to be, how the book retailing sector evolved along with them, and what their history says about the eBooks crisis of the early 2000s.

Today's major publishers of English-language trade books in the United States, almost all of which were defendants in *Apple,* began as small operations, often founded and maintained as family businesses or partnerships of two or a few partners. Each of them began under more or less similar circumstances in Europe or America; the first were founded in the early nineteenth century in London and the American Northeast. Those small firms operated in populous, atomistic markets, in times of fecund intellectual and commercial change. Another group of important firms was founded about a century later in New York, in similarly vibrant circumstances. Each of them had some claim to guardianship of high intellectual values. Their leaders were mostly studious, intellectual people who cared deeply about their institutions, and some of them were truly great figures.

Though an indigenous book industry was slow to get started in America, the earliest colonists were in fact a bookish people. The Pilgrims valued literacy as an adjunct to religious devotion, mandated education by law, and counted among themselves more university graduates than in similar places in Europe. They also valued books and owned some of the largest personal libraries in the world, though those books were mostly imported from England. The first active printing press in America was set up in 1638 in what is now Cambridge, Massachusetts, to serve Harvard University and colonial authorities. For much of that century, however, printing was suppressed by colonial governments wary of sedition and rabble-rousing. A native book business did not really begin until the early to mid-eighteenth century, around the time Ben Franklin established his influential operation in Philadelphia in 1728. John Peter Zenger—the defendant in the most famous American libel case—founded a similar outfit in New York. But that early industry was hardly a publishing endeavor in today's terms. For a long time it mostly put out reprints of English books rather than original publications by American writers. That was partly because it took a while for a homegrown literature to establish a readership, but it was also because US copyright law protected only domestic authors until the 1890s. American publishers could put out pirated copies of foreign works, paying their authors no royalties. They could profitably compete by selling those books at much lower prices than domestic books, whose authors had to be paid royalties. Publishers found the more expensive, poorly selling domestic books of less appeal.[6]

Even as larger indigenous publishing operations began in Philadelphia, New York, and Boston during the late eighteenth century, printing and distribution of books remained an adjunct to various other work that printers commonly did. They published legal and financial documents, government materials, and other ephemera, and many published their own newspapers and pamphlets. The book publishing they did still mainly comprised reprints of British authors.

Modern trade publishing as we know it began in the first part of the nineteenth century. In America, the religious fervor of the Second Great Awakening drove a huge new market in the expanding nation for printed religious works and above all, bibles.[7] In the nations of the North Atlantic, there were several trends that contributed to literacy and popular interest in reading and book ownership. Reading communities, which dated to the urban coffeehouses and salon culture of the late eighteenth century, became more prevalent. As the publishing sector gathered steam, communal reading played a new role in circulating societies and community purchasing arrangements of various kinds. (Tax-funded libraries came later; they first appeared in Boston in 1854, and became common only later in the century.) Americans were reading multiple books, rather than rereading only bibles and religious works.[8] Around the same time, the publishing business began to professionalize, with the entry of many young, more business-oriented book-trade entrepreneurs and substantially improved production technology to meet the growing demand.

By about midcentury, the industry's financial model had matured to its modern state, with publishers, rather than authors, funding production and distribution of their books. Accordingly, publishing is sometimes thought of as the act of taking the financial risk of bringing a book to market, and that would have implications in the *Apple* debate. But that was not always the case. There was a time when authors routinely took the risk, and prominent authors sometimes preferred it. Another key midcentury innovation, which would become important as firms established their own distinctive identities, was the branding of their books and the launching of book series with distinctive bindings and trade markings.[9]

The appearance of so many small publishing firms in America reflected the blossoming of competition and opportunity in the midcentury American economy. Among the new firms were several that many years later were either one of the named *Apple* defendants or one of the imprints they now own as subsidiaries, including Harper & Brothers, Henry Holt, Scribner's, John Wiley, and G. P. Putnam & Co. England's experience during this period was somewhat different, though it did see the establishment of the still very prominent Macmillan.[10]

Despite the growth of the industry in America, nineteenth-century publishing was an economically tumultuous affair. For example, the publisher J. P. Jewett brought out one of the bestselling books of the century, Harriet Beecher Stowe's *Uncle Tom's Cabin*, in 1852, but was bankrupted just a few years later in the depression of 1857. Ticknor and Fields, one of the country's most esteemed literary institutions, also experienced several bankruptcies, and finally was acquired out of insolvency in 1878 by the entity that became Houghton Mifflin. Later in the century, the family that had long operated the venerable Harper & Brothers surrendered it in insolvency to J. P. Morgan. In fact, the late century would prove to be a watershed in American publishing, and result in lasting reorganization. Both Philadelphia and Boston had been major centers of American trade publishing, but they would not last out the century. Following the depression of 1857 and the Civil War, only the New York industry remained prominent. Publishing in Philadelphia was largely done for, and the only major Boston firm to survive was Little, Brown.[11]

Meanwhile, some other firms that would be included among today's dominant English-language trade publishers were established on the Continent. In their broad outlines they were not unlike their American and British counterparts. In early 1820s Paris, Louis Hachette, the son of a peasant family who had won entrance to the École Normale Supérieure, was caught in political winds. He was among a group of students expelled in a political purge of the school, and found himself without a stable position, supporting his mother and younger siblings. He studied law for a few years, but made a fateful choice when the opportunity arose to purchase a small bookstore and its ancillary publishing operation. He proved to be a canny and tenacious competitor, quickly building a large business selling schoolbooks to the less extreme government that assumed power in 1830 and—as softcover publishers had done in Britain in the 1840s—securing a monopoly on railway bookstalls just as the railways were expanding in the 1850s. Over time, he built his firm into France's largest publisher. It would one day figure as one of the defendants in the *Apple* conspiracy.

Price-fixing and other trade restraints were common throughout publishing history. Due to our stricter competition rules it was not as open or long-lasting in America as in Europe, but it was nevertheless prevalent, and during much of the nineteenth century it was apparently effective. From early in the century, American publishers restrained competition among themselves through a voluntary norm they called "trade courtesy." To some degree it reflected problems with copyright. Congress had adopted a copyright law in the late eighteenth century, but it only protected American authors; American law would give no protection at all to foreign authors until 1891. The result was the peculiar circumstance that works by American authors were sold for $1.00 or $1.50 whereas pirated editions of comparable British works sold for ten or twenty cents. Under the rule of trade courtesy, when one publisher brought out an edition of a foreign work, all other publishers refrained from publishing their own editions. Often, publishers paid foreign authors directly for their works or employed agents in Britain to purchase "advance sheets" of new foreign works—manuscript pages of books not yet bound and distributed—to stake their claim and give them a few days' lead time to get their books into print. They had to do that before cut-rate houses that did not adhere to the gentlemen's agreement of trade courtesy could bring out cheaper pirate editions. Many publishers also believed that trade courtesy required them to refrain from soliciting any author, American or foreign, who had already published with another firm. They therefore abstained from bidding against other firms or negotiating over price with a previously published author entertaining a switch to another house. Notably, Harper & Brothers bucked this tradition throughout its life, but otherwise, among major firms, adherence to trade courtesy was the norm.

During the Civil War, an acute bout of vigorous price rivalry followed the introduction of "dime novels"—very cheaply printed popular stories priced at about ten cents. The "cheap books movement," as it was known at the time, was made possible in part by new kinds of inexpensive paper and low postal rates. It was mostly the work of smaller, maverick firms, though the recidivist trade-courtesy violator among the major firms, Harper & Brothers, jumped on it early. Some of the other established publishers participated, too. A precursor of the pulp fiction industry of the twentieth century, it began with popular fiction by new American authors who would grow to great fame, including Horatio Alger. It also published a great number of very cheap foreign reprint editions and popular American books no longer in copyright (at the time, the term of domestic copyright was much shorter than today, typically only twenty-eight years).[12]

Unsurprisingly, in an industry that had maintained trade restraints for decades, one major reaction to the cheap books movement was renewed efforts at establishing horizontal cartel. Leading publishers organized in 1874 as the American Book Trade Union, later renamed the American Book Trade Association, to restrain output and prevent discount retailing, but the effort was short-lived because it attracted popular disapproval as a conspiracy against the public. Vigorous competition also drove the creation in the late nineteenth century of two separate book "trusts," or mergers of many competing publishers into one firm to quell competition. The "cheap books" publishers themselves, at the urging of one of their own leaders, formed the United States Publishing Company in 1889, and for a time it was the largest publishing entity in the country. Schoolbook publishers also formed a trust, the American Book Company, and in its time it controlled as much as 90 percent of its market.[13]

Publishers were not unique in their cooperation and trade restraint, incidentally. Similar trade restraints were relatively common throughout the nineteenth century in a variety of sectors. They came naturally to a people accustomed to solving problems through private association, acting under an economic consensus that increasingly supported notions of ruinous competition.

Another group of publishers that would be foundational to modern trade publishing in English got their start somewhat later. They had their origins in a different generation, but they were similarly devoted to cultural values. That time was another important transition in publishing and in American society, and the tenor of the times would color those firms' early years. By the turn of the twentieth century, the American publishing industry had become centralized in New York. Many firms had come and gone, but the business was still dominated by the genteel, Anglo-American elites who had run it for a long time. In the 1910s and 1920s a class of young Jewish intellectuals pursuing art and literature found themselves unwelcome in those traditional publishing firms. They established new companies that quickly gained intellectual dominance, including Alfred A. Knopf, Viking Press, and later, Pantheon, Schocken Books, and Grove Press.[14]

One of the earliest of these firms was Boni & Liveright, which later spawned two of the five massive publishers that now dominate the United States—Random House and Simon & Schuster. Boni & Liveright was founded by the troubled but intellectually respected Horace Liveright and a young colleague, Albert Boni. They met while working at a stock brokerage, but Boni was a Greenwich Village bohemian who'd run a book-shop, and Liveright was a born impresario who had secured financial backing for the firm from his industrialist father-in-law. Boni soon departed over personal differences, and Liveright eventually wrecked the firm with his drunkenness and financial risk-taking. But before he did, he built Boni & Liveright into one of the country's most influential literary institutions. During his professional life he also became a great bon vivant among the New York literary elite, and the firm's offices were a social hub for a circle that included Eugene O'Neill, Dorothy Parker, and the screenwriter Ben Hecht.[15]

The firm's most significant contribution was the creation of the Modern Library, a series of affordable, high-quality titles that aimed to bring highbrow literature to American readers in low-cost editions. The Modern Library introduced Americans to works by, among others, Fyodor Dostoyevsky, Anatole France, Henrik Ibsen, and Oscar Wilde, as well as writers who furthered the founders' radical politics, like Leon Trotsky and Sigmund Freud. The firm provided a home for emerging American stars as well, giving important early exposure to Sherwood Anderson, E. E. Cummings, Theodore Dreiser, Ernest Hemingway, Dorothy Parker, William Faulkner, and Eugene O'Neill.

As Boni & Liveright was falling apart, one of its young employees was planning a new venture that would become one of the world's great publishing firms. Bennett Cerf had just graduated from Columbia University when he joined the firm as a junior editor. As Boni & Liveright declined, along with Liveright's personal life, Cerf arranged to buy the Modern Library. With his friend Donald Klopfer, aged twenty-three, Cerf used the series as the foundation on which to build Random House. Their personal friendship was a legendary inheritance of the firm's internal culture. From the time they opened their first small office in 1925 and throughout their entire long partnership, the two shared an office and sat at desks facing each other.[16]

Another of today's largest publishers, and also an *Apple* defendant, also had its origins in Liveright's firm. Simon & Schuster began with a rather less lofty literary foundation, capitalizing on the popular craze of the time for books of crossword puzzles. Richard Simon and Max Schuster, who began their careers with Liveright, distinguished themselves as aggressive marketers of their books, investing much more in advertising and promotions than had been traditional. But it was not all marketing at the expense of substance. During its growth into one of the world's major publishers, Simon & Schuster would bring out a long list of very distinguished books.

A theme that runs through this history is the old tension between the publishers' cultural significance and the commercial pressures they faced. Those commercial pressures appeared much sooner than the contemporary commercialization of publishing is thought to have begun. For example, the owners of the esteemed Ticknor and Fields found that they simply could not operate profitably, and so they merged their press with a better-run firm. Likewise, when the insolvent Harper & Brothers was taken over by J. P. Morgan in the late 1890s, it was placed under the control of Colonel George Harvey. Harvey had worked in journalism, but his main competence was having made a fortune in street railways, and his apparently helpful innovations at Harper & Brothers mainly consisted of making it run more like a railroad. Another of the traditional attitudes that publishers would shed during the twentieth century was the nineteenth-century view that advertising for books was unseemly and ineffective. When the young Simon and Schuster were building their new firm, much of their success owed to their aggressive investments in advertising. Even the legendary Alfred Knopf marketed his esteemed list of books in seemingly crass and sensational ways, sometimes paying men to promote them by wearing sandwich boards.[17]

Still, the modern commercialization and corporate reorganization of publishing was something else entirely. Both the financial pressures that publishers face and their guardianship of literary values began to change due to a course of events that began in the 1960s.

It is important to note the significance of these small firms in the arts and culture of their times and the devotion of their leaders to literature and literary culture. This was true of both the older generation of the nineteenth century and the intellectual bohemians who arrived in the early twentieth. In addition to books, they also published the celebrated and popular *Harper's* magazine (Harper & Brothers) and the *Atlantic Monthly* (Ticknor and Fields).[18] In France, Louis Hachette, who came to lead one of his nation's most prominent commercial enterprises, remained devoted throughout his life to humanitarian causes, writing popular works and building organizations to benefit the poor.[19] More generally, publishing executives have always counted themselves in company with the artists, scientists, university professors, and other esteemed authors they publish. Many were major scholars in their own right. One well-known example is Henry Charles Carey, the Lincoln administration economic advisor famous for his "American system" of international trade policy. He and his father, Matthew, proprietors of the great nineteenth-century firm Carey & Lea, were both noted scholars whose treatises on economics and sociology were leading works of their day.[20] And indeed, some publishing figures, including Liveright, Cerf, and many others, were genuinely heroic. From his daytime perch as an editor at the Paris publishing house Gallimard, during the Nazi occupation of France, the young Albert Camus risked his life to edit the clandestine resistance newspaper *Combat*.[21] Other publishers led important campaigns in service of literary values. Horace Liveright defended his edition of a bawdy Roman classic, *The Satyricon*, against a lawsuit by New York's infamous Society for the Suppression of Vice.[22] Barney Rosset of Grove Press battled censorship to publish *Lady Chatterley's Lover* and *Tropic of Cancer*, and Bennett Cerf of Random House similarly fought to bring out *Ulysses*.[23] The esteemed editor André Schiffrin, after his controversial, forced exit from Random House in 1990, founded a successful new nonprofit, the New Press, to publish serious books he felt were discouraged under the commercialism transforming the major trade publishers.[24]

Yet, this long history obscures a great deal of change, much of it driven by the publishers' own choices, which had more to do with their problems of the twenty-first century than they would care to admit. By the time of the *Apple* conspiracy, none of the significant trade publishers remained the small, private, arts-minded mavericks they had once been. By most accounts, the crucial change began in the early 1960s. The founding generation of several of the major firms reached retirement age around that time, and they needed to begin cashing out their substantial equity and planning their estates. They did so through sales to other firms and through going-public transactions, setting in motion the transformation of what had been a gentlemanly but not hugely profitable business.[25] Since then, the industry has seen many hundreds of mergers and acquisitions, all part of larger trends of vigorous acquisition activity that ran throughout the US markets.

Although there had already been some smaller acquisitions in publishing, the first major step was the decision by Random House, the largest American trade publisher, to go public in 1959. Shortly thereafter, Random House acquired two revered publishing houses, Alfred A. Knopf in 1960 and Pantheon Books in 1961, as well as the textbook publisher L. W. Singer in 1961.[26]

That kicked off several decades of mergers and acquisitions and expanding corporatization generally, in which the leading publishers acquired other firms and were themselves acquired by yet larger ones, many times over. Some of them were occasionally spun off again.[27] By the mid-2000s, as the trade publishers were bracing themselves for the coming struggle with Amazon and eBooks, virtually all of trade publishing in English had become concentrated the hands of only six firms, each of which was the subsidiary of either a publicly traded corporation or a large corporate family. The firms were Simon & Schuster, HarperCollins Publishers, Hachette Book Group, Random House, Macmillan Publishers, and Penguin. Since the *Apple* litigation, that number has narrowed to only five. In 2013 Penguin and Random House merged into a joint venture owned by the media holding companies Pearson and Bertelsmann, creating Penguin Random House, the single largest publisher in the world.[28]

To blunt the disagreeable cast of all this consolidation, the major publishers are quick to say that in Anglophone countries there are in fact thousands of publishing firms. That is strictly true, but those thousands of firms are minuscule and do not provide meaningful competition on any dimension.

A problem with both publicly traded firms and subsidiaries of corporate families is their preoccupation with short-term profits and pressures from parent firms to match the performance of other divisions.

Those pressures do not reflect differences in their products or the costs of making them. Often, the same products are produced by nonpublic firms as well, and free-standing private firms tend to be less focused on the short term. The emphasis on short-term profits is widely believed to reflect the obligation of publicly traded firms to make frequent public disclosures of their financial performance; the expectations of passive, highly liquid public stockholders concerned only with their own share value; and the stock options and other performance-based incentives that now comprise a large part of the compensation paid to most large companies' top management.[29]

More generally, the evidence shows that mergers and acquisitions have not done much good in any sector, and there is nothing to indicate that book publishing has been an exception. Many of the publishers' financial troubles may simply reflect the same problems that follow acquisitions everywhere. Though researchers have long sought evidence that acquisitions generate efficiencies of some kind, to explain why companies keep doing them, for the most part they have not found it. Their general approach has been to deploy econometric analysis on large datasets and ask how acquisitions affect the stock returns for shareholders of firms that participated in them, compared to stock returns for similarly situated firms. A broad consensus has emerged that consolidation among publicly traded firms generally has not generated the promised benefits. There is even some strong evidence that, on average, consolidation among public firms generates systematic shareholder *losses*.[30]

No one knows why mergers on the whole would have such disappointing long-term results. One common explanation is problems in implementation. Another is that there just might not be much to gain in most consolidations. In book publishing, for example, the evidence suggests that publishing does not exhibit large scale economies. Production efficiencies are fully exploited at relatively small firm size and should have been captured by each of the major publishers long before they became conglomerated giants. It stands to reason that the real motivation for consolidation lies elsewhere. No one seems to know why corporate executives have continued for such a long time to pursue so many transactions that plainly do their companies no good. That is the subject of its own economic literature, but one strong possibility is that while consolidation is generally not valuable to firms' shareholders, it is quite valuable to corporate executives and their bankers.[31]

In any case, publishing sector acquisition activity was heavily funded by debt, and that approach also put more pressure on profitability.[32]

Making matters worse was that the publishers not only participated in so many mergers but also became targets of conglomeration. They were frequent targets during both the economy-wide conglomerate merger frenzy of the 1960s and 1970s and the media-sector conglomeration that continues to this day. A "conglomerate merger" joins two firms that do not produce competing products, like a maker of consumer electronics and a maker of auto parts. Beginning in the 1950s corporations began to show interest in these mergers, and during the 1960s and 1970s that interest reached a massive fever pitch, generating one of the largest merger waves in US history.[33] There are various possible explanations for the trend. Executives and their advisors claimed that diversifying their lines of business would help them deal with risk. They were abetted with theoretical support from some economists, though it has more widely been thought that diversification is desirable for investors but not for individual companies.[34] Another explanation is that executives simply wanted to manage larger businesses, with more prestige and higher pay. It has also been suggested that because federal antitrust enforcement against horizontal and vertical mergers accelerated during the 1960s, firms turned to conglomeration for no better reason than that it was a convenient and legal alternative.[35]

In any event, conglomeration was a serious failure. True conglomeration—joining completely unrelated businesses under one corporate roof—was a disaster overall, and in the 1980s almost all of the conglomerate firms of the 1960s and 1970s either failed outright or unwound their holdings, spinning off assets that were too hard to manage profitably.[36] As leading market observers would say, it was "almost certainly the biggest collective error ever made by American business," a "colossal mistake" that left American industry "uncompetitive relative to international rivals."[37] Some even said that a later merger wave that began in the 1980s was driven by the large number of spin-offs of firms acquired during the conglomerate merger wave.

Book publishers first became targets for acquisition during the 1960s by acquirers in wholly unrelated fields. Early conglomerate buyers may have been drawn to the glamour of book publishing, which was already courting celebrity authors and working with Hollywood producers.[38] They also may have envisaged synergies with their computer and electronics businesses. Many thought that books could be integrated into electronic information programs and the boom in data processing driven by the Johnson administration's Great Society initiatives.[39] In any case, in an event that dwarfed Random House's 1959 IPO and its acquisitions of Knopf and Pantheon, in 1965 Random House itself was acquired by RCA, a firm that led the conglomerate movement and ultimately exemplified its failure. Years later, RCA's conglomeration strategy would tear it apart and result in the spinning off of many of the firms it had acquired. Once one of America's largest and most venerable companies, it would never recover.[40] When Random House unwound from RCA, it not was returned to the free-standing independence under which it had thrived for most of its life. RCA sold it in 1980 to the acquisitive media holding company Advance Publications, which was privately held by the Newhouse family, led by the media-firm collector S. I. Newhouse. It was already something of a media empire. Many tumultuous years later, Random House was merged with another publisher, the major UK firm Penguin. Together they formed the largest book publisher ever to exist, all of it majority-owned by the German media conglomerate Bertelsmann.

Much the same would happen to other major houses. International Telephone & Telegraph and Gulf and Western, two other emblematic leaders of the conglomeration era, each acquired major trade publishers (Bobbs-Merrill in 1966 and Simon & Schuster in 1975, respectively). They later spun them off to firms more narrowly concerned with media.[41]

In any case, while the general conglomerate mania died its dramatic death in the late 1970s, a different kind of conglomeration grew up in its place, and it has been especially prominent in media. In it, firms acquire not just any old business. They acquire seemingly complementary or related products that they will "co-brand" or "cross-promote" with their existing media assets. Media cross-promotion was not really new, and examples could be found from long prior. In one famous scheme of the nineteenth century, the American investor Horace Everett Hooper partnered the flagging *Encyclopedia Britannica* with the equally flagging *Times* of London, advertising mail-order sales of the former in the pages of the latter in exchange for a commission to the *Times* on each sale of the *Encyclopedia*. He later attempted to expand the program substantially with his *Times* Book Club, an innovative lending-library scheme for *Times* subscribers. Interestingly enough, that book club was later opposed by one of the first major price-fixing cartels in English book publishing, and it precipitated a struggle known as the "*Times* Book War."[42]

Cross-promotion has been common in media enterprises because media products seem like good candidates for it, at least superficially. A media product can carry an advertisement for some other product, so its distribution seems synergistic because it reduces the total cost of advertising the two and perhaps reaches broader audiences. Indeed, it often amounts to advertising that consumers pay to receive.[43] With this strategy in mind, major book publishers have frequently been acquired by media conglomerates interested in using books to promote or tie in with their other products, especially their more profitable entertainment offerings. In principle, a media conglomerate could use cross-promotion not only to better market its profitable entertainment properties but also to boost the comparatively low margins earned in trade publishing.

As one might guess, media conglomeration has many detractors. Particularly where news or academic resources have been combined with commercial ones, critics have savaged the threat to independence in publishing and journalism.[44] In some number of glaring examples, executives plainly compromised editorial principles for business goals. Notoriously, Rupert Murdoch caused HarperCollins, the trade publisher owned by his company NewsCorp, to produce a hagiography of a Chinese head of state at a time when NewsCorp was seeking favorable regulatory treatment in China.[45] But on a commercial level at least, media conglomeration has apparently been a mostly successful strategy. It has sometimes been spectacularly successful, as in the case of the Disney corporation and the organizations operated by Martha Stewart and Oprah Winfrey.

Successful, that is, except in the case of books. Cross-promotion has not had the same synergistic marketing pizzazz for general interest trade publishers as for other media. That is in part because cross-promotion works well in media products that are advertiser supported. Books are usually not advertiser supported and make money only through their own purchase price. Another reason is that cross-promotion in entertainment media is particularly successful when it involves the creation of unified, highly recognizable symbols, generalizable across a range of products. That is especially true for children's movies and action or science fiction entertainment, which lend themselves to repackaging of characters and stories in different formats and merchandise.[46] It is also true for books in some cases, and in the early years of media conglomeration it was expected that firms would focus on cross-promotional book-movie tie-ins.[47] The problem is that the kind of cross-promotion that works well with books is only of a certain, narrow type, like a tie-in with some established franchise. It holds no value for the many thousands of discrete titles the trade publishers bring out every year that have no connection to any film or franchise, and on which most of their business is based.

Accordingly, conglomerates that own major trade publishers have struggled to figure out how to make book publishing tolerably profitable as part of their diverse media operations. The results have generally been poor, and occasionally ridiculous. Consider the regrettable *Stacked,* a Fox Television sitcom that aired in 2005 and 2006. As awful as one might guess, its title being a crass pun, *Stacked* featured the buxom actress Pamela Anderson as a free-living young woman who trades her life of inebriate dissipation to work in a family bookstore. NewsCorp, the parent of Rupert Murdoch's media empire, owned both Fox Television and the trade publisher HarperCollins, and it devised *Stacked* to sell HarperCollins books. The show's scripts were sprinkled with mentions of HarperCollins. In one episode, for example, one store employee asks another, "Is the HarperCollins shipment in yet?" All the posters covering the store's walls were of HarperCollins books, and the books on its shelves were all HarperCollins best sellers. Aside from its abject embarrassment on an aesthetic level, and its sad commentary on corporate guardianship of our shared intellectual lives, this foray also apparently didn't work. The show was cancelled after two lackluster seasons.

So, a first major challenge during the publishers' modern history was a series of organizational changes, made either by them or by new owners who'd acquired them, which generated new pressures for short-term profits. Unfortunately, trade publishing presents few avenues for large, quick profits, other than to secure blockbuster best sellers. According to many critics, the hunt for those titles became a seriously distracting preoccupation. Finding them is difficult, unpredictable, and risky, often entailing very expensive bets on celebrity books—many of them with multimillion-dollar advances—which frequently fail commercially.[48] And more importantly, those books generally have no value as "backlist" titles. A publisher's backlist is the books it owns that are no longer new releases, and which have earned back the initial costs of their production. Even when they succeed initially, popular best sellers, and especially celebrity books, often have appeal only for a short time. So in the very expensive race for spectacular short-term success, publishers have to some degree given up on one of the most important components of their own traditional business model—continually replenishing the backlist with new titles that could provide stable, continuing revenue.

Along with these corporate changes came important changes in leadership. Whereas the major trade publishing firms originated in small partnerships managed by bookish and scholarly founders, by the mid-2000s they were mostly in the hands of MBA graduates trained at elite universities, a class of professionals not generally given to cultural values as their priority. Some of these appointments were controversial and had serious consequences. That was true of the decision at Random House, following its acquisition by the Newhouse family, to force out Robert Bernstein, the revered successor to Bennett Cerf, and replace him with an Italian finance executive named Alberto Vitale. That move was soon followed by the firing of André Schiffrin, the venerable director of the high-profile Random House unit Pantheon Books. Studs Terkel, a longtime Pantheon author, famously said at the time that "the barbarians have taken over at Pantheon, and they might as well be producing a detergent."[49] Likewise controversial was NewsCorp's appointment of Anthea Disney, a member of the extended Disney family whose major managerial experience had been publishing *TV Guide*, to be chief executive of HarperCollins.[50] Media conglomeration has been driven by a fascination with superstar CEOs since at least the 1980s, and generally it has not done the business firms any great favors.[51] The trend has affected several different sectors, though it is especially visible in media, and some have associated it with shareholder frustration in the 1980s over a long-standing decline in corporate profitability. But in any case, it has also been shown to have very mixed results.[52]

The budget obligations and short-term profit pressures associated with merger and acquisition, as well as the profit pressures imposed by cross-promoting media conglomerates, weighed heavily on the *Apple* defendants at the turn of the twenty-first century. The most common diagnosis from within the industry was that their changing managements had discarded the industry's long-standing priority of building durable backlists. Traditionally, new releases were not meant to generate short-term windfalls, though that was welcome when it occurred. They were meant to replenish publishers' backlists with new titles that could produce reliable long-term revenue. In addition to earning recurrent if not spectacular revenues, cultivation of the backlist was also important to the publishers' traditional role in building the reputations of new authors, both for the authors' sake and for the publishers' profit. While it is frequently true, as publishers stress, that individual titles are unprofitable in the short term, that fact is misleading. An author's potential to generate long-term revenue usually depends on publishing at least a few of his or her books. Often, a first book that is not initially profitable will later become reliably profitable once subsequent books are in print and the author's name is better established. As Alfred Knopf once said, "A book is gone today and here tomorrow."[53]

And so, even if we follow Michael Korda's advice from the beginning of this chapter, and take the publishers with a grain of salt when they say the sky is falling, they probably did face serious problems at the turn of the twenty-first century. By the time that Amazon introduced the Kindle in 2007, and launched the conflict that became *United States v. Apple,* the major firms felt profit pressures they could not satisfy. No one doubts it, and evidence of it fills recent histories of the industry.[54] But whatever financial pressures they faced seem unlikely to have reflected cost changes in their product, or the growing bargaining power of their retail distributors, or any other particular changes in their market's fundamentals. Instead, these pressures followed from the internal mandates of their own shareholders and acquisition-related debt service.

This history relates as well to a separate major theme that ran through the *Apple* litigation. The publishers' roles in safeguarding literary and cultural values are deeply complicated at best. It has no doubt driven many individual women and men in publishing, and it appears to have been sincerely, deeply engrained in earlier generations of industry leadership. But it can no longer explain the behavior of the major trade publishing firms themselves. When consolidation first began, there was a sense that the coming corporatization would damage the quality of the industry's output. When he sold his firm to Random House in 1960, Alfred Knopf justified his concession to pecuniary gain by saying that "the level of American publishing is already so low that the journey to Wall Street will make no difference."[55] During the rise of the chain stores Borders and Barnes & Noble, the major trade publishers were criticized for allowing their publishing agendas to be controlled by the chains' purchasing officials.[56] The destruction of traditional literary commitments in favor of short-term profits is the deepest regret expressed in the many recent memoirs by industry veterans. In its wake, the leading trade publishers' lists are now devoid of contemporary poetry, serious academic works in science, social science, or the humanities, and political work other than polemical, current-events potboilers written by celebrity pundits.[57] That has followed not because of the pressures of rapacious capitalism or the conniving of monopolists like Amazon, but because of decisions made by the publishers themselves.

8

Bookselling and the Birth
of Amazon

THE OTHER HALF of the book business, distribution, has also undergone substantial change. During *Apple,* justifications of the eBooks conspiracy depended heavily on claims about the damage that Amazon had done to book retailers. It is largely taken for granted that independent bookstores are finished. They were suffering and rapidly failing when Amazon introduced the Kindle, and even before then, Amazon was being blamed for store closings. By that time even the large brick-and-mortar chains were flagging, and most of them, too, would eventually succumb. With the loss of bookstores we lost a sense of place and culture that many of us miss dearly.

Yet, the idea that Amazon single-handedly caused all this loss is misleading. As a component of book distribution, independent bookstores had always been a comparatively small part of the overall distribution network. Moreover, their fate was shared by essentially all small-scale, independent retail stores. No small retailers could adequately cope with the large technological strides in distribution logistics that began in the 1970s. When Amazon went live in 1995, the already deeply imperiled independents faced just another escalation of the long-standing threats to their existence.

The good news is that the reports of the death of the independent book-store appear to have been premature.

Bookselling arose as an independent business much later in the United States than in Europe. People in America were more sparsely spread across a broad and expanding territory. American publishers before the Civil War commonly operated their own bookstores and other distribu-tion operations, and many of them were more booksellers than publishers. When independent sales channels did develop, they rarely took the form of physical locations dedicated to book sales.

Retail bookstores were not common in the United States until late in the century, and those were mainly in larger cities. Instead, books were sold in general stores, by mail, or by direct, door-to-door solicitation. Eventually a wholesale sector developed, consisting of a few larger firms such as McClurg & Co. and the American News Company, as well as countless smaller jobbers. Publishers began to advertise regionally and nationally, and several of them began to publish their own general-interest magazines, such as *Harper's* and *Putnam's Monthly,* to publicize their books. But until late in the century, most Americans would never have vis-ited a bookstore. And when retail bookstores did become more common, they were not the places for browsing and literary indulgence that we've come to know. As in all other retail shops, stock was kept behind the counter and retrieved for customers by clerks. In bookstores, the stock was arranged not by topic but by publisher.[1]

The bookstore as we now know it was a twentieth-century phenom-enon. The first independent bookstores offering stock curated by their proprietors and serving as literary and community resources appeared in the early decades of the century, and most of them were associated with university campuses. One of the first was the Hampshire Book Shop, a venture founded in 1916 by the widely respected Marion Dodd in coop-eration with Smith College in Northampton, Massachusetts. When book-stores became more common, they competed with the increasingly fa-miliar department stores and with mail order, book club, and subscription models that persisted from the nineteenth century. Book clubs in partic-ular flourished during the first half of the century, performing a mediating function that suited the cultural aspirations of the day. Another development of the early twentieth century was the rise of extremely cheap softcover books. They were printed on essentially disposable-quality paper and distributed at newsstands and drugstores by wholesalers whose main business was magazines and newspapers. By midcentury there also came to be some chain bookstores, notably Doubleday, Brentano's, and Kroch's.[2] The first serious financial problems for independent booksellers began not that much later. Decades before Amazon went live, they were already suffering at the hands of discounting bookstore chains founded in the 1960s.[3]

The proliferation of automobiles is generally said to have driven suburbanization and the rise of suburban shopping malls during the 1950s. The malls presented a new opportunity for marketing books to wider audiences, and a generation of bookstore chains arose to exploit it. Chain bookstores were not a completely new phenomenon. The legendary Brentano's, which originated as a New York City newsstand well before the Civil War, had expanded to ten stores nationally by 1930, and nearly thirty by 1980. Likewise, a firm called Bookland, still thriving today under the name Books-a-Million, began in small-town Alabama in 1917. Founded as a newsstand built from piano crates by a fourteen-year-old boy after his father's death, it began expanding nationally in 1950 and by 1980 had fifty stores. But much more significant were two chain store brands that arose in the 1960s and located their stores in malls to exploit the heavy foot traffic. Waldenbooks and B. Dalton Booksellers both maintained large, nicely appointed stores featuring creative in-store displays and comfortable furnishings. They were quick successes and they posed a serious threat to competing booksellers, and also to publishers.

The mall stores were the first to introduce aggressive retail price promotions, and they used their market share to force publishers to fund them. They generally priced hardcover best sellers at 15 to 25 percent off the publisher's suggested list price. By doing so, they gained substantial power and commandeered a good portion of the publishers' profit margin. In their day, the mall stores were feared by the publishing establishment as its final doom.[4]

Building on the mall store model, the next generation of chain stores appeared in the early 1970s. Borders, Barnes & Noble, and Crown Books all began during this period, and each of them grew rapidly during the 1980s and 1990s to operate many hundreds of stores. From the mall stores they inherited the model of large, nicely appointed stores, but they took it much further, operating free-standing, warehouse-sized stores with hundreds of thousands of titles in stock. The superstores also expanded on the price-promotion efforts of the mall stores. They offered 10 percent off all hardcovers and up to 30 percent off selected best sellers. They promoted those bargains at especially desirable locations at the fronts of their stores.[5] At the same time, other big discounters, including Walmart and Kmart, began selling limited lists of best-selling books at deep discounts, and they also took substantial share from independent bookstores.[6]

So, during the 1970s and 1980s the original mall-store chains and other book retailers were growing rapidly at the expense of independent bookstores. During the 1990s, before Amazon rose to dominance, the retail market share held by independents fell dramatically.[7] At that time, the independents were already raising the same complaint that Apple and the publisher defendants would raise about Amazon—that the power of a large retailer selling at unreasonable discounts was killing them.[8]

The retail chains' growth also attracted federal regulatory attention, and it generated a set of remarkable and widely watched legal events. Late in 1988 the Federal Trade Commission sued a group of publishers— several of which were *Apple* defendants or their predecessors—for giving improper wholesale discounts to the ascendant mall stores. It was one of the Commission's increasingly rare actions under a controversial, Depression-era law called the Robinson-Patman Act, about which we shall learn more later. Robinson-Patman is a price discrimination law driven by the anti–chain store sentiment of that earlier time. It was meant to limit chain store power by keeping manufacturers from giving them unfair discounts. The Commission's suit against the publishers was all fairly remarkable, as at the time the agency leadership was comprised entirely of Reagan appointees. Robinson-Patman had become disfavored, especially by the economic conservatives that then dominated the antitrust agencies. In fact, it would be among the federal government's last major Robinson-Patman actions, ever. Not long thereafter, the American Booksellers Association filed its own private suit on behalf of independent bookstores, alleging the same harms against several publishers and adding Barnes & Noble and Borders as defendants. It might seem strange that the *publishers* would be sued for this price discrimination, since they had so bitterly complained of powerful retailers and since they probably were pressured into the discounts by the retail chains. For what it may be worth, the publishers defended the litigation vigorously, and at least in public statements claimed that their pricing merely reflected the lower cost of serving the high-volume chains. But they then settled both actions with agreements that would sharply restrict the discounts. They may very well have taken Robinson-Patman litigation as their opportunity to free themselves from the power of their distributors, as the settlements would permit them to end the wholesale discounts of which they so complained. In a final unexpected twist, however, the Federal Trade Commission failed for some years even to review its own settlements for approval, and then a panel of commissioners that included new Democratic appointees rejected them and dismissed the case, with a lone, unexpected, and strongly worded dissent from a very conservative commissioner.[9]

Whether or not it was enabled by the failure of the Robinson-Patman litigation, the pressure exerted by the superstore chains continued to grow. They forced publishers to give them deeper wholesale discounts than they gave to independents or the mall stores, and progressively demanded more of the publishers' cooperative promotional allowances, mainly to fund deep discounts on best sellers.[10] They also returned as unsold inventory a significantly larger percentage of the books they ordered. The practice of bookseller returns, almost unique in retail, dates to the Great Depression, when Simon & Schuster introduced it to encourage retailers to carry more titles.[11] By the time the superstores had gained dominance in the mid-1990s, their returns amounted to about 30 percent of their purchases, whereas independent booksellers returned only about 20 percent.[12]

Given the adversarial bitterness with which the publishers viewed Amazon at the time of the eBooks controversy, it may come as a surprise that their relations for many years were friendly. In its early years, Amazon did not deal directly with publishers. It made the bulk of its purchases through the major book wholesale firms. From the publishers' perspective, Amazon provided welcome retail capacity for their goods and retail competition with the uncomfortably powerful Borders and Barnes & Noble. Better yet, Amazon returned essentially *none* of its books as unsold inventory.[13] When it first began distributing hard-copy books through its online store, the publishers welcomed it as their savior.[14]

Things began to change in about 2004, when Amazon started flexing its growing muscle in negotiations with publishers. By 2010, not only was Amazon no longer their savior, but they had begun to refer to the new iPad, and the iBookstore through which it would distribute eBooks in competition with Amazon, as the "Jesus tablet."[15] In the mid-1990s, though, relations with Amazon were mutually warm. Indeed, Amazon did something for the publishers that even the superstores with their huge stores and inventories would never be able to do. It displayed *all* their books in print, including profitable backlist titles that even the superstores would not carry.[16]

When it began, Amazon was one of the first serious attempts of any kind, in any sector, to commercially exploit the still-new internet. In 1994, before Jeff Bezos founded the firm and became its CEO, he was a rapidly rising vice president at D. E. Shaw & Co., an elite quantitative hedge fund. At the time, the internet as a commercial phenomenon was new, but the technology was not. The "internet," the system of geographically remote, interconnected computers, went live in 1969, and conceptual antecedents to it were first described as early as 1945. However, the predominantly commercial, user-friendly, visually stimulating resource familiar to users today came into being only in the early 1990s. It resulted from development of the "web," or the system for finding and sharing hyperlinked documents, as well as from the US government's relaxation of strict rules against its use for commercial purposes. Both changes occurred at about the same time. After that, the internet's simplicity and commercial potential developed rapidly over a period of about three years.[17] As they watched it unfold, Bezos and others at D. E. Shaw began serious discussion of exploiting its promise by creating an "everything store."

Though the same business considerations drove the business models for the other online book-selling pioneers, some critics found Amazon's decision to begin by selling books to be bloodless and calculated. As Bezos perceived, books are particularly suitable for online retail because any two copies of the same book are interchangeable, online bookselling could exploit the existing network of book distributors, and the huge variety of titles in print could offer customers a range of selection that harnessed the new medium's true power.[18]

For all its extraordinary success, Amazon has succeeded less by generating genuinely new ideas than by perfecting the ideas of others. Bezos famously stated as its founding philosophy that Amazon would be best among its competitors, but not the best innovator.[19] That is not really a criticism; indeed, that theme runs through the history of technology, and applies to firms and proprietors generally remembered for their innovation. It figures, for example, in the legendary Silicon Valley story that the young Steve Jobs essentially stole the technology and design concepts that would make the Macintosh so groundbreaking.[20] It also figures in the stories of many of the most important inventions in our history, each of them wrapped in folklore of breakthroughs by heroic individuals, including the lightbulb, the airplane, and the telephone. Simultaneous invention, building as it does on cumulative contributions of many people over time, is also very common.[21]

Like many other innovations that achieve worldwide significance, Amazon's original online bookstore had predecessors, and Bezos and his original team were well aware of them. The first was Book Stacks Unlimited, better known by its website address, Books.com. Book Stacks was launched by the Cleveland e-commerce visionary Charles Stack in 1992, about three years before Amazon shipped its first book, in the earliest days of the commercial internet. Indeed, Book Stacks first went live as a dial-up bulletin board service (BBS) before there was a World Wide Web. Stack himself wrote the code for that original BBS site, as well as for the website that went live in 1994. He had honed his technical skills as a law student at Case Western Reserve University in the 1980s, computerizing the operations of Cleveland law firms as personal computers were just hitting the market.[22]

Book Stacks was not the only online Amazon competitor. Even before Amazon went live, there were others, including WordsWorth of Cambridge, Massachusetts, and AbeBooks, a firm still in operation today. By the time Amazon had become a significant force in the late 1990s, there were dozens or hundreds.

The first decade of Amazon's growth was a difficult time in bookselling. Independent bookstores suffered visible losses and their widespread failure drove much of the new fear of Amazon. In just the five years following Amazon's entry into the market, the number of independent bookstores in America was cut almost in half. The large chains suffered even more, as several of them closed hundreds of locations and Crown Books closed for good in 2001. It is hard to say how much of that can be blamed on Amazon, because bitter price competition flowed from so many sources. The superstores in particular enjoyed wholesale advantages that independents could not overcome, and added to the mix was very vigorous competition from Kmart, Walmart, and other discounters. In any case, the carnage spread, and by 2011 only Barnes & Noble and Books-a-Million still stood among the major chains. Borders ended its US operations in 2011 and also closed its subsidiary Waldenbooks. B. Dalton, by then a subsidiary of Barnes & Noble, was liquidated in 2009.

Yet, brick-and-mortar bookselling did not completely die out, and in fact independent bookstores seem to be staging a comeback. While most of the large chains were liquidated in 2010 and 2011 and Barnes & Noble appeared to be on the ropes in 2018, there was a resurgence in the number of independent stores beginning in about 2009. It occurred, oddly enough, at the peak of the drastic eBooks pricing blitz by which Amazon triggered *United States v. Apple,* at the peak of the eBook market share it rapidly compiled, and well before the *Apple* conspiracy took control of the eBook prices that were allegedly killing the independents. Their numbers increased by about 35 percent, replacing a good portion of their losses from the 1990s and 2000s. Early research suggests that the independents have found success by emphasizing values that they are well-suited to supply, like physical atmosphere, customer attention, and sense of place built on community events, author presentations, and the like. That is to say, they may have found commercial viability by providing exactly those values that critics claimed were destroyed by Amazon. If so, then vigorous price competition did not wreck those things. That is so because when people want something, by and large, healthy markets will supply it.[23]

9

Publishers, Booksellers, and the Oldest Problem in the World

> The evils of underselling and the possibility of countering them were and for many years had been a constant subject of discussion when I first went into business. From an article which appeared in *Fraser's Magazine* in June 1852, it would seem that the question was a burning one at that date.
>
> —Sir Frederick Macmillan, *The Net Book Agreement, 1899, and the Book War, 1906–1908*

DESPITE THEIR RHETORIC, the publishers' conflict with Amazon was not a new kind of occurrence and it did not arise in circumstances new to the industry. The first serious conflict between English-language publishers and their retailers, and the first time publishers conspired to discipline price-cutting booksellers, had occurred more than two hundred years earlier. There followed a largely unbroken history of conflict in the book trade, with periods of aggressive retail price competition alternating with industry-wide price-fixing to constrain it. Some of those conspiracies were similar to the one in *Apple,* and several were long-lasting and effective. Though there is no explicit evidence that the connection was a conscious one, it seems unlikely that the *Apple* defendants were not aware that their arrangement mirrored the so-called Net Book Agreement, the industry-wide price-fixing plan that dominated British bookselling for nearly the entire twentieth century. As the astute industry watcher Paul Carr wrote in 2010 when news broke that the publishers had notified Amazon of their terms: "Hey, 1997—Macmillan called; they want the Net

Book Agreement back."[1] The long struggle over price-fixing had also played out in legislatures, both in the United States and overseas. Book industry players pressed for and secured legislation to limit retail price competition, and in some nations retail book prices are now fixed directly by governments.

This situation is not unique to the book industry. Conflict between makers of goods and their distributors is as old as mass-market capitalism, and has been one of its most visible features for well over a hundred years. Industry-wide agreements to set retail price floors appeared in a range of industries during the nineteenth century. They proliferated throughout retail across the United States and Europe, apparently in reaction to new vigor in retail price competition, driven by technological and organizational innovation. Price-fixing was short-lived in the United States due to antitrust law and popular opposition, but even here, throughout a century of change and uncertainty in law, bouts of resale price-fixing resurfaced from time to time and it never completely disappeared. What is striking in this history, had one heard only the *Apple* defendants' version of events, are the similarities between the modern *Apple* conspiracy and much older book industry conspiracies, including one in Britain in 1829 and one that bridged the Atlantic in 1901.

On some level, thinking about these matters requires thinking about the economics and law of "vertical" relationships. To recap, a vertical relationship is between firms at different levels in the chain of distribution of the same product. For example, a manufacturer of televisions, such as Sony, is in a vertical relationship with the retailer that distributes its goods, such as Best Buy. In the eBooks case, the vertical relationships among the defendants looked like the first figure below.

By contrast, horizontal relationships are between firms at the same level of a chain of distribution. Sony, for example, is in a horizontal relationship with other television makers, and Best Buy is in a horizontal relationship with other electronics retailers, such as Walmart. In the eBooks case, the horizontal relationships looked like the second figure below.

For what it may be worth, there is not actually a logically necessary reason to distinguish between horizontal and vertical restraints of trade

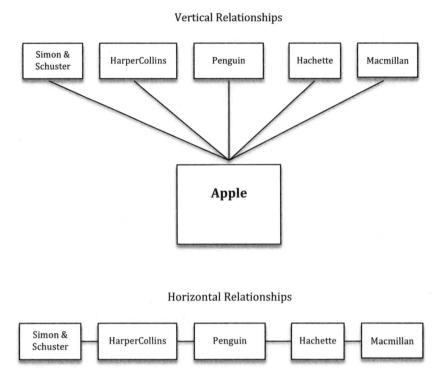

Vertical Relationships

Horizontal Relationships

in either law or economics, at least so fully as we do. The antitrust stat-utes make virtually no mention of the distinction, and the Supreme Court did not draw it sharply before 1963.[2] In terms of economic substance, all trade restraints have both horizontal effects (between rivals) and vertical effects (between suppliers and their distributors).[3] Yet, as both law and economics have developed, we distinguish between them quite a lot. Because their differences played such a role in *Apple*, it is important to understand them and the theoretical controversy they have engendered.

Strictly speaking, *Apple* was not a "vertical case," as lawyers normally conceive them. The Justice Department did not challenge any vertical agreements, and no court in *Apple* predicated liability on them. The gov-ernment challenged only the horizontal agreement among the publishers to fix the retail price of their products, a kind of agreement that is auto-matically illegal in US law and the most serious of all antitrust violations. With regard to Apple, the Justice Department challenged only its work in coordinating the horizontal conspiracy. Obviously, Apple was in a vertical relationship with each of the publishers—it took products they made and sold them to consumers—but the conduct challenged was its effort to facilitate the agreement among the publishers. Apple was shown to have proposed the agreement, shuttled between the publishers and communicated messages between them, and taken various steps to ensure that they would agree horizontally on terms relating to their own retail prices. Antitrust considers that conduct to be "horizontal" as well. For some time, the law has taken the view that any person who aids in coordination of a horizontal conspiracy is subject to the same degree of liability as the conspirators themselves. Antitrust has a special term for this kind of conduct, and it got a lot of use during the *Apple* litigation. Such an arrangement is known as a "hub-and-spoke" conspiracy. Like most hub-and-spoke deals, the one in *Apple* involved a set of vertical contracts— each publisher individually agreed to a bilateral contract permitting Apple to sell its eBooks. Those contracts were important to proving that the horizontal agreement existed, but they themselves were not challenged or found illegal. Had the vertical agreements been directly challenged, they would not have been subject to per se treatment and likely would have been upheld as lawful.

Still, the case, the relationships between the publishers, Apple, and Amazon, and the politics that underlay it all can't be fully understood except in their broader economic context. That context is the familiar and inevitable struggle between the makers of goods and their distributors—a context we normally think of as "vertical."

A few things are key. First, it is important to understand the tensions between the publishers and their various channels of distribution and the different motives at play. Though *Apple* wasn't a vertical case in legal terms, it was a case in which manufacturers wanted keenly to control their own retail prices. Second, it is important to understand the ideological issues running through the vertical economics literature. We need to understand the arguments by which, in the early twenty-first century, that literature had become so deferential to business that many people viewed the *Apple* conspiracy as a proconsumer, procompetition correction to serious market defects. They persisted in that view even though the extensive evidence at trial showed that it could have had no plausible consequence other than drastic price increases that would cost consumers hundreds of millions of dollars.

One simple fact captures a lot of current thinking. To borrow from Herbert Hovenkamp, "Firms generally prefer neither to purchase from monopolists nor to sell to them. . . . Those who buy from monopolists must pay higher prices; those who sell to monopolists . . . must receive lower prices than a competitive buyer would pay."[4]

A fact basic to this sort of thinking is that with respect to any particular good, there is some finite, maximum amount of revenue that can be gotten from selling it. That is, there is some maximum amount that consumers will pay for it before so many of them choose to switch to alternative products, or just do without the good altogether, that further price increases—by any firm in the chain of distribution—will stop increasing overall profits and will instead begin to reduce them.

To think this through, imagine that Sony, the maker of televisions, decides to distribute its televisions directly by opening its own retail stores and setting up a network of warehouses and trucks to get its goods from the factory to the stores and into consumers' hands. In this simple scenario, Sony must find some price that will give it the most profit that it can get. Whether Sony faces competition or not, that price will be the point at which the amount of profit it gets from selling one more unit would actually be less than the profit it got from selling the previous unit. Assume for now that Sony is a monopolist in the making of televisions. There are no other makers of televisions at all, and no good alternative products that consumers could substitute for televisions. Any consumer that wants a television must buy a Sony. Even in that situation, Sony can't just keep raising the price, infinitely. There will be some point at which so many consumers decide to live without televisions that it's less profitable to price them that high. Losing some sales is not always a problem. Any price increase causes a seller to lose some sales, and every price increase the monopolist makes, up to its profit-maximizing price, will cause some consumers to do without televisions. But losing customers through raising prices is actually *more* profitable than selling more units at lower prices, as long as each price increase makes the total amount of profit the seller earns larger than it was before.[5]

Now assume, much more realistically, that Sony distributes its goods through a wholesaler, which then further distributes them through various retailers such as Best Buy and Sears. That fact does not change the pricing strategy. Even if we keep our assumption that Sony is a total monopolist at the manufacturing level, the maximum amount of revenue it can get from selling its televisions would still be achieved by setting the retail price at that same monopoly-maximizing point. Let's say that that price, the highest retail price before Sony will begin losing total profit, is $200. Since third-party distributors are involved, Sony will have to compensate them for the distribution service they provide. They provide warehouses, trucks, retail space, and workers, and insure the goods against loss or theft and the cost of unsold inventory. In the common, simple scenario in which the distributors buy the goods outright from the manufacturer, their compensation takes the form of wholesale price. Assume that the cost of the services Sony gets from all the wholesalers and retailers and other distributors it deploys totals $50 for each television that they get to market. If those downstream actors lack any market power, Sony's wholesale price for each television would be $150, and all the downstream players—the wholesaler, other distributors, and the ultimate retail store—will have to divide among themselves the remaining $50 they can earn from each television.[6]

A crucial fact follows from this analysis: manufacturers and their distributors are necessarily adverse to one another. The $200 in revenue, which is the total that can be gotten from selling a single Sony television without losing profit, is fixed, and struggle over it is a zero-sum struggle. Each player involved in its distribution would like to get as much of it as they can, but for each one of them, taking more of it means taking some from the other players.[7]

So how do we know how much each player will take? That is a question of market power. Most firms at most levels of distribution have at least a little market power. Except in the most vigorously competitive sectors, sellers have at least some ability to raise price over their own costs. And firms in a vertical chain of distribution will use whatever bargaining leverage they have—that is, their market power—to squeeze out as much of the profit for themselves as they can. If one player at any given level in the chain holds substantial market power and the others do not, it will take the lion's share of whatever profit there is.

Imagine again that televisions can be sold at a monopoly-maximizing retail price of $200, and the cost of distributing them is $50. If Sony is a monopolist and its distributors have no market power, the wholesale price will be $150 and the retail price will be $200. But let us now flip the facts. Assume that Sony faces a lot of horizontal competitors, but must sell through a distribution system dominated by one retailer—say, Best Buy, a total monopolist. Best Buy is likely to keep the retail price high, but it will push the wholesale price down to the lowest price at which television makers can cover their costs and stay in business. In a more realistic real-world scenario, neither Sony nor Best Buy is a monopolist, but neither faces so much competition that they have no market power at all. Rather, each of them has some protection from vigorous horizontal price competition, and therefore has some market power. In that case, it's harder to say what the wholesale and retail prices will be, but the process by which they are reached is the same. First of all, the retail price will no longer be the fully profit-maximizing monopoly price, because Sony is no longer a monopolist in manufacture. There are other televisions consumers can buy, and perhaps substitute entertainment products that might do as well. But the price will be higher than it would be in perfect competition, so there is a bit of excess profit, and the firms in the chain of distribution will fight among themselves to divvy it up. Each firm will use the leverage it has to get the most it can of that finite pie of revenue. To the extent that one of them has market power, it can say to the other, if you don't like my price, go see if you can do better with my competitors. Since both players usually have some market power, both would likely have trouble doing much better with competitors. So, where both a manufacturer and its distributor have some market power, the retail price will likely be higher than the competitive price, and the only real questions are how high and how much of the resulting profit each of them takes.[8]

Another observation follows from this, and it was quite significant to how people thought about *Apple*. Other things equal, a manufacturer should want a downstream marketplace that is more competitive, not less so. This observation has often been overstated, and critics believe that it mischaracterizes many real-world situations. Nevertheless, loss of competition downstream can be bad for a manufacturer in two ways. First, in cases where the good is not already being sold at its monopoly-maximizing retail price, any player in the stream of distribution that acquires market power will likely use it to force up its own price. That in turn will push up the ultimate retail price, which will cause some lost sales. That is fine as far as the player with market power is concerned, but for the manufacturer it is bad, because if it lacks market power, it will lose sales on which it could have earned some return. Second, even if the retail price is already the monopoly price, any player that acquires more market power will keep more for itself from that ultimate, finite share of revenue that is received from consumers.[9]

This might seem to present some mystery in the *Apple* case, where the pressure to limit retail competition came from the manufacturers. If retail competition is good for manufacturers, one would expect that the publishers would want *low* retail prices, to increase sales.[10] And if so, it would have made more sense to use their conspiracy to raise their wholesale price. But the publishers had strong and clear-cut motives to oppose cheap eBooks, which are familiar from other contexts in history. We will get to them in due course.

American antitrust law has vacillated over the years with regard to vertical restraints. At one time it treated them harshly and briefly even outlawed them altogether, but today they are more or less always legal. Though *Apple* was not really a "vertical" case, the long controversy over vertical restraint rules and their underlying politics was central to the defendants' legal strategy and to the rhetoric of some of their supporters. Interestingly, during the periods when antitrust law has most vigorously attacked vertical restraints, and especially when it outlawed vertical price-fixing, critics on both the left and the right have savaged it. Critics on the right think that vertical restraints are often needed so that manufacturers can structure their distribution strategies efficiently and give consumers what they want. Critics on the left have argued that vertical restraints (and especially vertical minimum price-fixing) could be used to control big businesses and protect small ones. Both arguments ran through *Apple*. According to critics, a coordinated set of vertically imposed price re-

straints was needed to fix a problematic market, and was the publishers' only hope for protection from the voracious Amazon.

The law's most important early statement was the Supreme Court's 1911
decision in *Dr. Miles Medical Co. v. John D. Park & Sons Co.*, which held
that RPM would be per se illegal.[11] Though *Dr. Miles* itself is well-known
among lawyers today, the lengthy and important history behind it is not.
The case was the climax of a major, international effort by retailers to control price competition and to dampen the cost advantages that some
large retailers seemed to be gaining through size and organizational innovation. *Dr. Miles* largely ended that effort in the United States, though
it would resurface in various forms during certain periods and get a significant boost from time to time from Congress.

In an interesting twist, *Dr. Miles* was sandwiched between two other
Supreme Court decisions that both arose from a turn-of-the-century price-
fixing crisis in the book industry. Both of those cases were fought successfully by the doggedly litigious Straus brothers, the proprietors of the
then-aggressive discounter Macy's, in their long-running opposition to the
RPM movement of the day. First, *Bobbs-Merrill Co. v. Straus* held in
1908—before *Dr. Miles*—that American copyright law does not in itself
authorize price restraints on resales after a book is first sold.[12] *Straus v.
American Publishers' Ass'n* dropped the other shoe in 1913, after *Dr. Miles*,
holding that RPM imposed by contract is illegal under antitrust, even if
imposed by the holder of a copyright.[13]

After that seemingly devastating ending for American RPM, however,
there followed a long and complex history that still has not worked itself
out completely. The courts struggled to respect the rule of *Dr. Miles*, but
also to accommodate the routine interactions of parties to distribution arrangements, as well as the growing view among economists that at least
some restraints imposed on those relations could be desirable. Throughout
the century the courts fashioned exceptions and carve-outs, and ultimately began peeling back *Dr. Miles* itself. That long period finally culminated in reversal of *Dr. Miles* altogether, in *Leegin Creative Leather
Products v. PSKS* in 2007.[14]

The ideological backstory of these events was important in *Apple*.
Leegin was something of an end point to a long, dramatic struggle. The
most cherished rallying cry of the Chicago School antitrust critics had

been to attack the vertical restraints law of the 1950s and 1960s. They counted it among their most important successes when the Supreme Court decided *Continental T. V. v. GTE Sylvania* in 1977.[15] While technically *Sylvania* did no more than relax the antitrust treatment of nonprice vertical restraints, it did so by adopting the "free-riding" reasoning of the Chicago economist Lester Telser, described earlier in this book. In addition, the Court explained its decision in a whole new language of skepticism of antitrust enforcement and deference to business. In that, it was more than a watershed in vertical restraints law; it was one of the first breaks with the unforgiving antitrust rigor of the Supreme Court under Chief Justice Earl Warren, by a Court that had been drastically repopulated by Presidents Nixon and Ford. It was the first visible step in turning what had lately been the most proenforcement antitrust Court in American history into the most antienforcement.

But in any case, a number of other important changes were still to come in the Court's evolving treatment of vertical relationships, and in its turn to the right on antitrust. In the course of it, the Court would face bitter reaction from Congress and critics. *Leegin* so far remains the Court's last statement on the matter, and it has left vertical relationships more or less immune from any real antitrust challenge. Over the thirty years between *Sylvania* and *Leegin,* the Court frequently wrote in almost laudatory terms of the social benefits of vertical restraint, with sometimes sharp criticism of earlier, stricter precedent. In its cases the Court relied at length on the economic literature on which the conservative critique was based. In *Leegin* it stressed that now that *Dr. Miles* had finally been reversed, *all* vertical restraints would be subject only to the rule of reason, and it set out once again a miniature economic symposium to explain why that was important and good.

As a consequence, many people have come to believe that any sort of arrangement that could be characterized as "vertical" would be addressed under the rule of reason, and would be given broad deference. The defense team in *Apple* made this argument at length.

Efforts to control retail prices on an industry-wide basis have been well documented since the 1880s. Vertical price-fixing had happened before then—and in fact had happened in the book industry—but it became almost a movement late in the nineteenth century in both Britain and the United States, and in Britain it dominated a wide range of retail sectors. It also became a matter of much popular debate.

Sometime around the time of the Civil War, retail price competition in all kinds of consumer products grew more vigorous in most Western countries. In the United States it was partly because a once sparsely populated country was slowing its territorial growth and becoming more urban. Small merchants who had enjoyed local pockets of shelter from competition came to face low-price challengers more often. But it was also because major retailers were growing larger and were beginning to innovate in distribution and cost control. At the same time, mass transport and industrialization drove the rise of geographically massive new markets. These matters were controversial. Tense political conflict over retail innovation would roil the United States throughout the first half of the twentieth century. Indeed, the story of twentieth-century distribution politics can be understood as a conflict between different methods of distribution. Newer and typically larger-scale means of distribution threatened smaller ones. Change especially challenged the traditional wholesalers and jobbers, who ordinarily took title to the goods they carried and then resold them to single-location stores.[16] One of the most important innovations was multilocation chain stores that could buy directly from suppliers and perform their own wholesale functions, cutting out wholesalers and jobbers altogether. Also important were the beginnings of branding, modern trademark law, and new distribution methods, including an expanding mail-order sector.[17]

Though it is hardly the kind of thing that is free from controversy, the changes that drove this new competitiveness would seem to most economists today to be desirable. Market share achieved by lower prices, which a seller can offer because by some innovation it's been able to lower its own costs, is a chief benefit of price competition, and a reason competitive markets are thought to be good. The short-term benefit to consumers—the lower prices they pay—is one advantage. Probably more important in most circumstances is the incentive for sellers to innovate in the quality of their products and their manner of doing business, which they will do if they must to keep up with competitors. Markets that lack competition, by contrast, not only hurt consumers in the short term with higher prices but also generate lower-quality goods and wasted resources. These are not trivial concerns, and even if we gain some benefits by restraining competition sometimes, the consequences can be serious. For example, before the larger grocery chains of the early twentieth century introduced price competitiveness and organizational efficiency, food for most city dwellers was expensive and low in quality, and in particular their access to fresh produce was limited.[18]

Dr. Miles involved one of the several industry-wide price maintenance arrangements of the era, this one in pharmaceuticals. As it happened, the free-wheeling, colorful, and often fraud-ridden patent medicine industry not only made groundbreaking antitrust law in *Dr. Miles,* it also pioneered many of the new merchandizing and promotional methods that would lead to widespread RPM. In the 1880s and 1890s, as other businesses were just coming to advertising, trademark, and differentiation, patent drug makers were actively building national markets with vivid advertising and psychologically shrewd promotional maneuvers.[19] The business was also fiercely competitive, and when collusion came to tame the cutthroat pricing, the form it took was like the RPM schemes that later appeared in many other sectors. In 1881 the Dr. Miles firm helped found the Proprietary Association, which acted as lobbyist before Congress and state legislatures and also as a complex price-fixing cartel. The Proprietary Association set up a restrictive, nationally coordinated RPM organization, in large part by drafting and distributing standard form contracts to manufacturers and retailers. It also acted generally as cartel coordinator and enforcer.[20]

The Proprietary Association was one of the earliest and most effective RPM groups, but it was only one of many, and the diversity of products sold by these groups is striking. The only commonality was that all were protected by intellectual property or differentiated by advertising, because unbranded, fungible goods effectively can't be made subject to RPM. There were RPM plans for medicines, books, tires, chewing gum, farm machinery, gramophones, bathtubs, grocery items, Ford automobiles, and many other products.

It is not easy to generalize the interests of the major antagonists. For example, several of the large department stores, such as Marshall Field, Jordan Marsh, and especially Macy's, aggressively opposed restraints on retail competition, but others, such as Bloomingdale and Gimbels, favored them.[21] Likewise, some of the major RPM schemes uncovered during this era did not originate with wholesalers or retailers and were opposed by them. In the "Bathtub trust," for example, an extensive plan of RPM imposed on hundreds of jobbers of enameled bathtubs throughout the United States was plainly meant only to police an otherwise purely horizontal cartel at the manufacturer level.[22]

Popular fear of big businesses and especially of retail chain stores prompted Congress and the state legislatures to undertake a long reform effort immediately after *Dr. Miles*. Attempts to legalize vertical price-fixing by statute began in 1914, but they got nowhere in Congress for many years, and no state would pass an RPM law until California finally passed one in 1931. Many states quickly followed California—forty-two had laws by the mid-1930s[23]—and the federal government, too, followed shortly thereafter. Many states also adopted other antichain provisions, consisting mainly of punitive taxes on firm size and number of locations. The federal government explicitly authorized some RPM as early as 1933, by way of the ill-fated National Recovery Administration.[24] After the NIRA and the "codes of fair competition" that it authorized were held unconstitutional, Congress reentered the area in 1937 with adoption of the Miller-Tydings Act.[25] That law closely followed the state RPM laws that preceded it, having been secured by the same lobbyists who had earlier persuaded the state legislatures. Under the Miller-Tydings law, individual states could authorize resale price maintenance contracts for intrastate sales.[26] A related statute of the era, the Robinson-Patman Act of 1936, served the same goals.[27] By prohibiting some "price discrimination," the act was meant to keep large retailers from getting better wholesale prices than their smaller competitors could get. It reflected the thinking of the time—which seems to be shared by many in our time, too—that large retailers and the damage they have done to social values have reflected not so much their better efficiency as their market power. That is, they can charge lower prices only because of the unfair discounts they can coerce from their suppliers.[28] As we saw in the last chapter, among the last major uses of that law happened to involve the book industry, in suits filed in the late 1980s.

Both the Federal Trade Commission and a private suit alleged that publishers had acceded to the demands of the growing retail chains for discriminatory wholesale discounts. Those lawsuits no doubt reflected the continued public alarm over powerful distributors, but their peculiar circumstances and their ultimate failure suggest the continued American ambivalence over that power and the controversy that has always surrounded the Robinson-Patman law.

These laws and the agitation for them were not creatures of the book industry. Robinson-Patman and the chain-store taxes were pushed mainly by advocates for the grocery trade, and the Miller-Tydings Act and state fair-trade laws were pushed mainly by the drug industry.[29] But publishers and booksellers made use of them. As early as the National Industrial Recovery Act, some of the codes of fair competition affecting books included RPM rules. Publishers also attempted to use fair-trade contracts for books during the Miller-Tydings period, in the 1930s and 1940s, though apparently without much success.[30]

Overall, use of RPM in America was rare, though the firms that did use it were large and that may have been significant.[31] That it was not more systematically in use during the Miller-Tydings period raises some interesting questions. It should have generated benefits to *someone*—RPM should be profitable if it is anticompetitive, or generate consumer benefits if it is procompetitive. And yet, RPM was not only uncommon under Miller-Tydings, but also highly unstable. Manufacturers used and then abandoned it, and producers of similar products chose to use it in some places but not others.[32] One important reason seems to be that RPM is quite expensive and difficult for manufacturers to oversee. Distributors who benefit from fixed prices have an incentive not to provide the desired promotional services, and just to pocket the extra margin of inflated price.[33]

After many years of the Miller-Tydings regime, an odd thing happened in the mid-1970s, and it had broad significance. Congress and the courts swapped their views more or less completely with regard to RPM, and their switch would change the law and politics of distribution entirely.

As we shall see, that shift concerning the narrow issue of vertical restraints mirrored a much larger shift in economic policy. It occurred at the beginning of a long American turn to the right that continues to this day.

Whereas for much of the century Congress had been quite tolerant of RPM, and was persuaded that vigorous retail should sometimes be dampened in order to protect small businesses, its views flipped in the 1960s and 1970s. Riding the general wave of proconsumer enthusiasm of the 1960s and supported primarily by Democrats, Congress entered its most productive period of antitrust legislation since 1914. The effort was led by the two antitrust subcommittee chairs, Senator Philip Hart and Congressman Pete Rodino, both careful students of the law and supporters of enforcement.[34] In 1976 Congress adopted the Hart-Scott-Rodino Antitrust Improvements Act, which established the now-familiar system of federal merger review.[35] Congress also adopted measures to encourage private and state-government enforcement, created a system of antitrust settlement review meant to prevent political favoritism in enforcement, and passed another important law in 1980 to reverse very restrictive Supreme Court interpretations of the Clayton Act.[36]

Largely the same coalition, with the same rationales, also initiated the era's "deregulation" movement, which undid much of the rate-and-entry regulatory apparatus of the Progressive Era and New Deal years. The new antitrust coalition thought those regimes had little effect but to raise prices and enrich the regulated firms. Finally, during this period, and for the same reasons, the antitrust coalition of the 1970s repealed the Miller-Tydings law in 1975.[37] By doing that, Congress explicitly reaffirmed *Dr. Miles* as the law of the land.

Meanwhile, just as the elected branch was staking out a position on price competition that was arguably stronger than anything in a century, the federal judiciary made one of the sharpest ideological shifts in its history. The effects on antitrust would be profound. The courts were led in this change by a Supreme Court repopulated by an unusually large number of nominees of Richard Nixon.[38] While the courts reworked antitrust in all its substantive areas, one of its first and most important tasks was a reconsideration of vertical restraints. The courts were soon joined in the effort by Reagan administration and later Republican enforcement officials, whose agenda was aggressive and fueled by the new conservative academic consensus. From the very beginning of his service, President Reagan's first antitrust chief, former Stanford University antitrust professor William Baxter, raised eyebrows. On vertical restraints, for example, he informed the House oversight committee at his first appearance that "there is no such thing as a harmful vertical restraint."[39]

The Supreme Court spent the next thirty years chipping away at its own vertical restraints rules, making the plaintiff's case harder in certain ways and partially reversing the per se rule of *Dr. Miles* itself in one important case.[40] Then, in *Leegin* in 2007, the Court finally did away with per se treatment altogether, effectively holding all vertical restraints subject only to the rule of reason. To be clear, it did not hold them beyond challenge, and it acknowledged various respects in which they could still be found illegal under the rule of reason. But it made them much more difficult to challenge, and it also changed the tone of the debate.

Defendants in subsequent cases—including most emphatically the defendants in *Apple*—have tried to squeeze as much out of these opinions' rhetoric as possible. They draw from the tenor of the Court's opinions that legal challenges to distribution arrangements must be very careful and deferential, and they have argued that anything even remotely resembling vertical relationships must enjoy rule of reason treatment under that same careful standard.

Yet, the Court's new assessment drew much criticism. As several scholars have demonstrated, the Court systematically exaggerated the potential for good in vertical restraints, especially with regard to RPM. The courts also did something appellate courts ordinarily do not do: they made decisions on the basis of factual claims without record evidence in the cases to support them.[41] In *Leegin,* the Court by a narrow majority overturned the long-standing precedent of the *Dr. Miles* rule, though Congress had expressed a strongly contrary intent. As recently as 1975, Congress had repealed the Miller-Tydings law, reinstating *Dr. Miles* as the law of the land. It did so following hearings that aired all the arguments on which the courts would rely in these cases, and it rejected them.[42] More remarkably, as recently as 1985, Congress had explicitly, emphatically reaffirmed its commitment to the rule of *Dr. Miles* during a controversy with the Reagan Justice Department.[43]

10

Price-Fixing in Books

The cultural merits ascribed to [price-fixing in books] have
almost reached mythical proportions.

—Marcel Canoy, Jan C. van Ours, and Frederick van der Ploeg,
"The Economics of Books"

AND SO, WITH ALL that as background, the story of distribution in the
book industry is not really so special. One of the earliest known resale
price conspiracies in any sector, anywhere, was in the English book trade
in the early nineteenth century. If anything about price maintenance in
British books is surprising, it is only that it was so open, unconcealed,
effective, and long-lasting. The first industry-wide agreement was established in 1829 and lasted for more than twenty years, and a second one
lasted nearly a century, from its founding in 1900 until the British competition authority ruled it illegal in 1997. The history of those British book
conspiracies is instructive, because it confirms the economic analysis set
out in previous chapters. An intricate account by the Indian economist
Russi Jal Taraporevala, with contributions by Basil Yamey, the great
English scholar of distribution, shows that both the conspiracy of 1829
to 1852 and the Net Books Agreement of 1900 to 1997 were driven by the
interests of book retailers and imposed on generally resistant publishers.[1]
While in some important respects the circumstances were different in the
Apple case, this history also shows how little was new in the eBooks
conspiracy of 2010.

The story appears to begin with a particular price-cutting London
bookseller, James Lackington, who sold books at deep discount as

something of a maverick in the late eighteenth century.[2] There were some book trade associations set up to dampen price competition as early as 1802, and from about that time, leaders among retail booksellers attempted to convince their publishers to coordinate and enforce a sector-wide system of fixed retail prices.[3] They finally succeeded in 1829, and established a system that remained in place until 1852.

Quite in contrast to the views of authors during the latter-day eBooks dispute, the 1829 agreement was opposed by most authors, including the writers Charles Dickens and Thomas Carlyle, the economists John Stuart Mill and Charles Babbage, and William Gladstone, already a prominent politician and later, prime minister. Why authors saw things so differently in 1829 than they did in the 2000s is not clear. It may reflect their interest in the wide distribution of their books for the sake of prestige and influence, even if it meant lower prices. Authors are also comparatively large consumers of books, so they like them to be cheap. Interestingly, academics and authors also opposed formation of the strong price-fixing organization set up in the German book trade in the late nineteenth century. In the end, the most remarkable part of the story of the first British agreement is that, following extensive internal conflict and popular objection, the industry agreed to appoint a tribunal in about 1852 to consider whether the agreement should be continued. A panel of three esteemed arbitrators found the plan on the whole to be negative and decided it should be discontinued.[4]

Although America had its own book cartels during the nineteenth century, they mostly lacked the significance of those in Britain and continental Europe. In fact, the only American book cartel of consequence was the long-running system of "courtesy," the informal understanding among publishers not to solicit each other's authors or compete with their uncopyrighted works. When more formal cartels such as the American Book Trade Association were formed to challenge the aggressive discount books that appeared late in the century, they were mostly ineffective. That association, for example, folded quite quickly, the victim of bad public reception and a critical press. What might have been a much more significant effort, the attempt at the turn of the century to adopt a US version of the British Net Books Agreement, quickly foundered under the Sherman Act and the rule of *Dr. Miles*.

The most significant RPM cartel in English-language publishing, then, was the Net Books Agreement. Considered by its proponents to be the "Magna Carta of the book trade," it governed British books for nearly one hundred years.[5] It required active oversight by a major organization of publishers and another of booksellers to sustain its elaborate enforcement mechanism and frequent bouts of renegotiation and conflict. The details are complex and they evolved continually over the Agreement's lifetime, but generally they consisted of the kinds of enforcement measures familiar from all sorts of other cartel situations. Members of price cartels commonly find control of price-cutting cheaters to be a chief problem, and indeed, cheating on the Net Books Agreement's terms was a persistent problem. The Agreement was able to flourish because English law permitted it, so its administrators could undertake the necessary cartel enforcement quite in the open.

One surprising part of the story often noted by defenders of vertical price-fixing involved the Cambridge economist Alfred Marshall.[6] The new "marginalist" thinking was already well known in the 1880s, but Marshall's chief work, the *Principles of Economics* (1890), synthesized it and disseminated it to Europe and America, with revolutionary consequences. It was significant, then, that when the publisher Frederick Macmillan first initiated the effort to form the Net Books Agreement, he persuaded Marshall to allow the *Principles of Economics* to come under the Agreement and be one of the first books sold at a fixed retail price in Britain since 1852. Macmillan made a point of this when he advocated for the Net Books Agreement, and he later pointed to it as proof of the Agreement's economic wisdom.[7] But Macmillan's claims were misleading. It was later discovered in correspondence between the two men that Marshall objected to the Net Book Agreement once he knew what it entailed, and had agreed to Macmillan's pricing proposal only because he had misunderstood it. Macmillan's letter initially proposing the arrangement was a circuitous, reticulated exercise that made no mention that prices would be fixed.[8]

Like the earlier British arrangement, Net Books was predominantly an effort of booksellers, though it was begun by a publisher—Frederick Macmillan of Macmillan & Co. The initial Net Book proposal stated that it was "drawn up in the interest of the booksellers, as urged by the majority of them," and therefore enforcement of its terms would be their responsi-bility.[9] British publishers by and large opposed the agreement, at least in its first years, and were at odds with the booksellers for decades. Yet, it is not surprising that members of the same trade might disagree about their collective best interest, and a minority among the publishers supported retail price-fixing. They made a claim like one that drove the *Apple* con-spiracy: that vigorous competition at the retail level might lead book-sellers to demand lower wholesale prices.[10] And while most publishers opposed the arrangement and accepted it only grudgingly, in their public rhetoric they told a different story. Participants in the Agreement, both publishers and retailers, mostly spoke of it positively in public statements.

It is not coincidental that American publishers and booksellers exe-cuted a similar agreement, with similar terms, in 1901, the year after the British Net Book Agreement. For the purpose of restraining retail prices, much of the American book industry came together to form the Amer-ican Publishers Association and the American Booksellers' Association, which are still dominant in their respective sectors. Between them, they included about 95 percent of American publishers and 90 percent of American booksellers.[11] Consciously borrowing from their British col-leagues, their American agreement set up a "net pricing system" largely identical to the Net Book Agreement. According to public pronounce-ments of the publishers association, the American agreement was "un-dertaken at the earnest solicitation of booksellers of all classes in order that those handling books might be afforded a living profit."[12]

The US agreement was immediately the target of antitrust action that succeeded fairly quickly. The protagonists of the opposition were the brothers and business partners Jesse and Nathan Straus, owners of the Macy's retail stores, which at the time was an aggressive discounter. Macy's began selling books in 1869 and had become a leading bookseller by the time the 1901 agreement took effect.[13] The Straus brothers were ac-tive litigants and used the courts in a long and mostly successful campaign to empower retail price competition, which put them in conflict with the national movement for retail protectionism (of a variety of products, not just books).[14] They were also prominent in Democratic Party politics. During the 1920s Jesse was an important political ally of Governor

Franklin D. Roosevelt, and he later served as President Roosevelt's ambassador to France.

In their fight to sell discount books, the Straus brothers were locked in legal struggle with American publishers for nearly four decades. The Strauses and their counsel, Edmund Wise, appeared frequently before congressional committees and hearings of the Federal Trade Commission.[15] They made two successful trips to the US Supreme Court and several to state supreme courts as well, establishing along the way the important "first sale" doctrine in copyright law.[16] They were finally defeated, after many years, under the "fair trade" policy of the Miller-Tydings Act and the popular animus of the day against chain store retailers.

The conflict began with an antitrust claim that the Straus brothers brought against the American Publishers Association in New York state court, challenging the 1901 price-fixing agreement. That action was only partly successful. In 1904 New York's highest court held the agreement in violation of New York's state antitrust law, but only to the extent that it covered uncopyrighted books.[17] The publishers and booksellers immediately revised the 1901 arrangement so that it covered only copyrighted books, and brought their own action against the Straus brothers.[18] Specifically, the named plaintiff in that case, the Indiana publisher Bobbs-Merrill, alleged copyright infringement by Macy's in their sale of *The Castaway*, a novel by a controversial and best-selling author of the day, Hallie Erminie Rives. Rives, the daughter of a Confederate war veteran, drew attention among other things for seeming to take a favorable view of lynching. *The Castaway*, a fictionalized account of the life of Lord Byron that dwelt on his affair with the teenage Jane Clairmont, bore a notice that purported to fix its resale price. Printed on the copyright page, the notice prohibited resale of the book at less than one dollar. Macy's carried the book and sold many copies, which it had gotten mainly from wholesalers. It had no contractual or other relationship with Bobbs-Merrill. Although it was aware of the purported copyright restriction, Macy's sold the book at eighty-nine cents. The publisher plaintiff in *Bobbs-Merrill* asserted that resale of the book at terms other than those in the notice, even in the absence of contract between Bobbs-Merrill and Macy's, violated the publisher's copyright and entitled it to an injunction.

The Court disagreed. In a seminal opinion establishing what is now known as the "first sale" doctrine in American copyright law, the Court held that once a copyright owner has sold the protected item, it can impose no further conditions on the buyer's use of it.

However, *Bobbs-Merrill* asked only whether a copyright owner's resale limits were enforceable against persons—such as Macy's—with whom it had no contract. It left open the question whether imposing those limits by contract was itself illegal.[19] That would be decided three years later in *Dr. Miles.* But *Dr. Miles,* too, left open a question, because the medicines in *Dr. Miles* were not patented. That question was whether retail price-fixing contracts would violate federal antitrust where the articles in question were covered by intellectual property. The Court answered that a few years later, in a subsequent chapter of the Straus brothers' fight with the book industry. *Straus v. American Publishers' Association* held in 1913 that resale price maintenance in copyrighted books would be per se illegal.[20] The attempts by American business to secure legally permissible RPM had seemed to fail at every turn.

Other Western countries have legally sanctioned the fixing of retail book prices, in some cases since the nineteenth century. The German book industry established a well-organized, highly effective, nationwide price maintenance system in the 1870s, and secured explicit approval for it by statute. That system has governed ever since, and in 2002 the German government formally mandated RPM for all books, even while it forbids RPM in other products. The Netherlands likewise requires RPM in books in the Dutch and Frisian languages. But France is more protective of booksellers yet. The French government itself sets minimum retail book prices by law.[21]

This history suggests an interesting counterpoint to the argument that underlies this book. Price-fixing has been common in the books industry, perhaps more so than in others, and the degree to which some nations have formally supported it is unusual. It is also intriguing that a large, formal arrangement should have arisen so early in books. The British cartel of 1829 existed well before RPM organizations arose in other sectors in Britain and America. If indeed price-fixing is more common in books than in other sectors, it seems hardly likely just to reflect some tradition of peculiar wrongdoing. Nothing about publishers or booksellers indicates they are more or less avaricious or conniving than other businesspeople. So perhaps the prevalence of price-fixing proves that there is something special about the book business, some special fragility or dysfunction that requires it to operate differently than other industries.

The better explanation on the evidence is that the incidence of RPM in books is not as unusual as it seems. For one thing, while it is true that the Net Books Agreement was prominent and long-lasting, RPM was more common throughout British industry than in America during the twentieth century, simply because it was more broadly legal in Britain. For another thing, if books really are so economically special that they require RPM for their commercial viability, then the book sectors in Britain and America should have had very different experiences. The British industry enjoyed a plenary and well-administered RPM regime while its American counterpart survived largely without any RPM at all, but their experience over time has not been markedly different.

11

Content and the Digital Transition
in Historical Context

WHEN THE KINDLE HIT book publishing in 2007, it was at the center of three interrelated streams of technological and economic change. The first was the decades of organizational change in the publishing sector, which was left with heavy short-term profit pressures and a risky predilection for high-payoff best sellers. The second was change in book distribution, where first the large chain stores devastated independent booksellers and cut into publishers' margins, and then in turn, they were threatened by the new bookseller Amazon. Even as the major publishers struggled under these pressures, a third change was afoot. As consumer electronics evolved and proliferated, and then the internet became a commercial reality in the mid-1990s, they made possible different modes of distribution of all kinds of things, and especially artistic and literary content. Anything that could be "digitized" soon would be, because digital products offer significant quality and cost advantages. The consequences came much earlier to music, video, and news than to books, and the policy and legal struggles that played out in those other sectors would be important in *Apple*.

A lot of contemporary writing about digital distribution, especially writing preoccupied with whether it is "disruptive," overstates or misconceives its nature. Its chief economic consequence is a reduction in costs. It is much cheaper to distribute anything digitally, if it can be done, than to distribute it in hard copy. Artistic or intellectual works distributed in hard copy require the manufacture of some physical medium such as disks or tape recordings or paper; they require warehouses and trucks to carry the products; they risk unsold or damaged inventory; and they entail either direct-mail shipping costs or physical retail locations. Digitization avoids these costs altogether, and after creation of the initial master copy, distribution requires only the cost of transmitting a secure electronic file and arranging for payment. In fact, in the American economy, consumers own or pay for much of the distribution infrastructure themselves. The buyers download content onto devices they have purchased, using internet access paid for by themselves or by third parties (e.g., via coffee shop Wi-Fi or access provided by the consumer's employer).[1] Strictly speaking, even that fact does not distinguish digitization in kind so much as degree from other kinds of commerce. Consumers also own other components of the distribution infrastructure that sometimes have enabled major economizations. We own cars and pay taxes for public transit, and use them to travel further to big discount stores than we used to travel to the local grocery or hardware store. The difference in degree, however, is substantial.

Accordingly, a firm that can digitize enjoys a massive advantage, at least in cost terms, over competitors attempting to sell the same content in hard copy. The result is short-term dislocation for traditional firms, entailing typically painful changes in personnel and settled investments. Still, for all the drama the resulting changes can hold, digital economization is not in itself much different from other technological innovations that generate cost advantages, including some that seem very mundane and have occurred many times before. They give some firms competitive advantage, and other firms react with whatever strategic responses are available. Incumbent producers choose from the same short menu of defenses, which includes collusion, boycott, acquisition of the innovating competitor, and appeals for government protection. Indeed, there is nothing even very interesting about the fact that some change is *technological*. The coming of eBooks and the other digital transitions, for example, were similar in economic terms to the rise of chain stores in the early twentieth century.

That transition was to some degree just a change in organization and strategy.

One different issue runs through the history of content digitization, and it will prove illuminating. The history of the content industries is in some sense a history of their efforts to control piracy, and to use the law and other barriers to keep new distribution technologies from facilitating it.[2] But there is an important lesson in the following fact. By historical accident, piracy was never an important concern for electronic books. By the time of the Kindle's introduction in 2007, technology and legal changes put in place for music and video also made piracy in digital books very difficult. There was some evidence of it in the early years—pirated electronic versions of Harry Potter books, for example, turned up on widely used file-sharing sites[3]—but they weren't digital copies that a user could easily create and share with a click. Anticopying software had already made that nearly impossible, so the copies that existed were laboriously scanned or retyped transcriptions. Thus, by the time Amazon began eBook negotiations with the publishers in the mid-2000s, piracy was no longer a concern.[4]

And yet, in books, too, even absent the piracy that had threatened music and video, settled incumbent interest was threatened by an innovation with a cost advantage. Hardback new releases—the publishers' most important and profitable products—faced effective substitutes that were much cheaper, so the incumbents took steps to try to contain the threat. In some ways the steps they took differed from the actions the music and video industries had taken, but only in their details. In general terms, the incumbent firms in those prior periods of transition used conspiracy, forcible exclusion, litigation, or lobbying to keep out substitute products. In all those cases, they would ultimately yield to some degree and find ways to adapt. The losses they generated along the way were borne mainly by consumers. All that happened in industries facing digitization, whether piracy was an issue or not.

And so one lesson is that "piracy" is a somewhat misleading metaphor. On closer examination, this thing we presume to be immoral and undesirable is not so obviously distinguishable from other kinds of competition. It differs from other kinds of competition less in kind than in the normative freight with which we fill it. After all, so far as economic theory is concerned, the selling of precisely the same good that another person sells, with the goal of taking their revenues and making that money your own—"piracy," if you like—is what one is supposed to do. Not only is it not disfavored, it is the highest purpose of markets and a service to the public weal. What Amazon began to do in 2007 when it offered much cheaper alternatives to the publishers' high-priced new release hardcovers was in a way the same as what "pirates" do. It was also not meaningfully distinguishable from any other quality-adjusted price competition, and so it was the thing that in our system competitors are supposed to do. Accordingly, what is "piracy" and what is not is a matter of policy choice. Deciding to treat some kinds of competition as illicit may very well be a necessary or desirable choice, and it is not in issue here whether and when we should prohibit copying in any particular case. But it is not a distinction of kind inherent in meaningfully different kinds of conduct. Moreover, because the consequences of the choice are difficult to measure, it is always to some degree an exercise in speculation, and it is often probably rather arbitrary.

So isn't it then the most interesting insight that intellectual property policy is really a question how much competition is too much? In other words, intellectual property law instantiates yet another of our many perceptions of destructive competition. Generally, it is said to be needed because without protection from uncompensated copying—which is to say, protection from competition by sellers who didn't have to bear the cost of the initial creation, and who can therefore sell at lower price—innovators won't be able to earn enough to make their creativity worthwhile. It is just one of the dozens of adjustments we make to unbridled price competition. Despite our tendency to render it a moral question, it really is just one more problem in technocratic and inevitably somewhat arbitrary policy.

In any case, whether or not piracy should be permitted or whether it is ever desirable is not the point. The consequence of all technological innovation is just a matter of cost or other competitive advantage, and none of it is inherently distinguishable from other kinds of price competition. Wherever competition through innovation occurs, it tends to work itself out in more or less the same ways, regardless of the moral clothing in which we wrap it.

Like the other digital revolutions, the digitization of music has its roots in developments that occurred many years ago, long before the conflict over online music distribution erupted in the bitter courtroom and policy fights of the 2000s. Technology for converting analog audio signals into digital files originated in the early 1970s, in efforts to achieve high-quality speech transmission over phone lines. Though it would take a while for the threat to become apparent, analog-to-digital transformation was alarming to the music industry because it made possible the creation of successive copies that did not deteriorate in quality. Even copying onto cassette tapes, which improved on prior technologies, degraded sound quality during recording, and subsequent recordings from cassette to cassette get worse and worse. But the potential to copy from one digital copy to another was a very significant concern to record companies, because any number of digital copies can be made of a digital recording without loss of quality.

The threat surely became apparent with the commercial availability of compact discs in 1982, and high-quality CD-to-tape recording technology a bit later. The threat was keen because a 1984 Supreme Court decision was thought to render home copying for personal consumption a legally permissible fair use.[5]

But none of that matched the threat the industry perceived when music files became shareable over the internet. To make that happen, decades of frenetic work in labs in several countries was required to overcome the massive size of digital audio files. The most important breakthroughs were made by German computer scientists, aided by a project of the European Union, that resulted in the development in 1991 of the "MP3" data compression format. Thereafter, new hardware devices and software for MP3 playback on personal computers were rapidly commercialized—a series of events that became a multiply repeated pattern during the development of digital markets. Quick technological advancements and a flurry of new business start-ups were followed by the entry of some firm that would then dominate the category. This is fairly significant for the story of eBooks, because a series of strategic efforts began at least as early as 2003, among West Coast firms that would vie for dominance in digitization of books. It was very much part of the struggle that played out in the *Apple* conspiracy, and it was just like what had happened during earlier transitions.

In music, from its first few, wildly developing years, Apple would come to own the category. It was an interesting chapter in Apple's evolution as a company, and Steve Jobs' strategic mastery in bringing it about was key in his own personal story.

First came digital music playback software for desktop and laptop computers, including RealPlayer and Windows Media, as well as several portable hardware devices for playing MP3s, the most popular of which was the Diamond Multimedia company's Rio player. In a pattern that repeated several times over the next decade, a major step forward would be Apple's entry in both these categories, after the many other small aspirants that had clamored for market share were acquired or failed. Apple introduced its first digital playback application, iTunes, in January 2001. It was immediately successful, and quickly displaced the several other MP3 software applications that had been popular with Mac OS users. More important yet was Apple's introduction of the groundbreaking iPod device later that year. Technologically, the iPod substantially outpaced its competitors. The other handheld MP3 players had extremely limited storage and were counterintuitive to navigate and use. The iPod had huge storage by the standards of the day, and the user experience was one of the first and greatest successes of Apple's legendary chief designer Jony Ive. It could also be easily integrated with the iTunes music player on the user's Apple desktop or laptop to take advantage of those devices' much more powerful storage capacity. The iPod offered an easy, fast synchronization of songs and playlists using Apple's "FireWire" product.[6]

Meanwhile, another development in online music distribution would strike many as altogether darker. At about this time there arose the music industry's great bêtes noires, the "peer-to-peer" (P2P) sharing sites Napster, Grokster, Gnutella, Kazaa, and their ilk. As soon as consumer technology was widely available to rip CDs and store their data as MP3 files, the world of digital music became an unrestrained Wild West. The P2P sharing sites varied in their particulars, but their basic function was to radically increase the ease and value of file sharing. They facilitated not only one-to-one sharing between individuals, but very large networks of users who each made their collections of music files available to all the others. The industry's desperate, aggressive efforts to stop this activity over the coming decade would prove significant in many ways.

Apple introduced a much bigger innovation in music a few years later. The iTunes Music Store, launched in April 2003, was a major step forward in the organization of the music business, a reimagining of how content would be sold. The store offered a very large, comparatively unrestricted library of music at relatively low prices. Among its biggest innovations was that every song in its library was available for individual purchase without purchasing an entire album—a breakdown that the recording industry had long resisted. Again, Apple's music store had predecessors. Among them were the first downloadable music sales services, Diamond Multimedia's RioPort and a subscription service established by RealNetworks, both launched not long after the initial iTunes software in 2001.[7] But once again, Apple displaced those competitors. It quickly became the largest music retailer in the United States, and a few years later, the world.

Interestingly, it was by Apple's more-or-less wholesale reinvention of music distribution that the firm first reemerged from a period of ignominy in the 1990s, and it was a key chapter in Steve Jobs's own remarkable personal story. He launched the firm's new music business not long after returning to run the company in 1997, having been forced out a decade earlier by CEO John Sculley and his successors. Their generally disastrous tenures were associated with huge losses, product flops, and a narrow escape from insolvency just after Jobs's return. Further pressure was added as the tech sector in general endured the dot-com crash. Jobs saw the firm's salvation in a reorientation of its product focus. He ended several of his predecessors' failing product lines, including a variety of desktop peripherals and the expensive and ill-fated personal data assistant, the Newton. In their place, he expanded the focus from the traditional personal computing hardware to a broader set of devices and software to coordinate digital media, as a unified system. Sensing that the personal computer had matured and was no longer at the leading edge, he made Apple's new music business one part of a strategy to reinvent the PC as a "digital hub." It would still be a PC, but it would also become the core of a seamlessly integrated set of devices and applications to handle the user's entire digital life.[8]

The commercialization of online music was a complicated endeavor. It required the orchestration of technologically superior hardware, a very well-designed consumer experience, and shrewdness in coaxing the cooperation of content owners. Jeff Bezos later replicated that feat in digital books, and in fact he consciously modeled his effort on the success of iTunes. The record companies, like the publishers with whom Bezos would deal, vigorously opposed ceding control of their product to third parties from a very different sector they did not understand. The main lever Jobs worked to secure their content was their fear of online piracy, from which he would protect them just by making their products available in a format customers wanted. They were keenly aware, too, of their own lack of the skills needed to build online distribution of their own.[9]

Incidentally, a point that to some would prove significant during the *Apple* litigation is that Apple's music distribution agreements—like those it later negotiated in video and software—were similar in key respects to the eBook agreements it would negotiate years later. Indeed, they were negotiated by largely the same Apple personnel, presumably with similar goals in mind. To critics of the *Apple* case, it was more proof of the government's wrongheadedness that it would challenge agreements that had operated in Apple's other businesses for years without incident. But there were some important differences. Chief among them was that in books the government had evidence that the terms were negotiated as part of a horizontal cartel that would control not only Apple's prices, but all retail prices.

From the introduction of the first commercially available digital music in the early 1980s, the recording industry tried to control the threat to its model. The firms colluded in a variety of ways, and were successfully sued by the Federal Trade Commission over a large price-fixing agreement covering retail CD sales. It was apparently driven by their fear that the much more physically durable CDs would give stiffer after-market competition than vinyl and tape recordings.[10] They also tried to contain the threat of the developing copying and replay technologies. For example, when writeable CDs and technology to rip and burn them first became widely available in the mid-1990s, consumers were surprised to find that the blank CDs for burning music files were very expensive, whereas blank CDs for storing computer data were much cheaper. The higher price was the result of an agreement between the recording industry and the makers of writeable CDs, to pay the recording industry royalties on blank CD sales to compensate them for risk to their interests.[11] The industry also secured legislation to impose restraints on some digital home recording technology, and unsuccessfully sought to use it to block sale of the new MP3 player technology of the late 1990s.[12]

An important part of the story of industry reaction was "digital rights management" technology (DRM). DRM is software or other technology that prevents copying or sharing of digital files. CBS Records developed such a technology as early as 1987, and the recording industry was eager to use it to control the new world of compact discs. It was technologically difficult to incorporate it into the already existing platform of music CDs, which was not designed with DRM in mind, but that did not stop record companies from trying, with disastrous results. Sony BMG infamously tried to install DRM software in users' personal computers by secretly including it in music CDs, disclosing it only in extremely veiled license language. When consumers played the discs on their computers, the CDs surreptitiously installed the new software code. The software was largely indistinguishable from harmful virus software, and was widely thought to be illegal. Sony BMG ended up settling litigation and agreeing to serious remedies.[13] But for later-developing technologies, such as DVDs and eBooks, DRM did not pose similar problems. Those technologies were built from the ground up with DRM in mind.[14]

Essentially the same issues were rehashed with the online distribution of music, initially because it introduced the unbundled sale of individual songs. That became a major sticking point in negotiations over the iTunes Store.[15] Digitization also made possible P2P file sharing, even easier copying of songs, and more recently, the streaming of music over internet radio. The industry's response has combined lobbying, litigation, and consolidation.

With regard to P2P, the industry reacted with an aggressive push to suppress it completely, through lobbying and litigation. On the one hand, the industry successfully sued the P2P sharing sites in a set of lawsuits, first challenging Napster for "contributory" copyright infringement, and later succeeding before the Supreme Court against two Napster copycat products, Grokster and Morpheus.[16] In one of the more glaring episodes of the story, the industry also litigated aggressively against private individuals. That effort was always fairly ill starred, as it was unseemly in the popular eye, and also apparently ineffective. It was ended after suits against some thirty thousand users had no meaningful impact on P2P file sharing.[17]

The near-term future of music distribution seems to be in internet radio and similar online streaming services. Those innovations, like cheap ripping-and-burning of CDs or free P2P sharing, might have reoriented control of the revenue stream produced by music distribution, and might have led to lower prices, greater variety, and new features for consumers. But it appears that for now, the balance of power has been maintained by a very large consolidation and reorganization of the recording industry, and by litigation and efforts in the special federal court that oversees most music licensing.[18]

Video has undergone a broadly similar transition. In many details and peculiarities it is a story all its own, but the themes are essentially the same as those that played out in music. On the one hand, the problem of private piracy was simpler in video because DRM technology had been better developed by the time DVDs became commercially available.[19] On the other hand, video's transition was again mainly a series of technological developments with the potential to free up new distribution and make extensive benefits available to the public. It was followed by strategic retrenchments to protect incumbent content owners and distributors. In this case, the threatened incumbents were the major film and television studios, and then increasingly the cable television industry, and ultimately broadband internet service providers. As each innovation and new-entrant business has appeared, either incumbent firms or other powerful actors have resorted to familiar strategies to keep technological disruption from bringing competition back or distributing benefits to consumers.

Things of value besides literary and artistic content can be digitized and distributed electronically, and in those cases the developments and consequences have been similar. For example, a mad scramble occurred in recent years to control markets in digital maps and driving directions.[20] The same dynamic of digital innovation met with incumbent retrenchment also operates in ongoing struggles in sharing economy markets, where traditional firms in hotel and taxi cab dispatch have invoked a variety of defenses against firms such as Uber and Airbnb.

None of these conflicts were peculiar to digital technology. They have parallels in a long and sordid history of exclusionary struggle between content industries and technological innovation that stretches into the nineteenth century. Consider the huge publishing industry response to the invention of photocopying. There were predictions of dire threats to publishing and related businesses and several major lawsuits during the 1970s, including a large challenge to federal research libraries for merely photocopying journal articles for distribution to their own researchers.[21] Photocopying also played a major role in the complete overhaul of American copyright in 1976. Or consider the sheet music industry's reactions to the gramophone and, of all things, the player piano. The conflict began in 1895, when the major publishers of sheet music formed an umbrella group and collectively made one player-piano manufacturer their exclusive licensee. In exchange for exclusivity, that manufacturer agreed to finance infringement litigation against competing player-piano makers. The affair became a cause célèbre, with Theodore Roosevelt declaring the arrangement a "giant music monopoly," and it ultimately called for resolution by the Supreme Court.[22]

Similar cases with no connection to intellectual content or digital technology are also routine. One recent example is the acquisition of the popular urban car-sharing service Zipcars by the car-rental firm Avis. One imagines it was not irrelevant in Avis's calculus that Zipcars posed some threat to traditional car rental firms.[23]

One important theme in stories of digital transition was that incumbent firms, in addition to the private restraints and lawsuits and other steps they took to forestall disruption, looked to Congress for protection. Congress obliged, particularly in the form of copyright amendments. An important story in itself is the degree to which the making of American copyright law has been controlled by incumbent content firms. Beginning around the turn of the twentieth century, Congress began to defer in the drafting and updating of copyright legislation to ad hoc groups composed mostly of content-industry participants. The several major revisions for which they have been responsible have ordinarily focused on just the kind of content-technology conflicts discussed here. Beginning with turn-of-the-century fear of the gramophone and the player piano, recurring with the mid-1970s reaction to photocopying, and then repeating with more frequency in the 1980s and 1990s, copyright has extended ever-more extravagant protections to content holders to assuage their asserted fears of piracy or loss.[24]

One final point before moving on, and on some level it implicitly previews much of the argument to come. Although in all these changing contexts the incumbent firms claimed a need for protection, widespread evidence suggests that disruptive technological changes quite frequently *increase the profits of the incumbents.* For example, a persistent theme in most of these areas is the fear of piracy. But new copying and distribution technology, even if it facilitates illegal copies to some extent, has often increased sales and profitability for incumbent content owners.[25] As one of many examples, in the early 1980s the movie industry predicted its own demise at the hands of the new VCR device, but in fact, the ability to display films at home opened huge new sales opportunities for the studios.[26] Likewise, peer-to-peer music file sharing is thought to have increased actual purchases because it exposed music to new listeners on a song-by-song basis, and similarly, fair-use quotations from books in book reviews or the like helps book sales.[27] And sure enough, although publishers vigorously resisted the threat of low-priced eBooks, there is evidence since the end of the *Apple* conspiracy that competitively priced eBooks have been surprisingly profitable for them.

12

The Promise and Threat
of Electronic Books

> On the removal of an artificial protection in any department of
> industry some distress immediately follows; but the wholesome
> principles of commerce, when acted upon, ere long bring a
> remedy.
>
> —Report of a panel of the Booksellers Association, 1852, urging repeal of
> resale price maintenance in the British book trade

NEITHER APPLE NOR AMAZON nor any of the publisher defendants in
United States v. Apple invented the electronic book. By the time of the
Apple conspiracy, people had been conceptualizing eBooks for nearly
eighty years, making them for forty, and trying to make a commercial go
of them for twenty or more. The years it took for them to come into their
own resulted neither from lack of effort, nor, at least until the turn of the
century, suppression or obstruction. It was mainly technological happenstance. Certain problems in making reading devices that people would
actually want to use made the digital distribution of books harder to commercialize than had been the case for music or video. But in any case, it
was not until Amazon got ahold of them that eBooks became a commercial reality. When Amazon unveiled the Kindle in 2007, it effectively
brought the market into being by force, through substantial, clandestine
research investments to overcome weaknesses in prior efforts and through
a pricing and promotions approach aggressive even by Amazon's standards. To be sure, Amazon is like most successful companies in that its

important contributions have built on (or, if you like, appropriated) other people's work. That was a big part of the story of Amazon and eBooks. The firm also happened to enjoy several strokes of technological and marketplace luck.

And so, as a commercially viable phenomenon, books were latecomers to digital distribution. Prior struggles in music and video had already more or less run their course, and the digital music business in particular had settled into established channels. Besides just the technological challenge of developing desirable reading devices, other factors may have contributed to the delay, but it is hard to say. For years an unspoken wisdom had held that after music and video had become fully digitized, books would be "the last one in."[1] That was so even though, technologically, simple text should be the easiest content to digitize, and even though incumbent producers of other media had just as much reason to resist the change. For their part, the publishers were largely unprepared for the transition, and one can hardly fault them for it. Failures to foresee big developments are the stuff of business history legend. In the early 1990s, even as he led the world's most powerful tech firm, Bill Gates famously underestimated the significance of the coming internet.[2] In fact, Jeff Bezos himself apparently misunderstood the significance of content digitization until late in its evolution, and narrowly avoided losing the eBooks market to Apple. Moreover, the technology required for making both viable e-readers and a commercial eBook market were the work of some of the greatest minds in electronic commerce—Jeff Bezos and Steve Jobs—and it called for competencies and resources beyond any publisher's ordinary repertoire. So the publishers were more or less destined to be caught flat-footed. They were surely aware of the eBook technology of the day and the possibility of its growth, and had been thinking about eBooks since the mid-1990s.[3] But apparently they had no specific plans for how to secure that new market or control its consequences. As Jeffrey Toobin put it, even the year of the Kindle's introduction, they still viewed eBooks with "simultaneous lethargy and panic."[4] Meanwhile, a fact of which they seemed unaware was that the fate of their industry had been discussed for years among the leaders of Amazon, Apple, and Google, who were planning how they would carve up ownership of books among themselves as part of the new digital landscape.

A significant theme in the history of electronic books also runs through the history of information technology, and indeed technology in general, and it is important to competition as a public policy. Innovators have often been much less concerned with near-term efficiencies and other mundane matters than with the larger social consequences of innovation. That may be even more true in books and information than in other sectors. Something peculiar in the nature of information seems to have intensified the dreams of the great computer pioneers, given the social power of knowledge and education. Thus, the planners and entrepreneurs who foresaw the eBook's evolution often imagined it as a tool of nothing less than social emancipation. But running through all histories of technology are more complex problems. We have already seen the human loss that accompanies even positive change, in lost livelihoods and cultural inheritances. And at work in all stories of technological progress, with their mix of human promise and inevitable loss, one key force to opposes it—the investment-backed interests of incumbent producers. Facilitating the greater benefits of change is an important goal of competition policy, and threatening them has frequently been a goal of the anticompetitive conduct in which incumbent producers engage. And so, the goal of enforcement in *Apple* was not really to make books cheap, but to let markets work out those innovation gains for the greater good.

With that in mind, it is worth thinking about just how much promise there might be in digitizing text and what it might mean for society if it could proceed without constraint. The real question in *Apple* was whether the coming of eBooks was on the whole good or bad. The way Amazon introduced them may have caused various harms, and much of this book attempts to measure their gravity. But in counting up the costs and benefits, we must keep in mind that the *Apple* defendants, like the incumbent firms in other content industries during the digital revolution, worked to slow or stop the innovation and prevent it from getting to consumers as quickly or at all. Even just by keeping eBooks expensive, the scheme would limit their diffusion and commercial viability, and thereby slow their technological development and the derivative innovations that would flow from them. So in counting up the costs and benefits of the coming of eBooks, we should think seriously about what social benefits the publishers forestalled, over and above the higher prices they charged. Likewise, care will repay us in counting up the costs that eBooks themselves may have imposed. Many fears surrounded changes to the physical nature of books, their authorship, and their content once they became unbound. But as we shall see, many of those changes are really only to phenomena that themselves are more merely constructs than they seem.

One should forecast all these things with caution. Projections about the impact of the eBook often sound like predictions during the 1990s that the dot-com economy could not fail, or later, that securitized mortgages and cryptocurrencies and whatever else are immune to traditional market realities.[5] They tend to be made with a lot of confidence, and they tend to find many believers, but they also tend to extremes. So far, during the ten years of their widespread availability, eBooks have not radically transformed society, and it seems rather early to judge the many claims that they will rival the Gutenberg press. In fact, despite their very significant price advantage, eBooks sales have been shrinking and they remain in the substantial minority of books sold.[6] On the brighter side, it seems unlikely they will deliver on their critics' worst fears. Authors have not become, as John Updike predicted, "surrogate birth mothers, rented wombs in which a seed implanted by high-powered consultants is allowed to ripen and . . . be dropped squalling into the marketplace."[7] And so it is still too soon really to measure the impact of eBooks. Elizabeth Eisenstein, one of America's great historians, wrote in 2005 that her work on the social consequences of the Gutenberg press remained "tentative [and] provisional," merely "an extended essay and not . . . a definitive text."[8] She wrote that thirty years after she largely invented the social-historical study of printing, and 500 years after the press itself came into being. We probably should take her cue as to a trend that has existed for only a decade.

Still, with due caution, the potential for good from digitized text seems really substantial, and the threat to settled interests more than adequate to drive strictly avaricious obstruction. The mundane benefits are obvious. Besides their affordability, eBooks enable new amenities and consumer features such as portability and small size, the ability to resize or customize the page to one's aesthetic liking, and the ability to read books on different devices (a capability available on most eBook platforms). eBooks also already have prodigious storage power, and that will increase. The entirety of all physical or electronic documents that humans have produced—ever—is estimated to constitute about fifty petabytes of information. Experts expect that within the comparatively near future, storage capacity of that size will be possible even with handheld devices.[9]

More significant at present is the fact that a book whose text can be searched is more than just the same content in a different medium. As a minor matter, shoppers can browse books online, leafing through titles or using content search to discover books they otherwise might never have encountered. In encouraging publishers to supply Amazon with digital content, Jeff Bezos stressed that electronic browsing would help their sales—it would be the online equivalent of dipping into physical books in a terrestrial bookstore.[10] Digitized books also expand the prowess of academics, journalists, and other researchers. One can now type search queries into individual books, and search the text of whole databases of books. Indeed, digitized books have transformed search itself. Every search typed into Google's search engine now invokes the computing capacity of its roughly one million servers, blistering algorithmically through the full text of tens of millions of books that together represent a large portion of the entire extant store of human knowledge.[11] With digitization of books, search itself gets better.

Larger yet, at least in aspiration, is the potential for fast, cheap information access. That gain is potentially humanitarian in scope, and many technological pioneers have believed that eBooks would do much more than just make books affordable or searchable. By universalizing information and the social power it entails, they thought that the costless, instantaneous sharing of eBooks anywhere in the world could destabilize settled regimes of power, wealth, and inequality.[12]

But on some level, the greatest potential of eBooks, and surely the most fascinating and most often discussed, lies in their ability to change writing itself. If one will pardon the imagery, digitization can render books unbound. An exciting feature of disruptive technological change is its purely intellectual power to unravel settled conceptions. New technology tends to dissolve definitional boundaries that were arbitrary or that reflected constraints that no longer apply. The fact that a certain thing is produced in a certain way or sold through certain means may distort or limit how we think about it. Change to technology can open our eyes to possibilities that probably were always there but that we failed to see. The experience can be like the literary phenomenon of metonymy—calling something by a name that is really only a small part of the overall thing. We sometimes refer to the entire federal government as "Washington," for example. We mean not just the city, but also all the women and men who work in government, the agencies, the courts and Congress, the red tape, and so on. We refer to food that is served as a "dish," though the word really just denotes a plate, we refer to the judiciary as "the bench," and so on. Physical technology can have an effect like this, and when it does, our conceptions of it can constrain our sense of possibilities.

This problem of physical technologies obscuring the real nature of underlying phenomena has often had fairly serious economic consequences. For example, shipping of cargo is ancient, but it was not until the mid-twentieth century that it overcame a central, centuries-long driver of its own costs: the fact that cargo was not shipped in standardized units, and could not be easily transferred between different transport "modes" such as truck, rail, and ship. The technological solution known as "containerization"—packing cargo into large, standardized, metal boxes that can be easily transferred between modes—enabled huge savings and logistical improvements. It demonstrated that the business is not really three different modes at all, but one business of "transport" or "logistics." But containerization was delayed for decades, in part by the difficulty businesspeople and regulators had conceiving it outside the categories defined by the different technologies.[13]

And so it is with books. By that same metonymic process as with so many other objects of physical technology, we tend to think of the *content* of a book as having aspects that are not essential to it, and which actually follow only from the physical technology within which it has traditionally been contained. Histories and philosophies of the book are often criticized for this incaution.[14]

The concept "book" ends up being both significantly overinclusive and underinclusive. In a recent essay, the technology writer Kevin Kelly offers the simple but blinding insight that we absentmindedly think of a telephone book as a book, even though it is only a list of numbers with no rhetorical or symbolic content. Indeed, we think of a blank sketchbook as a book, though it has no content at all. In both cases we think of them that way only because they consist of pages bound between covers.[15] We think of other things as not being books, and substantially differentiate them from the contents of a physical book, because they aren't bound between covers, even though their substantive content is book-like. Some of these distinctions may have value in some respects, even if they are not logically necessary, while others seem less desirable, and in any case, there is no good reason to let any of them limit our conception of what written works must be.

Fundamentally, we conceive a book to have a certain fixity. We think of it that way at least in part because fixity is a trait of the physical book. First, it is fixed in spatial terms. It consists of the specific content printed on its pages. Second, it is fixed in temporal terms. It does not fully exist until the author "completes" it and the publisher renders it a physical object. After that, the author cannot add or subtract from it except by issuing another edition, which we think of as a different book. We so reflexively conceive of writing and literature deploying these fixities that we weave it in to our very metaphors and poetry. When something is conclusively established or agreed to by all, we might say, "so it is written." So, when we say "book" metonymically to refer to the intangible, substantive content, we mean some sufficiently large, discrete unit of symbolic content that is fixed in time and space.[16] These features may or may not be desirable, depending on the circumstances. But they are not logically necessary.

Some other phenomena associated with books are to some degree constructs, and reconceiving written content as separate from physical form renders them more fluid as well. To question the concrete fixity of the book is also to destabilize the concept "author" and the closely related concept "authority." As they are now produced, books can have different kinds of authorship, and we make significant judgments about their content based on whether they are written by one or a few authors, or collect the previously, published occasional works of an author, or discrete items written by different authors. The "authority" that these works carry, under our current conventions, largely depends on who their "authors" are and the faith we place in their expertise or talent.

Unbinding the "book" is not just a conceptual exercise. It is something we can do in the real world, by way of emerging digital distribution and sharing technologies. We have only begun to realize the available gains, though in truth a lot more has been accomplished than we often recognize. The first and probably still the most astounding demonstration is one that is hard to appreciate, because we are now so embedded in it. Early expectations for the World Wide Web were often dismissive and skeptical, and many thought it would remain a commercially insignificant curiosity. Populating it with content that people actually wanted to see or read seemed like a huge job that would be very expensive and laborious. Who would do all that for free? It seemed like someone would have to, because it would be too hard to keep content from being copied and shared once it was online. Of course, users themselves have generated the bulk of the material, for free and voluntarily, and the internet as we know it came into being largely because of their work. It was an early demonstration of the power and significance of distributed contributions. Other applications are only just beginning, such as Wikipedia, popular forums, and other resources with distributed or crowd-sourced material. eBooks, too, may come to have distributed features. Amazon already includes a "popular highlights" feature in Kindle eBooks, by which readers of a given book can display the text most frequently highlighted by other users. Other applications might include notes or marginalia of leading authorities, or audience voting to establish writers of prominence or authority.

All these things have been delayed to some degree by the legal and illegal conduct of content-industry incumbents, who probably would have preferred to stop at least some of them altogether. All of them would have proceeded more quickly had markets been more free, and it is a basic antitrust policy aspiration to make them so.

Nevertheless, there may be respects in which a book really is and should remain a "book." That is, there is value in preserving some of the traits we've traditionally attributed to books, and it may be desirable to keep them fixed, at least in some electronic simulacrum of the traditionally bound book. Authority seems important, and its destabilization could be very serious. It could be jeopardized by digital unbinding, especially by widely distributed authorship, and in particular by anonymous distributed contributions in the manner of Wikipedia. Authority is a sorting tool that serves as a compromise with human epistemological limits. We cannot always know for certain which things are true or which opinions we should trust. Few of us could personally consume and interpret enough information to make authoritative judgments on such things on more than one or a few topics. When an author or institution that has generated public esteem for authority on some topic speaks about it, it helps us make assessments amid what could otherwise be a paralyzing cacophony of information and argument. Authorship is also personally important to individual authors, in that it secures the pecuniary and moral rewards of writing.

A related problem is that expertise serves as a component of civic stability. Democracies need some basic epistemological ground rules, because the peace that follows from debate rather than conflict must have at least some shared premises. We have learned some hard lessons in recent years that that sort of agreement is at risk when technology distributes authority carelessly. The result is that we are less sure what to believe in a world of Wikipedia, proliferating sites purporting to report "news," and technology by which charlatans can give themselves the appearance of authority.

Digitization could also invite commercially motivated trends we might regret. Perhaps publishers will develop a means of computer-aided writing that is optimized for profit without regard to substance, perhaps changing in real time to reflect changing popular reactions. As Updike feared, maybe they'll manage to exclude human authors altogether. Such fears seem rather premature, so long as eBooks persist alongside physical copies, and at least for now, such complex, data-driven feats would have to be accomplished by a still-dominant publishing sector that didn't even know eBooks were coming until they hit them over the head. There could be other, more miscellaneous losses. For example, the evolution of a manuscript is itself a historical fact, and knowing how it evolved has intellectual value. With fixed text, it is comparatively easy to work out how any given manuscript evolved from draft to draft and edition to edition. Malleable digital text does not necessarily preserve any record of changes over time.[17]

Finally, one potentially very serious problem concerns preservation. Physical books pose preservation problems of their own, including costly storage, physical deterioration, and loss by theft or damage. But at least we know how to preserve them, in terms of both maintenance of the individual books and redundant holdings at disperse repositories. And for the moment, an individual copy of a physical book remains substantially more durable than any electronic representation of it. Physical books properly cared for can last hundreds of years, and remain fixed and unchanging. These are properties that no individual electronic record of a book can match.[18] By contrast, we have been unsystematic and, some critics say, reckless or cavalier in the preservation of digital content.[19]

Finally, the question is not whether the various problems posed by digitization are real—because they do seem real and serious. The question is whether it is a good solution to insist that books remain books in physical form, or in some form that mandates book-like attributes. That seems infeasible, so the question of social policy is whether we should let competitive markets handle whatever problems digitization creates. That is the solution that economic theory favors and that antitrust takes for granted. But they could also be handled by private restraints or government planning. A broader question yet is whether problems like these ultimately cast doubt on markets, because they are problems created by innovation of a kind that follows from markets in operation. If we decide that market evolution is either inevitable or better than its alternatives, how bad should it seem?

13

How Electronic Books Came to Be, and What It Would Mean for the *Apple* Case

AGAINST THIS BACKGROUND STANDS a surprisingly long history of efforts to make books mechanical or electronic. Though no devices before the Kindle were commercially viable or widely used, they long predated it, and they were mostly united by their visionary and humanitarian ambitions. The eBook pioneers, like most people involved in the early decades of the computer revolution, were captivated by the unique nature of information and its power. They envisioned the spread of free information not only in technological terms, with computational power and telecommunications unleashing new possibilities in usefulness and service, but also as economically and socially liberating, sometimes describing it in almost messianic terms.

The book as we know it is an ancient technology. One of the most dramatic aspects of the story of the eBook is that the technology of books was apparently satisfactory enough that it went broadly unchanged for several centuries. Specifically, a sheaf of paper or parchment bound between two covers is a "codex." For a few thousand years before the codex became common, people had written on all kinds of things, including clay and wax tablets, broken pottery, and for important or official documents, scrolls made of papyrus, an expensive predecessor of paper. The codex arose in Rome in the first century AD, and then dominated writing technologies for two thousand years. Even the technology of its production, after it became routinized during the century following Gutenberg, remained broadly stable until the twenty-first century.[1]

This archaeology of books, which is fascinating in its own right, contains a delicious episode that it is relevant to this story of technological innovation. From about 3000 BC, people throughout Asia Minor and the Mediterranean did some of their writing on papyrus. Papyrus is made by treating and pressing the reeds of the papyrus plant into flat sheets. But the plant would not grow in many of the countries where it was used, so papyrus sheets had to be gotten from Egypt, where the technology originated and the plants were native. With a certain dreary predictability, Egyptian governments controlled the product tightly and charged high prices for it. In a commonly recorded (though possibly apocryphal) conflict of the second century BC, the Egyptian ruler Ptolemy V finally refused altogether to provide papyrus to his rival Eumenes II of Pergamon. It seems that Pergamon, a rising city-state in Asia Minor and an important cultural center of the Hellenic world, was building a library that had come to rival Ptolemy's own Library of Alexandria. Opposing Ptolemy's trade restraint with the same kind of defiance that has generated many other innovations in history, Eumenes perfected and switched to another technology, known as parchment. The English word *parchment,* in fact, comes from the name of Eumenes's kingdom, Pergamon, though it did not actually originate there.[2]

The adoption of parchment made the codex both possible and eventually necessary. Papyrus cannot be bound very well, because bending and sewing it at the spine tends to make it crack. Parchment works well for this purpose. Conversely, the scriveners at Pergamon found that they could not use the newly dominant parchment in the form in which papyrus had been used, the scroll. Papyrus sheets can be glued together into scrolls of unlimited length, and then rolled up. But because parchment is made of animal skin, one sheet can only be about as big as the average sheep, and the sheets can't be glued together very effectively. Thus, Eumenes's decision to switch to parchment inadvertently abetted the rise of the codex. That change in turn prefigured the end of Egypt's jealous prize export of papyrus. (For reasons that remain unclear, the rise of the codex is also closely linked to Christianity. By the second century AD, virtually all extant Christian books were in codex form, while most other books were scrolls. But by the fourth century, the codex was the dominant model for all books.[3])

The codex has enjoyed largely uncontested dominance since then, probably because of its dramatic technological advantages. In contrast to scrolls, unbound sheets, tablets, and oral history, the codex compiles a great deal of information in a very compact and portable form that can be stored and retrieved with ease. It is also very durable. Properly cared for, physical books can survive for hundreds of years.

The earliest known conceptual description of an eBook was in a bizarre, ecstatic, futurist manifesto of 1930 called *The Readies,* by the writer and entrepreneur Bob Brown. Brown was an extraordinary figure who gained national fame as one of the most successful writers in the pulp fiction magazines of the day, but he also had success in a wild range of other efforts. As it happens, a serialization of one of his pulp fiction stories, first in a leading magazine and then in a series of movie installments, was one of the first cross-promotions in media history.[4]

Inspired by the then-phenomenal new invention of the "talkies"— motion pictures with sound—and by the spirit of the machine age, *The Readies* was utopian in its goals. Its basic idea was to describe a new machine envisioned by Brown that he called the "reading machine." It would be effectively a specialized microfilm reader, designed for high-speed reading. An artifact of the age is the book's inspiration by microfilm, now a homely old technology. In its time, miniaturizing photography was a magic-seeming breakthrough that promised a large advance over the ancient technology of the codex. Brown captured the revolutionary future he saw for his machine in lyric and seemingly clairvoyant imagery, imagining a day when "pocket reading machines will be the vogue" and reading matter could be transmitted electronically, such that "words will be recorded directly on the palpitating ether."[5]

Brown saw the codex, by contrast, as an archaic albatross, and the traditional means of writing it contained as "old-fashioned, frumpish, beskirted." By 1930, he thought, "all the arts" but writing "[we]re having their faces lifted," and he saw his machine as playing a key role in bringing change to writing as well.[6] Crucially, he envisioned change in both writing and the aesthetic experience of reading itself, in which the role of his machine would be inseparable from a new notation system he described as "optical writing." One of his more bizarre aspirations, optical writing displays texts according to a set of symbolic simplifications, something like shorthand. The system would excise quite a number of common words from writing altogether, as Brown considered them superfluous. However, neither the machine nor optical writing were ends in themselves. They worked together to facilitate the reading of words that were literally in motion. Merely looking at a static text composed in optical writing would miss the point.[7]

Brown made efforts to commercialize his machine, and produced a prototype in 1931. Along with it he collected a set called *Readies for Bob Brown's Machine,* comprising a few dozen texts provided to him and composed using his optical writing system. Among them were several from leading literary figures in his circle such as Gertrude Stein and Ezra Pound. Brown's biographer, Craig Saper of the University of Maryland, has created a website to simulate the experience of using it, allowing readers to scroll through the whole content of the *Readies for Bob Brown's Machine* and view them in an online display that replicates the experience of reading on the device.[8] It is jarring and the texts are largely inscrutable, or at any rate not very recognizable as traditional writing. That was also true of the sample "Story to be Read on the Reading Machine" that Brown included in *The Readies* itself.[9] It is so unusual that one wonders whether he meant the whole thing as a practical joke, but apparently he did not, nor did his literary circle.

Though Brown never said so and he seems not to have perceived it, his machine perhaps embodied the sadly inspiring sense that Virginia Heffernan captured, in a bittersweet mediation on technological change, as "magic and loss."[10] As she says, and as we have seen in this book already, technological change combines promise and regret. In that, too, Brown's vision prefigured much that was to come in the history of information technology. In his derision for the old, he expected that physical books would become antiquarian curiosities, but his devotion to the culture they transmitted was plain. He would make its exploding new volume and potential humanly manageable by transforming the very words in which it was written. He would privilege the content well above its traditional vessel, and not just the vessel of the codex. He would sacrifice some of the words themselves, and would give up some of the dancer to see more dance. In that, he anticipated a philosophical perspective that would influence several other pioneers of electronic reading projects, though there is no evidence that any of them were influenced by Brown himself. The central tension of the new age would reflect the increasing volume of ideas and knowledge and the challenge to find some means beyond human memory to exploit its potential.

Like Brown's reading machine before it, the first truly portable reading device to be produced in physical form was not electronic but mechanical. And like his machine, its aspirations in some respects prefigured the eBook and captured some of the pioneers' larger goals. Devised by the Spanish writer and schoolteacher Ángela Ruiz Robles in 1949, the "mechanical encyclopedia" or "automatic book" was a small, portable machine that used compressed air to run reels of preprinted content between spools. A reform-minded altruist, Ruiz Robles aimed mainly to help schoolchildren carry their reading material, and also to spread literacy and access to books. She built a working prototype, which looked a bit like a child's metal lunch box, containing the spool mechanism within it. She won substantial recognition for her work in Spain, and some units of the device were manufactured by the Spanish military in the 1960s, but she never secured funding to commercialize it.[11]

Another precursor is sometimes said to be a set of annotations to the works of Thomas Aquinas, begun in 1946 by an Italian priest named Roberto Busa. Over a period of about thirty years, he collected his work in one large electronic document, in a project sponsored by IBM. His groundbreaking goal was to create a text-searchable form of Aquinas's entire output. The project was completed in the 1970s and was released on CD-ROM in 1989 and online in 2005.

In terms of lasting influence, a popular article in 1945 by the MIT engineer Vannevar Bush would prove much more important than these other projects. Bush served as a government official during World War II, overseeing military science research. His article "As We May Think" considered the future of civilian science after the war. It cast long shadows, particularly for its conceptualization of a hypothetical information machine, which Bush called the "memex." Like Brown, his key concern was the need in the new age to process so much information. To meet that need, he imagined a "device in which an individual stores all his books, records, and communications," again on microfilm, "and which is mechanized so that it may be consulted with exceeding speed and flexibility." In the memex, Bush imagined nothing less than a revised infrastructure for human knowledge. Up to that point in history, retention of society's memory was the job of human academics, professionals, and librarians. Other than the ancient technology of the codex itself, they had never had any meaningful mechanical adjunct. That was fine in its way, but Bush thought the rapid expansion in the store of knowledge would soon become unmanageable by humans alone. The key contribution of the memex would not be storage capacity, which books already possessed, but Bush's idea of "associative indexing." It would be a system of internal links among materials stored on the device "whereby any item may be caused at will to select immediately and automatically another." This power of the memex to connect one document to another, including its power to let the user create these links as needed, would set up a "mesh of associative trails" to serve as an "enlarged intimate supplement to [humankind's] memory," and allow masses of ideas to be interrelated.[12] That idea was realized to some degree about five decades later, though not by way of microfilm. The memex largely anticipates the system of "hyperlinks" envisioned by several later thinkers and finally given useful life by Tim Berners-Lee in 1992, when he created the World Wide Web.

Serious attempts to distribute books electronically began during the 1960s. Two similar, mainly conceptual efforts developed independently at about the same time. Neither produced an actual reading technology, but they prefigured electronic libraries and anticipated their social significance.

In 1960 Theodore Nelson, a brilliant but eccentric Harvard philosophy student, first conceived of a project he called Project Xanadu, which he envisioned in terms similar to what would become the World Wide Web. Throughout his career, Nelson remained something of an itinerant mystic, holding several short-lived teaching jobs and doing stints at various technology companies and a publishing firm. Although he oversaw a long-running programming project, staffed over time by a series of talented and devoted volunteers, he never produced a working computer system.[13] His influence lay mainly in two countercultural manifestos that became legendary among programmers in the 1970s and 1980s.[14] As the journalist Steven Levy wrote in a widely read history, the first of Nelson's books was "the epic of the computer revolution, the bible of the hacker dream."[15] As for Project Xanadu, Nelson often likened it to Bush's "As We May Think," and in its humbler manifestations it seemed like mainly a convenient tool of organization.[16] But his vision was economically and socially subversive. He imagined a global, universally accessible publishing system that would undermine both the for-profit publishing industry and any possibility of censorship. (Nelson did not intend for information or use of it to be completely free. His very intricate vision included a system of automated micro-payments to be paid every time a user used a document created by someone else.) At times, it was like Brown's vision, in that Nelson imagined a destabilization or evolution in writing itself. Xanadu would be organizational, but unlike other systems for organization it would be built around the human, biological process of writing itself, as an augment to the internal architecture of human creativity that otherwise remains suspended within the thinker's own mind.[17] Above all, it built on a vision of the interconnectedness of things that Nelson said appeared to him in a childhood epiphany.[18] His eccentricity aside, it is a testament that he was able to hold the interest of computer science professionals even while personally lacking the technical competence to demonstrate that his ideas were feasible. Along the way, he advanced both his own project and other computer science efforts by working through a number of important technical challenges.[19]

Nelson's contemporary Douglas Englebart independently developed a similar system, though again only in concept. Englebart was much more a figure of the computer science establishment, and he contributed several pathbreaking conceptual and hardware innovations that would become commonplaces of personal computing. Writing from his post at the Stanford Research Institute during the 1950s and 1960s, Englebart described a communications network he called the oN-Line System, or NLS. Like Project Xanadu, it anticipated much of what would one day become the internet. He wrote that he meant to accomplish nothing less than "augmentation of human intellect" through technology.[20]

Nelson's Xanadu and Englebart's NLS shared with Bush's memex a key concern, and a key insight about how to solve it. The problem was the expanding mass of information produced by an increasingly productive population. The solution would be a new, flexible, computer-powered system of organization and sharing. Coordination of so much information would not be much improved by a simple hierarchical outline or index, which would be very cumbersome and time-consuming for users. Instead, all three men envisioned a "mesh of associative trails" of the kind Bush described, which was eventually realized in the World Wide Web. Remarkably, they did so at a time when computing still consisted of mainframe computers much less powerful than today's handheld devices. Indeed, even before those primitive machines had been connected by the first precursors of the internet, each of these men predicted several of the most important developments to come in information technology, including the personal computer, cutting-and-pasting of text, the graphical user interface, and other innovations.

Another purely conceptual forerunner would also cast long shadows. The Dynabook was a project developed as an idea by the computer scientist Alan Kay in the late 1960s. Though a few physical prototypes were produced over the years, the Dynabook was never commercialized, and its importance lies entirely in Kay's elaborate description.[21] It helped to shape the concepts and design of personal computing, and it is widely thought to have influenced Jeff Bezos, Steve Jobs, and the whole field of tablet computing.[22] Above all, Kay meant for the Dynabook to change education and effect broad social advancements. Notably, he foresaw its potential to make books and computer programs highly interactive and unbound, and very easily manipulable by users, including children. While his primary concern was education, he plainly saw the wide availability of information and easily manipulable computers as more generally significant.

None of those projects ever distributed a digital book. The first to do that is usually said to have been Project Gutenberg, a free, nonprofit digitization project begun in 1971 by a college freshman named Michael Hart.

The son of two professors at the University of Illinois, Hart was intellectually prodigious like his mother, who had earned three university degrees before she turned eighteen. He attended university courses as a teenager and finished an undergraduate degree in computer science at the University of Illinois in two years.

He did not, however, have the career of elite success that other computer science pioneers enjoyed. Like many others who linger in their college towns after their schooling, he supported himself with casual jobs, fixing stereos in Urbana and other towns where he lived and briefly as a street musician in San Francisco. Above all, though, Hart was an idealist. Accounts of the 1971 summer evening on which he inaugurated the eBook often stress the sense he felt of larger obligation. At age twenty-four, having just returned to college to begin his freshman year in computer science, he had been given access to the university's mainframe computer. Later, he estimated the value of that computer time at $100 million and said he felt obliged to put it toward something of social value: "I decided I had to do something extremely worthwhile to do justice to what I had been given."[23] His vision was revolutionary in cultural and economic terms, and he meant to accomplish it through what the technology writer Glyn Moody termed "digital abundance." Once created, a product in digital form can be replicated and transported at almost no cost, almost anywhere. Hart later described digitization projects as "replicator" technologies, borrowing from a science fiction program to which he was devoted, *Star Trek: The Next Generation*. He envisioned them destabilizing inequality, redistributing wealth, and empowering the weak. As he put it:

> I am hoping that with a library this size that the average middle class person can afford, that the result will be an even greater overthrow of the previous literacy, education and other power structures than happened as direct results of The Gutenberg Press around 500 years ago.
>
> Here are just a few of the highlights that may repeat:
>
> 1. Book prices plummet.
> 2. Literacy rates soar.
> 3. Education rates soar.
> 4. Old power structures crumble, as did The Church.

5. Scientific Revolution.
6. Industrial Revolution.
7. Humanitarian Revolution.[24]

In the early 2000s the attorney and distinguished law professor Lawrence Lessig initially named Hart as plaintiff in a case that would become an important constitutional copyright challenge, *Eldred v. Ashcroft*.[25] The goal of the case was to challenge the constitutionality of the Sonny Bono Copyright Term Extension Act of 1998, which had established extraordinarily long copyright terms.[26] That law was known by its detractors as the Mickey Mouse Protection Act, because it was adopted at the behest of interests including the Disney company. In short, the *Eldred* plaintiffs argued that Congress had gone too far. Copyright is authorized under a clause in the Constitution anticipating that it will "promote the Progress of Science . . . by securing [to Authors] for limited Times" the rights to their works.[27] In plaintiffs' view, the very long terms under the Bono Act were unconstitutional because they were not for "limited Times," and also because they violated the plaintiffs' free speech rights. The Supreme Court ultimately disagreed, and let the law stand. Hart and Lessig clashed, at any rate, and parted over their differing visions for the case. Hart left the case before its conclusion and was replaced by another plaintiff. To Hart, its purpose was nothing less than to "challeng[e] the entire social and economic system of the United States."[28]

As given to grand symbolism as the name "Gutenberg" implies, Hart launched the project with fanfare and ambition. Fittingly, it began on the evening of the Fourth of July, and for his first work Hart chose the Declaration of Independence. As he later told the story, he was in the computer lab that night only because he "had been hitchhiking on my brother's best friend's name, who ran the computer on the night shift."[29] Having gotten his account just that evening, he decided to spend the night in the computer lab rather than walk several miles home in the summer heat. On his way to the lab after watching a fireworks display, he stopped to buy some groceries for the evening. When he arrived at the university and dumped out his bags, he discovered that the grocer had also given him a complimentary copy of the Declaration of Independence on faux parchment paper. When it fell out, "the light literally went on over my head like in the cartoons and comics. I knew what the future of computing, and the internet, was going to be. 'The Information Age.'"[30]

That first book reached a grand total of six readers, going across the primordial internet ancestor known as ARPANET. The ARPANET was a fragile patchwork of computers established and overseen by the US Department of Defense as part of its preparedness for Cold War catastrophe. To put it into context, the year of that first eBook's distribution was also the year that the very first email was sent over ARPANET. Hart initially intended just to email the document directly to each of the roughly one hundred ARPANET users at the time, but he was warned by a colleague that such an email—consisting of about five thousand characters in the simple "Plain Vanilla ASCII" text format—would crash the entire network.[31]

Other early titles that Hart would type and distribute over the next decade included the Bill of Rights, the Gettysburg Address, and the US Constitution. Beginning in 1981 with the help of volunteers, he undertook more ambitious efforts such as the collected works of Shakespeare and the King James Bible. Hart said that during his lifetime he hoped to see the project contain ten thousand titles, a goal he achieved in 2003 with the addition of the Magna Carta.[32] Project Gutenberg would later be one of the first major projects to digitize books using optical scanning technology, which in terms of efficiency was a dramatic improvement over retyping manuscripts at the keyboard.

While Project Gutenberg remains active and significant—by the time of Hart's death in 2011, it contained thirty thousand titles in sixty languages, logged tens of thousands of downloads per day, and had distributed millions of free books—certain problems prevented the realization of most of Hart's vision. They deserve a detour, because they are key to the story of innovation and obstruction. Toward the end of his lifetime, Hart's vision even in its grander forms would have been within technological reach, but American copyright law made it impossible. That was a consequence of an accumulation of decades of barriers and preclusions, erected purportedly in the interests of writers and the reading public.

Naturally, books currently in copyright could not be included without permission, and would have required some arrangement for royalties.

Paying royalties for so many works would have crippled a project such as Gutenberg, but the more significant problem was logistical. For one thing, rights holders, which often means not the original authors of works but their publishers, would require elaborate assurances that digitizing their works would not risk piracy. That kind of assurance would not be possible without the digital rights management technology that was not common in books until the introduction of the Kindle. A much worse logistical problem would be determining for each book whether it is even subject to copyright and if so, who currently owns it. While strictly speaking, no one knows how many books there are, one very elaborate estimate put it at about 130 million.[33] Moreover, copyright terms are now very long, different nations' laws vary in their details, and the terms of existing works have been extended several times over the years. The number of works that *might* be under copyright is therefore both vast and very uncertain. With eBooks, the uncertainty is made worse by the fact that publishers and authors never thought until recently to negotiate digital rights. For perhaps millions of books still covered by copyright, digital rights were never negotiated. For these reasons, it is thought to be a multibillion-dollar project just to identify the current owner of each book that might currently be in copyright.[34]

One poignant consequence is the problem of the so-called orphan works. For many books, the copyright holder might be deceased or no longer exist, or otherwise be too difficult to locate. The likelihood of such an author coming forward to assert an infringement claim is very small, but it poses severe legal risk. An author that can prove infringement need not prove any actual harm. The author automatically enjoys damages that can be in the six figures for each infringement. The orphan works problem was to some degree created by US statutory relaxations in 1976 that made it harder to know who owns a particular copyright—among other things, because works no longer must be registered to enjoy copyright—and aggravated by term extensions.[35] So, while only about 10 percent of books are thought to be both in copyright and in print, another substantial number—perhaps several million more—*might* be in copyright, but one cannot know without locating their owners.[36] The poignant irony is that copyright is meant to encourage the availability of creative works, not to limit it. The vast majority of orphan works are out of print. Of all books in copyright, only about 25 percent are still in print, and most of the rest are thought to be effectively orphans.[37] Accordingly, no one currently earns money from them or has any prospect of doing so. Those works are also substantially harder to find in hard copy than more recent works. Thus, even though they are of no current value to their rights-holders, their legal protection has an effect precisely the opposite of our copyright goals. It keeps them scarce and unobtainable.[38]

For these reasons, it is effectively impossible for an effort such as Project Gutenberg to include full-text works produced any more recently than the 1920s. Hart's grand revolutionary vision, announced on the Fourth of July with an electronic Declaration of Independence, could not amount to more than a limited data-entry project. It endowed the items in its collection with magical digital-abundance properties, but ultimately, it consists of a small selection of old and often esoteric books. And that, once again, was the result of the unending struggle to defend the value of incumbent investment.

A number of other nonprofit digitization projects followed. As their promise and aspirations continued to grow, so too did their conflicts with settled investment. While several of them represent extraordinary accomplishments and contributions of extensive resources, their inability so far to attain their grand goals was foretold by Project Gutenberg.

One important and altruistic effort is the Internet Archive, founded by the internet search pioneer Brewster Kahle. After developing the early search engine WAIS in 1989, he went on to generate a substantial fortune. He sold WAIS to America Online in 1995 for $15 million, and his subsequent search engine Alexa to Amazon in 1999 for $250 million. He used the proceeds of the first sale to found the Internet Archive in 1995, initially with the goal effectively to back up the internet. In the early 2000s he turned his attention to books. To date, his project has scanned about five million books, which generate about fifteen million user downloads per month.[39] Kahle and the Internet Archive have been important advocates for freer distribution and copyright reform, and it was apparently Kahle who coined the term "orphan work."[40]

The other major nonprofit contributors have been public and university libraries. In 2008 the libraries of the Big Ten universities and the University of California system founded an online repository, HathiTrust. Taken from the Hindi word for elephant (pronounced "HAH-tee"), the name suggests both the size of the undertaking and the elephant's long memory.[41] HathiTrust was an outgrowth of the founding libraries' work on the Google Books project (see Chapter 14), with which they had collaborated since about 2004. It now includes several dozen contributing institutions from North America, Europe, and Australia, contains nearly fifteen million volumes, and adds about one million volumes annually. The entire depository is searchable, and about five million volumes are in the public domain and available in full text to the public.[42] Another major project, the Digital Public Library of America, was begun by a consortium of libraries and other institutions in 2010 as a central platform to collect and distribute the digital collections being produced by various digitization projects, including HathiTrust and more than one thousand individual libraries and institutions. Based in the Boston Public Library, its goal is extraordinarily ambitious—to "bring[] together the riches" of all of "America's libraries, archives, museums, and cultural heritage sites, and mak[e] them freely available to students, teachers, researchers, and the general public."[43]

These digitization projects have done more than just copy books and post them (though that itself is a massive accomplishment). About two dozen HathiTrust member libraries have contributed personnel for several years for the laborious work of copyright duration research. They have brought hundreds of thousands of works into the public domain and made them available digitally, when they otherwise would have been inaccessible. They also provide their entire digital collections to users with print disabilities.[44] The Internet Archive has recently pioneered the use of a little-used copyright exemption for libraries under the Sonny Bono Act, potentially freeing up digital distribution of a few decades' worth of orphan books, and it could result in digitization of tens or hundreds of thousands of books that are largely unavailable.[45] These institutions also store and make available digital materials other than books, including millions of images, videos, and audio files, and the Internet Archive's nearly three hundred *billion* archived web pages.

14

Google Books

TWO OTHER DIGITAL BOOK efforts deserve special attention. Both were for-profit efforts, and both were led by Silicon Valley giants: first Amazon, several years before Bezos even conceptualized the Kindle, and then Google. They were significant in the technological and legal events that led up to the fight over the Kindle, and more importantly, they triggered the extraordinary fear that gripped East Coast publishing that digitization would spell its doom. Indeed, if anything, Google's effort struck more fear into publishers' hearts than the Kindle did a few years later. That was ironic, because it likely would have served their own best interests. In any case, the Google project launched a decade of litigation.[1] Its experience was much the same as those of Project Gutenberg and the other nonprofit digitization efforts. Technology promised truly significant social advancements, but they were kept out of reach by policies and tactics designed to protect the financial interests of a relatively small group.

It is often forgotten amid the glamour and controversy that surrounded the Google Books project, but Amazon's digitization project apparently predated Google Books by several years. Amazon anticipated many of the design and legal issues that would affect later digitization, and it pioneered some of the solutions that Google would later employ. To conceive and execute the project, Jeff Bezos recruited a cutting-edge computer scientist named Udi Manber, a University of Arizona professor renowned for his work on algorithms. In the early 2000s Manber led the Amazon research unit known as "A9" (the letter *A* followed by nine other letters, which stood for "algorithms," and as Manber liked to point out, could also stand for "Alexandria"). Just as Google would later do, Amazon scanned the individual pages of physical books, then processed the scans with optical character recognition software to render them searchable. Amazon began scanning in early 2003 and publicly announced its project that October—a full year before Google acknowledged the Google Books project. Amazon's new library contained 120,000 books, every page of which was searchable and capable of online display.[2] But there were important differences between the two projects. Amazon's early effort was never meant to become an eBook business, and the scans themselves would never be sold. From its earliest planning, Amazon intended book search and display to be only a marketing tool for its hard copy book business. Nevertheless, like many Amazon innovations driven by Bezos himself, the book scan project was envisioned in very big, long-range terms. It was conceptualized as a tool to improve product search and create a base from which to challenge Google in its home territory, internet search.

Amazon also conceived the legal arguments that Google would later use to settle its long litigation over Google Books. Large-scale digitization posed a fraught and enormous legal problem, and posed uncertainties that had never been faced, mainly under the law of copyright. Before the Google Books litigation, it wasn't clear whether scanning constituted copyright infringement. In Manber's view, copying and search displays were not infringement because Amazon would retain the digital copies and never display more than short snippets. Users would see only the text that they searched for and a few pages before and after. Moreover, the snippet was not actual text but a picture of it, so it could not be copied. Amazon took several other steps to prevent customers from getting more text than that by making repeat visits or engaging in other shenanigans. Merely digitizing a book that one already owns should not violate copyright, Amazon's argument went. As Manber told the press, there would be no copyright problem because "This is not an ebook project!"[3]

In 2006 Manber was lured away to Google to head its entire search program. The move came during a wave of high-profile defections from

Amazon to Google that threw a harsh light on an internal Amazon culture increasingly seen as poisonous.[4] Without its visionary leader, Amazon's grand plan for book digitization—and its foray into general search to challenge Google—came to an end.

Though technologically similar to Amazon's project, Google Books was in many ways a different animal altogether. It had different goals, broader scope, and much more substantial impacts on law and policy. Unlike Amazon, Google never intended to be a major retailer of print or electronic books, and though it did eventually set up a capacity for retail sales of scanned eBooks, its digital books business has always been small.[5] Instead, its digitization project was all about making search better.

In late 2004 Google announced that in partnership with several major libraries, it would begin digitizing hard-copy books, incorporate them in its search process, and make at least some of them available for download. Google's interest in book digitization may have originated in Page and Brin's student days, when they both worked on a federally funded Stanford project to organize books and other hard-copy information in digital form. They informally discussed including books in Google's database when they founded the company in 1998.[6] Google began discrete planning for a books project as early as 2002, knowing that university libraries were interested in digitization for preservation and that some of them had already begun that work.[7] While not the first digitization project, Google Books was breathtaking in its ambition. By 2008 Google was working with more than forty preeminent libraries and about ten thousand publishers to supply it with content for digitization, and reportedly it was scanning as many as thirty thousand books per week.[8] Google estimated in 2010 that there are about 130 million distinct book titles in the world, and it intends to scan them all.[9]

Also breathtaking, to some, was Google's view of its duties and freedoms under copyright law, and so for all its promise the project was extraordinarily controversial from the start. Google contemplated scanning most books still in copyright, with or without the copyright owners' permission, and delivering copies in various forms to third parties.

By far the most controversial part of the plan was the "Library Project," under which Google would digitize the entire holdings of Stanford University and the University of Michigan, as well as smaller collections at

Harvard, Oxford, and the New York Public Library. Google did not intend to provide full access to copyrighted works without permission, but it would make the full text of public domain works available online, and provide the fully digitized copies of all the books it scanned to the libraries that provided them. Much more controversially, it planned to make the entire depository publicly searchable, and the search results it provided to user queries would include some text of the copyrighted works. To respect the rights of works still in copyright, Google would display only "snippets" of text, as Amazon had done, consisting of a sentence or so before and after the user's search term, and would apply certain other limitations to prevent user abuse.[10] Responding to objections after its announcement, Google also agreed to withhold any in-copyright work whose owner requested it.

The project generated a cluster of massive, long-running copyright lawsuits. Over a period of many years starting in 2005, the Authors Guild, a group of major publishers, and other plaintiffs pursued lawsuits against Google, as well as a suit against the HathiTrust for its work on the Google Books project. Plaintiffs claimed that digitizing even a book that one owned in hard copy, for one's own use, was an infringement, and they sought to block even the library members of the various consortia from making private digital copies solely for preservation purposes. The suits generated many hundreds of pages of judicial opinions and a small library of popular and academic commentary. The judicial opinions largely vindicated Google's view—and Udi Manber's, and Amazon's—that full-text copying for search, as well as display of short bits of text in reply to user queries, were fair use and did not infringe copyright. The parties then attempted settlement, and had it survived judicial review their arrangement would have been one of the most spectacular class settlements in American history. As it happened instead, the entire affair wound up with something of an inconclusive fizzle.

Because most of the suits were class actions, settlement of them would resolve the rights of all persons that the court determined were properly part of the class of plaintiffs.[11] In these cases, the effect would have been to determine the rights of potentially many thousands of authors and publishers who did not participate in the litigation and might not even have known about it. Therefore, under class-action law, the settlement required court approval. The parties first attempted a global settlement among Google, the authors, and the publishers in 2008, and revised it in 2009 following substantial criticism. The trial court rejected the settlement in 2011, for various reasons raised by many objectors.[12]

Whatever else, good or bad, that the settlement might have accomplished, it would have been a financial boon for Google. It would have allowed Google to display up to 20 percent of all out-of-print, copyrighted books (a large proportion of all books in existence), to run ads alongside the displays, and to sell access to the full text to institutions and individuals. Worse yet, to many objectors, was that Google would likely have monopoly control over the new asset it would own: a complete digital library of effectively all books, with legally binding rights to license it. There was no prospect of any other firm developing a competing asset. Indeed, other major firms had tried, with disappointing results. While some earnestly argued that the settlement would still be hugely procompetitive, to many others it seemed too big a risk.[13]

Yet, the settlement also would have created some truly spectacular new possibilities, and no one doubted it could have generated huge public gains. The settlement would have effectively made Google a compulsory collective rights organization to license rights to in-copyright works. In principle, it would be like the familiar ASCAP and BMI entities that collectively license rights for composers of music, albeit with some key differences. The most significant result of the settlement would have been to make *all* books, including all in-copyright books whose owners did not affirmatively opt out, available in digital form. Google would have done that by making available institutional and individual subscription options—blanket licenses like the ones that ASCAP and BMI provide for music. Google would gain financially, but it would share that new, previously infeasible revenue stream with publishers and authors who would have no other way to monetize their rights.

Moreover, for publishers and authors the settlement would represent a heretofore unheard-of marketing tool. In fact, many publishers did take Google up on a separate, voluntary program that didn't require court approval, under which it digitizes in-print books with the rights holders' permission. That program now includes several million in-print books. Their full text is searchable, and when a title is found in response to a user query, Google provides the user not only bibliographic material and a short section of the relevant text, but also links for purchase of the book from the publisher. It is, effectively, an extraordinary, free marketing service, providing the opportunity for any person in the world to leaf through every publisher's entire book list, including all the backlist titles that would never get shelf space in any terrestrial bookstore. Those search results appear on Google, by far the dominant portal for popular search queries.[14]

Most tantalizing of all, all the benefits of the Google Books settlement could finally have been accomplished by one court order, whereas other private solutions and even legislative reform had seemed persistently hopeless.

By no means were all the objectors to the Google Books settlement just protecting their own selfish interests. On the contrary, the objectors included the Justice Department's Antitrust Division, Brewster Kahle of the Internet Archive, and plenty of devoted, good-faith academics and activists with nothing to gain but confirmation of their own views of better social policy. They objected mainly to the very large amount of power and lucre that would be concentrated in Google's hands, as well as to the settlement's sweeping resolution of the rights of the many, many authors and rights holders who were not parties to the action.[15]

But for the purposes of this book, what is important is not whether the settlement was good or bad, or even whether Google Books would have been beneficial to society. The important issue is that we, as a society, have found ourselves in such a predicament. The technological means to create a universal digital library, including essentially *all* books, perhaps all extant books ever written, was very close at hand, but neither the might of a powerful firm such as Google nor the influence of the many governments who've tried to intervene by legal reform have been able to bring it into being. The impediment is the pressure to preserve the fairly lavish protections for the interests of the tiny minority of rights holders whose books still have commercial value. Millions of other books are no longer under copyright and the vast bulk of them no longer earn money for anyone, but they are sheltered by the wall of various nations' copyright systems, and especially by the great uncertainty of their long and varying terms. That legal system, in turn, is only one manifestation of the unending struggle between incumbent investment and the broader social concern, and it is in that respect quite like the conspiracy in *United States v. Apple*.

Thus, much of what the eBooks visionaries foresaw still eludes us. We remain leagues away from the anarchic, transformational emancipations foreseen by Bob Brown, Alan Kay, Ted Nelson, and Michael Hart. Only books produced before the 1920s can safely be distributed without permission. And to a great extent, the books themselves remain quite the same as they ever were. The eBooks that now proliferate in their millions merely mimic the physical books they channel.

15

The Kindle

THE FIRST MEANINGFUL ATTEMPT at a *commercial* eBook was the Sony Data Discman, introduced in 1990. A small, clunky device with a clamshell design—the top flipped open like a laptop, with a reading screen above and a keyboard below—the Data Discman read books from cartridges inserted in a slot below its keyboard. It suffered several problems typical of all the early readers. It had poor battery life, a small, hard-to-read LED screen, and above all, a very limited selection of titles. Though Sony would release a dozen or more models of the Data Discman over the ensuing decade, the product never sold well and was discontinued.[1]

Somewhat more successful dedicated readers emerged later in the 1990s, including the SoftBook by SoftBook Press and the Rocket eBook of NuvoMedia, which would play a part in Amazon's eBooks story. Proving that the major publishers were not oblivious to digital transition, SoftBook Press was financed by Random House and Simon & Schuster. The Rocket eBook was well-received by critics, and in 1997 Jeff Bezos reportedly said its display technology "was finally good enough."[2] Yet, all of the early readers suffered from a series of problems, and none were commercially successful. They were unpleasant to read and hold, and downloads were slow. Many were also very expensive. One model of the Rocket eBook retailed in 1998 for $1,200, and some could download content only through expensive subscriptions or special internet access accounts.[3] But their chief weakness was their limited catalogues of titles, and on this account Amazon's Kindle would put them to shame.

Several other steps moved the world closer to digital distribution in the years leading up to the Kindle. In 2004 Stephen King, an early eBook enthusiast, released a short novel in electronic-only form with his publisher Scribner, an imprint of Simon & Schuster. *Riding the Bullet,* the world's first mass-market eBook, sold more than five hundred thousand downloads. While the document was readable only on personal computers and the limited device options of the day, and while it suffered encryption and technological problems, it did more than just make commercial eBooks seem feasible. It was an early demonstration of digital distribution as a challenge to corporate publishing. As King later wrote in an open letter to readers on his personal website, he had been inspired to try another electronic-only book, and this one he would publish entirely himself, with no publisher intermediary. Telling his fans that "we have the chance to become Big Publishing's worst nightmare," he began to self-publish an online serialized novel, *The Plant.*[4] It tells the story of a potted plant sent by an author as a gift to a struggling publishing firm that had rejected his novel. The plant turns out to be a magical being that causes the publishing house's fortunes to turn around, but also a demon that requires human sacrifices to sustain the firm's success.

There were also various preliminary experiments with other technologies or delivery models, which for the most part were unsatisfactory. Some firms tried distributing books in PDF or other formats readable on general-purpose computer devices. Notably, Microsoft marketed a service to distribute such books enshrouded in its own digital rights management (DRM) tools. Those efforts were disappointing. Amazon ran its own eBookstore in the early 2000s, selling PDF and Microsoft-format eBooks to be read on computers or PDAs, but sales were so poor that Amazon executives had already planned to close it by the time Bezos began secretly planning the Kindle.[5]

Some firms attempted other models to monetize for-profit distribution. One important pioneer was based, like the venerable Amazon predecessor Book Stacks, in Cleveland. Overdrive was founded in the mid-1980s to perform the then–cutting-edge but now prehistoric business of converting analog documents into digital form and distributing them on CD-ROM. As its fortunes evolved, Overdrive developed a niche in managing digital book portfolios for public libraries. The firm was later acquired by the Japanese online commerce and financial services conglomerate Rakuten (which also owns the Canadian eBook retailer Kobo), and it is now the leading provider of this service to libraries.

One rather different effort attempted to combine the format of physical books with instant, worldwide distribution and the internet's power to offer catalogs of indefinitely large variety: on-demand printing. Around the turn of the century, a device was developed that could print individual, on-demand physical copies of books, including hard-to-find and out-of-print titles. About the size of a large photocopier, the machine can print and bind one physical copy of a book from an electronic file in about five minutes, and in principle, it can print any book it can access in electronic form. Jason Epstein, the long-time Random House editor and founder of the firm On Demand Books, predicted its service would supplant traditional publishing entirely.[6] It failed of that grander vision, and only a few print-on-demand services remain active and vigorous. Epstein's On Demand Books and its Espresso Book Machine still exist and sell books in several dozen locations. A more impressive business is Lightning Source, a unit of the major book wholesaler Ingram, which has generated a niche distribution service aimed mainly at smaller publishers. Lightning Source promises to put an end to risky excessive print runs, to monetize esoteric backlists that cannot feasibly be marketed, and to meet unexpected surges in demand. Lightning Source made news several times with titles whose publishers ordered very small print runs and later saw big spikes in demand following unexpected events. Among them was a book about Sarah Palin written just before her vice presidential nomination.[7]

The penultimate event was Sony's re-entrance in the eBooks market in 2004 with a product called the LIBRIé. A relatively sleek tablet that in design anticipated the original Kindle, the short-lived LIBRIé's only significant contribution was a new display technology called electronic paper. That innovation, like several others already discussed, was associated both with Xerox's famous PARC operation and with the prestigious MIT Media Lab. Now known as E Ink, the technology is a super-thin, transparent film comprised of microcapsules filled with clear fluid and electrically charged white and black particles. Energy is applied in pulses to arrange the black and white particles in combinations to make text or graphics appear. The effect on the screen is more like reading ink on paper than reading a computer screen, and it has important advantages. It is easier to read, and can be read easily in different levels of light, including direct sunlight. Designers of e-readers later incorporated very low-power, low-glare lighting innovations so that E Ink displays could be read in the dark. E Ink is also extremely thin and lightweight, and because it requires only a tiny pulse of energy to rearrange particles when a page is turned, it improved battery life dramatically.

But it was only when Amazon got ahold of it that the electronic book became commercially viable. Creating the market was an extraordinary achievement that overcame decades of commercial and technological barriers. The Kindle's origins date to as early as 2003, during a struggle between Apple, Amazon, and Google for control of digital content distribution. It was made possible by substantial research and development investments, as well as some bravado on the part of Jeff Bezos, but it also borrowed heavily from the work of others and was on the receiving end of a significant stroke of commercial luck.

Amazon had considered taking some position in eBooks for many years. A near-miss occurred in late 1997, when the fledgling firm Nuvo-Media approached Amazon with an e-reader prototype. That product, later commercialized as the Rocket eBook, was one of the first dedicated e-readers with any real chance of success. Not long after launching it, the firm's founders approached Amazon and spent a few eventful weeks in Seattle attempting to secure its support. They ultimately broke off negotiations over Bezos's demand for certain exclusive rights and a veto over future investors.[8] Rebuffed, NuvoMedia's proprietors turned to other sources of funding, and quickly inked a deal with Amazon's archrival Barnes & Noble. What happened next may have preserved Amazon's opportunity to make an eBooks market of its own.

In his biography of Amazon, *The Everything Store,* Brad Stone argues that the Rocket eBook could have been the breakthrough product, given its design and technological improvements. As he notes, the product's retail price was falling and its quality was improving; had it found a better footing, events might have unfolded very differently. But for reasons personal to the firms' founders, they decided against continuing their partnership with Barnes & Noble and instead sold the Rocket eBook to a peculiar Southern California firm called Gemstar International. That firm's main businesses had been publishing *TV Guide,* a brand it acquired in 1999, and providing an onscreen programming technology to cable and satellite television companies. Gemstar was not peculiar because of its products, but because of its CEO. Henry Yuen was both an attorney and a Cal Tech–trained PhD in mathematics, and he had invented an electronic scheduler to record television programs with a VCR. He was notorious for his ruthless acquisition and enforcement of patent rights, and was known in his industry as "the patent terrorist."[9] At length his career ended when he was found to have inflated Gemstar's earnings, evidently to preserve his own bonus compensation, and he fled prosecution (he remains a fugitive).[10] Gemstar acquired not only the Rocket eBook but also the one other commercially feasible e-reader then available, the SoftBook product of SoftBook Press. Both of them would fail, and Gemstar pulled them from the shelves in 2003. At a minimum, that turn of events spared Amazon a few years' breathing room to get the Kindle right.

Meanwhile, a portentous meeting occurred in early 2003 between Apple and Amazon executives at the Apple campus in Cupertino, California. Amazon's team were there to propose a joint venture between the two firms that would allow iPod owners to buy digital music downloads from Amazon. On arrival, they were surprised to be greeted by Steve Jobs himself. He was unamused by their proposal. Though the iTunes product was still merely a file-handling tool, and not yet a music store, at that meeting Jobs made a remarkable boast that would prove accurate: he told them that Apple would soon overtake Amazon in music sales. In fact, Apple did just that, in one of the great coups of the digital transition. Amazon was reportedly blindsided, and took the event as a serious blow. A firm that was one of the first, great e-commerce innovators had been seriously outmaneuvered for failure to grasp fully the digital transition happening around it. As Apple was busy building some of the most powerful businesses in that transition, and eating other firms' lunches in the process, Amazon's business was still founded predominantly on mail-order delivery of hard-copy books and compact discs. By 2004 Amazon executives feared that Apple would not only secure the same dominance in eBooks that it had in music, but also destroy Amazon's core business in hard-copy books.[11]

So Bezos resolved to build his own e-reader. His vision was characteristically ambitious. Patterning the new business on the iPod's extraordinary success, Bezos foresaw an affordable, extremely consumer-friendly reader device with a comprehensive library of downloadable titles priced just as aggressively as iTunes songs had been. He launched the program over substantial internal resistance at Amazon. Developing consumer hardware was something Amazon had never done, and it would demand substantial competencies that it did not have.[12] To give the project life, he established a secretive research-and-development program based in Palo Alto, known as Lab 126. (The name refers to the first and twenty-sixth letters in the alphabet, i.e., Lab *A* to *Z*.) The existence of the Kindle, as well as a viable eBook sector, is in large part due to a series of technological innovations developed there. Lab 126 still exists as a research juggernaut with a budget of several billion dollars per year.

The original Kindle device got a mixed reception from critics and consumers. Its product development suffered from conflict among design teams and from time pressures imposed by Bezos.[13] As a matter of design and features, it was unhandsome. "The early 90s called and they want their device back," wrote one reviewer.[14] The machine had the "design panache of a Commodore 64," and once the iPad became available, switching from its eBook app to reading on the Kindle "was like going from a Mini Cooper to a white 1982 Impala with blown shocks."[15] Many readers also found the Kindle ungainly to hold and use; it did not live up to Bezos's frequently quoted ambition that, like a real book, it should "disappear while you read it."[16] For years, product reviews of the early Kindle editions were very mixed.[17]

But none of that really mattered. The Kindle succeeded because it solved several problems of earlier devices, including their unpleasant reading experience, high prices, poor title selections, and cumbersome downloads. The Kindle also introduced certain truly groundbreaking features, and for them, Amazon must be credited with creating a commercial reality that did not previously exist. First, and surely most breathtaking, the Kindle gave users free wireless broadband access for book downloads. That feat was widely thought to be impossible, even within Amazon, but Bezos pulled it off through a partnership with Sprint wireless called Whispernet. Second, the Kindle has always offered a large selection of books—ninety thousand titles by the time of the Kindle launch, and many more thereafter. Importantly, the Kindle combined these features for the first time in one device.

But the Kindle's most radical innovation—and for this book, its most relevant—was Amazon's extraordinary pricing. For this reason, the arrival of the Kindle and viable eBooks was a story not only about technology, but also about strategy and organization. Pulling it off posed a delicate problem for Amazon, because it needed to secure access to the publishers' content as electronic files. That was complicated by the publishers' increasing wariness of Amazon, which had been taking a more aggressive stance in negotiations over wholesale terms for hard-copy books. Bezos sold the eBooks project to them as a way to expand sales that would not undermine conventional book sales and would not risk piracy. He bolstered those claims with evidence that earlier Amazon innovations the publishers had feared in fact had helped them sell books. These included online customer reviews, used-book sales (including display of available used books alongside search results for new titles), and personalized recommendations.[18] Meanwhile, Bezos kept the Kindle development project a strict secret. Even as he negotiated with the publishers for electronic rights to sell in a new digital store, he didn't let on that the sales would be made on Amazon's own, dedicated e-reader. The negotiations were tense, mainly because of the strict time constraints Bezos imposed for delivery of the electronic files. The publishers could not understand the rush, because so many eBook projects had come and gone without success.

Eventually, Bezos revealed to them that Amazon intended to launch an e-reader product, and even shared its primitive outlines. But he kept secret another strategic decision, because Amazon executives knew it would be explosive. Bezos had decided, evidently unilaterally, that Amazon would drastically discount popular eBooks to drive substantial initial sales and establish a large installed base of Kindle owners. It was Bezos who determined, over internal objections at Amazon, that the price of new-release best sellers would be a flat $9.99, which roughly matched what Amazon initially paid for rights to the books. Incidentally, the fact that $9.99 was initially a break-even price is significant, given later claims that the firm sold its eBooks at a predatory loss. The publishers initially discounted their ordinary wholesale rate by 20 percent for eBooks, to reflect the lower costs of supplying them (hard-copy books were generally sold to distributors at half the publisher's suggested retail price). The wholesale price was raised significantly above $9.99, causing Amazon to suffer some loss on many eBook sales, only later. But even in the beginning, the flat $9.99 retail price was still essentially arbitrary and quite risky, and the only real reason for it was that it struck Bezos as having the eye-catching, consumer-friendly feel of the iTunes price of $0.99 per song.[19]

The pricing decision was not announced until the Kindle's formal product launch event in New York City in November 2007. Many executives from the major publishing houses were in attendance.[20] By all accounts, they were caught completely off-guard. What had seemed like a sleepy, probably premature effort by Amazon to revise a technology that had failed badly several times already was suddenly revealed to be a radical and dangerous assault on their industry.

For its part, Amazon pushed the effort so aggressively because it understood what the publishers apparently did not. Content itself was in the midst of a dramatic transition to digital distribution, and although the processes and the results would vary for different content products, the transition would have zero-sum consequences. Digital books would be dominated by someone, and it seemed clear it would be either Amazon, Apple, or Google. Amazon had been demanding and impatient in its negotiations with publishers because its own future was at stake. In the end, eBooks have not spelled the end of physical books in the same way the iPod devastated records and CDs and streaming video seems likely to do to DVDs—at least not yet. But that couldn't be known in 2005 and 2006, and for Amazon, the threat was to its core business, the sale of books.

The technology watcher and former publisher Paul Carr later wrote, immediately after the *Apple* conspiracy went into effect:

> Before e-readers, publishers didn't care about ebooks. You could tell
> this by the fact that they gave authors really generous royalties on their
> electronic sales. It was an easy item to appear generous over—so they
> could fuck you on the paperback royalty. No one read books on their
> computer so it was no huge loss. For the same reason, publishers were
> happy to release ebooks at the same time as hardbacks—it wasn't like
> the sales of the former were cannibalizing the latter.[21]

In court filings in the *Apple* case the publishers admitted that before they
were negotiating their first eBook distribution deals with Amazon, they
hadn't given eBooks much thought.[22] Indeed, although some immediately
expressed frustration and worry over Amazon's $9.99 pricing, the in-
dustry was still divided for years over whether eBooks even *mattered*.
Many insisted they were just a passing fancy, and not without reason,
given the history of failed eBook ventures. There was no particular reason
to be believe that even Amazon would fare better than others had. For all
its dominance in its core businesses, Amazon had launched some widely
noticed failures, including an early plan to improve distribution in New
York City by paying college students to store merchandise in their apart-
ments, and an attempt to compete with eBay with an auctions site that
struggled for years.

The publishers changed their minds when there was a drastic uptick
in eBook sales around the holidays in 2009—perhaps in connection with
Christmas sales of Kindle readers—which set off a two-year climb that
left the major trade publishers with as much as 20 percent of their total
sales in eBooks.[23] By then, the lesson had been learned: books do in fact
compete on a price basis, and obey the law of supply and demand. That
was further confirmed during the *Apple* conspiracy, when the publishers
managed to get prices of their eBooks up across all platforms and sales of
them fell.

But by then it was too late for the publishers. The race to own the space
for eBooks had been lost to Amazon, or at any rate to the West Coast technology sector. Lost, that is, but for one last gasp—the period of the conspiracy they hatched with Apple, when they hoped to stave off Amazon's
threat, or at least wrest some control over the industry's transition.

16

The eBooks Conspiracy

*If you want to make the right decision for the future, fear is not
a very good consultant.*

—Markus Dohle, Chairman and CEO, Random House, Inc., on his
firm's decision not to join the eBooks conspiracy

AS 2008 BEGAN, in the wake of the Kindle's introduction and publishers' deepening horror at Amazon's pricing strategy, the book industry was already in disarray. For reasons to some degree of their own making, the publishers found themselves under heavy pressure to improve short-term performance. Amazon's dominance in hard-copy book sales had contributed to the uncertain future of brick-and-mortar book sales even at the major chains, and for a time it seemed to have caused the demise of independent booksellers. Meanwhile, Amazon had caught the publishers unawares with its creation of a digital book market, having secured their content before unveiling the bitter surprise of its pricing strategy. And with the arrival at long last of viable electronic readers, the industry would have to face the trauma of digital content transition, an ordeal that music and video had suffered through years earlier.

The industry's response would evolve haltingly and mostly ineffectively over the next year or so, but it ended with a scheme that for a few years was *very* effective. During that period, the defendants built up—unwittingly, one presumes—a spectacular evidentiary record of smoking-gun admissions and conduct. There was much more explicit evidence of conspiracy than is usually available in price-fixing cases, and it painted an unmistakable picture of the publisher cartel and Apple's knowing initiation and coordination of it. The trial record eventually included several dozen incriminating statements in emails, other written documents, depositions, and in-court admissions, which made the government's job of proving illegal conspiracy easy. The defendants met in private rooms of posh Manhattan restaurants without attorneys present and openly talked of prices and their relations with distributors. They traded cloak-and-dagger talk, including things like advice from one conspirator to another to "double delete" their email communications. Meanwhile, impolitic public comments made by Steve Jobs shortly before his untimely death, which were widely reported in the press, all but openly acknowledged the conspiracy.

Steps approaching conspiracy first percolated in the minds of different executives at about the same time, independently, on two coasts. For their part, the trade publishers had been discussing collective action for some time, since at least the Kindle debut. In fact, they had tried out a few other collaborations, some quite serious and a few perhaps independently per se illegal, though none of them in themselves were ever formally challenged. It may have been a coincidence that the publishers were right in the middle of one of them, their "windowing" initiative of late 2009, when Apple first approached them. It was not a coincidence, however, that the publishers in New York and Apple's team on the West Coast were both planning collective action around eBooks, or that they met when they did. When Apple's top management finally resolved to build an eBooks business into the iPad, in time for the iPad launch in early 2010, they were well aware of the publishers' conflict with Amazon. They had been considering some strategy to include books in the iPad for a year, and figuring out more generally where eBooks belonged in a digital ecosystem had been on the minds of Apple executives for several years. And while the publishers were by all accounts taken by surprise when Apple first made contact, their thoughts on eBooks turned out to be quite sympathetic to those of their Silicon Valley benefactors.

The history of all that planning, when all the details are laid out, was starkly anticompetitive on both the East and West Coasts, the various business leaders most concerned with how to hang onto as much excess profit as possible and keep it from being competed away for consumer gain by the likes of Amazon. What is most striking about it is that eBooks seem to have been an afterthought to Apple. Their inclusion in the iPad was a last-minute grab at a low-hanging profit opportunity. At most, it was just a volley in Apple's ongoing struggle over digital content with Amazon, and not one intrinsically important to Apple. It was surely no more than trivially meaningful to the iPad as a product line, which would have launched with or without an iBookstore. Even if it had lacked its own eBook sales capacity, it still would have been used widely as a reading device for books purchased on other platforms.

Some facts in the publishers' history help to explain the ease with which they colluded in the years following the Kindle launch. They have long shared a camaraderie, dating at least to the days of trade courtesy of the nineteenth century, and it may well be more intimate than that in other industries. By 2007, communications among the leadership of the Big Six publishers had apparently been friendly and frequent for many years. After the Kindle launch, however, they grew in urgency and common cause.

Their first steps toward coordination were some of the most surprising, because they seem so likely to have been illegal themselves, had they been challenged. Under pricing conventions that have been standard throughout most of American publishing history, publishers sell their hardcover new releases to booksellers at a wholesale "trade discount" price of one-half their "list" or suggested retail price. When they first agreed to give their books to Amazon in digital form—before they realized how drastic its retail pricing would be—the publishers offered Amazon additional discounts of about 20 percent to account for their own cost savings in supplying digital content rather than printed books. The government's evidence suggested that they made their first formal agreements to share information and coordinate their conduct in December 2008, about a year after the Kindle launch. Those agreements were likely legal, but by February 2009 they were already acting in concert to eliminate the 20 percent additional discount they had offered to Amazon. If they did that collectively and by explicit agreement, as it appears they did, then it almost certainly would have been per se illegal.

Amazon, however, was resolute, partly no doubt because it had heavily promoted its $9.99 price and it could renege only by breaking well publicized commitments to its customers. Moreover, aggressive pricing of content was key to Amazon's effort to establish a large base of Kindle owners. The books were cheap, but the Kindles were still relatively expensive. Without that base, the new eBook sector might not have come to be.

The publishers attempted various other schemes. Among them was a would-be marketing joint venture called Bookish.com, which by their own admission was designed not so much to compete with Amazon as to pressure its retail prices by limiting its market share. Somewhat later, they agreed to "window" the eBook release of popular new titles unless Amazon relented in its pricing. That is, they would not give Amazon their eBook titles until several months after the hard copies had been available. Again, the windowing strategy was not challenged by any plaintiff, but it was a naked, horizontal output restraint that appeared to have been coordinated by explicit agreement, and so it was almost certainly illegal.

In any case, the windowing strategy did not move Amazon's pricing or have any other real effect, and it was short-lived. Industry analysts and the publishers themselves were aware that it would be unpopular with consumers, would encourage piracy, and would sacrifice profits at a key moment in a book's initial sales.[1] Delays in publication tend to encourage piracy because fans who prefer digital versions but don't want to wait will at some point actually invest in the work of creating pirate copies. This is demonstrated, for example, by the fact that illegal translations are more common than other kinds of book piracy, because legal translations tend to take a fairly long time. And anecdotally, fans often report that they read pirated copies not because they are free, but because they are immediately available.[2] When Apple entered its negotiations with the publishers it flatly refused to permit windowing, because it knew from the experience of digital music that it would lead to piracy and consumer alienation.[3]

Meanwhile, in California, a different group of executives in a different industry had also spent much of 2009 thinking about eBooks. In fact, though Apple's first serious preparations for an iBookstore appear to have begun in about February 2009, that was not the first time Apple had considered eBooks. Recall the fateful meeting of about six years earlier, when Jobs himself confronted an Amazon negotiating team in Apple's offices in Cupertino. While Apple's eventual entry into eBooks was intricately entwined with the launch of the iPad, its interest in book publishing predated that development by several years.

That 2003 meeting in Cupertino was in many ways remarkable. Typically, competing firms do not tell each other their plans, particularly in quickly developing times of change. On the contrary, they go to extraordinary lengths to keep their own secrets, they fire and litigate against employees who disclose them, and they employ corporate spies to pry loose the secrets of their rivals. In this case, though, Jobs had a perfectly sensible reason for telling Amazon his plans for digital music. Even at that early date, he foresaw the major platform firms not competing in digital media but dividing it up into fiefdoms. At that early meeting, before digital books were even viable, it appears that Jobs already intended to propose that Amazon leave music to Apple, and Apple would leave books to Amazon. That was corroborated some years later, when Apple was once again seriously thinking about books in 2009. As an early solution to the digital problems, Apple made a patently anticompetitive suggestion hardly fitting the savior of traditional values that the publishers would someday imagine it to be. It proposed to cut the traditional publishers out of the planning altogether. Apple and Amazon would each remain in their respective domains of digital music and books, and each "own the category." Judge Cote interpreted this as a "proposal to Amazon that they simply divide the e-market for books and music." That arrangement, too, would have violated antitrust per se.[4]

Apple's entry was one small adjunct to a much bigger project. It was nearing its launch of an entirely new product sector that many other firms had tried and failed to establish—tablet computing. As with eBooks, people had been trying to make a commercial go of tablet computing for a long time. At least as early as 1992, companies including IBM, Fujitsu, AT&T (through its subsidiary EO), and Apple itself (with a product called the Newton) had produced devices with forms and functions similar to today's tablet computers. The most successful was probably Apple's Newton, but its price and widely derided technological problems limited its sales. One of Steve Jobs's early decisions after his fabled return to the firm in 1997 was to cancel the Newton project entirely.[5] Tablet computing had also been foreseen much earlier in a number of well-known theoretical prognostications, including in the elaborate exploration of Alan Kay's Dynabook, the conceptual eBook forerunner.[6]

Three Apple executives led the breakneck period of design and negotiations that produced Apple's new iBookstore, and they also eventually served as key hostile witness for the government in the *Apple* trial. Most important was Eddy Cue, senior vice president of Internet Software and Services at Apple. By the time the iBookstore was first planned, he was a twenty-year Apple veteran and a key architect of its several groundbreaking content businesses. He had played major roles in creating the Apple Online Store in 1998, the iTunes store in 2003, and the App Store in 2008. Since 2004 he had been responsible for all of Apple's digital content stores, and he led negotiations with all digital content providers.[7] With Cue throughout the development of the iBookstore was Kevin Saul, an associate general counsel at Apple and the lead business lawyer supporting Apple's Internet and Software Services division, as well as Keith Moerer, a director of iTunes at Apple.

Cue and his staff began initial planning for an iBookstore in early 2009. They quickly discovered the publishers' conflict with Amazon and their desire to be free of its eBook pricing. They believed an iBookstore was a potentially profitable opportunity, but only if it could avoid unrestrained retail competition with Amazon. When Cue and Jobs began seriously discussing it in February 2009, they were already focused on Amazon and aware that competing at its very aggressive price point would not be worth Apple's time. A fact significant enough that Judge Cote listed it as the very first of her extensive findings of fact was that this team knew, before they first made contact, that the publishers wanted to raise eBook prices and that they had already been acting collectively to bring it about. An analysis performed by Cue's group had determined as early as February 2009 that "the book publishers would do almost anything for us to get into the e-book business."[8]

Still, Jobs did not seriously consider creating an iBookstore until November of that year. The delay seems to have reflected his doubts about the quality of electronic reading technology and the effect that a poor technology would have on the Apple brand. It wasn't until November—only a few months before the iPad launch date—that the legendarily meticulous Jobs was persuaded the device could deliver a sufficiently desirable reading experience.[9] That left Cue and his team less than two months, spanning the winter holidays, to build the iBookstore and secure a competitively meaningful menu of content. (This tight time frame apparently explains their initial focus on trade books only, leaving until after the iPad launch the goal of adding textbooks and other nontrade items.) It also put heavy pressure on the technology and design teams, and Apple engineers began creating the online infrastructure for the bookstore only in mid-December.

The negotiations that ensued in New York were the stuff of now-legendary brinksmanship. Over the space of just a few weeks, with the iPad launch looming desperately near, Cue first made contact with the Big Six, arranged a series of meetings and communications among them, and hammered out the details of a set of agreements that would transform the industry and cause hundreds of millions of dollars of consumer injury over the course of two years. Most of the most important evidence in the *Apple* trial was built up during these weeks. While it seems that Cue and his team never met or communicated with more than one of the publishers at a time, the publishers communicated among themselves extensively, and Cue shuttled messages and assurances between them.

Apple never managed to secure the agreement of all six of the Big Six—Random House did not join the initial conspiracy—but the parties seemed to agree that five participants would be enough. A fact absolutely key to understand is that no agreement could have been made unless all or most of the publishers joined it. No one publisher could take the risk of demanding higher retail prices from Amazon unilaterally. Amazon would simply refuse, and blacklist the books of a publisher that persisted. That was confirmed when the first of the publishers confronted Amazon with the terms of the new conspiracy—Amazon rejected the higher prices, halted sales of the publisher's books, and posted notices on its site that the books were unavailable because the publisher had attempted to raise price. But if the publishers acted together, and cut off supply of their eBooks, Amazon's hugely popular new Kindle market would be crippled, and it would have no choice but to comply. The publishers and Apple were acutely aware of these dynamics. The government proved this at trial by submitting dozens of the defendants' emails and other admissions explicitly acknowledging it.

The publishers' problem was the problem that all price-fixing conspirators face. Competitors can see that their collective interests are best served if they all raise their prices. But if any one of them chooses not to, that firm will take all of the business with its lower rates. So all of them have an incentive to stand pat if the others raise their prices, and no one of them will take the risk of raising price alone, hoping the others will follow. The only way to be sure that all of them act, and everyone benefits, is to agree among themselves that they will do it. But of course, that would violate antitrust, and so it is usually done only in secret and at serious risk.

The entire arrangement came to depend on the agreement of the fifth of five of the publishers, the HarperCollins unit of Rupert Murdoch's News Corp. Apple did not secure that agreement until the day before the iPad launch. On that day, Jobs made a personal appeal to News Corp's chief operating officer and Rupert Murdoch's son, James Murdoch. In a lengthy email peppered with other explicit admissions, Jobs elaborately explained the plan and the pressure it would exert horizontally to raise price, and urged Murdoch to "throw in with apple and see if we can all make a go of this to create a real mainstream ebooks market at $12.99 and $14.99."[10]

The Apple eBook agreements were not identical, and they involved some complexities that figured in arguments made during the litigation. First, the publishers and their supporters made a great deal of the fact that the contracts were "agency" contracts. Superficially, they provided that the publishers would set their own retail prices, and Apple would take a fixed commission on each sale. In other words, they were structured as if Apple were the publishers' mere "agent" in reselling the books. That was a significant change, and in the publishers' relations with Amazon it went to the core of their conflict.

In American markets—unlike in Britain and some other European countries—publishers have almost always sold books on a wholesale basis. The publisher identifies a "list" or suggested retail price, then sells the book to the bookseller at some fixed discount. The bookseller is then free to charge the retail price it likes. The new "agency" model changed that practice. The publishers agreed with Apple that they would now decide the retail price at which each eBook would be sold, and Apple would take a 30 percent commission on that price. A fact not much discussed during the litigation is that the term "agency" was also used in the famous British Net Books Agreement of the twentieth century, and in the short-lived American version of it that the Supreme Court held illegal in *Bobbs-Merrill.* It therefore had a basis in history and was familiar to the publishers, and one imagines that history was on their minds when they designed the new plan.

There were various arguments that something special about the "agency" nature of the arrangements, or the value to the publishers or taking back control of their own prices, served some procompetitive or socially desirable purpose. The hard evidence that emerged made any such benign explanation seem extremely unlikely. It seems clear that the agency structure was just designed to impose fixed prices on Amazon, without the publishers having to make an explicit agreement among themselves that obviously would have been illegal. In fact, Apple's intention until late in the negotiation had been to preserve the longstanding wholesale model, and indeed, it resisted the agency model when the publishers first suggested it.[11] It was agreed to only as a tool to ensure that prices overall were raised substantially. Amazon would not relinquish retail pricing discretion to one publisher, but it might comply if they all demanded it, by each demanding a switch to agency pricing.

The agency strategy took another significant step with an innovation added by Apple in-house lawyer Kevin Saul. A problem with the agency strategy, standing on its own, was the same problem that all cartels face. Members of a cartel have an incentive to "cheat" on the cartel by selling their products at slightly less than the cartel price, and if one of them can get away with it while the other cartel members obey the agreement, the chiseler will steal the sales. The publishers' deal would not work for any of them unless they could be certain they all would impose the same price on Amazon that all of them charged Apple. The obvious problem was that antitrust would forbid explicit agreement to that effect. Saul therefore suggested what all agreed was an "elegant solution." The publishers would each individually agree with Apple to a "most-favored-nation" (MFN) clause: while they could set their prices on Apple and any other platform wherever they wanted, they could not set them lower on any other platform than on the Apple platform. That had the effect of fixing the prices.

Finally, a peculiarity to many was that the publishers also agreed to a set of retail price caps and a commission structure with Apple that would cause them to earn *less* money than they had been making on their original deal with Amazon. Where these caps would be set was the focus of much bickering between Apple and the publishers over the course of their few weeks of negotiation. The publishers plainly wanted to set the prices very high, and Apple wanted them to be as low as the publishers could stand. In the end, the caps were set at roughly the same prices the publishers were then charging Amazon at wholesale for the same books. But critically, Apple demanded that it get a 30 percent commission on each sale, so the publishers would actually earn substantially *less* on each eBook sale to Apple than they were then earning with Amazon. To many critics, that was proof that the publishers couldn't have intended an *anti-competitive* outcome. No one would enter into a deal that loses money, without some good reason.

But the explanation for it is simple enough. The parties elaborately, laboriously negotiated schedules of prices for eBooks subject to the agreement, meaning mainly important new releases. Those schedules nominally left the publishers with pricing discretion, up to fixed maximums. However, because the publishers were left with only 70 percent of the resulting revenue, they would have little interest in charging anything less than those maximum prices. And the effect of the MFN clauses was to mandate that the same prices be charged everywhere else, lest the publishers give up even more revenue. The reason the publishers agreed to such a seemingly self-defeating plan was carefully explained by Jobs himself in that long, last-minute email to James Murdoch to secure the final publisher's agreement. As Jobs said, the alternative to making a deal with

Apple was that Amazon would continue to expand its eBook market share and eventually demand that it be given lower eBook wholesale prices. The continued expansion of drastically low eBook prices would erode pricing for the publishers' much more important products, the high-priced hardcover new releases.

Although some critics portrayed them as procompetitive means to ensure Apple's entry or improve quality or innovation, the agency and MFN terms were plainly just designed to impose much higher retail prices on Amazon. The contracts were elaborately designed to look as if they left the publishers with freedom to set their prices where they wished, and to avoid the appearance that they had conspired horizontally or restricted their pricing freedom. But in practical effect they had very little freedom at all. Once the deals were executed and their terms were imposed on Amazon, their effect was that the price maximums would become the fixed retail prices for most important new releases, for Amazon, Apple, and all other retailers. And indeed, precisely that happened, and it remained so for the duration of the conspiracy.

There is no doubt that the publishers wanted back control of their prices, and in fact it was their desperate passion. To many outsiders that gave their agreement the feel of a plausible and good-faith plan of self-defense. As it was put by Hachette CEO Arnaud Nourry after the Justice Department consent decree expired and the publishers could set their own retail prices again, "When you lose control over your price point you are on the way to death. We have to be very careful and never think it is behind us. We are still concerned. And I am glad that there is a consensus among major publishers that we should keep control."[12] But it is critical to understand why they wanted that control and from whom they wanted it. They ultimately wanted their freedom from the ordinary working of price competition. While it may very well have posed dangers to them and threatened their settled interests, that is the oldest story in commerce, and distinguishes them from any other price cartel not at all.

Another point that frustrated or confused many observers was that the eBook agreements seemed similar to Apple's arrangements with music publishers in iTunes and with software developers in the App Store. In both businesses, Apple takes a 30 percent commission on sales, and App store developers also enjoy agency pricing discretion. Apple has also experimented with MFNs in some other contexts.[13] But these similarities are superficial and misleading. The most important distinction is that in those cases, there was no evidence that the content providers colluded on retail price or that Apple coordinated any such conspiracy. More importantly, Apple has not coordinated a conspiracy to impose its own preferred pricing on competing retailers.

Less than twenty-four hours after Jobs sealed the eBooks deal with his last-minute email to James Murdoch, Apple hosted a gala iPad product launch at the Yerba Buena Center for the Arts in San Francisco. It was the sort of event for which Jobs had become famous, ever since the groundbreaking 1984 launch event of the original Macintosh computer, held at the same venue. As was customary in Apple product presentations, the event showcased the iPad's sleek design and exceptional user experience features. Among so many other things, the iPad provided a much more sophisticated reading experience than the Kindle and other readers then on the market, which were black-and-white and displayed only text.[14] It is a full-color device that can display high-quality illustrations and photographs on a backlit screen, and it offers sound, video, and touch-screen controls.

Among the first and most striking indications that there had been a conspiracy occurred at the launch event itself. There already had been some inklings of it. The existence of the negotiations between Apple and the publishers and the detail that agency pricing was under consideration had already been leaked in the press on January 18, before any agreements had been reached and before Amazon had heard anything about them.[15] But at the launch event itself, in a flourish that got much attention (and later played a role in the *Apple* litigation), Jobs introduced the iBookstore by being its first customer. From the stage, with the iBookstore page open on a massive screen in the theater, Jobs used his own credit card to purchase an eBook of Ted Kennedy's memoir, *True Compass*. While it was not at all something emphasized in the presentation or mentioned by Jobs, a careful observer could see that the price he paid was $14.99, the maximum new-release price the publishers had negotiated with Apple. After the presentation, the *Wall Street Journal*'s veteran technology columnist Walt Mossberg was captured on camera asking Jobs some follow-up questions. The video, shot by the technology reporter and Mossberg's friend Kara Swisher, circulated online and eventually found its way into the evidence in *Apple*. Mossberg asked Jobs why someone would buy iBookstore books at the higher price Jobs had paid for *True Compass* when Amazon sells them for $9.99. "That won't be the case," Jobs replied, "The prices will be the same." If they weren't, he said, the "publishers will actually withhold their books from Amazon . . . because they're not happy with the price."[16] Two days later, having seen press accounts of the video, Simon & Schuster general counsel Elisa Rivlin told the company's CEO Carolyn Reidy that Jobs's comments were "incredibly stupid," and by that time, the publishers were already receiving customer inquiries about their meaning.[17]

If Amazon was not already aware of the scheme, it immediately would be. In order for the publishers to put the agreement into effect, they needed to confront Amazon with its terms, along with the other retailers to whom it would apply. The same week of the iPad launch, Macmillan became the first of the publishers to confront Amazon. Macmillan's CEO John Sargent flew to Seattle to deliver the news in person. He told Amazon that unless it agreed to the new agency model, Macmillan would withhold new releases for seven months (the length of time books were denoted "new releases" under the Apple agreements, and subject to its pricing terms). It was a nice historical coincidence that Macmillan was the first to deliver that message. The champion of the British Net Books Agreement, probably the greatest success in the history of fixed book prices, had been Frederick Macmillan, a scion of the venerable Macmillan publishing family and leader of the one-time parent and namesake of Sargent's company, Macmillan Ltd.

After Sargent's visit to Seattle, events were followed very closely in the press.[18] It was clear to many in the industry what was going on, though the details were still essentially secret.[19] Amazon initially resisted vigorously and publicly, but only during the brief period when it seemed that only Macmillan was making demands. When the other publishers came forward and demanded the same terms, Amazon relented. By the time the iPad began retail sales that spring, agency pricing with fixed price caps was in place at Apple, Amazon, and other eBook retailers.[20]

Government interest in the conspiracy was quickly aroused as well. In early June, news leaked that both federal agencies and several state governments had begun investigations.[21] The federal agencies had presumably been at work much earlier, at least as soon as the agreements took effect in April, and probably as soon as Amazon alerted the FTC, in January or February.[22]

Not long after it took effect, the conspiracy expanded to cover the entire trade sector. As they were effectively driven to do by the MFNs, the publisher defendants eventually negotiated agency agreements with the other major eBook retailers of the time—Google, Barnes & Noble, and the Canadian firm Kobo.[23] And in early 2011, Random House, the only one of the Big Six publishers that had not joined the original conspiracy, relented and executed its own agreements with Apple and its eBook distributors.

The Justice Department filed suit in federal court in New York on April 11, 2012. By that time, the arrangement had been in operation almost exactly two years. The government initially sued Apple and each of the five publishers that joined the original agreement. (It did not sue Random House, even though it eventually switched to the agency model and adopted terms essentially the same as its rivals, because its only relationship was a bilateral, vertical relationship with Apple. It had no role in the original horizontal arrangement.) Each of the publisher defendants settled before trial, but Apple stuck it out until the bitter end, exhausting its appeals all the way to the Supreme Court.[24]

To make its case, the government had to prove "conspiracy" of two different kinds. Antitrust plaintiffs suing under Sherman Act section 1 must always show some kind of conspiracy or multilateral conduct, because section 1 applies only to "contract[s], combination[s], . . . or conspirac[ies]." Courts have long read that language to require some proof of actual agreement between two or more persons to restrain trade. It does not apply to unilateral efforts to restrain trade, or even to parallel, interdependent behavior. Absent some sort of agreement, the plaintiff's only alternative for antitrust relief is under Sherman Act section 2, which reaches unilateral conduct and requires no conspiracy showing, but imposes a very heavy factual burden. Section 2 plaintiffs must show competition-protected market share so large that it constitutes "monopoly."

In *Apple,* these were not problems for the government. While much ink would spill during the litigation over proof of conspiracy and its legal particulars, and some critics alleged that sufficient evidence was lacking, the evidence of both conspiracies the government alleged was explicit and overwhelming. For whatever reason, these particular defendants, despite some evidence that they knew their conduct was illegal, made relatively little effort to keep it secret.

The first conspiracy the government had to show was that the publisher defendants conspired among themselves. This kind of conspiracy is said to be "horizontal"—it is between firms that are at the same level in the chain of distribution of some product. Second, the government had to show that Apple *coordinated* the horizontal conspiracy—that Apple, though it was not actually a horizontal competitor, got the horizontal competitors to agree on their prices.

The government did not challenge and Judge Cote did not impose liability for any vertical agreement. Though Apple was in a vertical relationship with the publishers, the conduct for which it was sued was coordinating horizontal conspiracy among the publishers. That is, while its relationship was vertical, the conduct with which it was charged was horizontal conduct. The parties even explicitly so stipulated before trial.[25] There was some debate in the *Apple* litigation about the applicable legal rule—that is, whether such hub-and-spoke conspiracies had ever been properly held per se illegal, and if so, whether that rule would still be applied by the Supreme Court today. However, while the state of the law involves some complexity, acting as the hub in a hub-and-spoke price-fixing arrangement is widely held to be per se illegal, and ultimately the *Apple* case itself has come to be an important precedent affirming that rule.

Proving the purely horizontal part of the conspiracy—the publishers' agreement on the retail prices they would set—was easy. Typically, antitrust plaintiffs must prove price-fixing conspiracies with little evidence in hand, for the simple reason that parties to plainly illegal conspiracies usually keep them secret. The courts, recognizing that fact, have long permitted proof of conspiracy on relatively limited direct evidence, or even on circumstantial evidence with no direct proof at all. So, despite what the defendants and their supporters frequently claimed, the evidence of conspiracy in *Apple* was extraordinary by comparison to the usual antitrust case. In fact, by the time of trial, proof of the horizontal conspiracy was essentially undisputed.

First, the government had substantial direct evidence, including dozens of emails and testimony by the publishers explicitly admitting that they meant to fix their prices.[26] There was also substantial direct evidence that they knew they must act in a coordinated manner because none of them acting alone could force Amazon to do anything.[27] It is not legally necessary to prove the defendant's motive in price-fixing cases, because unadorned horizontal price agreements are always illegal. But where there is strong evidence of motive, it can be relevant in deciding whether there was a conspiracy.

The government also presented extensive circumstantial evidence of conspiracy. First, there was a history of explicit agreements among the publishers to cooperate in various ways and share information.[28] Courts often consider it serious if there is a large amount of otherwise unexplained communication between horizontal competitors, particularly if the amount of it increases at a time when a conspiracy was thought to have been reached. Judge Cote included as an appendix to her opinion a Justice Department trial exhibit showing calls among the publishers in December 2009 and January 2010. While the content of the calls is unknown, they spiked at key moments during that period, especially on January 21 and 22, the deadline Apple had set for the publishers' commitment.[29]

It was also important to Judge Cote that the defendants had plainly been coordinating on various other matters before the actual price-fixing conspiracy, all with the purpose of getting Amazon's retail prices up. During the entire period from the Kindle launch in late 2007 through the Apple negotiations in January 2010, they coordinated their activities, and they made many promises to one another that they would collaborate, and generated plenty of admissible evidence to that effect.[30]

Proving the other conspiracy—that Apple played a role in coordinating the horizontal conspiracy among the publishers—was also easy. Again, the direct evidence was overwhelming. Judge Cote found that beginning on December 8, 2009, in the very first phone calls to request meetings, Cue and his team gave the publishers several assurances that Apple would be meeting with all of them. In Apple's first round of New York meetings with the publishers on December 15 and 16, 2009, it individually assured each of them again that it would not launch the iBookstore unless it could sign them all.[31]

And again, the explicit evidence was corroborated circumstantially. One of the facts that persuaded the courts that Apple had actively coordinated the horizontal conspiracy for its own ends was that before it ever contacted the publishers, Apple was aware that they feared Amazon and would conspire to retaliate against it. When first researching the possibility of an iBookstore in early 2009, Cue wrote to Jobs that "all the content owners hate Amazon." He attributed their animosity to Amazon "leveraging [its] force in physical [books] to force [the publishers] into bad deals" in eBooks. As a result, "it would be very easy for [Apple] to compete with and . . . trounce Amazon by opening up our own ebook store," because "[t]he book publishers would do almost anything for [Apple] to get into the ebook business."[32] More significant was explicit evidence that Apple needed Amazon's retail eBook prices to rise in order for its own iBookstore to be economically worthwhile. At the beginning of their negotiations with Apple, the publishers were selling eBooks to Amazon at the same wholesale price they charged for hard copies, having long since taken back the 20 percent discount they initially gave Amazon for eBooks. In the case of better-selling books that price was well in excess of Amazon's $9.99 retail price. Apple had no interest in *losing* money on eBooks, but it would, at least on some titles, if it faced retail competition at Amazon's going price while paying publishers the hard copy wholesale price. And indeed, in an email to Cue concerning the publishers' various demands and complaints, Jobs wrote that he could "live with" their preferred pricing "as long as [they] move Amazon to the agen[cy] model too."[33]

So there was substantial proof that the conspiracy occurred, and that Apple coordinated it. Even a judge who wrote a strongly worded dissent on appeal did not dispute it as a factual matter. More controversial was whether the conspiracies *should* be illegal, and under what legal standard they should be judged.

To be clear, there is no question that a nonhorizontal participant in a horizontal conspiracy *can* be held liable. The language of the Sherman Act unequivocally applies to such conduct to some degree, because it says that "*every* person who shall make *any* contract or engage in *any* combination or conspiracy hereby declared to be illegal shall be deemed guilty."[34] But the statute does not address whether the nonhorizontal player should be judged with the same harshness as the horizontal ones. However, the facts of *Apple* were more or less squarely on point with a long and well-established line of authority involving hub-and-spoke arrangements that holds that a nonhorizontal player who coordinates a cartel is just as responsible as the cartel member. That case law includes an important Supreme Court decision and a celebrated Seventh Circuit case finding hub-and-spokes per se illegal.[35]

Following Judge Cote's ruling, legal events pertaining to the case unfolded gradually over some years, as these affairs do, but they were mostly unremarkable. The only really big event was Judge Cote's final judgment on the merits of the fact and legal issues. When a "fact case" like *Apple* (where there isn't much uncertainty about the applicable legal rules) has been tried on the merits all the way to final judgment, the odds are heavily against anything changing on appeal. With the exception of one unexpected dissent, that's how things played out. Apple appealed the ultimate finding on liability, but it lost. Both the majority and a bitter dissent affirmed all of Judge Cote's fact rulings.[36] The appellate decision was noteworthy for only one thing—the tone of the disagreement between the majority and the dissent by Judge Dennis Jacobs.

Judge Jacobs is an interesting figure, and his dissent deserves a digression, both because it was legally peculiar and because *Apple*'s critics clung to it. More than anything else in this story, his views captured the peculiarity of the case. In its tone and reasoning it could have been taken almost word for word from arguments by left-leaning critics of the case, and it could also have come from the anti-bigness rhetoric of a Progressive Era trustbuster like Louis Brandeis. But on any other measure, Judge Jacobs could not have had less in common with them.

Perhaps a bit of a maverick as Republican appointees go, Judge Jacobs has ruled for criminal defendants in some important cases, and he notably wrote the lower court decision in *Windsor v. United States,* the epochal case in which both he and the Supreme Court recognized a constitutional right to same-sex marriage.[37] His sympathy for the publishers might also have had something to do with his own literary background. He earned a master's degree in English literature at age twenty-one and taught English before attending law school.[38] But above all he seems very conservative in affairs of business and economic regulation. A veteran corporate defense lawyer, his economic regulatory rulings are overwhelmingly for defendants, including all but one of his antitrust opinions.[39] A few of those rulings were particularly antiplaintiff in their language and outcomes.[40] He also has drawn negative attention for public comments about plaintiffs, as when he issued an opinion in an en banc matter, joined by no other judge on his court, in which he openly ridiculed an ACLU lawsuit that many observers considered gravely serious, or when in a speech he seemed to deride pro bono legal service and cause lawyering.[41] In a more sober moment he also spoke of his apparently serious dislike for "things that need and use lawyers, enrich them, and empower them vis-à-vis other sources of power and wisdom." He thinks a preference for those things—that is, a preference for solutions to social problems that entail the interference of lawyers, courts, and government—is an unspoken ideological bias held by most judges.[42] Given the manner in which all lawsuits are necessarily begun, one wonders if this antipathy translates into an unspoken ideological bias against plaintiffs. In short, Judge Jacobs seems to be ill-disposed to the barn-burning, anticorporate populism of the left-leaning pundits who took the *Apple* defendants' side. And yet, they saw the case in exactly the same way, at least superficially. To both the vehement Brandeisian populists who defended the agreement and excoriated the government, and the genteel, very conservative Republican judicial appointee, the real villain in the case was

Amazon. The case was a perversion of the antitrust idea, an attack on smaller and less powerful firms, at the behest of a threatening monopolist.

The real-world effects of the conspiracy were significant and stark. Prices for defendants' books rose drastically as soon as the agreements were executed, both on Apple's iBookstore and on Amazon. Their prices were essentially identical, and they stayed high for the two-year duration of the conspiracy even as average prices for other eBooks were falling.[43] Shortly after the publisher defendants settled with Justice Department, their prices fell back to preconspiracy levels.[44]

Apple's experts offered evidence attempting to mute the apparent damage, mainly consisting of descriptive statistics showing that during the period of the conspiracy the quantity of eBooks went up and their overall prices went down. But the government's experts presented regression evidence—a standard technique of statistical inference that controls for variables and isolates specific economic effects—showing that while overall eBook prices fell, the prices fixed by the conspirators went up substantially and stayed there for the agreement's duration. That was particularly damning evidence. If the price of a price-fixed good stays high while similar products are falling substantially, that clearly demonstrates anticompetitive effect.[45]

The Justice Department's case against Apple was not the only legal challenge to the eBooks conspiracy. There were two other cases in the United States, another major action brought by the European Union, and another by the government of Canada.[46] In the United States, nearly every state joined in a parens patriae action seeking money damages, and a private class action sought damages on behalf of eBook consumers.[47] Both of these cases was assigned to Judge Cote, though only the Justice Department suit against Apple reached trial. The other cases settled, and Apple and the publishers agreed to damages payouts to the states and consumers. In all, the conspiracy wound up costing Apple and the publishers well over a half-billion dollars in damages, plus their own attorney fees and costs.[48]

One minor mystery remains why Apple fought the case so doggedly and for so long. Its codefendants all settled before trial, and the case against it was strong on the facts and the law. An intriguing possibility is that defending its actions in the *Apple* case may have been important to other business models then in planning, which notably included streaming music and video products.

Others have explained it as reflecting the techno-libertarian defiance that is a Silicon Valley tradition. As his biographer noted, Jobs himself notoriously defied laws and constraints, driving his car for many years with no license plates and routinely parking in spaces reserved for disabled drivers.[49] In high-tech markets more generally, defiance goes along with an overall culture devoted to "disruption" of technologies, markets, and settled ways. Indeed, Judge Cote's frustrations with Apple's intransigence sometimes echoed the famous complaints of Judge Thomas Penfield Jackson in the seminal case *United States v. Microsoft.*[50]

Separately, Apple's leadership may have felt genuinely wronged by the affair, much more so than the publisher defendants. They seemed certain that they had done nothing wrong and were convinced they would find sympathy once they were beyond Judge Cote's sole oversight. One notable indication was a very bitter bout of appellate litigation immediately after Judge Cote's initial finding of liability. The remedy she imposed on Apple was the appointment of a monitor to investigate and oversee some of Apple's business operations for a few years, to ensure the company's compliance with the antitrust laws. The monitor she appointed was an attorney named Michael Bromwich. A partner in the prominent New York City firm Fried Frank, Bromwich had formerly been inspector general of the Department of Justice and would later play a role defending parties in litigation surrounding President Trump. He was both very aggressive in his role and very expensive, and Apple was responsible for paying his fees. Apple objected bitterly, and according to Bromwich, it refused to cooperate. That surprised many, because once the finding of liability had been made and attempts to modify the remedy order failed, it was clear that Apple was just pointlessly aggravating both Judge Cote and a monitor who wasn't going away and had extensive oversight powers.[51] By all appearances, the company's leadership had a great deal of trouble accepting that they had done something wrong.

But at some point, at least after Apple lost at trial, continued exhaustion of legal avenues probably came to serve more practical goals. In the months following Judge Cote's liability ruling, Apple negotiated a rather unusual settlement of the private claims still pending against it by the states and private parties. Unlike the Justice Department, those parties could recover money damages for their injuries. Under the settlement, Apple agreed to pay them nearly $500 million, but only if it was unsuccessful in the appeals it took from Judge Cote's judgment in the Justice Department case. That is, whether Apple ever had to pay the private plaintiffs depended on whether it won in the separate case against the government. The Apple team probably did not believe its chances were great before the Second Circuit, because federal appeals courts affirm much more often than they reverse, and they rarely reverse in fact cases. And it could not seriously have expected the Supreme Court to take the case. The Supreme Court has discretionary jurisdiction, meaning that it is not required to take most cases that are appealed to it, and indeed it takes only a small fraction of them. The Court almost never takes cases like *Apple,* that raise only fact questions. In due course, the Court rejected Apple's petition to hear the case on March 7, 2016.[52]

But Apple's reason for sticking it out may have been purely financial. Just by seeking Supreme Court review, which would not have been very expensive in terms of legal fees, Apple could delay payout on a $500 million obligation for many months. The savings Apple made by delaying the payment were in the tens of millions of dollars.[53]

In the years since *Apple,* not only have physical books not yet disappeared, but now ten years after the introduction of the Kindle, eBooks still represent only a minority of trade sales.[54] While both ownership of e-readers and reading of eBooks has increased, sales of print books have remained healthy, and reading of print books remains very common.[55] Market research suggests that readers have not switched to eBooks in larger numbers because they are suffering "digital fatigue"—they don't like reading on screens as much as some had predicted. Moreover, the publishers appear to have been more worried about their new-release best seller profits than was necessary. Even before the Apple agreements took effect in April 2010, when new-release eBooks were still selling for $9.99 and eBook sales were expanding very rapidly, they stole sales much more significantly from paperbacks than from hardcovers.[56] It appears that hardcover book demand is less elastic than paperback demand, even when very low-priced electronic versions are issued at the same time as hardcover and the paperback won't be available for some time. In any case, it is plain that readers still love the experience of holding, reading, and owning traditional books.[57]

One of the more remarkable twists of the whole saga was the financial performance of the publishing firms once eBooks and eBook pricing had become established. It appears that the publishers did *better* under the regime of Bezos and the Kindle. Print book sales have fallen, but eBook sales have taken their place on a unit basis, and while revenues have stayed flat—because although eBook sales are robust, their prices are lower—the drastically reduced costs of the eBook business seem to have improved profits.[58] This could be because eBook sales reach some consumers who otherwise wouldn't buy books at all. During both the windowing experiment of 2009 and the price increases of the conspiracy of 2010 to 2012, many of the customers who were dissuaded from buying eBooks did not turn to print copies. They chose not to buy any edition of the book at all. Lower-priced eBooks might actually serve publishers the same way paperbacks do, as a trick of profitable price discrimination.

If these trends are as they appear to be, and if they hold, they would be consistent with a pattern commonly seen in disputes between content owners and distribution innovators. Innovations are met with fear and opposition, and content owners try to stop them with aggressive lobbying and legal responses (and, as *Apple* shows, sometimes with illegal responses). Yet, if new means of distribution are allowed to take root, they usually result in content owners making *more* money.

PART III

COMPETITION AND ITS
MANY REGRETS

17

The Long Agony of Antitrust

At one major house, there is a running joke that the second book published on the Gutenberg press was about the death of the publishing business.

—Ken Auletta, "Publish or Perish"

BENEATH ITS STUDY of the *Apple* case, this book's theme has been America's long effort to make peace with competitive markets, which have seemed so important in the nation's philosophy but often seem so regrettable. Popular reaction to *Apple* captured the issues in microcosm. To summarize some of the key ideas with which the book began, the tension in that case reflected the fact that *markets in their ordinary operation are machines for producing pain.* Accordingly, to different people in different circumstances, *some markets seem special, because sometimes competition seems destructive.* When antitrust has required firms to compete in circumstances where competition seemed to be destructive, antitrust itself has seemed like a failure. The theme of the book is in some sense the intellectual history of this particular regret. *Apple* was not the first case to raise it.

Narratives of the policy's failure are not only not new, they have cyclically recurred throughout its history. The Sherman Act was initially disdained by most economists, and much of the public took it as a symbolic gesture of no consequence.[1] Since then, many on the left have said that it merely gives political cover to the business class, who continue to do as they please.[2] Many critics on the right are sure that it can do good in only the narrowest circumstances, and some reject it completely.[3] Other critics, from across the spectrum, have thought it might not work for institutional reasons or because it has too many unintended consequences.[4]

In that long history of criticism and second thoughts, a recurrent theme has been the law's apparent ironies. Its consequences in particular cases can seem to be in tension with its own objectives, or with other values important to society. In fact, certain purported ironies have been something of an obsession among critics, hence the title of the best-known book on the subject, Robert Bork's *The Antitrust Paradox: A Policy at War with Itself*. The specific irony that preoccupied him was the view that while antitrust should aspire to maximize economic efficiency, some specific doctrinal rules arguably retard efficiency, typically by protecting competitors in one way or another from price competition. But as *Apple* and many other cases show, the same reaction is often at work in other ways and with critics of all kinds of other persuasions.

The rest of this book deals with these questions, using *Apple* to illustrate the faults or ironies critics perceive in many antitrust actions, and showing that similar tensions have been present in all kinds of other cases in the past. Certain problems tend to inhere in all antitrust, and to have a competition rule at all seems to require making peace with them. We will work through them in rough order of increasing plausibility. At the end, we will reach some problems that seem very challenging, or ought to, and consider some ways policy might cope with them. This chapter begins with some that are very common, but not ultimately very persuasive.

The most visible critiques of competition are also often the simplest and least substantive. Lay critics of the famous monopolization case against Microsoft, for example, thought it was simply an attack on Bill Gates for succeeding in business.[5] That was not true. Categorically, the government did not sue Gates or Microsoft for making a lot of money. There may be disagreement on the merits, but the case culminated in a unanimous per curiam opinion finding illegal monopolization, through an elaborate series of exclusionary devices.[6] The opinion issued by the en banc DC Circuit—not exactly a den of the radical left when the case was decided in 2001—apparently was written by a judge who is a peerless antitrust expert and a Reagan appointee.[7] It elaborately explained how pernicious, deliberate, and anticompetitive Microsoft's machinations were, and its findings were in large part responsible for Microsoft's subsequent agreement to well over $4 billion in settlement payments. The *Microsoft* opinion also demonstrated how emphatically the suit was not an attack on the firm or Bill Gates for their success. As far as American law is concerned, anyone can make any amount of money and can capture as much of a market as they like, so long as they do it by selling things of better quality or lower price. No one has been sued successfully in antitrust merely for succeeding in business in decades if indeed it ever happened. Incidentally, while many critics doubted the remedy actually gotten in the case could make anything any better in practice, there is reason to believe that even the watered-down remedy imposed by the administration of George W. Bush had significant benefits in constraining Microsoft, opening up competition in operating systems and making room for innovation.[8]

A deeper manifestation of the same instinct is the tension between antitrust and individualism, or the closely related phenomenon of private property. Antitrust has struggled with this for a long time. A fact often overlooked in economic debate is that, in and of itself, the mainstream price theory on which contemporary antitrust builds has no concern at all for individualism or property rights. In fact, standard welfare economics is rather radically collectivist in such matters. Standard theory asks only how we can optimize the *aggregate* welfare. It takes for granted that to do that, we might sometimes need rules that disadvantage some for the benefit of others. For example, making the most of society's overall welfare might sometimes require the government to take property forcibly from some for public use, perhaps even without compensation.[9]

Antitrust has not been so radical. Perhaps it would be if courts and policymakers suffered no epistemic limits, but in what can be explained as a compromise with the limits of human institutions, and with the individualist values we generally protect with things such as procedural due process and the plaintiff's burden of proof, several antitrust rules have evolved to protect individual freedom.

For example, while it can be illegal to "monopolize" a market, it is never illegal in American law simply to have a "monopoly." Sellers enjoy a strong right to set their own prices, even when they hold monopoly power and even when the prices they charge are monopoly prices. There are a few limits on pricing freedom, but they are very difficult to enforce and they leave sellers with very broad freedom. First, prices that are below cost may be illegal if they can be shown to be predatory. That is, they are illegal if they can be shown to be part of a seller's plan to exclude competitors and then later recover the losses of the predatory campaign. But the courts have made proof of predatory prices so difficult that no plaintiff has won a case on that theory in decades.[10] Second, discriminatory prices can violate the Robinson-Patman Act, but that law has fallen into such disfavor with courts that it is largely a dead letter.[11]

Sellers may also deal with whomever they choose, except in unusual circumstances, and they cannot violate antitrust by merely earning excessive profits, no matter how allocationally inefficient or abusive.[12]

These rules are best explained by individualist values, and not strictly economic ones. That point is hard to prove, because the same antitrust rule can usually be justified in more than one way. These rules in principle might serve an "economic" purpose if very strict liability for monopoly would chill procompetitive conduct or be more costly to administer than the benefits it could bring. And indeed, that is how courts and academics have often defended them.[13] But they are otherwise hard to square with economic goals. For example, the rule that large market share alone is not illegal cannot in itself serve the economic goals of allocational efficiency or consumer welfare. Except in the empirically unlikely circumstance that it is disciplined by very quick, equally efficient potential entry, a firm with a monopoly share rationally raises price, regardless how it got that share. So a competition law concerned only with allocational efficiency or consumer welfare would ban or regulate monopolists without exception.

So the explanation for such rules might not be economic at all—there might be a purely libertarian, political explanation. Perhaps we have them because they let business owners use their property as they wish, until someone can make a substantial demonstration of illicit market power. That seems implicit in the common view of courts that imposing liability for merely having a monopoly, which was not gotten through illicit exclusionary means, would be "unfair."[14] That may or may not be, but the economic theory the courts claim to embrace has no concern whatsoever for "fairness."

We also have not infrequently established antitrust rules to reflect the "rights" of individual defendants, another concept foreign to economic theory. Admittedly, much of that "rights" talk dates from the law's early years. There was a time when American courts very explicitly, unapologetically explained antitrust results with reference to noneconomic, libertarian values, long before the modern consensus began to allege that antitrust law serves purely economic values. For example, in the famous *Dr. Miles* case, which established the rule against resale price maintenance, the Court justified its rule on the individual rights of retailers to do what they liked with items they'd bought from manufacturers.[15] More significant is the decision that soon followed in *United States v. Colgate,* and the modern courts' continued use of the *Colgate* rule—that despite *Dr. Miles,* a manufacturer could refuse to sell to retailers that wouldn't maintain minimum prices.[16] *Colgate* established the "right" to refuse to deal, because the Sherman Act "does not restrict the *long recognized right of trader or manufacturer* engaged in an entirely private business, freely to exercise his own independent discretion as to parties with whom he will deal."[17] But what is interesting about this reasoning in *Dr. Miles* and *Colgate,* which otherwise might be written off as the antiquated reasoning of a pre-economic era in antitrust, is that have we repeatedly reaffirmed the right of refusal to deal in modern cases, stating it explicitly in terms of the seller's "rights."[18] In fact, we've made it stronger than it ever was, without any additional economic reasoning and only rote citations to *Colgate.* In its most recent *Colgate*-style cases, the Court has conspicuously quoted *Colgate*'s key rights-talk without *Colgate*'s own qualification that a refusal to deal must be undertaken without an anticompetitive purpose.[19]

The point of this philosophical digression is not whether particular antitrust rules are good or bad. It is that the "liberty" objections that some critics raise to antitrust ought not seem too serious. They are already elaborately accommodated.

Another highly visible criticism of antitrust is that it contributes to business failure. If antitrust is enforced and firms are forced to compete, some of them may be forced to exit, and perhaps to liquidate completely. That could happen if they cannot keep up with their competitors' cost advantages. Workers would lose jobs, productive assets would be shuttered, and shareholders would lose money. For example, when mergers are challenged as anticompetitive, the merging parties often claim that if they don't merge, one of them will fail. When on occasion the government challenges acquisition of a genuinely failing or already insolvent firm, the public may find that action hard to understand.

The problem of business failure was prominent in *Apple*. The publishers claimed that they needed the Apple pricing model in order to survive the transition to digital distribution. They feared that if Amazon's low prices on eBooks drove consumers to no longer value hardcover new releases at the higher prices the publishers had charged, they would be unable to remain in business. Specifically, because eBook prices would erode the consumer perception that hardcover new releases are worth the prices they had traditionally enjoyed, the publishers would lose earnings they needed to stay afloat.

Fear of business failure is not a very good reason to doubt antitrust. The most basic recommendation of economic theory is that if a firm cannot survive a change in a market's cost structure, then it *should* exit. In this particular case, the publishers' complaint was not about some inherent economic defect in their market that made it too hard for them to compete. There simply had been a technological change that significantly reduced the cost of producing a closely competing product.

The only revenue an intermediary can earn in an efficient market is a competitive rate of return on capital invested in order for the intermediate service to exist. In book markets, the product can now exist in a form that consumers appear to find acceptable, at least at the very low prices charged by Amazon, without the investment in traditional production and marketing that was the publishers' reason for being.

Separately, there is not much reason to believe that restraining retail price competition helps more firms stay in business, however obvious the instinct might seem. When Congress repealed the Miller-Tydings Act in 1975, thirty-six states had laws that permitted some resale price maintenance. Of those, twenty-three prohibited "nonsigner" clauses, meaning that a manufacturer could not impose fixed resale prices on any distributor that did not personally agree to them. Congress found that rates of small business failure were higher in states with fair-trade laws, and the highest in those with the most restrictive, nonsigner provisions. Likewise, rates of new business formation were substantially lower in fair-trade states. Although the study that found those results was not rigorous in social science terms—it consisted of descriptive data from Dun & Bradstreet, collected by the Library of Congress at a Senate committee's request—it makes a case that retail price restraints actually hurt retailers, or at any rate that they do not help. The thirteen states with nonsigner clauses, where business failures were the highest, were diverse. They were scattered geographically and differed widely in size, population, and local economy. One obvious reason fixed retail prices may cause overall harm to retailers is that at higher prices, consumers will buy less of the product. If there is less business to go around, there will be fewer sellers to provide it.[20]

There may very well be important reasons why business failure is a more serious problem in publishing than elsewhere. Publishing may require special policy treatment, and the rest of this book is largely devoted to asking whether it does. But the publishers' argument in *Apple* that they needed to preserve high hardcover prices for their own sake is not a good one. Preserving demand inelasticity based on differentiation, for no reason other than to preserve an industry structure built on prices that were supracompetitive even before eBooks, is not a goal that anyone need take seriously.

A subtly related argument critics often make of enforcement actions is that conduct must not be anticompetitive if the defendants aren't making any money. Monopolists, the argument goes, should at least be profitable. If firms are struggling financially, or they can persuade outsiders that they are, then it is hard to believe that they are engaging in anticompetitive conduct, and trying to do as monopolists do. But, first, claims of poor performance have often been overstated by firms threatened with government intervention. And indeed, while the trade book publishers claimed during *Apple* to be suffering, they have in fact remained profitable, and it appears that eBooks have actually improved their bottom lines.[21] But even were it otherwise, there are well understood reasons why firms could suffer even while earning supracompetitive revenues. Wasteful investments in retaining market power and "X-inefficiency" are common explanations.[22]

In any case, none of those very basic ironies or misunderstandings was what drove opposition to the *Apple* case. There are more serious tensions, none of which is so easy to dismiss, all of which involve some degree of empirical uncertainty, and a few of which are seriously troubling. As they manifested in *Apple,* they all in one way or another reflected the sense that something about books, or something about the business of selling them, is special. The ultimate goal of thinking through all these arguments is not to prove any particular point about books or publishing, or to show that the *Apple* case was a good one. The analysis will show that the same arguments raised to show that books are special have been made in all kinds of other cases before, throughout the history of antitrust. There has never been a defendant that didn't think its market was special. The history of competition policy has been one long, case-by-case assessment of their claimed needs for relief from the rules of competition. Close examination of those arguments in the case of publishing, and a showing that they are just the same arguments that all defendants make all the time, is in effect a broad and general defense of competition as a policy.

18

So Are Books, After All, Special?
Is Anything?

> Information, that slippery and strange economic good, is, in fact, handled very well by market institutions. The reason is that real markets are much more creative than those simple competitive markets studied in Econ 1. The fact that real-life markets can handle a good as problematic as information is a testament to the flexibility and robustness of market institutions.
>
> —Hal Varian, "Markets for Information Goods"

WHETHER BOOKS ARE SPECIAL and need protection from unbridled retail competition is at least two questions. First, on a practical level, several specific economic problems are said to infect books, such that markets with ordinary competition won't produce them in efficient numbers and variety. Books are "experience goods," in that consumers must use them before being able to properly value them, and when that is the case, there can be well-known market problems.[1] But that problem is accommodated pretty well by author reputation, an active sector for book reviews and awards, word of mouth, and branding by publishers. Accordingly, book purchases are actually fairly transparent. Also, to whatever extent consumer search is a problem in books, digitization might radically improve it. Amazon, Google Books, and some other outlets make digital excerpts available for browsing from hundreds of times more books than could be displayed in any physical bookstore. Amazon's "Look Inside the Book" program, for example, displays preselected excerpts and searchable text for millions of books, at no cost to publishers or authors.[2] That program and others like it have been promoted to publishers as marketing tools, and publishers now voluntarily opt in to them in very large numbers, despite having bitterly opposed digital excerpts in the Google Books dispute. Presumably, display of free, searchable excerpts in a massive online library is highly desirable to their sales. Digitization and online distribution have also enabled massive coordination of user reviews, which for whatever new problems they may pose are a consumer search tool that never existed before.

Many claim that publishers take a particular kind of risk that calls for some shelter from rivalry. This is the problem that the economist Richard Caves famously called the "nobody knows" problem.[3] Because each individual book title is differentiated—every title is a unique product—each one of them poses a problem of predicting success.[4] As the great publisher George H. Putnam once said, "The history of publishing is a record of erroneous judgments."[5] But that is true of a lot of products. Risk is common to all products, and it generates returns to managerial expertise in planning. In the case of books, it is misleading to imagine the risk is extraordinarily different from the risks in businesses with larger runs of interchangeable products. The run of an individual new-release book makes up a much smaller portion of a publisher's total output than the production runs of a manufacturer that makes a narrower range of more interchangeable goods. (A specific hardcopy title becomes a larger part of a publisher's production if it begins to sell well, but by then it is no longer unusually risky.) It may be that each individual new title poses risks like a brand-new product introduction. The publisher's business is therefore unlike the manufacture of widgets, where the producer brings out a product line, establishes it once, and then produces it in large numbers. Yet, because each individual title is a much smaller part of the publisher's overall production, it is a much smaller part of the publisher's overall capital commitment. The publisher diversifies all of those comparatively smaller individual risks by bringing out a variety of books and by cultivating reliably stable, long-term revenue from backlist titles. Thus, while there are local differences between publishing and other markets, there are actually local variations among *all* products, and their varying details do not make them all subject to their own fundamental economic laws. Publishing requires a different set of skills than in other manufacturing, but that does not mean other manufacturing is unskilled or that the skills needed for other sectors are not also specialized to assess particular risks that may be idiosyncratic and market-specific. Publishers perform the same basic function in capitalism as other entrepreneurs, and they earn market-based returns for their managerial contribution.

A different market problem might affect books when they are made electronic, and it is a problem characteristic of all digital products. Digital goods may be costly to develop, but they are very cheap to reproduce. A book, for example, might entail hundreds of thousands of dollars in author advances, editorial preparation, and publisher's overhead costs, but once the manuscript is prepared and exists in digital form, making each copy of it is largely costless. The problem is that if firms offer digital products in competition with each other, they might be tempted to fight for sales by undercutting each other's prices, and standard economic theory predicts that they will do so in the short term until price is equal to marginal cost. But the marginal cost of a digital book—the cost to the publisher of printing one further copy—is nearly zero. If publishers competed in that manner they would be unable to cover their fixed costs, and would quickly find it better to quit the market altogether. No more books would be published at all.[6]

But that has not happened, and it will not, even in digital media markets with many competitors and vigorous rivalry. For one thing, digital technology has also reduced fixed costs to some degree, or at least it could, depending on how it is implemented.[7] But more importantly, the problem is no more real than the purported risk of destructive competition among high-capital industries at the turn of the twentieth century. While many economists believed those markets were prone to disastrous, recurrent rate war, in fact they weren't, for the simple reason that new entrants would not enter markets without having assessed whether their fixed costs could be covered, taking into account the amount of capacity already present in the industry. In other words, firms typically choose not to enter markets that already have sufficient capacity, as long as those markets are reasonably competitive. And once firms do enter particular markets, they ensure they can cover their costs by doing the same thing that all firms in all real-world markets do under competitive circumstances. Unlike the hypothesized firms of perfect competition, they do not attempt to price at marginal cost, because in reality marginal cost cannot be known. Instead, they work out heuristic estimates of their average total costs, knowing that competition at lower prices quickly becomes unsustainable. Competitors in digital markets do so, just as other types of firms do.[8]

There is a second idea built into the claim that books are special and should not be left to the rigors of ordinary competition, and to the *Apple* defendants and their supporters, it was probably more important than these practical economic problems. On the most intuitively obvious level, books have cultural significance that seems not "economic." Books convey the life of our culture. If they are left to cold capitalism, many important works might not be published.

Economists have a way of conceptualizing these kinds of problems, and it seems as good as other ways. To an economist, the issue can be very serious, and the frequent possibility that real-world markets may be unable to preserve important values can seem like one of economic reasoning's thorniest and most trenchant failures. Specifically, economists acknowledge that markets sometimes fail to preserve a value that is important to real people, even though they might be willing to pay to support it. The problem is typically understood as an "externality." Values are "external" when the parties that participate in market transactions do not or cannot internalize that value and take it into account when they decide the prices and quantities at which they will do business. A good example is the problem of pollution. Imagine that a steel factory produces harmful smoke. People living in its region likely see it as a health concern, a danger to their environment, and a danger to their real estate investments, and the factory owner might, too. But imagine that controlling the pollution would require the installation of technology that costs, say, $10 million. If the factory owner pays for it, either it will be done as charity or the cost will somehow be incorporated into the price of the steel. If it is figured into the steel price, the owner will likely face competitors who can sell for less because they avoided the clean air technology. As for steel purchasers, even if they would prefer to buy environmentally friendly steel, and therefore might subsidize the cost of pollution control, they will have their own competitors. The odds are that at least some of them will buy cheaper, environmentally unfriendly inputs, because they just don't care. And what about the factory's neighbors and other third parties, who do care about the environment? They might want to subsidize pollution control, but organizing them and getting them each to contribute enough to fund the project may be difficult. As a theoretical matter, this "collective action" problem is especially hard where large numbers of people are needed to contribute, even if the individual contributions are small.

Pollution is just one example; any number of externalities can be imagined in all kinds of markets. Accordingly, real-world markets leave many significant social values out of consideration. Most honest economists acknowledge they have no very encouraging solutions for these problems, because fixing them often depends on regulatory interventions funded with taxes, and those policies pose many problems of their own.

Book markets seem likely to have nontrivial externalities. Every time a book is bought and sold, the transaction has an effect (good or bad) on third parties, which the main parties to the transaction don't personally feel. Because they don't internalize that cost or benefit, the prices they accept don't incorporate them. The externalities that might affect books all suggest that they are underproduced in ordinary competition, because if their real social value could be incorporated into their prices, publishers would produce more of them. Namely, books preserve a culture that it is good for a society to have, even though few individuals would spend their own money on it. It is good, for example, that books of avant-garde poetry and esoteric learning *exist*—in a library or university, perhaps—even if so few individuals would buy them that they could not feasibly be distributed commercially. Books store knowledge, and having them in some broadly dispersed ownership has a social value over and above the value that an individual person derives and will pay for. Likewise, a society benefits from its citizens' level of education and knowledge, and from greater communication. Books are also important for their role in preserving specific aspects of language and culture that are otherwise jeopardized.[9]

But the odds are good that those values are already accounted for by public spending and other policies, at least in most developed countries. There are many large libraries, universities, and research institutions that purchase books very widely. Some of them purchase essentially all new books as they are printed, and many more purchase voraciously, such that virtually any new book can be assured of at least some sales. And in fact, most new titles require surprisingly few sales to cover costs, so they will continue to be published. Also, governments and philanthropies subsidize writing by way of direct funding for the arts and sciences, and through university faculty salaries.

And finally, we can expect that writing of value will persist because most writing is not entirely or even partly commercially motivated. Some writers do support themselves by writing, and no doubt some writing would not be produced if it did not generate real financial rewards. But that is a different issue than whether handsome remuneration is *required* in order for society to get the amount and variety of writing that is *desirable*. In fact, it seems likely that significant rewards are not required. Writers do much of their writing for other reasons. For example, like many authors, I received no advance for this book, and the very slender royalties I'm likely to earn from it will not pay for the time I invested over more than five years.

A closely related concern is that books and other intellectual products may have "public good" features. Here the issue is not just that parties other than a buyer and a seller can benefit from the production of a book, but that third parties can enjoy the book without paying for it. When that is the case, use by those who might otherwise pay for the good may lead to serious underproduction if the good is produced privately. (And hence true public goods, such as national defense, public safety, and official statistics, are usually produced by government with tax revenue.) But physical books are not so different from other products in this respect, and they probably don't have features that ordinary markets can't adequately accommodate. An individual physical book is "rival and excludable," meaning that publishers can without unusual difficulty keep you from reading it until you've bought it, and afterwards, no one else can consume your copy, thereby evading purchase of their own, without your permission.[10]

Of course, the *content* of books can be copied and is at risk of piracy and exploitation, but that problem is accounted for by our copyright. By most accounts, the legal protection for copyright at present is extensive and perhaps excessive. The actual risk that piracy of physical books could ever have defeated optimal production was probably small. At least with respect to physical books, reasonably efficient production would not have been defeated even by open piracy and complete absence of copyright protection.[11] Indeed, books by foreign authors were sold in the United States throughout the nineteenth century without any copyright and were subject to extensive piracy, without destroying their authors' incentives to write. The risks of piracy and exploitation probably rise when the costs of copying and distribution go down, so one might expect that the risks have become more serious with easy digital distribution. But it is hardly a problem needing further correction in our current regime. Our copyright, in the extent of its protection and the length of its term, is notoriously protective, and it is now abetted by technological tools to make copying and distribution in digital form even more difficult. In the case of digital books, in any event, it is so little a concern that it was hardly mentioned during the *Apple* litigation.

19

The Virtues of Vertical and Entry
for Its Own Sake

> It's true that there are fewer independents than there were. . . .
> But the shops that are still around are better, fitter, and often
> bigger.
>
> —Tim Godfray, Chief Executive, British Booksellers Association, on the
> effects of the suspension of the Net Books Agreement in 1995

MUCH OF THE CRITICISM of *Apple,* especially from conservative academics and the antitrust defense bar, concerned the possibility that the defendants needed vertical restrictions to correct problems in their markets. If vertical arrangements deliver efficiencies that markets themselves can't provide, then government antitrust intervention can be counterproductive. To a large extent, critics delivered that message in the language of vertical economics, and to some, that body of theory has come to seem almost magical. Many people, including those ordinarily confident that markets are so powerfully self-correcting that antitrust is almost never necessary, are prepared to believe that vertical agreements are routinely needed to correct systematically persistent market failures. They often believe it even when an obvious purpose for some agreement would just be anticompetitive profit taking. In particular, the embrace of vertical economics by the federal courts, and above all, by the Supreme Court, has led many antitrust litigators to expect that any arrangement that can be plausibly characterized as vertical will be legal.

Some believe that in the particular case of books, additional benefits follow from limiting retail competition, over and above the correction to free riding or market failure described in the economic literature. In Europe, where state-sanctioned RPM in books is common, defenders claim that it preserves independent bookstores, access to variety and numbers of new titles, and in some countries, native languages and literatures.[1] Some a priori theoretical models suggest that RPM could, in principle, serve positive externality values such as these, specifically by subsidizing the publication of more titles. If higher retail prices generate higher profits, then publishers might publish and booksellers might carry at the margin some additional titles whose returns would not have supported publication at competitive prices.[2] But so far, those claims lack empirical verification.[3] Indeed, it appears that RPM in books throughout Europe has had little effect besides higher prices and possibly some protection for smaller booksellers.[4] That coheres with an emerging view of RPM generally, corroborated by recent empirical evidence, that its only real effect is increased retail prices.[5] In any event, the historical record suggests that many RPM arrangements in books, especially in Britain, were driven at least in part by more mercantile goals. They may have been meant to shore up retail-level cartel, which is likely the original motive in the British case, because the Net Books Agreement began emphatically as a project of the booksellers.[6] Or they may have been meant to prevent concentration of bargaining power in large retailers. As time wore on in Britain, that seems to have become the purpose of the Net Books Agreement, as publishers fought to save it in the face of discount sales by chains and supermarkets.[7] It was also the case in the *Apple* conspiracy. And in fact, even many of the more noble goals cited for RPM in books, like preserving smaller booksellers and subsidizing variety or quality, would not really distinguish it from any mundane retail cartel. Whatever its merits, a set of agreements to preserve firms that could not survive under price pressure sounds uncomfortably like a routine cartel outcome.[8]

In the particular case of *Apple* and eBooks, vertical limits were thought necessary for the somewhat unusual reason of enabling manufacturer entry. Some critics said that Apple needed RPM protected by a set of MFNs so that it could protect its up-front investment. It could lose that investment if it had to compete at Amazon's very low prevailing prices. To many defenders of the conspiracy, this all but conclusively proved its desirability. Entry *is* competition, the argument goes, so anything that encourages it must be good from the antitrust perspective.[9]

This argument is extraordinarily weak, and it is surprising that so many sophisticated antitrust watchers made it during the *Apple* case. It is sometimes thought that RPM could facilitate the entry of small, not-yet-established firms struggling to secure distribution.[10] The idea is that distributors might not carry a small entrant without the promise of some cushion of profit protected by RPM. The Apple computer corporation, however, is a uniquely implausible underdog. The world's largest company by valuation, the first company in history to be valued at $1 trillion, and frequently the most profitable company in the world, Apple was also the company that single-handedly created the present worlds of digital music, smartphones, tablet computing, and mobile software distribution. It has also seemed quite willing to risk entry into other markets, including the evolving markets for streaming music, streaming video, and payment systems. In those areas, it has done so—so far as anyone knows—without organizing cartels to restrain its own retail competitors.

Even leaving aside the fact that these were not just independent vertical arrangements—Apple orchestrated an industry-wide, horizontal scheme imposed on all retailers—the claimed need for entry protection does not make sense. The cost at the point of Apple's entry was very low. The publishers were already present, and Apple had only to develop a bookstore app and include it on the iPad. The iPad was already developed and it would plainly go ahead with or without a bookstore. Moreover, neither Apple nor Amazon nor presumably other eBook retailers offered anything in particular in marketing the eBooks themselves other than providing search capability, establishing a payment system, and streaming the data once the books were purchased.

But most fundamentally, it is simply not the case that Apple's entry, or the entry of any other firm, is unequivocally good. Entry is good only to the extent that it lowers price. Or, more accurately, it is good if it lowers price or raises quality to a degree that the quality-adjusted price is lower than before. If a firm can enter only by getting not only its own but also everyone else's prices way up, then its entry is not welcome. Accordingly, black-letter antitrust emphatically does not contain any rule that all entry is good, no matter what. The defense attorneys and others who stressed that entry must be good would sing rather a different tune if Amazon were their client, and would stress instead that antitrust does not protect less-efficient competitors from more efficient ones.[11]

Apple and the publishers raised various arguments that Apple's entry brought technological or quality improvements such that even though raw prices rose, quality-adjusted price may have improved. Strictly speaking, no such defense could be legally relevant, even if it had more weight. The best established rule in antitrust is that where naked horizontal agreement on price or output is shown, efficiency or cost-benefit judgments are no longer relevant.[12] In any case, those arguments tended to shift quickly as the government showed that each of them was either unsupported by evidence or legally irrelevant.[13] Moreover, there is no question that the iPad would have been used for reading eBooks whether Apple got into eBook retailing or not. Whatever technological improvements Apple could bring to e-reading, they were not contingent on Apple having an iBookstore.[14] Rather than offering anything new or better, it was just taking easy profits.

And, really, the most significant fact is just that Amazon had already pulled it off. Amazon itself made huge research and development investments in developing eBooks, a market that largely did not exist prior to its entry, and apparently saw no need for inflated prices to recoup them.[15] The conservative critics who said that Apple needed price protection are from the same school who have been saying for sixty years that "entry barriers" can never include costs that incumbent firms themselves had to bear.

In principle there could be other theoretical arguments that Apple's entry somehow required some kind of protection, but they seem implausible. It is sometimes said that in some high-tech markets, sellers must have large market shares to function efficiently, and that might conceivably explain Apple's need for RPM. Some critics of the *Apple* case seemed to say as much. The argument usually concerns "network" effects or network externalities, by which a product becomes more valuable as more people own it. A fax machine, for example, has no value unless a lot of people have machines that can talk to it, and VHS beat the Beta standard because distributors would produce videocassettes in a given format only if enough people owned players that could play them. If the network effects are very large, such that any firm selling the product must have a majority of the sales just to be efficient, then that competition is not for individual sales, it is "for the field." At any rate, if it is true in a given case that efficient production requires immediate establishment of a large market share, perhaps entry could require some protection from price competition to make getting that share feasible.

But again, even if this does exist in some real-world markets, the *Apple* case is an unlikely candidate for it. The technological features that typically create network effects aren't present in eBooks, because the usefulness and experience of a book don't change depending on how many other people use it. Reading a book is uniquely solitary. The only way anything like network effects would occur in such a product is if some firm created them artificially to extract excess profit. For example, imagine that Amazon sold a very large number of Kindles, far more than any competing technology, and that it used proprietary software so that books released for the Kindle can't be read on other readers. Publishers might not bother releasing eBooks for competing readers, and that could impede their entry. That was the means by which Microsoft monopolized computer operating systems in *United States v. Microsoft.* Even then, though, it's hard to imagine such a thing working in books, because releasing book files in different reader formats is easy, and indeed publishers have done it as long as there have been eBooks. In any case, Apple did not behave like a firm that needed to secure a very large share just to enter. It was unafraid to develop its new tablet device, and would introduce it with or without eBooks. It developed the iBookstore apparently as an afterthought, green-lighting it barely three months before launch and completing both negotiations and technological steps in just one or two. It seems extremely unlikely that Apple would enter a market with so little preparation if very large market share were mandatory.

A theory that strikes some as more plausible at the moment, because some people are coming to believe that it characterizes all kinds of high-technology markets, is that eBook distribution is a "platform" business, tending toward "platform" or "two-sided market" economics. Some economists argue that some special businesses don't just sell products to customers, but rather exist to connect different parties with each other. What makes platforms economically special, according to the theory, is not just that their proprietors interact with more than one set of market participants. That is true of all firms. A manufacturer, for example, converts inputs into manufactured goods, so in some sense it is a platform over which suppliers of raw materials are connected with downstream buyers. Rather, a platform seems special when its success in attracting participants on one side affects participants on the other side. For example, most successful computer operating systems have been technologically desirable in and of themselves, and suitable to their users' needs. In addition, they have also depended on sectors of third-party software designers willing to create content for their devices. A successful system marketed on this model will attract retail purchasers by delivering high quality and a range of desirable applications software. And by succeeding in attracting a large base of customers, the system in turn attracts more designers to provide more and better content compatible with the system, and so on. Platform effects are network externalities, in other words, amplified by the fact that there are at least two sets of network effects that mutually interact. In the literature, these mutual interactions are known as cross-platform externalities.[16]

Many now claim that these special effects characterize all kinds of other high-tech businesses, including media distribution, software delivery, third-party sales platforms such as eBay and Amazon Marketplace, and electronic payment systems. Platform theories can be present even where we don't refer to them as such, as in the theory of monopoly power in *United States v. Microsoft*.[17] The court found monopoly power because a critical mass of widely used applications software was available for Microsoft's system, and would continue to be made available as long Microsoft maintained its very large base of users. Meanwhile, challengers offering competing systems found expansion very difficult because consumers would not switch to a new system without some available range of useful software products, and third-party developers would not create those products until enough consumers had adopted the system. The familiar Catch-22 of platform economics was at play. And indeed, once the government sued Apple in the eBooks case, some explicitly said that eBook delivery over Amazon or the Apple iBookstore is a platform, and requires special antitrust treatment to attend to its special economics.[18] While it seems absurd that online distribution of book content should be treated differently than distribution of the same books in terrestrial bookstores, there is little in this theory, as it is now stated by some advocates, to prevent that result.

But the theory's flexibility and broad applicability is its most problematic feature. A serious question is how often these purported externalities distinguish platforms from other businesses. If in fact they characterize all kinds of businesses, then the discovery is not much of a discovery, and it shouldn't justify any special legal treatment. If any firms really are "platforms," they are not limited just to digital or high-technology products, and in fact these platform effects might really be quite common. Newspapers, for example, are widely acknowledged to have the same features, because they depend on attracting large circulation on the one hand, and that makes them desirable to advertisers on the other hand. They need to maintain substantial ad revenues to fund their competition for circulation, and need circulation to keep up ad revenue. If they experience losses on either side, they will lose on the other. The fabled newspaper "death spiral" may follow. Yet, antitrust has treated newspapers no differently from any other firms, throughout a long history. And when the Supreme Court recently accepted a platform argument for the first time, it explicitly held that newspapers would not be protected by its new rule.[19]

And so one might question whether digital platforms are so different from the "platforms" that seem to be all over the place, and whether, even if the phenomenon is real, it poses any problem that would be helped by special legal treatment. Since the theory was first given credence in an antitrust case in the Second Circuit in 2016, defendants in other cases have already claimed that the same platform theory should justify conspiracies or restraints in all kinds of unrelated areas.[20] Where will it stop? If the courts say that it applies in those cases, it might as well apply to regular old retail stores. No less than Amazon or an operating system, retail stores are platforms for bringing together suppliers of diverse products and consumers who want them. Should they be allowed to fix their input prices, in order to fund promotions that will keep their customer bases large?

In any case, theoretical justifications for price restraints to stop rough rivalry tend to have a familiar feel. They are literally just destructive competition arguments, in that their inner working mechanism is that low prices themselves will keep market participants from supplying things that society needs. They resemble the theory of the turn of the twentieth century that led many economists and other Americans to doubt that competition could work anymore, an argument that now holds no sway. Latter-day theories of vertical restraints and platform effects come to seem like a lot of other complex, specialized theories of market dysfunction—like Lester Telser's theory of the empty core and like theoretical justifications for extravagant intellectual property rules. While they might be helpful to the careers of the economists who invent them, they often do not explain real-world markets very well.

Ultimately, it is hard to imagine an efficiency-enhancing rationale for a horizontal agreement that did literally nothing other than raise retail prices across an industry. That so many argued otherwise in *Apple* shows the lengths to which some will go to doubt markets when it suits an ideological need. They raised the arguments discussed in this chapter, implying that the markets in *Apple* were so faulty they couldn't be trusted to perform their most basic function, which is to sort out the efficient amount and variety of goods and services that consumers want. Many of the critics who made those arguments were people who ordinarily find markets so super-strong that we have nothing to fear from massive, horizontal mergers and highly restrictive trade restraints.

20

Amazon

I think I have observed that not the man who hopes when others despair, but the man who despairs when others hope, is admired by a large class of persons as a sage, and wisdom is supposed to consist not in seeing further than other people, but in not seeing so far.

—John Stuart Mill

A MORE IMPORTANT THEME of the *Apple* case is the role played by Amazon. For many critics, Amazon and the law's failure to deal with it encapsulates everything wrong with modern antitrust. The publishers said that Amazon was already a monopolist—at the time of the eBooks conspiracy, it had about 90 percent of eBook sales—and that it was trying to get more and more power. They said that its aggressive eBooks initiative was meant to destroy them and take their place as the intermediaries of literature. Their specific theory of its danger in the eBooks case was that it had engaged in what lawyers and economists call price *predation*. That is, its prices were so low that it was sacrificing its own profits in order to destroy its competitors. They also stressed the fact—which to them looked like a smoking gun—that Amazon had encouraged the government to bring the lawsuit.[1] An old criticism of antitrust is that it really just helps competitors avoid competition, and to some, *Apple*'s paramount irony was that federal regulators were used in a game to benefit an aspiring monopolist. And the publishers and other critics also stressed social issues that reached beyond the scope of the case itself: that failures of publishing businesses would be accompanied by a loss of social values that neither Amazon nor others could supply in their place.

Their argument raises two questions: whether Amazon actually engaged in predation or some other anticompetitive strategy, as opposed to just selling better or cheaper products; and if it did, whether it would justify the publisher cartel. The first question is the easier of the two, because the factual case for predation is weak. The second question is more significant because it goes to the bigger question of whether antitrust can feasibly make up a holistic competition policy. It is obvious that even the success of a genuinely predatory monopoly would not justify the *Apple* cartel. For various reasons, it is a bad solution to monopoly to permit retaliatory cartels. But it poses a serious question about the current state of our law. If Amazon really were a monopolist, and a publisher price cartel is a bad response, what alternative can antitrust offer?

That returns us to an observation from the beginning of this book. Popular acceptance of competition policy as legitimate can't be secured by telling the public that they misunderstand the world. It requires recognizing when something is wrong in the policy itself. Even if it is true that the public systematically misjudges the consequences of ordinary competition and as a result, fails to give antitrust the support it needs, it is a separate problem if the policy itself is broken is some way. *Apple* demonstrates a serious flaw in current antitrust. Even if the specific criticisms of Amazon's eBooks business weren't very strong, the firm probably does pose serious risks. The extraordinary challenge of controlling such firms with our current laws signals the danger of a competition policy with a broken and unused monopolization rule.

The claim that Amazon was engaged in some genuinely predatory scheme seemed unlikely, even to most true believers in antitrust enforcement. Skepticism followed from a traditional theory according to which predatory pricing rarely occurs. That theory is the subject of vast literatures in economics and law, all stemming from a 1958 article by John McGee of the University of Chicago.[2] That article, however, is itself the target of a lot of criticism, and both the theory and its adoption by the courts are now widely thought to have been problematic. But it still makes a trenchant criticism of predation claims in reasonably competitive circumstances, including circumstances like those in *Apple*.

McGee thought that in the ordinary case, the purpose of price predation was to kill off all rivals, and once the predator had all the business,
raise prices for a nice profit. The problem is that raising prices after the
predatory episode would invite new entry, unless entry barriers precluded
it. In the absence of difficult entry, the predator would end up sacrificing
a lot of money by charging predatorily low prices, and then, to make the
episode worth it, would have to recoup the entire sacrifice through supracompetitive prices before earning any actual profits from it. If entry
occurred before all that could be done, then the predation would have
been self-defeating. Wherever there is reason to believe that entry barriers
are low, it seems irrationally risky to try it. In the meantime, predatory
attempts that fail actually *benefit* consumers. They enjoy low prices for a
while, and when the predator attempts to cash in, that invites new entry
to replace the competition it destroyed.

The claim that Amazon was a price predator seems unlikely according
to this theory and the facts of the company's history. For one thing,
eBooks seem to be a market in which the impossibility of recoupment
would make simple predation infeasible. That was shown in the facts of
the case itself. As soon as the conspiracy took effect and eBook prices
went up, Amazon's market share shrank dramatically.

Moreover, setting prices below its own costs was not even Amazon's
idea. There is no question that it sold some individual eBook titles at less
than its own costs; that fact attracted a lot of attention in popular debate.
Prior to the conspiracy, Amazon's retail price for some new releases was
indeed less than the wholesale price. But crucially, the $9.99 price was
initially about the same as its own wholesale cost for most titles, and it
was only in about January 2009, when the publishers jointly eliminated
their 20 percent wholesale discount for digital titles, that some of
Amazon's sales came to be below cost.[3] At that point, Amazon had already heavily promoted a flat $9.99 retail price, and the only way it could
have covered its wholesale costs under the publishers' increased prices
would be by breaking its own widely publicized promise to sell new release eBooks at $9.99. Amazon's prices were "predatory," then, only
because actions by the publishers left it little choice. In fact, those
actions—which stemmed from an apparently coordinated decision to
raise wholesale prices—were very possibly antitrust violations.

Furthermore, there were several reasons to expect that Amazon's overall eBooks program was profitable, or would be in the longer term, without any anticompetitive conduct. First, it also sold its own eBook reader device, the Kindle, which predated the iPad and other eBook-compatible products, and launched it at a time when there was effectively no market for eBooks.[4] Kindle sales might have made the eBook business profitable even if eBook sales themselves were at a loss. Amazon's own explanation is consistent with this motive. The Amazon executive in charge of Kindle content in the relevant years, Ross Grandinetti, testified that while Kindle sales did not "directly subsidize" eBook sales, Amazon looked at the program "holistically, as the sum of what the device business and the content business provide together."[5]

While the eBooks pricing was daring, it seems consistent with other daring bets for which Amazon was already legendary, and which probably drove much of its rapid growth. One famous example was its radical gamble to sell J. K. Rowling's fourth Harry Potter book, *Harry Potter and the Goblet of Fire,* at a 40 percent discount and with express delivery at standard delivery rates, so that preordering customers would receive it the day it was released. By knowingly sacrificing some hundreds of thousands of dollars of profits, the firm earned fawning press attention and consumer approval, and the plan is widely thought to have been a major success.[6] Another example was Amazon Prime, the risky and expensive gamble on free, two-day shipping and a variety of other benefits, paid for with a fixed membership fee. Prime has proven extraordinarily popular. While it probably incurred large initial losses, it seems unlikely that it would continue for so long (it was introduced in 2005) if it didn't at some point become profitable. If Amazon was able to generate a profitable new business by offering something consumers want, while sustainably covering its costs, that is probably just competition.

Another reason Amazon may have expected even very aggressive eBook pricing eventually to be profitable is that it could use the market share it gained to force down the wholesale prices it faced from publishers. That goal would be desirable from a social point of view, because "wholesale" prices for eBooks were to some degree fictitious. In competitive markets, prices are driven by some approximation to cost. Competition cannot generate marginal-cost pricing where fixed costs are large as a portion of total cost, and digital goods have the unusual property that fixed costs overwhelmingly dominate. But even where fixed costs are large, it's not as if prices are untethered from cost, as long as markets are competitive. Vigorous competition in high fixed-cost good should be able to push prices down, as long as they still cover long-term average cost.

Even Amazon's price of $9.99 was likely well in excess of the publishers' long-term average cost of an eBook produced under competitive conditions. The publishers made no effort to explain the "wholesale" price for eBooks on any cost basis; they explained it only in terms of needing to preserve their hard-copy book business. Their efforts to keep those prices up were an attempt to find some substantially supracompetitive price that the market would bear for their well-differentiated products, not a competition-driven effort to cover the economic cost of producing them.

Amazon might also have needed to establish a sufficient scale for profitability. In that case, aggressive pricing over the relatively short period it was alleged to have occurred would be part of the process of creating a new market. In other words, even a business run at a short-term loss would have made sense as part of a desirable, procompetitive means of doing business.

One final reason to doubt the predation story is just that Amazon has been accused of it so frequently, for so long, in so many sectors. Gaining market share through deep discounting funded by innovation in internal efficiencies is a long-term Amazon strategy, dating back two decades or more and evident throughout its large range of retail and other businesses.[7] It seems unlikely that the firm has operated on a genuinely predatory basis across so many of its lines of business for such a long period. For good or ill, Amazon appears to have developed significant cost advantages through technological and logistical innovation.

This all presumably explains why Apple failed to raise a predation argument in the one place it could actually have mattered—the courtroom. Apple's filings repeated throughout the trial that Amazon used eBooks as "loss leaders," and occasionally came close to saying its prices were literally predatory in a legal sense. Yet, despite having hired several internationally renowned economic experts, Apple produced no proof that Amazon's eBooks program was an overall loss.[8] The government, meanwhile, presented evidence that it was profitable overall, even prior to the *Apple* conspiracy, when it was still charging $9.99.

What *Apple*'s critics really meant by this emphasis on predation was that the government had sued the wrong defendant. But, largely following the theoretical critique that began with John McGee, the courts have stacked the American law on predatory pricing overwhelmingly against enforcement. So blaming the government for not (yet) suing Amazon as well as suing Apple is unfair, and could make for pretty bad policy. It might also be jumping the gun, because the government is still free to sue Amazon when it has a case for monopolization that could survive in court.

In making the law on predatory pricing, the Supreme Court has stressed certain special policy problems in addition to the basic economic critique. Unlike much other conduct challenged in antitrust, predation *looks like competition.* Predation is by definition the effort to take competitors' business by underselling them. When the authorities vigorously enforce a rule against predatory pricing, they run the risk of discouraging competition that isn't monopolistic and is in fact the conduct antitrust is meant to encourage. Moreover, enforcement implies a problem of remedy. If a firm is held liable for having charged certain prices, it may be discouraged from going forward and continuing to compete with the vigor that antitrust demands, taking the risk that the government will again think it's crossed a line, with serious legal consequences.

For these reasons, and following McGee, the Supreme Court in a handful of seminal decisions has made predatory pricing largely impossible to prove.[9] Most important was its seminal 1993 decision in *Brooke Group, Ltd. v. Brown & Williamson Tobacco Co.,* which established a demanding two-part standard to govern predation cases.[10] Plaintiffs must show that the challenged prices were below some appropriate measure of costs (typically assumed to be average variable costs, as a proxy for marginal cost), and that once the predator excluded its victim, it had a reasonable likelihood of recouping the losses of the predatory episode. In the twenty-five years since *Brooke Group,* predatory pricing plaintiffs have failed completely in almost every case. Actually, the trend even pre-dated *Brooke Group*. Predation plaintiffs almost always lost during the preceding decade, when most lower courts adopted some version of the test that was ultimately adopted in *Brooke Group*. Accordingly, no American plaintiff, government or private, has won significant relief on a predation theory in at least thirty-five years.[11] About fifteen years ago, the Justice Department itself brought an important, ambitious predation case, which it lost.[12] Even with a team of excellent lawyers and econo-mists and the investigatory power of the federal government, it could not meet the court's exacting evidentiary expectations of proof of defen-dant's costs.[13] Given the difficulty of proving predatory pricing, it was not fair to attack the government's failure to sue Amazon on the evidence that was available in the eBooks case.

It would be a poignant irony indeed if it could be a defense to price-fixing that some other person was pricing predatorily. If that were so, then two harmful courses of conduct would both be effectively immune from challenge. If antitrust claims must lose whenever the defendant is lowering price (which is effectively the case under current predatory pricing law), and *also* must lose when a conspiracy of that monopolist's trading partners then conspire to raise prices, then antitrust really is finally dead.

Wholly aside from whether the predation story is plausible as a factual matter and whether the government would have succeeded in chal-lenging it in court, there is another reason why alleged predation should not have stopped the Justice Department's lawsuit. For good reason, it is not legally relevant to a case against price-fixers that they needed their conspiracy as a defense against some third party. There is a reason that horizontal cartels and hub-and-spoke price conspiracies are per se illegal, even if they are organized to repel another party's antitrust vio-lations. A cartel will not serve the public interest. It will only serve its own interest, at public expense. In *Apple,* for example, there is no ques-tion that the cartel successfully raised price, by quite a lot and for a long time, but the defendants were unable to produce any serious evidence of having accomplished anything else. Only raising prices, and doing nothing else, is a serious social harm with no offsetting benefit at all. No regulator cares less about the public interest than a conspiracy of horizontal competitors.

This leaves a much more significant and pressing problem for our doctrinal antitrust to face. A piece of our contemporary policy is broken in a way that was evident in the *Apple* case. It is easy to say to critics of the case that a cartel is a bad way to deal with monopoly because it will only pad its members' wallets. But implicit in that response is that if Amazon really was a monopolist, then the right solution is for the government to sue both the publisher cartel *and* Amazon. And there is the problem, because any suit against Amazon would be a monopolization claim to challenge its unilateral conduct under Sherman Act section 2, and our law of monopolization is effectively dead.

The fact that Amazon may be an anticompetitive danger itself does not really provide any support for a supplier cartel, but it most definitely supports improvements in doctrinal antitrust. Specifically, the plaintiff's burden in single-firm monopolization cases should be made easier. The details of that law are complex and the subject of a substantial literature of their own. But it will help give a flavor of the changes that might be made if we think through the likely anticompetitive threats that Amazon actually poses.

Amazon seems most likely to be a danger as a monopsonist—that is, not a powerful seller but a powerful buyer. In the abstract, that is like what the *Apple* defendants said, because for eBooks it was their buyer. Amazon seems unlikely to intend harm as a seller because its output markets— mostly retail sales of consumer goods—tend to be extremely price-competitive. If it gets big market shares in those areas through aggressive price and quality, and then tries to cash in by raising retail price, it is likely to lose lots of sales to retail competitors. Just that happened in eBooks, when the conspiracy forced prices up. What seems more likely is that Amazon has built its market share to become a distributor that suppliers cannot do without, so it can force down the wholesale prices it pays. That is fine in principle, and as long as its suppliers can still cover their costs while supplying as much of their product as markets want, reducing input costs is something that competition is supposed to do. The problem arises if Amazon is able to force them *monopsonistically* low, meaning that it would pay less than the price for their product that they could get in competitive markets.

In economic theory, monopsony is usually thought of as a mirror-image of monopoly. It is just as harmful, and causes harm in essentially identical ways. Specifically, if they are paid less than they would be in competitive markets, then suppliers will either produce less or reduce quality, substituting cheaper raw materials. They also will lose incentives they might otherwise have had to innovate in production and design.[14] Generally speaking, while antitrust claims are almost always based on seller power, the law has always recognized that buyer power causes the same harms and is illegal in the same ways. Thus, there have always been successful claims for conspiracy, unilateral conduct, and mergers that enhanced or abused buyer power.[15]

The problem in using existing buyer-power rules against Amazon is the same problem we have with our law of monopolization generally. As part of their effort to rein in what they viewed as excessive antitrust and reduce the risk that it would "chill" desirable business behavior, the increasingly conservative federal courts since the mid-1970s have made it progressively harder to challenge single-firm conduct of any kind. Eventually, challenges under our basic monopolization rule in Sherman Act section 2 became all but impossible, and they rarely occur. Addressing a problem such as Amazon seems to call for reversing that trend and making a monopolization plaintiff's legal burden easier to meet. But the challenge is determining when a buyer's behavior merits legal correction, because in many cases buyers will kill off competitors and grow larger just by figuring out how to distribute things more cheaply or with better service. Short of instituting a simple anti-bigness policy, we can't have a rule that says a distributor is a danger just because it charges low prices, or that it is a monopsonist just because it has a big market share.

Amazon is a useful illustration of this. On the one hand, it has succeeded by doing desirable things, to some large extent. Its logistical innovations have been groundbreaking and revolutionary, and much of its market share in most sectors is explainable by having translated those gains into consumer benefit through lower prices. Moreover, its retail market shares in most sectors aren't even that large, by traditional standards, and they are often grossly exaggerated in popular discussion. On the other hand, despite what much of this book seems to imply, it has *not* succeeded *only* by selling a cheaper or better service. Just on the information available from public sources, it seems to have engaged in conduct that could support a monopolization challenge even under our current law, because it doesn't consist of "competition on the merits." There are many claims that Amazon has used its widely used platform and control of customer data to disadvantage retail competitors in various ways. Moreover, something not yet well understood is why so many suppliers consider Amazon a must-have distributor. It seems unlikely to be just because Amazon has big retail market shares. Its shares often aren't even that big, and there are several other mass merchants in America with bigger shares in lots of products, but evidently many suppliers do not consider them indispensable. So there seems to be something special about the particular market in which Amazon really is monopsonistically powerful, and it does not flow from any individual retail market share. It perhaps owes to its role in supplying "online logistics," or something like "in-home, next-day delivery," and it seems possible that it has gotten power there through conduct other than cost or service improvements. For example, in the emerging market in "smart home" products such as Amazon's Echo and Google's Nest, Amazon has aggressively sought to maximize Echo's penetration with the evident goal to control of in-home shopping. Among other things, when an Amazon Echo user asks Alexa for a specific product, Alexa appears to recommend only Amazon's own private-label products, or otherwise makes recommendations that discourage disfavored brands. *That* seems like the kind of conduct that is anticompetitive and makes a compelling case for monopsony. Through nothing that could be called competition on the merits, Amazon would establish a world in which suppliers must be recommended, literally, by Amazon's consumer search tool, and therefore must accede to whatever terms Amazon imposes.

Many of us take for granted that we *shouldn't* have an anti-bigness policy, but there is something to be said for the argument that we should. The efficiencies that come with higher volume production—the "economies of scale" on which monopoly and concentration are routinely defended—are fully realized in most sectors at relatively low levels of output. It is the rare market where there must be only two or three or four sellers in order to reach efficient production. Moreover, there is a growing empirical case that concentration is systematically correlated with anti-competitive injury. It leads to higher prices, lower output, and other social harms. It seems, in principle, that size itself is systematically correlated with net harm, perhaps closely enough that we could have a policy of breaking up big firms or setting caps on their size as a proxy for direct examination of the details of each given case. The dramatic benefit of such a rule, if the empirical claim proves true, is that it would make the policy much easier and cheaper to enforce.

So why not do it? Perhaps we should. We tried it a few times in the United States, and the results were arguably pretty good. We have also tried a few times to adopt more general anti-bigness rules, as when Congress in the early 1970s attempted to enact a no-fault monopolization law. But the idea presents a political problem. The policy would require new legislation, because there is no likelihood that such a change would be made by the federal judiciary for at least another generation. And at present, a new statute would have no political plausibility whatsoever, either in Congress as it is constituted or among the broader public. But even if such a thing were possible, would it work in practice? The problem with similar laws historically has been that they are very difficult to administer because they tend to invite dramatic political backlash. When the federal agencies attempted to enforce something like an anti-bigness program under the existing laws during the 1960s and 1970s, in response to pressure from a very successful popular movement led in part by Ralph Nader, the result was the crushing failure of antitrust overall during the Reagan administration and the near abolition of the Federal Trade Commission.

There was a different concern about Amazon and the social risk posed by its aggression. If it had put the traditional publishers out of business, certain socially valuable functions might have been lost, too. Media firms have traditionally performed intermediate functions needed to identify commercially promising works and take them to market, often including funding or organizing their creation. The process is expensive in comparison to digital distribution. Significant evidence in *Apple* showed the publishers' fear that Amazon, Google, or other major online distributors threatened entry as new publication venues that would compete *as* publishers.[16] Perhaps we should fear the technological change the publishers tried to deter, because it risks losing important functions that they perform.

In and of itself, this kind of disintermediation is not obviously bad. A lower-cost means of production or distribution *should* win out over more costly means, and aggregate welfare should improve. As ever, one can regard this kind of cold theoretical talk as bloodless and insensitive to the human cost of business failure. But the failure of the major publishers is economically undesirable only if their investment of resources is needed for the desired product to exist. To show that disintermediation is bad, there must be some important intermediary function, other than production of the literary works themselves, that disintermediated markets don't provide on their own.

One such function might involve the "risk capital" that media intermediaries often claim to supply. The development and marketing of new intellectual works involve some costs and a high frequency of commercial failure. We already saw this argument in Chapter 18; it is an aspect of what the economist Richard Caves called the "nobody knows" problem. Each new work is a differentiated and untested product, and its success is ordinarily difficult to predict. Ordinary capital sources without specialized expertise would find such investments hard to evaluate. Publishers argue further that they are specially suited to it because they invest in large inventories of books and can diversify the risk. The moral punchline of the argument is that traditional publishing supports works of high literary merit but unlikely commercial success. They cross-subsidize, in other words, to preserve art for art's sake.[17]

The loss of these functions seems not terribly significant in the case of digital disintermediation, because its main impact is to reduce the very costs that make the markets risky. The high-risk capital that publishing intermediaries front is needed mainly to fund their own operations. Much of those costs would be obviated by full digital distribution.

The publishers' largest single cost, for example, is returns of unsold inventory, and that cost with digital distribution is zero.[18] Moreover, the claimed riskiness of new publications is probably overstated. For one thing, while each individual book is unusually risky, each individual book is only a small part of the publisher's overall output. For another thing, taking risks on new authors is an important and financially rational component of building a publisher's backlist, which was traditionally a key strategy in book publishing. Authors often do not do well financially on their first book or two, but those initial books are necessary to establish an author whose reputation sells books, and when they are established, their initial, unprofitable books can become profitable backlist items.

There is a more significant problem. Traditional intermediation performs a legitimating or sorting function that is socially valuable. Being published by a prestigious intermediary such as an academic press or major commercial publisher means facing a screening or peer-review process. If authors could find a way to evade this screening and still widely distribute their work, and in particular if they could sell directly to consumers, then an information problem could arise. Actually, it is at least two problems. The first and seemingly less serious problem is the sorting of quality. With easy, disintermediated mass distribution, book markets might be flooded with works lacking authoritativeness or legitimacy, and consumers might be too overwhelmed for the markets themselves to sort out the works of real quality. Although authors have always been free to fund their own publications, it was traditionally expensive to distribute a new book without investment from an intermediary. The cost of vanity publishing was therefore a deterrent to a flood of products that could impede efficient consumer search.

But economically, this sorting or legitimizing function should be a simple matter of intellectual property, and it should be easy for disintermediated markets to replicate. It is a function of trademarks, and their reason for being. There is nothing to suggest that a trademark in eBooks, differentiated by a reputation for literary quality, requires investment of the kind the major publishers apparently find necessary for their own continued existence. On the contrary, if there is money to be made in eBook markets, and rents can be generated through quality-differentiated branding, authors will have strong incentives *not* to disintermediate all the way to direct, one-to-one sales to consumers. They would prefer to be published under the mark of some firm or cooperative that has been able to differentiate a brand for quality. In any case, online distribution should have an advantage in developing brands, given the internet's power to support user reviews, sharing or usage information, and other mass data collection.

Indeed, protection of the leading publishers from alternative intermediaries could deter desirable innovations, such as authors' cooperatives or book-buying guilds, or other nontraditional distribution forms that could brand their own reputation for quality. This sorting function is what Kevin Kelly recently described as "filtering." He explains how technology could improve it in many ways, as by exploiting the massively distributed nature of online content and making it algorithmic (and, as Kelly says, increasingly "cognified").[19]

The publishers themselves acknowledged that filtering might be performed by some free-standing technological solution. One of their several attempts to confront Amazon's retail dominance and the damage it had done to brick-and-mortar book retailers (which were also important for their filtering function) involved the creation of a filtering device of their own, a website called Bookish.com. Initially intended as a competing distribution alternative to Amazon, Bookish now exists only as a stylish and well-written literary newsletter, produced online and distributed to registered visitors through an email list. It operates in a very crowded field and in a sector—literary journalism—already dominated by the *New York Review of Books,* the *New York Times Book Review,* and other venerable periodicals. For now at least, filtering remains vibrant, and independent of the publishing firms.

The future of filtering is where it has been for many years, with the "recommendation engine"—a program that collects as much data as it can on each consumer's traits, purchasing history, and other habits, and crunches them algorithmically to recommend the products that are most likely to interest that consumer. Recommendation engines are now very common and increasingly sophisticated, and are used to sell all kinds of products. Among the most effective are two powerful and successful engines that exist for books. One of them is Amazon itself, which pioneered the idea and so far has developed one of the best of all recommendation products.

These innovations have their critics. Automated recommendations first arose during a controversial and difficult period in Amazon's history. From its beginnings, Amazon employed an Editorial group, comprised of human staff whose jobs were to post written book reviews and recommendations on the Amazon website. Editorial was no doubt meant to preserve the intellectual atmosphere of a terrestrial bookstore, but it was also meant to solve the problem of filtering that otherwise might be daunting for an online bookstore with an inventory of millions of titles and no physical displays for consumers to browse. The problem for Editorial was the limitations of its human staff in the face of the vastness of Amazon's inventory and its ambitions.

Amazon's solution was an early indication of Bezos's prescience as an e-commerce pioneer. Many other observers found the early internet's information content unimpressive and predicted that creation of new content would be slow because it is very costly.[20] What they failed to imagine was the power of distributed user contribution, and the fact that user content generated for free would come to make up the vastness of the internet.[21] Bezos saw that distributed contributions would be key to the now powerful recommendations and user ratings tools of electronic commerce.

As early as Amazon's initial capital fundraising efforts in 1995, Bezos promised investors he would one day offer each customer a personally tailored website.[22] By 1996 he had already established a team to begin doing it. The unit began with an early recommendations product known as Firefly, which like the Kindle's E Ink display had its origins in the MIT Media Lab. In those days of primitive search engines, it was considered to be among the most promising tools for sorting out the disorganized mass of information that was the internet. But Amazon's Firefly-based recommendations prototype did not work well, because it required customer input and most customers did not take the time to participate. So the personalization team started from scratch and built one of the first recommendation engines based on customers' own purchasing history.[23]

The engine, known as Amabot, was both a quick success and an offense to Amazon's human editorial staff. On Valentine's Day 2002 an anonymous Amazon employee placed a classified ad in a local alternative newspaper, reading:

DEAREST AMABOT
If you only had a heart to absorb our hatred. . . . Thanks for nothing, you jury-rigged rust bucket. The gorgeous messiness of flesh and blood will prevail.[24]

However much sympathy we might have for these human editors, they were not at war with a bloodless machine trying to render the quintessentially human function of judging art. Instead, it used human judgments—*millions of them*—to find that convergence with truth toward which the accidental wisdom of very large crowds asymptotically bends. The dominance of the company's recommendation engine would be implacable and inevitable, and the company appears to have built much of its brand and success on it.[25]

The other currently successful recommendation engine is the site Goodreads. As a consumer search tool, Goodreads does roughly the same thing as Amazon's recommendations, and arguably not as well—indeed, after a successful few years as a start-up, Amazon acquired it in 2013.[26] But it is interesting because of the success of its unlikely business model. From the customer-facing side, Goodreads appears to be just a blog and a social media site for book lovers to discuss books, with occasional, unobtrusive advertisements. But Goodreads earns revenue not just from advertising; it also takes a small commission when a user clicks from Goodreads to an online bookseller and buys a book. Publishers have good reason to financially support a service such as Goodreads, and not just because it generates some sales for them. Following the failure of most brick-and-mortar bookstores, publishers fear they've lost a filtering function useful to marketing their new books. Bookstores physically display books to bring them to the attention of customers who otherwise might not have known of them, giving prominent positioning to those they expect to sell the most, and allowing all of them to be browsed. Merely by stocking them, bookstores bring them to the fore from the sea of other information products competing for consumer attention. Goodreads's proprietors and the publishers who have worked with the site hope that it and businesses like it can preserve that function in the age of electronic commerce.[27]

Even if the branding needed for efficient consumer search can't be created by alternative intermediaries, the resulting need for sorting should simply shift demand curves outward for complementary products. Specifically, the need should drive more interest in artistic criticism or arts journalism, to take the place of the traditional publishers' quality-differentiated, trademarked imprints.

If some good or service is desirable, markets usually are robust mechanisms to provide it, even when changing circumstances frustrate older models. It could be that disintermediation really will destroy traditional publishers, rather than just forcing them to adapt to changing circumstances (which seems more likely). It could also be that the publishers performed functions that are still important. It seems likely, however, that disintermediated markets would manage to replicate those functions in one way or another, and probably at lower cost. The potential loss at issue here—the loss of the information contribution that publishers make by selecting books, at least in trade publishing and other ordinary retail markets—seems to be overstated. Particularly as trade publishing has become more concentrated and several of the major publishers now face pressure from public shareholders, they have long been under pressure to focus on only profitable titles, regardless of quality.[28]

Finally, a true monopolist bookseller, particularly one that destroys traditional publishers and takes their place, might be a dangerous censor. Many critics stress that Amazon's strength allows it to control what people can read.[29] Similarly, there have been allegations that powerful platform firms have suppressed conservative views.[30] In particular, former Facebook employees claimed (anonymously) that the platform suppressed right-leaning views in its "trending news" section.[31] Twitter has also been accused of censorship, and the Apple and Google app marketplaces have been accused of excluding social media or communications apps thought to facilitate hate speech.[32]

Amazon has sometimes refused to sell some books, as it did during its bitter negotiations with Hachette in the summer of 2014, though there is no evidence that it has ever excluded a book because of its content. There is a real risk that powerful content distributors might abuse their power to suit their owners' preferences or those of their allies. So, critics have urged government action against Amazon to keep it from suppressing disfavored content, and have specifically urged antitrust action.[33]

For better or worse, antitrust action to stop censorship is not legally feasible at present, because our law of monopolization—our only competition law that can reach unilateral abuses—just doesn't reach these circumstances. The law requires that a large amount of pricing power be gotten through exclusion of rivals, which effectively means exclusion of horizontal rivals that might have threatened its pricing power. By contrast, the government action these critics have in mind would challenge Amazon for restricting access in spite of anticompetitive exclusion. The concern would be the refusal to carry some products, not actions detrimental to horizontally competing book retailers. As far as American law is currently concerned, that would amount to a no-fault monopolization challenge.

A more interesting question is whether we should modify our antitrust to reach refusals to deal generally. Given the social importance of written content, perhaps we should have some special, specific rule against censorship by media monopolists. Or, perhaps we should have some sort of no-fault concentration caps or the like to ensure that diverse sources exist for sales of books. In fact, we did have a set of rules for the newspaper, radio, and television industries that were supposed to preserve diversity of content, and they were explicitly predicated on free speech and intellectual freedom. Under rules administered by the Federal Communications Commission, it was long prohibited for any person or firm to own too many licensed broadcasting entities, and also for the same entity to own any more than a few broadcasters and newspapers in the same geographic territories.[34] Those rules have been targeted by a sustained deregulatory effort, with pressure from Congress and conservative FCC leadership, but because deregulation has faced judicial challenge and popular objection, some part of those rules still exists.[35] In principle, there is no reason we could not extend a similar system of rules to book publishing, and while the FCC lacks jurisdiction to do it, Congress might adopt some such limits.[36]

While the risk of a monopolist bookseller suppressing books for their content should not be taken lightly, there are two reasons not to be too alarmed about censorship. First, merely refusing to carry a title is not censorship, and cannot by itself keep the title or its contents secret. At no time in history has it been easier or cheaper for any person who wants to disseminate ideas to do so, simply by posting them on the internet. And of course, however big it may be, Amazon is not the only book retailer. Second, suppression of books for their content is a sin not uncommonly committed by traditional publishers, whose demise at the hands of Amazon is said to have jeopardized intellectual freedom. Examples of suppression in book publishing date back generations, and it is widely thought to be more a problem now, in this age of very large publishers in very concentrated markets owned by much larger conglomerates with many conflicting interests.

21

The Threat to Writers and the
Threat to Cultural Values

There's a tendency among book publishers, especially when
making speeches on public occasions, to boast that the writer
and the publisher are both part of the same team. This, of course,
is pious nonsense. . . . A lot of people start out in book publishing believing that it's true, or at least that it ought to be true,
then have to waste time learning otherwise.

—Michael Korda, *Another Life: A Memoir of Other People*

ONE OF THE MOST poignant concerns in the eBooks controversy was
the possibility that price competition could hurt authors themselves.
Retail competition might push book prices so low that authors could
no longer earn remunerative pay for their creations, and would be
forced to seek other work that would keep them from writing. During
the eBooks case and earlier fights over digitized books, authors often
made this argument.[1]

In principle, these are serious concerns, and there is no question that
authors face the risk of exploitation by firms with power. But the evidence
is very strong that mere exposure to retail price competition won't diminish quality or quantity of writing. And with regard to the abuse of
authors by powerful firms, surely the least desirable solution is to give
publishers *more* power by allowing them to collude.

Whether authors have socially desirable incentives in given circumstances has been the subject of a rich academic literature on copyright.
Copyright law's main purpose is to ensure that authors have financial

incentives to create that are socially optimal. There is robust consensus among copyright scholars that to encourage socially optimal literary output, authors probably need less incentive than the protection they enjoy under current copyright, and a meaningful subset of those scholars have even questioned whether authors need much protection at all.[2] That is to say, most academics who study the issue think that authors would still have enough reason to keep writing if books were exposed to substantially more retail competition than they traditionally have been in the United States.

Traditionally, the argument was made as a function of the cost of producing paper books. The cost of copying and distributing paper copies would be high enough that with lead time and other advantages, publishers could recover their initial costs and continue selling copies competitively. That is, they would sell at something near their long-run average cost, and there is no reason to expect that competing firms selling their own copies of a publisher's works would have any cost advantage. The argument is bolstered by historical examples in which books have been sold profitably without any copyright protection at all.[3]

It may be that this argument was persuasive only in the days of hard copies. Back then, the cost and delay of making pirated physical copies kept copiers from denying publishers their fixed costs. Those costs fell with the rise of photocopying and other innovations, and even more now that books can be copied and delivered electronically. But to be clear, that is an argument about *piracy*, in the absence of copyright protection. Even if it really was a threat when other content industries faced similar challenges during the digital transition (a widely disputed claim), for legal and technological reasons it is not a threat in current book publishing.

Indeed, while most authors probably are disadvantaged financially— in the sense than they earn less than they might in a fully competitive market—it is not because of retail price competition, but because of the power of the publishers who set the terms of their compensation. Competition policy might have done something to improve the position of authors, but only by enforcing our merger rule during the decades of hundreds of publisher mergers. It would not help them to encourage a conspiracy among those publishers to make them more powerful yet.

It is also often argued that although *some* books will still be produced, *quality* will suffer. With tight margins, publishers will lack freedom to take chances on unknown authors or risky new projects, and will be forced to fund only the most commercially trustworthy products. But this argument is very weak. As with other products, where similar arguments have been made and disproven many times, where there is demand and reasonably well-functioning markets, demand will be satisfied. Moreover, the argument that the currently dominant Big Five publishers must be able to keep their margins in order to preserve quality is palpably absurd. There is no compelling reason to believe that publishers care about "quality" in any sense that is not incentivized by profitability—that is demonstrated by their own lists over the last several decades. As for authors, many scholars believe that nonmonetary incentives significantly drive literary production, and in some cases, more than monetary incentives. There is empirical support for that view.[4] As long as intellectual property rights are reasonably secure, it is hard to see why authors wouldn't be able to earn returns sufficient to generate socially desirable levels of creativity. And those rights are secure. Content owners have often argued that disruptive technological innovations had to be stopped because they would encourage piracy. But piracy has never been the problem that content owners predicted, and indeed, new reproduction and distribution technologies have ordinarily *expanded* sales and profits for content owners.

Finally, if the goal of limiting price competition is to support high-quality literary work, private price-fixing is not a good solution. In any chain of distribution, relationships up and down the chain are necessarily adverse to some degree. Within those chains, such excess rents as can be extracted from the ultimate sale of the product tend to be claimed by the participant with the most market power. In all except rare cases—the world's vanishingly small number of best-selling writers—meaningful market power in book distribution will not be in the hands of authors. In the case of trade publishing, it is likely to be in the hands of the five large firms that now dominate the publishing level, all of which were *Apple* defendants. Accordingly, only a very few authors will be able to represent their own interests. Where the publishers are able to give effect to their interests, they will lower output (like any other monopolist or oligopolist), which means that fewer authors will publish, and among them they will sell fewer books.

In short, authors' interests are better served by price-competitive distribution and retail markets. That competition may cost a tiny handful of the most popular authors some of their current earnings, but for others, output will increase and revenue will rise.

Authors themselves have watched this long history with rapt attention but widely varying views. If retail competitiveness and technological transition in book trades are bad for authors, one would expect them to object to those things consistently. But they have not. Individual authors' politics vary, of course, and their perspectives on markets in general are just as conflicted and complex as other people's are. But there are other reasons for their differences that might say more about whether competition in books is really so bad, or whether it threatens literary values.

Authors are not all the same, and their interests sometimes conflict. Established authors, and especially elite, top-selling authors, have a comparatively strong interest in maintaining the status quo and not much to gain from more price competitiveness in retail. Particularly now that so much of trade publishing depends on big, best-seller payoffs, top-selling authors command leverage over financial terms. They can enjoy something like bilateral monopoly bargaining power, in which case it is advantageous to them if retail prices are high. Retail prices raised to supracompetitive levels generate monopoly profits, and with substantial leverage, an author can secure a generous piece of that bigger pie. By contrast, newer and previously unpublished authors benefit from more competitive publishing and retail. Lower retail prices will mean more books sold, because regardless of their idiosyncrasies and their cultural significance, books respond to supply and demand just like other products.[5] When more units are sold, more new titles can be published as well. More opportunities will be available for new authors to find their audience. Separately, for many authors—me, for instance—the gains of authorship are really not pecuniary, or at least not exclusively so. For many, the benefits depend much more on broad exposure. For authors without star appeal who are mainly concerned with broad dissemination of their ideas, in terms of retail price, the lower, the better. Accordingly, as the publishing and retailing sectors have evolved radically, authors have had widely different opinions on the changes.

Often, authors have welcomed competitiveness and innovation. During the price-maintenance episodes in nineteenth-century publishing, authors were conflicted among themselves whether it was in their best interests. In particular, they largely opposed the major retail price-fixing arrangement in Britain and favored its repeal. Likewise, as the publishers have grown larger and more commercial over the past century, authors have ordinarily been adversarial. They have generally favored a less powerful, more competitive publishing sector. As long ago as 1947, the socialist writer James Farrell warned that because of the publishers' growth and commercialization, "in the future it will be impossible for writers to retain any integrity and . . . American writing will become merely a success chronicle of commercialized writing."[6] After consolidation in publishing took off in the 1980s and 1990s, it met sustained opposition from authors' groups. The Authors Guild, a major trade organization of writers, went so far as to argue in 1979 that further consolidation in publishing should be illegal, in part because it impaired the variety and quality of books published.[7] That was so even though the publishers already faced substantial pressure from their newly powerful distributors, the mall stores Waldenbooks and B. Dalton. That position is in tension with the view many authors took of the *Apple* litigation, when they seemed to regard the publishers as victims in need of protection and, above all, as their allies.

In these latter days, as self-publication has become much more feasible, those few prominent authors who've chosen to self-publish or to publish with disruptive alternatives have met with enthusiasm from authors and others eager to see change in traditional publishing. But the reaction is different when the alternative publisher happens to be Amazon. "When I signed with Amazon," said Barry Eisler, a best-selling novelist who left traditional publishing in 2011 to sign with an Amazon imprint, "those 'attaboys' turned to cries of 'Hypocrisy!' and 'Eisler is a sellout!' and that sort of thing."[8]

Even with regard to the *Apple* debate, in which formal authors' groups were uniformly opposed to the government's case, and many or perhaps most individual authors agreed, there were those who felt differently. Eisler, for example, berated the traditional publishers, arguing that Amazon's inauguration of discount eBooks was beneficial to both authors and the reading public. Eisler—a Cornell law graduate and formerly a covert CIA operative—became a best-selling spy novelist under deals with major firms. But he surprised many when he turned down a large advance from St. Martin's Press, an imprint of Macmillan, to take an alternative publishing deal with Amazon.[9] He is candid that his own motives are not heroic, and that he thinks the choice he made will be most lucrative. But he also plainly thinks as more authors follow him, it will benefit publishing and society.

More generally, the major authors' groups that have opposed digitization represent only a tiny percentage of authors with rights at stake. The Authors Guild, for example, represents only eight thousand authors, but hundreds of thousands of authors have books currently in copyright. The vast majority of them have very little expectation of earning further profits from their books, but more or less all of them have a strong interest in their books being ever more widely distributed and read.[10]

22

The Creeping Profusion
of Externalities

The village cobbler [is] more precious than a pair of boots.

—Archie Green, *Torching the Fink Books and Other Essays
on Vernacular Culture*

NONE OF THE TECHNOCRATIC points of detail that have consumed the last several chapters can explain the passion with which many opposed the *Apple* case, any more than they explain the long human struggle with capitalism itself. The case was so painful and so captured the popular attention because it was not really about cheap consumer goods. It was about the aesthetic and emotional significance of our habits of consumption, the physical and intangible decor of our intimate lives, and centers of community that preserve "the longstanding link between commerce and place."[1] Commerce is the vessel of social experience, it is the mechanism of class in America, and it occurs in modes and forums that define community. Change and loss within those traditions feel somber in ways that cold theory struggles to capture.

For example, technological change poses some threat to the paper book. Opinions are not uniform, but there is a fair consensus that we may see it decline to some degree in the near future.[2] At some point, production of new physical books may cease completely or become limited to narrow, specialty products such as fine art or photography books. The simple reason is cost. Bound paper books are expensive to produce and distribute. But books are cherished objects of almost mystical significance, and life without them would be qualitatively different. If they do disappear, other beloved institutions could be lost as well. Bookstores have cultural value far beyond their net receipts, as meeting places and literary centers. The comparatively expert persons who own or work in them represent special cultural assets.

These are local instances of much more general ravages of capitalism. The powerful discount retailers that arose in the middle and late twentieth century brought with them the death of downtown shopping areas, especially in smaller towns, and along with them we have lost ways of life, such as small entrepreneurship and the family farm. Many of us as consumers like all those things and mourn their loss, but we struggle to assume the cost of preserving them (in the face of lower-cost discount competition) as a component of our own willingness to pay. The fact that antitrust almost insists on competition in tension with these other values quickly devolves into a complex of other problems. Retail market participants fail to internalize the harms that their purchases impose on third parties, such as declines in product quality, loss of small-town neighborhoods, environmental injuries, and increased output of undesirable goods such as cigarettes, gambling, and junk food. Most poignant of all is a problem that at least superficially has the same contours as these others: labor and income inequality. Progressives who believe in competition policy struggle with our current solutions to inequality in labor, and in related areas such as family farm policy, where we have sought to protect the weak from abuse.[3]

I will not work through the dry tedium of economists' proposed policy solutions to these problems. Instead I will note that, in working out the inner tensions at the heart of the *Apple* case, which reflected the anxiety that has followed competition throughout its history, one realizes that a defense of the case becomes in some sense an apologetics for capitalism itself. And fittingly for problems that are essentially spiritual in nature, it seems useful to respond to them not with arguments but with a story.

The ocean sailing industry of the nineteenth century was storied, with great commercial significance since dim antiquity as well as an intimate link with humankind's own history and culture. Though the transition lasted through most of the nineteenth century, sailing ships were doomed by the coming of steam power. Historians differ over exactly how and when it happened, because it required decades of technological improvements and because certain factors other than technological change were at play.[4] The end began during a long period of technological improvements starting in about 1840, abetted by naval arms races in Europe and the American Civil War. It was necessary to advance beyond the paddle-wheel propulsion of the first steamships to screw-drive propellers, to build ships of iron instead of wood, and above all, to increase the power and efficiency of steam engines. The final step was the perfection in about 1870 of the compound engine, with steel boilers capable of high-pressure operation, which could deliver much more power, much more efficiently than its predecessors.[5] When all that was achieved, a model had been found that would spell the quick demise of the ancient sailing industry. For one thing, steam power allowed for ships made of iron, and iron ships could be made much larger (and thus with potentially much greater efficiency), without the structural problems that preclude wooden ships of more than about three hundred feet in length. Steamships can also travel the shortest route between two points, without regard to the winds, and technological improvements throughout the late nineteenth century steadily widened their dominance in speed. Most important was an advantage that sailing ships could never match. Unlike sail, which depends on the fickle wind for departure and arrival times, steamships can leave when they like and arrive with greater predictability. Steam carriers could therefore offer their customers the regular, predictable schedules they desired.

When they came into their own in the 1870s, the new steamships transformed shipping with a cruel and efficient brutality. It took some time, as sail developed its own technological and operational improvements and the perfection of steam technology took a few decades. But once effective steam competition was feasible, a bitter price war ensued. Sailing ship owners slashed their prices, but ultimately the conflict ended the business of sailing ships as a living industry.[6]

Sailing ships were vessels of commerce, but they were also many people's livelihoods, and they were entwined in literary and popular culture. Indeed, for whatever reason, sail took on a more significant role than other culturally prominent trades and technologies. In English literature it inspired an elaborate genre of fiction, especially during the nineteenth century, comprising work by Joseph Conrad and Herman Melville, among others. Even now it retains a certain romance that steam and diesel-powered shipping would never enjoy. Perhaps this is because the transition from sail to steam signified the overall social and aesthetic transformation of the coming machine age and the Industrial Revolution. In some respects it was wildly exciting and promising, like other technological watersheds were. (Likewise, the mystique of the machine age surrounded some of the earliest progenitors of electronic books.) But in other ways it was dark. It brought with it the demoralizing reduction and unitization of human workers in the face of mechanization and ever larger industry. The poignancy in a folktale of the day was that John Henry won in his heroic struggle against the steam-powered rock drill, but then collapsed and died.

And yet, our sense of moral loss over the transition probably would not compel us to prefer some other outcome. Most of us, at least at this historical remove, would not say that operators of steamships and sailing ships should have been allowed to collude to keep their prices up in order to preserve sail as a living technology. Advancing shipping technology was critical to the expansion of international trade during the nineteenth century, allowing for division of labor and specialization on an international level and enabling economic development in poor nations.[7] But even if the particular economic advancement were not important in purely economic terms, private self-help to preserve that older technology for its own sake would be self-defeating. It would be a chaotic and dangerous use of society's resources if we diverted perhaps many millions or billions of dollars' worth of efficiency gains every time some change jeopardizes other values, however sincere they might be. And for reasons we've seen before, it would seem unwise to leave those kinds of judgments in the hands of firms in the industry.

But perhaps this analogy is too simple and too clumsy. I do not mean to imply that because mechanized ocean ships were tolerable, unmediated, unbridled economic change is therefore also fine. After all, the cost of the great generalization is not in the loss of a specific technology itself. Many thousands or millions of individual technologies or ways of doing business have come and gone without any tears. It is not even the loss of some way of doing something. It is the human cost of those transitions. Sometimes they are small, sometimes they are large but tolerable, on balance, and then sometimes again they seem very large indeed.

Consider a different historical case, one that was culturally significant and wrecked another old tradition, and had perhaps more complicated implications. It certainly had close parallels to the facts in *Apple*. This time, the change was not strictly technological so much as organizational. At the turn of the twentieth century, retail distribution in the United States was mainly in the hands of very small retailers, and the vast majority of them owned and personally ran only one store. Much of what they sold was unbranded, and they got their goods from small jobbers and wholesalers who were not themselves manufacturers. That all changed radically over the next few decades. Empowered in part by the rise of branding and a variety of technological advancements, the size of retail organizations and the number of new "chain" stores had begun to grow in the late nineteenth century, and they increased rapidly after World War I. Among them was a firm that would become the largest retailer in America and hold that position for many years, the Great Atlantic & Pacific Tea Company (A&P). The damage the new chains did to traditional retailers and local communities gave birth to a political fervor that rivalled the agitation for the Sherman Act. Popular opposition to new, low-priced retail competition was so strong that in 1903 the Sears, Roebuck catalog promised shoppers that their mail-order items would be shipped in plain, unmarked wrappers.[8]

Though the extent and speed of its growth was not widely appreciated until congressional hearings in 1914 and 1915, and though it was judged by experts of the day to be still "in its infancy" as late as 1922, the chain store movement was already an issue in American politics by the turn of the twentieth century.[9] It was discussed in popular literature and was a formal presidential platform issue as early as 1912.[10] Even in its first decades, A&P was large. It operated seventy tea and coffee stores in the 1870s, and by 1900 it operated hundreds of stores and had integrated to perform its own wholesaling and produce many of its own products. But it was during the 1920s that the number of chain stores exploded.

At the time, small business was a more potent political force than it is now.[11] It waged a lengthy and not infrequently successful war against the chain stores, in both legislatures and courtrooms and through its own collective self-help measures. One success was a set of punitive tax laws adopted by a few dozen states during the 1930s that imposed taxes that got progressively larger the more stores a chain had. The movement also sought legal protections to neutralize the chain retailers' advantages. The chief complaint was that the chains, because of their size and the volume of their purchases, could extort unfairly low prices from their suppliers. Small business wanted legal protection against discriminatory wholesale prices, which they got in the Robinson-Patman Act of 1935.[12] They also wanted legal permission for RPM, to stop price-cutting competitors such as the chains. Sometime after the Supreme Court outlawed RPM in in 1911, small merchants and wholesalers secured federal and state fair-trade laws that largely reauthorized it.

Despite those successes, the opposition effort didn't really work, at least not in the long term. The A&P and other chains continued to grow, in spite of unfavorable tax rules and legal restraints on preferential wholesale terms. Small merchants and wholesalers managed to defend their territory throughout the 1930s and 1940s, but by the 1950s, the future for small merchants was largely written. Consumers found discount prices just too alluring.[13] Historians differ widely on whether this should be judged a failure in political terms, and on what its real consequences were. But at least on some levels, the Depression-era effort to stave off mass retail was something of a "rearguard action" meant to "preserve a dying society."[14]

Whether the changed marketplaces and communities that mass retail introduced were good or bad is a matter of perspective, but it is not a matter for simple judgments. On the one hand, mass retail changed cultural and community traditions and had impacts on labor and the distribution of wealth. That was manifested again more recently and all the more dramatically in the rise of very aggressive, very low-cost discount stores such as Walmart, and then discount club stores, and then, as if by some reductio ad absurdum, the dollar stores. These new chains have largely destroyed small-town downtown neighborhoods, and the products they sell seem to be ever-falling in quality. There is no doubt that they put massive and perhaps monopsonistic pressure on their suppliers. But the most serious injury may be their pay and labor standards. It has recently come to light that many retail workers require welfare assistance to survive.[15]

On the other hand, a rapidly expanding population depends on improvements in both technology and the distribution of goods, very literally for its survival. As a case in point, the small merchants of the turn of the twentieth century could not supply fresh produce at affordable prices, and it was not until the arrival of the chain stores that most city dwellers of the day had access to it.[16] There is also reason to question the standard account of cause and effects, at least with regard to the original anti–chain store movement and those who benefitted from it. The complaint was that chain stores could secure the same discount on their goods that manufacturers gave to wholesalers, because the chains could perform their own wholesale functions. So the main opposition to the chains came not from workers or local communities but from small wholesalers, who themselves contributed little to Main Street culture or local employment, and had no real reason to continue once other firms could do their work more cheaply. At this remove, it is useful to consider the conduct that was objected to during the political movement, and why anyone would try to stop such things. The state chain-store taxes, for example, sometimes punitively taxed particularly despised chain-store retailing innovations such as "self-service" grocery aisles, and federal prosecutions against A&P in the 1950s tried to stop it from doing things such as canning its own vegetables.[17]

There may also be something to the fact that in the rise of mass distribution was formed the consciousness of the "consumer" as a class. Nowadays we hear talk of "consumerism" as a debasement, involving loss of culture and turning average people into sheep.[18] Nevertheless, the rise of the consumer served as a counterbalance in American politics, and perhaps a more successful one than the Jacksonian populist ethos of small entrepreneurs entitled to protection of their own way of living.[19]

Conclusion

Real Ironies

The antitrust laws have not been effective in the real world. . . .
All antitrust law enforcement under any plan depends on the
public attitude.

—Thurman Arnold, "Symposium"

IT IS UNSETTLING that Thurman Arnold wrote those words years *after*
having served as the most celebrated, tireless, and influential antitrust enforcer in the nation's history. When he was appointed to run the Justice
Department's Antitrust Division in the late 1930s, Yale law professor
Arnold was already something of a celebrity. His widely read book *The
Folklore of Capitalism,* with its sardonic evisceration of common economic superstitions, had made him famous. His appointment to revitalize
the antitrust effort was a decisive break and a new direction in Franklin
Roosevelt's program to confront the Great Depression, marking the transition between Roosevelt's First New Deal and the second one. When the
Supreme Court in 1935 held the National Industrial Recovery Act unconstitutional, it threw out the initial New Deal's centerpiece. The NIRA had
effectively repealed the antitrust laws and replaced competition with
government-sanctioned self-regulation. It entailed a vision of central planning that largely rejected capitalism itself, identifying competition as
having been a cause of the Depression. But even before the Court rejected
it, the law seemed not to be working and had become unpopular. When
the economy dipped into a renewed recession in 1937, it became clear that

a new direction was needed, and Roosevelt changed the nation's course drastically.

Leaving behind almost entirely the planning focus of the First New Deal, Roosevelt installed Arnold in 1938. He also called for creation of the Temporary National Economic Committee, a massive, three-year undertaking to study the economy. The TNEC, on which Arnold and a dozen other leading lights served, issued a forty-three-volume report generally reviving concern for monopoly and calling to reestablish competition as the fundamental policy. Meanwhile, with the backing of a very personally engaged president and a sympathetic Congress, Arnold oversaw the largest increase in the Antitrust Division's size and budget in its history. During his five years in office, the Division brought hundreds of cases against firms throughout the economy, many of them grand affairs openly designed to restructure whole industries. The program enjoyed extensive courtroom success, and in the course of Arnold's work, the Division worked out a newly coherent and consistent theoretical vision for enforcement policy. It is largely the model still in place.

So one might wonder why Arnold, writing some years after his Justice Department service in that 1949 symposium of the American Economic Association, would say that the law had failed. His judgment may have been clouded by personal feelings, because by all appearances, he been forced out of government. Apparently, many people felt that his aggressive enforcement against basic industries jeopardized the American war effort as the nation geared up to join World War II. Eventually, he left the Justice Department for a judicial appointment to the federal appellate court for the DC Circuit, then left that post after only two years to return to a private litigation practice. Allegedly, he explained, in his very characteristic way, that he left that prestigious lifetime appointment because he would "rather talk to damn fools than listen to them." At any rate, his judicial appointment is now widely understood not as an honor but as a case of having been "kicked upstairs" to satisfy his critics. So maybe his judgment of antitrust failure is too harsh, and tainted by his own bitterness.

But in fact, the contributors in that 1949 symposium all largely agreed that antitrust had not worked well, and they included some of the most influential lawyers, economists, and enforcement officials of the day.

And importantly, it is not clear at all that Arnold was forced out over the war effort. Business interests lobbied continually for his removal during his time in office, and their arguments were not about war preparations. They complained that they could not perform well under competitive vigor. In other words, they made the same complaints about antitrust enforcement that we have seen in all kinds of sectors in examples throughout this book. And those complaints seem to have been effective, making it much harder for antitrust to work. Antitrust has never worked especially well on any sustained basis, it seems. And the cause is the public attitude.

This book has been about one basic problem: popular doubts of antitrust are based on criticisms of the wrong thing. They attack a microeconomic policy—the antitrust policy that favors competition and prohibits private steps to limit it. They say that the competition it protects destroys other values important to society, but the values most often of concern will not be better protected by deadening competition. In *Apple,* for example, permitting the publishers to bargain collectively with Amazon would not have resulted in better compensation for authors, the subsidizing of more and better literature, and the protection of small business—all of which were goals identified by the defendants. Instead, it would have just meant there were two monopolies instead of one, and neither of them much concerned about the public interest. The main function of such bilateral monopolies is to divide between themselves whatever consumer wealth they can confiscate.

Yet, competition indisputably causes harms to individuals and other losses that people sincerely care about. And some values probably are frustrated by marketplace dysfunctions such as externalities or informational problems. People will not support the policy if they systematically lose under it. Among the most serious of the losses that critics identify are wealth inequality and stubborn unemployment, especially during times of marketplace transition. Those problems seem to be side effects of unmoderated competition, and they are real. So a better approach, which could sustainably preserve competition policy in our democracy, is not to attack competition but also not to ignore its regrets. The better approach is to favor competition while also reestablishing a safety net to protect its economic losers.

Moreover, there are sometimes genuine problems in the doctrinal law of antirust that require correction. One of them was important in this book. Without a viable monopolization rule, there was no satisfying answer to the *Apple* critics' complaints that however bad price-fixing might seem, Amazon seems dangerous, too. Without a monopolization law (and effective merger program), an economy will be prone to accumulations of power in individual firms that can be exercised unilaterally, leaving buyers and suppliers no resort to protect themselves other than collective self-help. But that is no good reason to give up on competition as a policy, or to decide that markets are the problem; it is a reason to fix the law and enforce it for real.

Instead of telling the public that losses caused by markets are irrelevant, or denying that the law to preserve them is imperfect, we should make an appeal to popular consensus that focuses on the good that markets do while acknowledging their discontents. A democratically sustainable and humanly decent competition policy could adopt measures to confront existing flaws, such as progressive fiscal and social safety net policies. We must recognize, too, that long-term sustainability requires that a competition law prosecutes not only low-hanging fruit such as the publishers' conspiracy in *Apple*. It must also constrain other accumulations of power, and must have vigorous monopolization and merger programs along with its prohibition of conspiracies. Those things are difficult and problematic, but without them there is reason to doubt whether we should have competition policy at all.

An approach like that would highlight that many popular doubts of individual antitrust cases are driven by fears of the wrong thing. They are fears of price competition and the legal rules meant to keep it rigorous, and so they presume that problems caused by competition will be fixed by making competition stop. But they should let competition do what it does well.

NOTES

ACKNOWLEDGMENTS

INDEX

Notes

Introduction

1. The term "eBook" has been rendered in many ways—ebook, eBook, Ebook, e-book, E-book, and probably other ways as well. At first I avoided writing it as "eBook," with a little "e" and a big "B" and no hyphen, because that seemed to preference a branding habit of the Apple computer corporation. That seemed somehow unfitting. But in the course of writing the book I learned that it was also the preference of the late Michael Hart, who founded the free, nonprofit digital library called Project Gutenberg in the early 1970s. Hart, a visionary and humanitarian, is widely said to have distributed the first electronic book. See Michael S. Hart, "Project Gutenberg Mission Statement," http://www.gutenberg.org/wiki/Gutenberg:Project_Gutenberg_Mission_Statement_by _Michael_Hart.

2. Steve Coll, "Citizen Bezos," *New York Review of Books,* July 10, 2014.

3. Sara Forden, "U.S. Sues Apple for eBook Pricing as Three Firms Settle," *Bloomberg,* Apr. 17, 2012, http://www.bloomberg.com/news/2012-04-17/u-s-sues-apple-for-ebook -pricing-as-three-firms-settle.html, quoting Herbert Hovenkamp.

4. Judith Resnik et al., "Constructing Courts: Architecture, the Ideology of Judging, and the Public Sphere," in *Law, Culture and Visual Studies,* ed. Richard K. Sherwin and Anne Wagner (New York: Springer, 2013), 515; Judith Resnik, "Courts: In and Out of Sight, Site, and Cite," *Villanova Law Review* 53 (2008): 771–810.

5. See, e.g., Thomas Catan, "Justice Department Confirms E-Book Pricing Probe," *Wall Street Journal,* Dec. 8, 2011; Barbara E. Hernandez, "Did Apple Collude with Publishers to Fix Prices on E-Books?," *Mediashift,* Oct. 3, 2011, http://mediashift.org/2011 /10/did-apple-collude-with-publishers-to-fix-prices-on-e-books276/.

6. See Charles E. Schumer, "Memo to DOJ: Drop the Apple E-Books Suit," *Wall Street Journal,* July 17, 2012; "The E-Book Price-Fixing Conspiracy," *New York Times,* July 13, 2013, A18; L. Gordon Crovitz, "Apple's 30% E-Book Commission Is 100% Legal," *Wall Street Journal,* June 9, 2013.

7. On all these points, see Chris Sagers, "#LOLNothingMatters," *Antitrust Bulletin* 63 (2018): 7–48, 14–20.

8. See, e.g., Barry C. Lynn, "The Real Bad Guy in the E-Book Price Fixing Case," *Slate,* Apr. 12, 2012, https://slate.com/technology/2012/04/e-book-price-fixing-amazon-is-the -real-bad-guy.html; Olivia LaVecchia and Stacy Mitchell, "Amazon's Stranglehold: How the Company's Tightening Grip Is Stifling Competition, Eroding Jobs, and Threatening Communities" (Institute for Local Self-Reliance report, 2016), https://ilsr .org/wp-content/uploads/2016/11/ILSR_AmazonReport_final.pdf.

9. See William E. Kovacic, "Failed Expectations: The Troubled Past and Uncertain Future of the Sherman Act as a Tool for Deconcentration," *Iowa Law Review* 74 (1989): 1105–1150, 1107–1109.

10. The public also disapproved of the breakup of the vertically integrated Hollywood studio system in the 1940s and was ambivalent at best about the breakup of AT&T in 1983. See United States v. Paramount Pictures, Inc., 334 U.S. 131 (1948); United States v. AT&T Co., 552 F. Supp. 131, 226–27 (D.D.C. 1982) (consent decree), aff'd sub nom. Maryland v. United States, 460 U.S. 1001 (1983). For discussion of these cases and their popular reception, see Tim Wu, *The Master Switch: The Rise and Fall of Information Empires* (New York: Vintage, 2010), 160–161. Much of the public also opposed a case that I discuss later, United States v. Microsoft, Inc., 253 F.3d 34 (D.C. Cir. 2001) (en banc).

11. There is some international comparative evidence that antitrust lowers real consumer prices and generates several other benefits. See Oz Shy, *Industrial Organization* (Cambridge, MA: MIT Press 1995); Jonathan B. Baker, "Market Power in the U.S. Economy Today," Washington Center for Equitable Growth, Mar. 20, 2017, https://equitable growth.org/market-power-in-the-u-s-economy-today/.

12. For a discussion of the difficulties of empirical antitrust study, see John E. Kwoka Jr., "The Attack on Antitrust Policy and Consumer Welfare: A Response to Crandall and Winston" (Northeastern University Department of Economics Working Paper No. 03- 008June 2003), 2–3.

13. Naked price cartels are prevalent, last longer than theory predicts, and cause significant harm. See Jonathan B. Baker, "The Case for Antitrust Enforcement," *Journal of Economic Perspectives,* Fall 2003, 27, 28–30, 42–45; John M. Connor and Robert H. Lande, "Cartels as Rational Business Strategy: Crime Pays," *Cardozo Law Review* 34 (2012): 427–490; Margaret Levenstein and Valerie Suslow, "What Determines Cartel Success," *Journal of Economic Literature* 44 (2006): 43–95. There is also growing evidence that mergers and acquisitions produce no significant benefits and that horizontal ones cause substantial harm at lower concentration levels than previously thought. See, respectively, Dennis C. Mueller, "Merger Policy in the United States: A Reconsideration," *Review of Industrial Organization* 12 (1997): 655–685; John Kwoka, *Mergers, Merger Control, and Remedies: A Retrospective Analysis of U.S. Policy* (Cambridge, MA: MIT Press, 2014).

14. On this complaint, see William E. Kovacic, "Rating the Competition Agencies: What Constitutes Good Performance?," *George Mason Law Review* 16 (2009): 903–926, 905; Kwoka, *Mergers,* 2.

15. See, e.g., George J. Stigler, "The Economic Effects of the Antitrust Laws," *Journal of Law and Economics* 9 (1966): 225–258, 236; Thurman Arnold, "Symposium," *American Economic Review* 39 (1949): 689–724. On the occasional bitterness of the controversy,

compare Robert W. Crandall and Clifford Winston, "Does Antitrust Policy Improve Consumer Welfare? Assessing the Evidence," *Journal of Economic Perspectives,* Fall 2003, 3; Baker, *Case for Antitrust Enforcement;* Kwoka, *Mergers;* Gregory J. Werden, "The Effect of Antitrust Policy on Consumer Welfare: What Crandall and Winston Overlook" (AEI-Brookings Joint Center for Regulatory Studies Related Pub. 04-09, April 2004); Jonathan B. Baker, letter in *Journal of Economic Perspectives,* Winter 2005, 243. See also Russell W. Pittman and Gregory J. Werden, "The Divergence of SIC Industries from Antitrust Markets: Indications from Justice Department Merger Cases," *Economic Letters* 33 (1990): 33-35.

16. See Clayton M. Christensen, *The Innovator's Dilemma: When New Technologies Cause Great Firms to Fail* (Cambridge, MA: Harvard Business Review Press, 1997); Kenneth Arrow, "Economic Welfare and the Allocation of Resources to Invention," in *The Rate and Direction of Economic Activity: Economic and Social Factors,* ed. R. R. Nelson (Cambridge, MA: National Bureau of Economic Research, 1962); Richard Gilbert, "Looking for Mr. Schumpeter: Where Are We in the Competition-Innovation Debate?," in *Innovation Policy and the Economy,* ed. Adam B. Jaffe et al. (Cambridge, MA: MIT Press, 2006), 159; Constantinos Markides, "Disruptive Innovation: In Need of Better Theory," *Product Innovation Management* 23 (2006): 19-25.

17. For a thoughtful mediation on this point, see Michael S. Jacobs, "An Essay on the Normative Foundations of Antitrust Economics," *North Carolina Law Review* 74 (1995): 219-266.

18. Arnold, "Symposium," 690-691.

1. The Great Generalization

Epigraph: Mark De Wolfe Howe, ed., *Holmes-Pollock Letters: The Correspondence of Mr. Justice Holmes and Sir Frederick Pollock, 1874-1932* (Cambridge, MA: Belknap Press, 1961).

1. See William Blackstone, *Commentaries on the Laws of England,* vol. 1 (Oxford, 1765), 60; Samuel von Pufendorf, *Of the Law of Nature and Nations,* trans. Basil Kennett (Oxford, 1672; London, 1729), 540; Perry Dane, "A Blegging Blog about Blood in Bologna," *ReligiousLeftLaw* (blog), Dec. 16, 2013, http://www.religiousleftlaw.com/2013/12/blood-in-bologna.html; United States v. Kirby, 74 U.S. 482, 487 (1868) (citing Edmund Plowden, *Commentaries* (1761)).

2. Frank H. Easterbrook, "Statutes' Domains," *University of Chicago Law Review* 50 (1983): 533-552, 535.

3. Frederick Schauer, "A Critical Guide to No Vehicles in the Park," *NYU Law Review* 83 (2008): 1109-1134, 1109.

4. H. L. A. Hart, "Positivism and the Separation of Law and Morals," *Harvard Law Review* 71 (1958): 593-629, 607.

5. Lon Fuller, "Positivism and Fidelity to Law—A Reply to Professor Hart," *Harvard Law Review* 71 (1958): 630-672, 663.

6. Compare Frederick Schauer, "Formalism," *Yale Law Journal* 97 (1988): 509-548, 526; J. E. Penner, "The 'Bundle of Rights' Picture of Property," *UCLA Law Review* 43

(1996): 711–820, 790; Abner S. Greene, "The Work of Knowledge," *Notre Dame Law Review* 72 (1997): 1479–1495, 1487–1488.

7. For an ambulance, see Lawrence M. Solan, "Law, Language and Lenity," *William and Mary Law Review* 40 (1998): 57–144, 79; Jeremy Waldron, "Vagueness in Law and Language: Some Philosophical Issues," *California Law Review* 82 (1994): 509–540, 537. For a baby stroller, see Richard H. Fallon, "The Meaning of Legal 'Meaning' and Its Implications for Theories of Legal Interpretation," *University of Chicago Law Review* 82 (2015): 1235–1308, 1256. For a wheelchair, compare H. L. A. Hart, *The Concept of Law* (Oxford: Oxford University Press, 1961), 104; Anthony D'Amato, "Legal Uncertainty," *California Law Review* 71 (1983): 1–55, 40n79. For an ice cream truck, see David A. Strauss, "Does Meaning Matter?," *Harvard Law Review Forum* 129 (2015): 94–97, 95. For a bicycle, see Adrian Vermeule, "The Cycles of Statutory Interpretation," *University of Chicago Law Review* 68 (2001): 149–192, 154. For a police bicycle, see Philip P. Frickey, "Faithful Interpretation," *Washington University Law Quarterly* 73 (1995): 1085–1094, 1085n2.

8. See generally American Bar Association, "Antitrust and Organized Labor," in *Handbook on the Scope of Antitrust* (Washington, DC: ABA Book Publishing, 2015), 193–206; Theodore St. Antoine, "Connell: Antitrust at the Expense Labor Law," *Virginia Law Review* 62 (1976): 603–632, 604–608.

9. See, e.g., Brief for Law and Economics and Antitrust Scholars as Amici Curiae in Support of Appellant, O'Bannon v. NCAA, 802 F.3d 1049 (9th Cir. 2015); cf. Peter C. Carstensen and Bette Roth, "The Per Se Legality of Some Naked Restraints: A [Re]conceptualization of the Antitrust Analysis of Cartelistic Organizations," *Antitrust Bulletin* 45 (2000): 349–436, 402–408.

10. Gary Becker, "The NCAA: A Cartel in Sheepskin Clothing," *Business Week,* Sept. 14, 1987, 24; Taylor Branch, "The Shame of College Sports," *Atlantic Monthly,* Oct. 2011, 80, 82; Roger D. Blair and Jeffrey L. Harrison, *Monopsony in Law and Economics,* 2nd ed. (Princeton, NJ: Princeton University Press, 2010), 1n3.

11. That long and controversial conflict has only partly been solved. See generally Gabriel A. Feldman, "The Misuse of the Less Restrictive Alternative Inquiry in Rule of Reason Analysis," *American University Law Review* 58 (2009): 561–632; Herbert Hovenkamp, "Competitor Collaboration after California Dental Association," *University of Chicago Legal Forum* 149 (2000): 149–190.

12. Currently, doctors who maintain their own practices cannot bargain collectively with anyone, because only "employees" come within the "labor exemption" from antitrust law.

13. Nitasha Tiku, "Publishers Could Get a New Weapon against Facebook and Google," *Wired,* Mar. 7, 2018.

14. Newspaper Preservation Act, Pub. L. No. 91-353, 84 Stat. 466 (1970). See generally John C. Busterna and Robert G. Picard, *Joint Operating Agreements: The Newspaper Preservation Act and Its Application* (Santa Barbara, CA: Praeger, 1993).

15. United States v. Addyston Pipe & Steel Co., 85 F. 271 (6th Cir. 1898), aff'd 175 U.S. 211 (1899).

16. Specifically, in United States v. Socony-Vacuum Oil Co., 310 U.S. 150 (1940).

17. On the simplicity of the product, see generally Technical Advisory Group, Cast Iron Soil Pipe Institute, *Cast Iron Soil Pipe and Fittings Handbook* (Chattanooga, TN: Author, 2006), 1–5.

18. See Naomi R. Lamoreaux, *The Great Merger Movement in American Business, 1895–1904* (Cambridge: Cambridge University Press, 1985), 46–62.

19. *Addyston Pipe,* 85 F. at 283–84.

20. *Addyston Pipe,* 85 F. at 291.

21. *Addyston Pipe,* 85 F. at 292–93.

22. *Addyston Pipe,* 85 F. at 284–88.

23. Nat'l Soc'y of Prof'l Eng'rs v. United States, 435 U.S. 679, 692 (1978).

24. United States v. Phila. Nat'l Bank, 374 U.S. 321, 371 (1963); see also United States v. Socony-Vacuum Oil Co., 310 U.S. 150, 222 (1940) ("Whatever may be its peculiar problems and characteristics, the Sherman Act . . . establishes one uniform rule applicable to all industries alike").

25. *Socony-Vacuum Oil Co.,* 310 U.S. at 222.

2. In the First Ships

Epigraph: Werner Sombart, *Why Is There No Socialism in the United States?,* trans. Patricia M. Hocking and C. T. Husbands, trans. (1906; London: Palgrave Macmillan, 1976).

1. For careful histories of American economic thought, see Carl N. Degler, *Out of Our Past: The Forces That Shaped Modern America,* 3rd ed. (New York: Harper Perennial, 1983); Joseph Dorfman, *The Economic Mind in American Civilization,* 5 vols. (New York: Augustus M. Kelley Publishing, 1946–1959); Herbert Hovenkamp, *Enterprise and American Law, 1836–1937* (Cambridge, MA: Harvard University Press, 1991); Thomas K. McCraw, "Capitalism in America," in *Creating Modern Capitalism,* ed. Thomas K. McCraw (Cambridge, MA: Harvard University Press, 1998).

2. See, e.g., John Higham, "The Cult of the 'American Consensus': Homogenizing Our History," *Commentary,* Feb. 1, 1959; Staughton Lynd, "The New American Historians," *Commentary,* Sept. 1, 1962, reviewing John Higham, ed., *The Reconstruction of American History* (New York: Harper, 1962); Irwin Unger, "The 'New Left' and American History: Some Recent Trends in United States Historiography," *American Historical Review* 72 (1967): 1237–1263; James Weinstein, "Socialism's Hidden Heritage: Scholarship Reinforces Political Mythology," in *For a New America: Essays in History and Politics from Studies on the Left, 1959–1967,* ed. James Weinstein and David W. Eakins (New York: Random House, 1970), 221; James Weinstein, "Anti-War Sentiment and the Socialist Party, 1917–1918," *Political Science Quarterly* 74 (1959): 215–239.

3. See, e.g., Weinstein, "Socialism's Hidden Heritage" (making this case); Unger, "'New Left,'" 1250–1251 (so characterizing the view of the left revisionists).

4. Higham, "Cult of 'American Consensus'"; Weinstein, "Socialism's Hidden Heritage," 252. Even some consensus-view historians disapproved of the lack of intellectual diversity. Unger, "'New Left,'" 1243–1244.

5. Or, indeed, that the "people" even exist. As Staughton Lynd says, the genuine radicals in American history declared that "my country is the world." Staughton Lynd, *Intellectual Origins of American Radicalism,* new ed. (Cambridge: Cambridge University Press, 2009), xix-xx. Cf. Isaiah Berlin, *The Hedgehog and the Fox: An Essay on Tolstoy's Theory of History,* 2nd ed. (1953; Princeton, NJ: Princeton University Press, 2013).

6. Except for slavery, but the point is that the class that dominated since colonial times was more or less a fully formed bourgeoisie. Marx himself said so. See Arthur M. Schlessinger Jr., *The Cycles of American History* (New York: Houghton Mifflin, 1986), 232, quoting Karl Marx, *From the Economic Manuscripts of 1857-59.*

7. Gary Gerstle, "The Protean Character of American Liberalism," *American Historical Review* 99 (1994): 1043-1073.

8. Hovenkamp, *Enterprise,* 4; see generally Richard Hofstadter, *The American Political Tradition* (New York: Vintage, 1989).

9. On economics in ancient cultures, see Joseph Schumpeter, *A History of Economic Analysis,* rev. ed. (Oxford: Oxford University Press, 1996), 51-72; Karl Polanyi, "Aristotle Discovers the Economy," in *Trade and Market in the Early Empires: Economies and History and Theory,* ed. Karl Polanyi et al. (Chicago: Henry Regnery, 1971), 64-94.

10. On the theory of value, see Raymond de Roover, "The Concept of the Just Price: Theory and Economic Policy," *Journal of Economic History* 18 (1958): 418-434; Raymond de Roover, "Monopoly Theory Prior to Adam Smith: A Revision," *Quarterly Journal of Economics* 65 (1951): 492-524. On monopoly and anticompetitive conduct, see de Roover, "Monopoly Theory," 498, noting the conception of some Scholastics that monopolization deprived the public of some supplies by creating an artificial scarcity. See also Ernesto Screpanti and Stefano Zamagni, *An Outline of the History of Economic Thought,* 2nd ed. (Oxford: Oxford University Press, 2005), 27.

11. See Polanyi, "Aristotle," 70-71, locating that idea in the French physiocrats. The process may not have been complete until Alfred and Mary Marshall renamed the discipline "economics," rather than "political economy." Alfred Marshall and Mary Paley Marshall, *The Economics of Industry* (London: Macmillan & Co., 1879), 2.

12. The problem was to explain why water, a precious substance, was free, whereas diamonds, with no practical use, were precious. See Bo Sandelin et al., *A Short History of Economic Thought* (London: Routledge, 2014), 23-24, which notes the problem's consideration by Plato, Copernicus, Galileo, and John Locke. Adam Smith began to give the problem its modern answer in 1776 in *The Wealth of Nations* (bk. 1, ch. 5), and it was refined substantially during the marginalist revolution a century later. See Herbert Hovenkamp, *The Opening of American Law: Neoclassical Legal Thought, 1870-1970* (Oxford: Oxford University Press, 2014), 29-30.

13. See William Letwin, *The Origins of Scientific Economics* (London: Routledge, 1964), 85-105. Letwin identifies the origins of meaningfully scientific economic writing in the 1680s and 1690s, as one reflection of the scientific spirit that flourished in Restoration England.

14. Dorothy Ross, *The Origins of American Social Science* (Cambridge: Cambridge University Press, 1991), 10. See also Gerstle, "Protean Character," 1070-1071.

15. Degler, *Out of Our Past,* 2.

16. See Theodore F. T. Plucknett, *A Concise History of the Common Law*, 5th ed. (London: Lawbook Exchange, 1956), 528–29, 538–39.

17. See A. W. B. Simpson, *A History of the Land Law* (Oxford: Oxford University Press, 1961), 224; Gregory S. Alexander, "The Dead Hand and the Law of Trusts in the Nineteenth Century," *Stanford Law Review* 37 (1985): 1189–1266, 1189–1193.

18. Dyer's Case, Y.B., 2 Hen. V, f. 5, pl. 26 (1415).

19. E.g., Mitchel v. Reynolds, 1 P. Wms. 181, 24 Eng. Rep. 347 (K.B. 1711).

20. Morton Horwitz, *The Transformation of American Law, 1780–1869* (Cambridge, MA: Harvard University Press, 1977), 110–111.

21. See generally Samuel Fleischacker, "Adam Smith's Reception Among the American Founders, 1776–1790," *William and Mary Quarterly* 59 (2002): 897–924. On the availability of *The Wealth of Nations*, reliance on it by founding-era Americans, and the influence of the Scottish Enlightenment, see Edward G. Bourne, "Alexander Hamilton and Adam Smith," *Quarterly Journal of Economics* 8 (1894): 328–344; Scott E. Casper and Joan Shelley Rubin, "The History of the Book in America," in *The Oxford Companion to the Book*, ed. Michael F. Suarez et al. (New York: Oxford University Press, 2010); Schlessinger, *Cycles of American History*, 221, n5, quoting Thomas Jefferson to T. M. Randolph, May 30, 1790; James Madison, *The Writings of James Madison: Comprising His Public Papers and His Private Correspondence, including His Numerous Letters and Documents Now for the First Time Printed*, vol. 6, ed. Gaillard Hunt (New York: G. P. Putnam's Sons, 1900), 19, 23–24, citing *Wealth of Nations* in an address to Congress concerning a national bank; Dorfman, *Economic Mind*, 1:243, 410. For Smith's view on the American colonies, see Adam Smith, *The Wealth of Nations* (1776; New York: Modern Library, 2000), 627–629. "To prohibit a great people, however, from making all that they can of every part of their own produce" is "a manifest violation of the most sacred rights of mankind" and the "impertinent badges of slavery imposed upon them, without any sufficient reason." See also Fleischacker, "Adam Smith's Reception."

22. Dorfman, *Economic Mind*, 1:410; Schlessinger, *Cycles of American History*, 231.

23. United States v. E. I. du Pont de Nemours & Co., 351 U.S. 377, 392 (1956).

24. One might wonder how sellers could survive earning only enough to cover their costs, leaving them with no profits. Surely all viable businesses must have some "profit," or there would be no point staying in the market. The answer lies in how economists define "cost" and "profit" for purposes of economic theory. To an economist, the cost of producing a good includes not only the costs of the raw materials, labor, etc., but also the payment of a return to the investors. So even a business earning "zero economic profits," as economists understand that phrase, will pay its owners attractive dividends. In fact, in perfectly competitive markets, the maximum a business can earn is zero economic profit.

25. Abrams v. United States, 250 U.S. 616, 624–31 (1919) (Holmes, J., dissenting).

26. Associated Press v. United States, 326 U.S. 1, 20 (1945).

27. See generally Ronald D. Rotunda and John E. Nowak, *Treatise on Constitutional Law—Substance and Procedure* (Eagan, MN: West Thompson Reuters, 2017), § 15.2.

28. On banks and communication policy, see "Banking and the Financial Sector," in *Handbook on the Scope of Antitrust*, 291–307.

29. Specifically, Congress adopted the Credit Rating Agency Reform Act of 2006, Pub. L. No. 109-291, 120 Stat. 1327 (2006), now codified at 15 USCA § 780-7.

30. See Thomas J. Fitzpatrick IV and Chris Sagers, "Faith-Based Financial Regulation: A Primer on Oversight of Credit Rating Organizations," *Administrative Law Review* 61 (2009): 557-610, 595-598.

31. America Creating Opportunities to Meaningfully Promote Excellence in Technology, Education, and Science Act, Pub. L. No. 110-69, 121 Stat. 572 (2007) (codified in scattered sections of 20 U.S.C. (2007)). See Chris Sagers, "A Statute by Any Other Name Might Smell Less Like S.P.A.M., or, The Congress of the United States Grows Increasingly D.U.M.B.," *Georgetown Law Journal* 103 (2015): 1307-1333, 1329-1330.

32. See Richard Monastersky, "Researchers Dispute Notion that America Lacks Scientists and Engineers," *Chronicle of Higher Education,* Nov. 16, 2007, A14.

33. See, e.g., Richard A. Posner, *Antitrust Law,* 2nd ed. (Chicago: University of Chicago Press, 2001); Oliver E. Williamson, "The Merger Guidelines of the U.S. Department of Justice—In Perspective" (speech, US Department of Justice, June 10, 2002), https://www.justice.gov/archives/atr/merger-guidelines-us-department-justice -perspective. See also FTC v. Whole Foods, 548 F.3d 1028, 1058-1059 (D.C. Cir. 2008) (Kavanaugh, J., dissenting) (arguing that antitrust became "modern" under conservative economic influence).

34. United States v. E. C. Knight Co., 156 U.S. 1, 16 (1895).

35. See generally Theodore H. Davis Jr., "Corporate Privileges for the Public Benefit: The Progressive Federal Incorporation Movement and the Modern Regulatory State," *Virginia Law Review* 77 (1991): 603-630.

36. See generally Ellis W. Hawley, *The New Deal and the Problem of Monopoly* (Princeton, NJ: Princeton University Press, 1966); Davis, "Corporate Privileges."

37. Public Utility Holding Company Act, 49 Stat. 803 (1935).

38. See generally Hawley, *New Deal;* Joel Seligman, *The Transformation of Wall Street,* 3rd ed. (New York: Aspen Publishers, 2003).

39. See "White House Task Force Report on Antitrust Policy," reprinted in *Antitrust Law and Economics Review* 2 (1968-69): 11-52; Kovacic, "Failed Expectations," 1126-1128.

3. And Yet, Uncertainty

1. Martin J. Sklar, *The Corporate Reconstruction of American Capitalism, 1890-1916: The Market, the Law, and Politics* (Cambridge: Cambridge University Press, 1988), 1 ("formative birth-time"); generally, ibid., and Joseph Dorfman, "The Role of the German Historical School in American Economic Thought," *American Economic Review Papers and Proceedings* 45 (1955): 17-28, 17.

2. See generally Lamoreaux, *Great Merger Movement;* Daniel T. Rodgers, *Atlantic Crossings: Social Politics in a Progressive Age* (Cambridge, MA: Belknap Press, 1998); Schumpeter, *History of Economic Analysis,* 759-760, discussing late nineteenth-century depression; Donald Dewey, "The Economic Theory of Antitrust: Science or Religion?," *Virginia Law Review* 50 (1964): 413-443, 417; Tony Freyer, "The Sherman Antitrust Act, Comparative Business Structure, and the Rule of Reason: American and Great Britain, 1880-1920," *Iowa Law Review* 74 (1989): 991-1018, 994; James

Livingston, "The Social Analysis of Economic History and Theory: Conjectures on Late Nineteenth-Century American Development," *American Historical Review* 92 (1987): 69–95, 72–73; Jeffrey G. Williamson, "Watersheds and Turning Points: Conjectures on the Long-Term Impacts of Civil War Financing," *Journal of Economic History* 34 (1974): 636–661; Jeffrey G. Williamson, "Late Nineteenth-Century American Retardation: A Neoclassical Analysis," *Journal of Economic History* 33 (1973): 581–607. Cf. H. L. Beales, "The Great Depression in Industry and Trade," *Economic History Review* 5 (1934): 65–75, questioning the dates and severity of the depression of the late nineteenth century.

3. Hovenkamp, *Enterprise and American Law.*

4. Gerstle, "Protean Character."

5. Ibid., 1046.

6. See generally Martha Banta, *Taylored Lives: Narrative Productions in the Age of Taylor, Veblen, and Ford* (Chicago: University of Chicago Press, 1993); Samuel Krislov, *How Nations Choose Product Standards and Standards Change Nations* (Pittsburgh: University of Pittsburgh Press, 1997); Ross, *Origins of American Social Science;* Robert W. Hamilton, "Role of Nongovernmental Standards in the Development of Mandatory Federal Standards Affecting Safety or Health," *Texas Law Review* 56 (1978): 1329–1484, 1368–1373; Marc A. Olshan, "Standards-Making Organizations and the Rationalization of American Life," *Sociological Quarterly* 34 (1993): 319–335.

7. Gerstle, "Protean Character," 1045.

8. Namely, Hugh Johnson, the first NIRA administrator. See Robert F. Himmelberg, *The Origins of the National Recovery Administration: Business, Government, and the Trade Association Issue, 1921–1933* (New York: Fordham University Press, 1993); Peter Irons, *The New Deal Lawyers* (Princeton, NJ: Princeton University Press, 1982), 22–34; Ellis W. Hawley, "Herbert Hoover, the Commerce Secretariat, and the Vision of an 'Associative State,' 1921–1928," *Journal of American History* 61 (1974): 116–140.

9. Sklar, *Corporate Reconstruction;* Louis Galambos, "The Emerging Organizational Synthesis in American History," *Business History Review* 44 (1970): 279–290.

10. Hovenkamp, *Opening of American Law,* 206–219. Dorothy Ross recounts the conversion to marginalism of John Bates Clark, America's greatest early economist, as essentially a religious experience. Ross, *Origins of American Social Science,* 118–122.

11. The books were *The Theory of Political Economy,* written by the Englishman William Stanley Jevons in 1871; *Principles of Economics,* written in German by Carl Menger in Austria, also in 1871; and *Elements of Pure Economics,* written in French by Léon Walras, then a professor of political economy in Switzerland, published in two volumes (1874, 1877). On the books' reception, see generally Screpanti and Zamagni, *Outline of the History of Economic Thought,* 146–147, 152–153. For the view that they were not simply bolts from the blue, see George J. Stigler, "The Nature and Role of Originality in Scientific Progress," *Economica,* n.s., 11 (1955): 293–302. The history of simultaneous and cumulative invention is nicely summarized in Mark A. Lemley, "The Myth of the Sole Inventor," *Michigan Law Review* 110 (2012): 709–760.

12. See Henry William Spiegel, *The Growth of Economic Thought,* 3rd ed. (Durham, NC: Duke University Press, 1991), 396.

13. See generally Dorfman, "Role of the German Historical School," 20–22.

14. See Milton Friedman, "The Methodology of Positive Economics," in *Essays in Positive Economics* (Chicago: University of Chicago Press, 1953), 3.

15. See generally Dorfman, "Role of the German Historical School," 19.

16. See generally Spiegel, *Growth of Economic Thought*, 396-409.

17. Before the wave of young Americans first went to study with them, the Historicists were known in the United States from controversial and widely read review essays published in American journals in the early 1870s. See generally Dorfman, "Role of the German Historical School," 20-22.

18. See generally Rodgers, *Atlantic Crossings;* Dorfman, "Role of the German Historical School."

19. On Veblen, see Hovenkamp, *Opening of American Law.* On Berle and Means, see generally Geoffrey M. Hodgson, *The Evolution of Institutional Economics: Agency, Structure, and Darwinism in American Institutionalism* (London: Routledge, 2004).

20. See generally Barbara Fried, *The Progressive Assault on Laissez-Faire: Robert Hale and the First Law and Economics Movement* (Cambridge, MA: Harvard University Press, 2001); Hovenkamp, *Opening of American Law*, 114-120; Alan Devlin and Michael Jacobs, "The Empty Promise of Behavioral Antitrust," *Harvard Journal of Law and Public Policy* 37 (2014): 1009-1064; Morris R. Cohen, "Property and Sovereignty," *Cornell Law Quarterly* 13 (1927): 8-30.

4. Uncertainty of Another Kind

1. Hovenkamp, *Opening of American Law*, 206-219; Lamoreaux, *Great Merger Movement*, 46-62; Eliot Jones, "Is Competition in Industry Ruinous?," *Quarterly Journal of Economics* (1920): 473-519, 473-474; O. W. Knauth, "Capital and Monopoly," *Political Science Quarterly* 31 (1916): 244-259, 245n2.

2. Barry Alan Shain, *The Myth of American Individualism: The Protestant Origins of American Political Thought* (Princeton, NJ: Princeton University Press, 1996).

3. See Alexis de Tocqueville, *Democracy in America,* trans. George Lawrence (1839; New York: Doubleday Anchor Books, 1969), 513-517.

4. See generally Alfred Chandler, *The Visible Hand: The Managerial Revolution in American Business* (Cambridge, MA: Belknap Press, 1993), 122-144; Robert L. Rabin, "Federal Regulation in Historical Perspective," *Stanford Law Review* 38 (1986): 1189-1326, 1199-1200. Both note that associationalism was extensive among businesses during the last half of the nineteenth century.

5. "People of the same trade seldom meet together, even for merriment and diversion, but the conversations ends in a conspiracy against the public, or in some contrivance to raise prices." Smith, *Wealth of Nations,* 137.

6. See generally Chandler, *Visible Hand,* 122-144 (railroads); Hovenkamp, *Enterprise and American Law,* 145-148 (railroads); J. A. C. Grant, "The Guild Returns to America I," *Journal of Politics* 4 (1942): 303-336; Rabin, "Federal Regulation," 1199-1200 (railroads); Chris Sagers, "The Demise of Regulation in Ocean Shipping: A Study in the Evolution of Competition Policy and the Predictive Power of Microeconomics," *Vanderbilt Journal of Transnational Law* 39 (2006): 779-818 (shipping); H. R. Tosdal, "Open Price Associations," *American Economic Review* 7 (1917): 331-352 (reviewing

the rapid World War I–era rise of the "open price association" form of horizontal cartel, devised by antitrust lawyer Arthur Jerome Eddy).

7. Schlessinger, *Cycles of American History*, 231–232.

8. Henry C. Carey, *The Harmony of Interests: Agricultural, Manufacturing, and Commercial* (New York: M. Finch, 1851); see also Schlessinger, *Cycles of American History*, 238–239.

9. Specifically, those that operate within the American National Standards Institute framework. See Hamilton, "Role of Nongovernmental Standards,"1342.

10. See Krislov, *How Nations Choose Product Standards*, 21, 27, 90–99; Hamilton, "Role of Nongovernmental Standards," 1368.

11. See generally Sklar, *Corporate Reconstruction*, 204–222.

12. See Russell Pittman, "Who Are You Calling Irrational? Marginal Costs, Variable Costs, and the Pricing Practices of Firms" (Economic Analysis Group, Antitrust Division, Department of Justice Discussion Paper EAG 09-3 2009), https://www.justice.gov/atr/who-are-you-calling-irrational-marginal-costs-variable-costs-and-pricing-practices-firms.

13. See generally Alfred E. Kahn, *The Economics of Regulation* (Cambridge, MA: MIT Press 1988).

14. See Himmelberg, *Origins of the National Recovery Administration;* Hawley, "Herbert Hoover," 116–140.

15. Arthur Jerome Eddy, *The New Competition: An Examination of the Conditions Underlying the Radical Change That Is Taking Place in the Commercial and Industrial World—The Change from a Competitive to a Cooperative Basis* (New York: Appleton & Co., 1912), 23.

16. See John D. Clark, *The Federal Trust Policy* (Baltimore, MD: Johns Hopkins University Press, 1931).

17. See generally Tosdal, "Open Price Associations."

18. See Clark, *Federal Trust Policy*, 139–164.

19. Bureau of Corporations, U.S. Department of Commerce, *Farm Machinery Trade Associations* (Washington, DC: Author, 1915); Henry R. Seager and Charles A. Gulick, *Trust and Corporation Problems* (New York: Harper & Brothers, 1929), 304–338; Tosdal, "Open Price Associations," 348.

20. Federal Trade Commission, *Control of Unfair Competitive Practices through Trade Practice Conference Procedure of the Federal Trade Commission* (Washington, DC: Author, 1940).

21. See Hawley, *New Deal;* Himmelberg, *Origins of the National Recovery Administration;* Hawley, "Herbert Hoover."

22. A.L.A. Schechter Poultry Corp. v. United States, 295 U.S. 495 (1935); Hawley, *New Deal.*

5. Tensions of the Latter Day and Some Unexpected Skepticism

1. See, e.g., Herbert Hovenkamp, "Post-Chicago Antitrust: A Review and Critique," *Columbia Business Law Review* 2001 (2001): 257–338, 266–267 (so characterizing conservatives and their critics).

2. See Lester Telser, *Economic Theory and the Core* (Chicago: University of Chicago Press, 1988); George Bittlingmayer, "Did Antitrust Policy Cause the Greater Merger Wave?," *Journal of Law and Economics* 28 (1985): 77–118; William Sjostrom, "Antitrust Immunity for Shipping Conferences: An Empty Core Approach," *Antitrust Bulletin* 38 (1993): 419–424. The theory was easily disproven in real-world markets. See Sagers, "Demise of Regulation," 779–818.

3. Ohio v. Am. Express Co., 138 S. Ct. 2274 (2018).

4. Richard A. Posner, "The Chicago School of Antitrust Analysis," *University of Pennsylvania Law Review* 127 (1979): 925–948, 926–927 (identifying vertical restraints theory as foundational to the Chicago School); United States v. Anthem, Inc., 855 F.3d 345, 376 (D.C. Cir. 2017) (Kavanaugh, J., dissenting) (identifying adoption of the theory by Supreme Court in 1976 as point at which antitrust became "economic"); Robert H. Bork, *The Antitrust Paradox: A Policy at War with Itself* 430 (1978; New York: Free Press1993), 430 (same).

5. See Lester G. Telser, "Why Should Manufacturers Want Fair Trade?," *Journal of Law and Economics* 3 (1960): 86–105. Telser cites earlier examples of these various arguments at 86n1, 89n4. Also see Matthew Moloshok, "Dr. Miles—A Rock of Ages," *Antitrust Source*, Feb. 2007 (noting early Supreme Court decisions recognizing economic defenses of RPM).

6. Telser, "Fair Trade," 90, 90n5; see also Benjamin Klein, "Competitive Resale Price Maintenance in the Absence of Free Riding," *Antitrust Law Journal* 76 (2009): 431–482, 435.

7. F. M. Scherer and David Ross, *Industrial Market Structure and Economic Performance*, 3rd ed. (New York: Houghton Mifflin, 1990), 551–555, surveying economic literature.

8. This point was made by economist Robert Steiner, based on his own experience as a consumer goods manufacturer. Robert L. Steiner, "Letter to the Editor: Free-Riding Explains Maybe 15%," *Antirust Law and Economics Review* 15 (1983): 7–8.

9. Robert Pitofsky, "Are Retailers Who Offer Discounts Really 'Knaves'? The Coming Challenge to the Dr. Miles Rule," *Antitrust*, Spring 2007, 61, 63.

10. See, e.g., Klein, "Competitive Resale Price Maintenance."

11. Ibid. Klein explains "incentive incompatibility" between manufacturers and retailers with respect to desire to provide promotions. See also Howard P. Marvel and Stephen McCafferty, "Resale Price Maintenance and Quality Certification," *RAND Journal of Economics* 15 (1984): 346–359, arguing that sales by high-quality retailers establishes a "quality certification" for which manufacturers might pay by way of RPM protection. For critique of these alternative models, see Warren S. Grimes, "A Dynamic Analysis of Resale Price Maintenance: Inefficient Brand Promotion, Higher Margins, Distorted Choices, and Retarded Retailer Innovation," *Antitrust Bulletin* 55 (2010): 101–150.

12. See Grimes, "Dynamic Analysis."

13. Ibid. See also Steiner, "Letter to the Editor."

14. Telser, "Fair Trade," 92–94. See also Richard M. Brunell, "Overruling Dr. Miles: The Supreme Trade Commission in Action," *Antitrust Bulletin* 52 (2007): 475–530, 506, 512.

15. See Grimes, "Dynamic Analysis," 114, 118–120; Stanley C. Hollander, "United States of America," in *Resale Price Maintenance*, ed. Basil S. Yamey (New York: Transaction Publishers, 1966), 65, 82; Benjamin Klein and Kevin M. Murphy, "Vertical Restraints

as Contract Enforcement Mechanisms," *Journal of Law and Economics* 31 (1988): 265–298, 266.

16. See Grimes, "Dynamic Analysis," 112–113; Warren S. Grimes, "The Path Forward after Leegin: Seeking Consensus Reform of the Antitrust Law of Vertical Restraints," *Antitrust Law Journal* 75 (2008): 467–504, 482–484.

17. Philip I. Areeda and Herbert Hovenkamp, *Antitrust Law,* vol. 8, 2nd ed. (Alphen aan den Rijn, Netherlands: Wolters-Kluwer, 2004), ¶ 1604b, 40, finding "the evidence persuasive on this point"; Thomas R. Overstreet Jr., "Resale Price Maintenance: Economic Theories and Empirical Evidence" (FTC Bureau of Economics Staff Report, Nov. 1983), https://www.ftc.gov/sites/default/files/documents/reports/resale-price-maintenance-economic-theories-and-empirical-evidence/233105.pdf, 160; Brunell, "Overruling Dr. Miles," 497, 497nn100–101; Grimes, "Path Forward," 481n60; Brief for William S. Comanor et al. as Amici Curiae, Leegin Creative Leather Products, Inc. v. PSKS, Inc., 551 U.S. 877 (2007) ("It is uniformly acknowledged that [resale price maintenance] and other vertical restraints lead to higher consumer prices"). Occasionally it has been suggested that in principle, RPM could sometimes *lower* retail prices. See Howard P. Marvel and Stephen McCafferty, "The Welfare Effects of Resale Price Maintenance," *Journal of Law and Economics* 28 (1985): 363–380. But circumstances in which RPM lowers prices should be rare, and the argument has no empirical support.

18. Under many plausible circumstances RPM will cause harm to "inframarginal" consumers—those who would have bought the product even without the promotional services supported by RPM. The harm to those consumers may be much larger than any good that it accomplishes by sales to buyers brought in by the promotions. William Comanor, "Vertical Price-Fixing, Vertical Market Restrictions, and the New Antitrust Policy," *Harvard Law Review* 98 (1985): 983–1002, 990–1000.

19. Ronald H. Coase, "Industrial Organization: A Proposal for Research," in *Policy Issues and Research Opportunities in Industrial Organization,* ed. Victor Fuchs (Cambridge, MA: National Bureau of Economic Research, 1972), 59, 67.

20. See George L. Priest, "The Limits of Antitrust and the Chicago School Tradition," *Journal of Competition Law and Economics* 6 (2010): 1–10. Admittedly, there are some efforts to demonstrate RPM's alleged benefits or lack of harm, but they tend to produce limited, indirect, and problematic inferences at best. See, e.g., James C. Cooper et al., "Vertical Antitrust Policy as a Problem of Inference," *International Journal of Industrial Organization* 23 (2005): 639–664.

6. Competition as a Living Policy, circa 2019

1. NCAA v. Bd. of Regents of Univ. of Okla., 468 U.S. 85, 104 n.27 (1984), quoting N. Pac. Ry. Co. v. United States, 356 U.S. 1, 4–5 (1958); Flood v. Kuhn, 407 U.S. 258, 291 (1972); *Socony-Vacuum Oil Co.,* 310 U.S.

2. See, e.g., "Comments, Reports, and Amicus Briefs," American Bar Association, Jan. 17, 2019, http://www.abanet.org/antitrust/at-comments/comments.shtml.

3. F. James Sensenbrenner, U.S. House of Representatives, press release, June 27, 2001, http://judiciary.house.gov/legacy/news_062701.htm.

4. Walter Lippman, *Public Opinion* (New York: Free Press, 1922), 122; Theodore Kreps, "Symposium," *American Economic Review* 39 (1949): 697.

5. For comprehensive background on that period, see Kahn, *Economics of Regulation*. For views of the Reagan administration "deregulation czar," see Christopher C. DeMuth, "Deregulation Review," *Antitrust Law Journal* 53 (1984): 189–192.

6. See, e.g., Goldfarb v. Va. State Bar, 421 U.S. 773, 787 (1975) (Congress meant "to strike as broadly as it could"); United States v. Southeastern Underwriters Ass'n, 322 U.S. 533, 553 (1944) ("language more comprehensive" than that in the antitrust statutes "is difficult to conceive").

7. On judge-made limits, see, e.g., United States v. Phila. Nat'l Bank, 374 U.S. 321, 350 & n.28 (1963); Associated Press v. United States, 326 U.S. 1, 20 (1945). On construing statutory exemptions narrowly, see, e.g., Union Lab. Life Ins. Co. v. Pireno, 458 U.S. 119, 126 (1982); FMC v. Seatrain Lines, Inc., 411 U.S. 726, 733 (1973); U.S. v. McKesson & Robbins, Inc., 351 U.S. 305, 316 (1956); Chi. Prof'l Sports Ltd. P'ship v. NBA, 961 F.2d 667, 671–72 (7th Cir. 1992).

8. See Antitrust Modernization Commission, *Report and Recommendations* (Washington, DC: Author, 2007), 338, 340–341; *Report of the Task Force on Productivity and Competition,* reprinted at 115 *Cong. Rec.* 15933, 15934, 15937 (June 16, 1969); *Report of the White House Task Force on Antitrust Policy,* reprinted at 115 *Cong. Rec.* 13890, 13897 (May 27, 1969); Attorney General's Committee to Study the Antitrust Laws, *Report* (Washington, DC: Government Printing Office, 1955), 269.

9. National Commission for the Review of Antitrust Law and Procedures, *Report to the President and the Attorney General* (Washington, DC: Author, 1979), 177–316.

10. For an explanation of this view of counting cases, see William E. Kovacic, "Rating the Competition Agencies," 908–909, 919–923. On the drop in enforcement, see Paul E. Godek, "Does the Tail Wag the Dog? Sixty Years of Government and Private Antitrust in the Federal Courts," *Antitrust Source,* December 2009, http://www.americanbar.org/content/dam/aba/publishing/antitrust_source/Dec09_Godek12_17f.authcheckdam.pdf; William Kolasky, "Antitrust Litigation: What's Changed in Twenty-Five Years?," *Antitrust,* Fall 2012, 9.

11. For the view that new filings have fallen because of increasingly strict legal rules, see Kolasky, "Antitrust Litigation"; Jonah B. Gelbach, Note, "Locking the Doors to Discovery? Assessing the Effects of Twombly and Iqbal on Access to Discovery," *Yale Law Journal* 121 (2012): 2270–2345.

12. On the repeal of rules of per se illegality, see Leegin Creative Leather Prods., Inc. v. PSKS, Inc., 551 U.S. 877 (2007) (reversing per se illegality of vertical minimum price fixing); State Oil Co. v. Khan, 522 U.S. 3 (1997) (reversing per se illegality of vertical maximum price fixing); Continental T.V. v. GTE Sylvania, Inc., 433 U.S. 36 (1977) (reversing per se illegality of non–price vertical restraints). See also Nw. Wholesale Stationers, Inc. v. Pac. Stationery & Printing Co., 472 U.S. 284 (1985) (restricting and moderating per se rule against "group boycotts"); U.S. Steel Corp. v. Fortner Enterps., Inc., 429 U.S. 610 (1977) (limiting the rule against tying, traditionally known as a "per se" rule). On the procedural rules on pleading, see Ashcroft v. Iqbal, 556 U.S. 662 (2009); Bell Atlantic Corp. v. Twombly, 550 U.S. 544 (2007). On class litigation, see ComCast Corp. v. Behrend, 569 U.S. 27 (2013); Wal-Mart Stores, Inc. v. Dukes, 564

U.S. 338 (2011); Kolasky, "Antitrust Litigation." On arbitration, see AT&T Mobility LLC v. Concepcion, 563 U.S. 333 (2011); Kolasky, "Antitrust Litigation," 15. On expert testimony, see James Langenfeld and Christopher Alexander, "Daubert and Other Gatekeeping Challenges of Antitrust Experts," *Antitrust,* Summer 2011, 21.

13. On the changes to standards governing mergers, see Sagers, "#LOLNothingMatters," 37–40. On monopolization, see generally Jonathan B. Baker, "Exclusion as a Core Competitive Concern," *Antitrust Law Journal* 78 (2013): 527–590. On the sub silentio repeal, compare Bigelow v. RKO Radio Pictures, Inc., 327 U.S. 251, 264–65 (1946) ("the wrongdoer shall bear the risk of the uncertainty which his own wrong has created,"), Zenith Radio Corp. v. Hazeltine Research, Inc., 395 U.S. 100, 123–124 (1969), and Perma Life Mufflers, Inc. v. Int'l Parts Corp., 392 U.S. 134, 139 (1968), rev'd on other grounds Copperweld Corp. v. Independence Tube Corp., 467 U.S. 752 (1984), with Kansas v. UtiliCorp United, Inc., 497 U.S. 199, 214–19 (1990). On the unusual chain of events, see Jim Rossi, "Lowering the Filed Tariff Shield: Judicial Enforcement for a Deregulatory Era," *Vanderbilt Law Review* 56 (2003): 1591–1662 (noting that the "filed rate" or *Keogh* doctrine, meant to protect rate-regulated firms from antitrust challenge to their prices, has actually been expanding, even as traditional rate-regulation has been rapidly repealed); Herbert Hovenkamp, "Antitrust and the Regulatory Enterprise," *Columbia Business Law Review* 335 (2004): 335–378, 341 (same).

14. See, e.g., Credit Suisse Secs. (USA), LLC v. Billing, 551 U.S. 264, 280–83 (2007); Bell Atl. Corp. v. Twombly, 550 U.S. 544, 557–62 (2007); Verizon Commc'ns, Inc. v. Law Off. of Curtis V. Trinko, LLP, 540 U.S. 398, 411–14 (2004).

15. The unanimous victories were N. Car. State Bd. of Dental Examiners v. FTC, 135 S. Ct. 1101 (2015), FTC v. Phoebe Putney Health Sys., Inc., 133 S. Ct. 1003 (2013), and American Needle, Inc. v. NFL, 130 S. Ct. 2201 (2010). The fourth of the five plaintiff victories also went only to a non-substantive procedural question. Apple, Inc. v. Pepper, 139 S. Ct. 1514 (2019).

16. 570 U.S. 136 (2013).

17. See Chris Sagers, "The 'Reverse Payment' Drugs Case: The Most Important Economic Issue You Never Heard of—And Why There Might Still Be Some Hope for Antitrust," *Huffington Post,* June 25, 2013, http://www.huffingtonpost.com/chris-sagers/the-drug -patents-case-the_b_3480866.html.

18. On the federal courts, see, e.g., Laura Kalman, *Right Star Rising* (New York: W.W. Norton, 2010); Erwin Chemerinsky, "Supreme Court's Conservative Majority Is Making Its Mark," *Los Angeles Times,* Oct. 4, 2010. On the Supreme Court, see Lee Epstein et al., "Ideological Drift among Supreme Court Justices: Who, When, and How Important?," *Northwestern University Law Review* 101 (2007): 1483–1542; Adam Liptak, "Court under Roberts Is Most Conservative in Decades," *New York Times,* July 25, 2010, A1; Nate Silver, "Supreme Court May Be Most Conservative in Modern History," *New York Times: FiveThirtyEight Blog,* March 29, 2012, http://fivethirtyeight.blogs.nytimes .com/2012/03/29/supreme-court-may-be-most-conservative-in-modern-history/#.

19. See, e.g., *Trinko,* 540 U.S. at 414; Matsushita Elec. Industrial Co. v. Zenith Radio Corp., 475 U.S. 574, 594 (1986).

20. See, e.g., FTC v. Phoebe Putney Health Sys., Inc., 663 F.3d 1369 (11th Cir. 2011), rev'd 568 U.S. 216 (2013) (holding a local hospital authority exempt from antitrust only

because state government had given it authority to make contracts); American Needle, Inc. v. NFL, 538 736 (7th Cir. 2008), rev'd 560 U.S. 183 (2010) (holding NFL member teams, though separately incorporated and with diverse economic interests, to be "single entity" incapable of violating Sherman Act §1); FTC v. Lundbeck, 650 F.3d 1236 (8th Cir. 2011) (holding a merger to monopoly that resulted in a 1,300% price increase exempt from antitrust challenge).

21. Jessica Litman, *Digital Copyright* (New York: Prometheus Books, 2001); Raymond Shih Ray Ku, "The Creative Destruction of Copyright: Napster and the New Economy of Digital Technology," *University of Chicago Law Review* 69 (2002): 263–324, 287–293.

22. See Seligman, *Transformation of Wall Street*.

23. Silver v. New York Stock Exchange, 373 U.S. 341 (1963).

24. 551 U.S. 264 (2007).

25. 422 U.S. 659 (1975); 422 U.S. 694 (1975); Credit Suisse Secs. (USA), LLC v. Billing, No. 05–1157 (U.S. Jan. 22, 2007) (Brief of U.S. Solicitor General).

26. See Ralph Folsom, "Antitrust Enforcement under the Secretaries of Agriculture and Commerce," *Columbia Law Review* 80 (1980): 1623–1643; Franklin D. Jones, "Historical Development of the Law of Business Competition," *Yale Law Journal* 36 (1927): 351–383, 366–367.

27. Cf. Victoria Saker Woeste, *The Farmer's Benevolent Trust: Law and Agricultural Cooperation in Industrial America, 1865–1945* (Chapel Hill: University of North Carolina Press, 1998) (laying out the earlier history of cooperative movement and the failures of federal cooperative policy to achieve its goals).

28. See Chris Sagers, "Competition Come Full Circle? Pending Legislation to Repeal the U.S. Railroad Exemptions," *GCP: Antitrust Chronicle* 9 (2009): 1–8.

29. Paul Stephen Dempsey and Andrew R. Goetz, *Airline Deregulation and Laissez-Faire Mythology* (Santa Barbara, CA: Greenwood Publishing Group, 1992), 227.

30. On energy regulation, see Richard J. Pierce, "Reconsidering the Roles of Regulation and Competition in the Natural Gas Industry," *Harvard Law Review* 97 (1983): 345–385. On shipping, see Sagers, "Demise of Regulation," 779–818, discussing the history of federal maritime agencies' laxity in oversight and their failure to use statutory enforcement authority.

31. See, e.g., Simon Johnson, "Bring in the Antitrust Division (on Banking)," *Baseline Scenario*, Apr. 16, 2009, http://baselinescenario.com/2009/04/16/bring-in-the-antitrust-division-on-banking/.

32. See *Too Big to Fail: The Role for Antitrust and Bankruptcy Law in Financial Regulation Reform: Hearing Before the House Judiciary Subcommittee on Regulatory Reform, Commercial and Antitrust Law*, 111th Cong., 1st Sess. (Nov. 17, 2009) (statement of Christopher L. Sagers); Letter from Albert A. Foer, President, American Antitrust Institute, to Harry Reid, Majority Leader, US Senate, May 11, 2010, https://papers.ssrn.com/sol3/papers.cfm?abstract_id=1648997.

33. See *Too Big to Fail* (testimony of Assistant Treasury Secretary Michael Barr).

34. Vivek Ghosal, "Regime Shift in Antitrust Laws, Economics and Enforcement," *Journal of Competition Law and Economics* 7 (2011): 773–774; "Criminal Program Update 2013," Antitrust Division, US Department of Justice, Spring 2013, http://www.justice.gov/atr/public/division-update/2013/criminal-program.html.

35. See Maurice E. Stucke, "Morality and Antitrust," *Columbia Business Law Review* 2006, no. 3 (2006): 443–548, 460–469.

36. See Robert Pitofsky, "Antitrust in the Next 100 Years," *California Law Review* 75 (1987): 817–833, 819 ("To a large extent, th[e] [Reagan] administration has only brought the same case over and over again—a long series of challenges to interrelated regional and local conspiracies in the construction industry").

37. See John M. Connor and Robert H. Lande, "Cartels as Rational Business Strategy: Crime Pays," *Cardozo Law Review* 34 (2012): 427–490 (large econometric study showing that price-fixing is hugely profitable despite criminal penalties and treble civil damages).

38. In many industries, only four or even three dominant firms control nearly all sales in the United States. For examples in communications and broadcasting, see Susan Crawford, *Captive Audience* (New Haven, CT: Yale University Press, 2013). For re-corded music, see Richard A. Feinstein, Dir., Bur. of Comp., FTC, *Statement in the Matter of Vivendi, S.A. and EMI Recorded Music* (2012), http://www.ftc.gov/os /closings/comm/120921emifeinsteinstatement.pdf (approving merger leaving previ-ously four-firm market with only three firms worldwide). For US domestic air travel, see United States v. U.S. Airways Grp., Case 1:13-cv-01236-CKK (D.D.C. 2013) (com-plaint). For more mundane sectors such as light bulbs and auto tires, see Andrea Al-geria et al., "Highly Concentrated: Companies That Dominate Their Industries," *IBISWorld Special Report,* Feb. 2012, 1. See generally Baker, "Market Power in the U.S. Economy" (collecting recent empirical evidence). It may also become an issue for English trade book publishing, where a merger consummated after the *Apple* case began has already reduced the Big Six to the Big Five.

7. The Old Business of Books

1. Marcel Canoy, Jan C. van Ours, and Frederick van der Ploeg, "The Economics of Books," in *Handbook of the Economics of Arts and Culture,* ed. Victor A. Ginsburgh and David Throsby (Oxford: Elsevier North Holland, 2006), 721, 723; Michael Szenberg and Eric Youngkoo Lee, "The Structure of the American Book Publishing Industry," *Journal of Cultural Economics* 18 (1994): 313–322. Szenberg and Lee write, "In recent years, the American book publishing industry has found itself caught sharply between financial constraints and obligations as the gatekeeper of the nation's culture" (313).

2. Canoy, van Ours, and van der Ploeg, "Economics of Books," 723–724; OECD, *Policy Roundtable on Resale Price Maintenance, DAF/COMP (2008)37* (2008), 23; OECD, *Policy Roundtable on Resale Price Maintenance, OCDE/GD(97)229* (1997), 10.

3. Quoted in Ken Auletta, "The Impossible Business," *New Yorker,* Oct. 6, 1997, 50.

4. Casper and Rubin, "History of the Book in America."

5. Charles A. Madison, *Book Publishing in America* (New Providence, NJ: R. R. Bowker, 1966), 8–46.

6. Ibid., 3–5; Eli Noam, *Media Ownership and Concentration in America* (Oxford: Oxford University Press, 2009), 144–145; Casper and Rubin, "History of the Book in America."

7. See generally Casper and Rubin, "History of the Book in America"; Leslie Howsam, "The History of the Book in Britain, 1801–1914," in *The Oxford Companion to the Book,* ed. Michael F. Suarez et al. (Oxford: Oxford University Press, 2010).

8. See Casper and Rubin, "History of the Book in America"; Howsam, "History of the Book in Britain."

9. See generally Casper and Rubin, "History of the Book in America."

10. Ibid.; Howsam, "History of the Book in Britain."

11. See generally Casper and Rubin, "History of the Book in America."

12. See generally Siva Vaidyanathan, *Copyrights and Copywrongs* (New York: NYU Press, 2003), 52–55.

13. See generally Madison, *Book Publishing in America*, 50–60; Vaidyanathan, *Copyrights and Copywrongs*.

14. Michael Korda, *Another Life: A Memoir of Other People* (New York: Random House, 1999), 46–49; André Schiffrin, *The Business of Books* (New York: Verso, 2000).

15. Bennett Cerf, *At Random: The Reminiscences of Bennett Cerf* (New York: Random House, 1977), 31–34.

16. Ibid., 57.

17. See generally Casper and Rubin, "History of the Book in America."

18. Madison, *Book Publishing in America*, 44.

19. Vincent Giroud, "The History of the Book in France," in *The Oxford Companion to the Book*, ed. Michael F. Suarez et al. (Oxford: Oxford University Press, 2010); Frédéric Saby, "Jean-Yves Mollier: Louis Hachette (1800–1864), le fondateur d'un empire," *Bulletin des Bibliothèques de France*, Nov. 1999, 105–107, http://bbf.enssib.fr/consulter /bbf-1999-06-0105-013.

20. Madison, *Book Publishing in America*, 22.

21. Herbert R. Lottman, *Albert Camus: A Biography* (Corte Madera, CA: Ginko Press, 1997), 301–329.

22. Tom Dardis, *Firebrand: The Life of Horace Liveright* (New York: Random House, 1995).

23. "Barney Rosset Dies; Publisher Fought Censorship," *Los Angeles Times*, Feb. 23, 2012; Cerf, *At Random;* Kevin Birmingham, *The Most Dangerous Book: The Battle for James Joyce's Ulysses* (New York: Penguin, 2014).

24. Schiffrin, *Business of Books*.

25. Ben H. Bagdikian, *The New Media Monopoly*, 20th ed. (Boston: Beacon Press, 2004); John B. Thompson, *Merchants of Culture*, 2nd ed. (New York: Plume, 2012), 104–107; Thomas Whiteside, "Onward and Upward with the Arts: The Blockbuster Complex-I," *New Yorker*, Sept. 29, 1980, 48.

26. Whiteside, "Onward and Upward."

27. Albert N. Greco, "Market Concentration Levels in the U.S. Consumer Book Industry: 1995-1996," *Journal of Cultural Economics* 21 (2000): 321–336. Greco finds 675 mergers in the US book industry from 1960 to 1994.

28. Three of the Big Five publishers are subsidiaries of publicly traded entities, two American and one French. The other two are subsidiaries of privately held German media conglomerates.

1. Simon & Schuster is a subsidiary of the television corporation CBS, a minority of which is publicly traded and the majority held by the holding company National Amusements, which is owned by the media magnate Sumner Redstone and his daughter.

2. HarperCollins is a subsidiary of the holding company News Corp, a majority of which is publicly traded but a large minority owned by the media leader Rupert Murdoch, who is also chair and CEO and has effective control of the firm.

3. Hachette Book Group is a wholly owned subsidiary of the French publisher Hachette Livre, which is itself wholly owned by the major French media conglomerate Lagardère, and that firm in turn is organized as a publicly traded limited partnership.

4. Macmillan is a subsidiary of the family-owned German holding company Holtzbrinck. Holtzbrinck is focused on newspaper, trade book, and academic publishing in Germany, the United States, and the United Kingdom. The US and UK operations are subsumed under the Macmillan name.

5. Penguin Random House is a joint venture owned by the British publisher Pearson and the German media conglomerate Bertelsmann.

29. The topic is actually more fraught than that makes it sound, and there are those who disagree fairly strongly. How one feels about it depends on how much confidence one has in the efficiency of public capital markets. See generally Aspen Institute, "Overcoming Short-Termism: A Call for a More Responsible Approach to Investment and Business Management" (Aspen Institute Business and Society Program Report, Sept. 9, 2009), https://assets.aspeninstitute.org/content/uploads/files/content/docs/pubs/overcome_short_state0909_0.pdf.

30. Lawrence A. Sullivan, Warren S. Grimes, and Christopher L. Sagers, *Antitrust Law: An Integrated Handbook*, 3rd ed. (Eagan, MN: West Publishing, 2015), § 8.1b (collecting empirical evidence).

31. See Szenberg and Lee, "Structure," 319-321. On problems of merger implementation generally, see Scott A. Christofferson, Robert S. McNish, and Diane L. Sias, "Where Mergers Go Wrong," *McKinsey Quarterly* 2 (2004): 92.

32. See Pankaj Ghemawat and Bret Baird, "Leadership Online: Barnes & Noble vs. Amazon.com" (Harvard Business School Case Study No. 9-798-063 1998).

33. See generally Jeffrey Church, "Conglomerate Mergers," in *Issues in Competition Law and Policy,* vol. 2 (ABA Book Publishing, 2008), 1503.

34. Yakov Amihud and Baruch Lev, "Risk Reduction as a Managerial Motive for Conglomerate Mergers," *Bell Journal of Economics* 12 (1981): 605-617; Gerald F. Davis et al., "The Decline and Fall of the Conglomerate Firm in the 1980s: The Deinstitutionalization of an Organizational Form," *American Sociological Review* 59 (1994): 547-570, 548.

35. Davis et al., "Decline and Fall," 547; Neil Fligstein, "The Spread of the Multidivisional Form among Large Firms, 1919-1979," *American Sociological Review* 50 (1985): 377-391.

36. See generally Scherer and Ross, *Industrial Market Structure,* 90-94; David J. Ravenscraft and F. M. Scherer, *Mergers, Sell-Offs, and Economic Efficiency* (Washington, DC: Brookings Institution, 1987); Davis et al., "Decline and Fall."

37. Davis et al., "Decline and Fall," 548, quoting "The Ebb Tide: A Survey of International Finance," *The Economist,* Apr. 27, 1991.

38. Albert Greco, "Mergers and Acquisitions in the U.S. Book Industry, 1960–89," in *International Book Publishing: An Encyclopedia,* ed. Philip G. Altbach and Edith S. Hoshino (London: Garland, 1995), 229, 230.

39. Whiteside, "Onward and Upward," 51–52.

40. Alfred D. Chandler Jr., *Inventing the Electronic Century: The Epic Story of the Consumer Electronics and Computer Industries* (Cambridge, MA: Harvard University Press, 2005).

41. Whiteside, "Onward and Upward," 49.

42. Frederick Macmillan, *The Net Book Agreement, 1899, and the Book War, 1906–1908* (Glasgow: [Glasgow] University Press, 1924), 35–36.

43. See generally Jonathan Hardy, *Cross-Media Promotion* (Bern: Peter Lang, 2010).

44. See, e.g., Bagdikian, *New Media Monopoly;* Hardy, *Cross-Media Promotion;* Ken Auletta, "Synergy City," *American Journalism Review* 20 (1998): 18–35.

45. Ken Auletta, "The Pirate," *New Yorker,* Nov. 13, 1995.

46. Hardy, *Cross-Media Promotion,* 65–87.

47. Thompson, *Merchants of Culture,* 23–25.

48. Jason Epstein, *Book Business: Publishing Past, Present, and Future* (New York: W. W. Norton, 2001), 58–60; Auletta, "Impossible Business," 50, 52, noting that in 1996 Penguin wrote off $20 million in unearned advances, Simon & Schuster wrote off $35 million, and Random House wrote off more than $50 million. See also Thompson, *Merchants of Culture,* 2–3 (noting that in 2007 a previously unknown author named Randy Pausch was paid a $6.75 million advance for his book *The Last Lecture*); Doreen Carvajal, "HarperCollins Cancels Books in Unusual Step for Industry," *New York Times,* June 27, 1997 (recounting that comedian Jay Leno was paid an advance of $4 million for an autobiography that performed poorly); Ken Auletta, "Publish or Perish," *New Yorker,* Apr. 26, 2010 (noting that the industry's second-largest expense has become royalty advances); Whiteside, "Onward and Upward," 48, 49 (noting that million-dollar advances had become commonplace by 1980).

49. Szenberg and Lee, "Structure," 314.

50. Edwin McDowell, "New Publisher Named in Shift at Turbulent Random House," *New York Times,* Oct. 31, 1990; Edwin McDowell, "Random House Swept by a Rash of Rumors," *New York Times,* Nov. 6, 1989; Glenn Collins, "After Disappointments, a New Chief for HarperCollins," *New York Times,* Mar. 4, 1996.

51. Rakesh Khurana, "The Curse of the Superstar CEO," *Harvard Business Review* 80, no. 9 (Sept. 2002): 60.

52. Jonathan A. Knee, Bruce C. Greenwald, and Ava Seave, *The Curse of the Mogul: What's Wrong with the World's Leading Media Companies* (New York: Portfolio Books, 2009); Khurana, "Curse of the Superstar," 62.

53. Schiffrin, *Business of Books,* 126, quoting Knopf, and discussing the backlist strategy generally.

54. See, e.g., Thompson, *Merchants of Culture.*

55. Quoted in Korda, *Another Life,* 103.

56. See, e.g., Szenberg and Lee, "Structure," 314; Whiteside, "Onward and Upward," 48.

57. See, e.g., Epstein, *Book Business;* Korda, *Another Life;* Schiffrin, *Business of Books.* See also Thompson, *Merchants of Culture;* Steve Wasserman, "The Amazon Effect," *The Nation,* June 18, 2012.

8. Bookselling and the Birth of Amazon

1. See generally Casper and Rubin, "History of the Book in America."
2. Ibid.
3. Schiffrin, *Business of Books,* 121–124.
4. Peter Osnos, "The Incredible Resilience of Books," *The Atlantic,* June 19, 2012 (recollections of a publishing veteran of industry sentiments when he began his career in the mid-1980s).
5. See Ghemawat and Baird, "Leadership Online."
6. See Auletta, "Impossible Business," 50, 60.
7. Ghemawat and Baird, "Leadership Online"; Whiteside, "Onward and Upward," 48, 91–93.
8. Whiteside, "Onward and Upward" 91–93.
9. *In re* Harper & Row Publishers, Inc., 122 F.T.C. 113 (1996) (Commission order dismissing suit); American Booksellers Association, Inc. v. Houghton Mifflin Co., Inc., 1995 WL 787394 (S.D.N.Y. 1995) (approving settlement in private Robinson-Patman suit); Donald S. Clark, Secretary, Federal Trade Commission, "The Robinson-Patman Act: Annual Update" (April 2, 1998), https://www.ftc.gov/es/public-statements/1998/04/robinson-patman-act-annual-update; Sandra Sugawara, "FTC Hits Publishers' Book Pricing," *Washington Post,* December 23, 1988, D1.
10. See Ghemawat and Baird, "Leadership Online," 7; Whiteside, "Onward and Upward," 92.
11. "A Brief History of Simon & Schuster," Simon & Schuster, http://about.simonandschuster.biz/corporate-history/.
12. Auletta, "Impossible Business," 57–59.
13. Ibid., 62 (noting that in 1997 Amazon's return rate was about 2%).
14. Brad Stone, *The Everything Store: Jeff Bezos and the Age of Amazon* (New York: Bantam Press, 2013), 240. See also Coll, "Citizen Bezos"; Keith Gessen, "The War of the Words," *Vanity Fair,* Nov. 6, 2014.
15. Auletta, "Publish or Perish."
16. Ibid.
17. Tim Berners-Lee, *Weaving the Web: The Original Design and Ultimate Destiny of the World Wide Web by Its Inventor* (New York: HarperBusiness, 2000); "A Little History of the World Wide Web," W3C, 2000, http://www.w3.org/History.html. For the earliest, purely conceptional suggestions of what a networked communications system might one day be, see Vannevar Bush, "As We May Think," *The Atlantic,* July 1945. On Bezos's early years at D. E. Shaw, see Stone, *Everything Store,* 17–24.
18. Stone, *Everything Store,* 25; Coll, "Citizen Bezos" (remarking on this fact unflatteringly). As evidence that other online booksellers chose books for quite similar reasons, see, e.g., John Soeder, "Cyberscene: Book Sale," *Inside Business,* Mar. 1998

(discussion of Charles Stack, founder of the venerable internet bookseller Book Stacks Unlimited).

19. See Stone, *Everything Store.*
20. See Walter Isaacson, *Steve Jobs* (New York: Simon & Schuster 2011).
21. See generally Lemley, "Myth of the Sole Inventor," 709–760.
22. Dustin S. Klein, "Visionary in Obscurity: Charles Stack," *Smart Business,* July 22, 2002; Soeder, "Cyberscene."
23. On the difficulties facing Barnes and Noble, see "Barnes and Noble Hangs Up 'For Sale' Sign," *CBS News Money Watch,* Oct. 4, 2018, https://www.cbsnews.com/news/barnes -noble-hangs-up-for-sale-sign-stock-surges/. On the resurgence of independent book-sellers between 2009 and the present, and explanations for their success, see Frances X. Clines, "Indie Bookstores Are Back, with a Passion," *New York Times,* Feb. 13, 2016, A20; Husna Haq, "Indie Bookstores Are on the Rise: What's behind Their Come-back?," *Christian Science Monitor,* May 28, 2015; Ryan Raffaelli, "Reaffirming Collec-tive Identity in Response to Multiple Technological Discontinuities: The Novel Resur-gence of Independent Bookstores" (Harvard Business School Working Paper, Nov. 2017), https://hbswk.hbs.edu/Documents/pdf/2017-11-15%20Indie%20Book-store%20Resurgence_Ryan%20Raffaelli_Extended%20Abstract_HBSWK.PDF.

9. Publishers, Booksellers, and the Oldest Problem in the World

1. Paul Carr, "NSFW: Hey, 1997—Macmillan Called, They Want the Net Book Agree-ment Back," *Washington Post,* Feb. 7, 2010.
2. Admittedly, at times, antitrust statutes have made the distinction. Two antitrust laws that specifically regulate agreements between sellers and buyers survive today, though both are largely vestigial and unenforced. Section 3 of the Clayton Act of 1914, ch. 323, 38 Stat. 730, 731 (1914), now codified at 15 U.S.C. § 14, prohibits some exclusive distri-bution arrangements and package deals where they can be shown to be anticompeti-tive, and the Robinson-Patman Act, ch. 592, §§ 2–4, 49 Stat. 1526 (1936) regulates price discrimination. Likewise, from 1937 until its repeal in 1976, the Miller-Tydings Act explicitly exempted vertical price-fixing contracts where authorized by state govern-ments; see ch. 690, 50 Stat. 693 (1937). On the Supreme Court's distinction, see White Motor Co. v. United States, 372 U.S. 253, 259 (1963).
3. See Areeda and Hovenkamp, *Antitrust Law,* vol. 7, ¶ 1503a, 392; Sullivan, Grimes, and Sagers, *Antitrust Law,* 302–303;. Mark Lemley and Christopher Leslie, "Categor-ical Analysis in Antitrust Jurisprudence," *Iowa Law Review* 93 (2008): 1207–1270, 1265.
4. Herbert Hovenkamp, "Mergers and Buyers," *Virginia Law Review* 77 (1991): 1369–1384, 1370.
5. In technical terms, the profit-maximizing price will be the price that causes Sony's mar-ginal cost of making televisions to be equal to the marginal revenue it earns from selling them. Past that point, if Sony sells even one more television, the increased output will push total profit down, for two reasons. First, where more supply is available, con-sumers move further down their demand curve and will pay less for the good. Second,

it will push up Sony's marginal cost. At any scale of output at which production is efficient, marginal cost will be constant or rising. So, even producing one more unit past the point at which MC=MR would cause Sony to begin reducing the total amount of its profit.

This point is usually made in connection with the theory of monopoly. A monopolist sets price where MC=MR. However, it is actually true of all rational sellers, even in perfect competition. The seller's best price under all circumstances is the one that causes MC=MR.

6. A monopolist manufacturer distributes through third parties—thus giving up some of the overall revenue—when it is cheaper than doing the distribution work in-house. Under the strong assumption here—that the manufacturer is a total monopolist and all downstream markets are competitive—it does not reduce the monopolist's *profit*. In any case, in real-world practice, manufacturers usually do not perform very much of their own distribution, and rarely do they integrate all the way to the retail level. Generally speaking, it appears to be more costly to integrate than to sell through third-party distributors. They typically integrate all the way to the final point of sale only for highly differentiated luxury items. Preserving consumer perception of a luxury brand's quality is thought to require a high degree of control at the retail level, and so only then does it justify the high cost of integration to retail. See generally Robert L. Steiner, "The Evolution and Applications of Dual-Stage Thinking," *Antitrust Bulletin* 49 (2004): 877-910; Robert L. Steiner, "The Prejudice against Marketing," *Journal of Marketing*, July 1976, 2.

7. For more on the inherent rivalry of vertical relationships, see Steiner, "Dual-Stage Thinking"; Grimes, "Path Forward," 467, 473-474.

8. I've made an arguably significant simplifying assumption about what happens in this case with regard to the *retail* price. I've assumed that where both an upstream and a downstream player have some market power—as is ordinarily the case—the retail price will be at least somewhat elevated, and that where one or both of them hold a lot of market power, the price will be elevated a lot. Technically, economists are less certain about what happens to retail price where there is power at more than one level in distribution.

But it is not a bad assumption. The only case in which players in less than full competition will nevertheless act to set retail prices at the competitive level would be a so-called noncooperative game, in which they both make their price and output decisions without thinking about how the others will react. Nowadays, any such assumption is thought naive, and it is taken for granted that the players will ordinarily engage in cooperative strategies in which the goal is to maximize joint profits. In conditions of diminished competition, each player can be confident that its individual profits will be maximized if joint profits are. See, e.g., Hovenkamp, "Mergers and Buyers," 1374-1376. Note that "cooperative" in this context does not mean "friendly"; vertical relations will remain adversarial. The play is "cooperative" only in the sense that players assume their own actions will elicit reactions from others, and they take those anticipated reactions into account in making their own decisions.

9. All these points, often referred to as the "one monopoly profit" argument, were elaborated in Robert H. Bork, "The Rule of Reason and the Per Se Concept: Price Fixing

and Market Division Part II," *Yale Law Journal* 75 (1965): 373–476. Bork's article and its impact on vertical restraints law were controversial, and in some respects it seems incorrect and overstated. See, e.g., Einer R. Elhauge, "Tying, Bundled Discounts, and the Death of the Single Monopoly Profit Theory," *Harvard Law Review* 123 (2009): 397–481 (surveying criticisms and noting circumstances in which relaxation of Bork's strong assumptions led to different results); J. R. Gould and B. S. Yamey, "Professor Bork on Vertical Price Fixing," *Yale Law Journal* 76 (1967): 722–730. Still, no one seriously doubts that as long as its fairly strong assumptions are met in a given case, Bork's argument is correct in the abstract. See also Telser, "Fair Trade," 86, 86n1 (with citations to earlier work recognizing the same issue).

10. See generally Telser, "Fair Trade," 86–87.

11. 220 U.S. 373 (1911).

12. 210 U.S. 339 (1908).

13. 231 U.S. 222 (1913).

14. 551 U.S. 877 (2007).

15. 433 U.S. 36 (1977).

16. See, e.g., Joseph Cornwall Palamountain Jr., *The Politics of Distribution* (Cambridge, MA: Harvard University Press, 1955).

17. Marc Levinson, *The Great A&P and the Struggle for Small Business in America* (New York: Hill and Wang, 2011); Palamountain, *Politics of Distribution,* 5–23; Basil S. Yamey, "The Origins of Resale Price Maintenance: A Study of Three Branches of Retail Trade," *Economic Journal* 62 (1952): 522–545.

18. Levinson, *Great A&P.*

19. See Rudolph J. R. Peritz, "'Nervine' and Knavery: The Life and Times of Dr. Miles Medical Company," in *Antitrust Stories,* ed. Eleanor M. Fox and Daniel A. Crane (Eagan, MN: Foundation Press, 2007), 61, 64–65.

20. See generally Mark D. Bauer, "Whither Dr. Miles?," *Loyola Consumer Law Review* 20 (2007): 1–31; Peritz, "'Nervine' and Knavery."

21. H. R. Tosdal, "Price Maintenance," *American Economic Review* 8 (1918): 28–47, 34, 34nn21, 23.

22. United States v. Standard Sanitary Mfg. Co., 226 U.S. 20 (1912). The restraints on jobbers, and their objections to them, are elaborated in the lower court opinion. 191 F. 172, 176–77 (C.C.D. Md. 1911).

23. Overstreet, "Resale Price Maintenance"; E. Raymond Corey, "Fair Trade Pricing: A Reappraisal," *Harvard Business Review* 30, no. 5 (Sept. / Oct. 1952): 47; H. R. Tosdal, "Price Maintenance," 45–46.

24. Hawley, *New Deal;* Daniel Scroop, "The Anti-Chain Store Movement and the Politics of Consumption," *American Quarterly* 60 (2008): 925–949.

25. Ch. 690, 50 Stat. 693 (1937).

26. 50 Stat. at 693–94.

27. Ch. 592, §§ 2 to 4, 49 Stat. 1526 (1936), now codified at 15 U.S.C. §§ 13a–13b.

28. See generally Levinson, *Great A&P,* 151–166.

29. Palamountain, *Politics of Distribution,* 59; Herbert Hovenkamp, "Progressive Antitrust," *University of Illinois Law Review* 2018 (2018): 71–114, 81–83.

30. Casper and Rubin, "History of the Book in America."

31. A short paper of 1959, one of few empirical efforts on point, claimed that only about 1 percent of American businesses ever used legally sanctioned RPM. E. S. Herman, "Statistical Note on Fair Trade," *Antitrust Bulletin* 4 (1959): 583–592. However, although that study has been cited repeatedly without comment (e.g., Overstreet, "Resale Price Maintenance," 113), it contains a severe methodological flaw and should not be relied on. Cf. Herman, "Statistical Note," 584n4.

32. Grimes, "Dynamic Analysis," 105.

33. Grimes, "Path Forward," 489–490.

34. See, for example, Rodino's erudite critique of Reagan administration enforcement policy. Peter W. Rodino Jr., "The Future of Antitrust: Ideology vs. Legislative Intent," *Antitrust Bulletin* 35 (1990): 575–600.

35. Pub. L. No. 94-435, 90 Stat. 1383 (1976), now codified at scattered sections of 15 U.S.C. The law also enhanced the investigatory and enforcement powers of the federal antitrust agencies and gave new powers to the states, creating the modern regime of enforcement of antitrust law by state attorneys general.

36. Antitrust Procedures and Penalties Act, Pub. L. No. 93-528, 88 Stat. 1706 (1974); Antitrust Procedural Improvements act of 1980, Pub. L. No. 96-349, 94 Stat. 1154 (1980).

37. Consumers Goods Pricing Act of 1975, Pub. L. No. 94-145, 89 Stats 801 (1975).

38. On the significance of President Nixon's appointments, and ideological change in the courts generally, see Sagers, "#LOLNothingMatters," 20–21.

39. *Oversight Hearings on the Antitrust Division of the Department of Justice: Subcommittee on Monopolies and Commercial Law,* House Comm. on the Judiciary, 97th Cong., 1st and 2d Sess. 7 (1983).

40. Monsanto Co. v. Spray-Rite Serv. Corp., 465 U.S. 752 (1984) (adopting pleading requirements for vertical restraints claims); Business Electronics Corp. v. Sharp Electronics Corp., 485 U.S. 717 (1988) (increasing the pleading requirements); State Oil Co. v. Khan, 522 U.S. 3 (1997) (holding that vertical *maximum* price-fixing would be subject only to the rule of reason).

41. The Court deviated from norms against commenting on cases not before it, and its vertical restraints cases included record evidence contrary to the Telser model. Grimes, "Path Forward" (noting that the Supreme Court did just this in *Sylvania, Sharp,* and *Leegin*).

42. Leegin Creative Leather Prods., Inc. v. PSKS, Inc., 551 U.S. 877, 918–23 (Breyer, J., dissenting).

43. Congress adopted budget rules and resolutions against agency guidelines and amicus briefing urging limits on vertical restraints law. Pub. L. 99-180, tit. VI, § 605, 99 Stat. 1136, 1169–70 (1985).

10. Price-Fixing in Books

1. Russi Jal Taraporevala, *Competition and Its Control in the British Book Trade, 1850–1939* (Bombay: D. B. Taraporevala & Sons, 1973).

2. Taraporevala, *Competition and Its Control,* 14–15.

3. H. R. Tosdal, "Price Maintenance in the Book Trade," *Quarterly Journal of Economics* 30 (1915): 86–96.

4. On opposition to the German plan, see Tosdal, "Price Maintenance in the Book Trade," 94–95.

5. Macmillan, *Net Book Agreement,* 30.

6. See, e.g., Overstreet, "Resale Price Maintenance," 7n2; Tosdal, "Price Maintenance in the Book Trade," 98n1.

7. Indeed, Macmillan reprinted his correspondence with Marshall in his 1924 book defending the Agreement. Macmillan, *Net Book Agreement,* 13–17.

8. Basil S. Yamey, "Retail Price Competition and the Origins of the Net Book Agreement," in Taraporevala, *Competition and Its Control,* 32–34.

9. Macmillan, *Net Book Agreement,* 29–30.

10. Macmillan, *Net Book Agreement,* 34–35.

11. Bobbs-Merrill Co. v. Straus, 139 F. 155, 158–60 (S.D.N.Y. 1905).

12. "Work of the American Publishers Association," *Publishers' Weekly,* July 20, 1901, 87.

13. Thompson, *Merchants of Culture,* 26.

14. See, e.g., Straus v. Victor Talking Machine Co., 243 U.S. 490 (1917); Straus v. Am. Publishers Ass'n, 231 U.S. 222 (1913); Bobbs-Merrill Co. v. Straus, 210 U.S. 339 (1908); Straus v. Am. Publishers Ass'n, 177 N.Y. 473 (N.Y. Ct. Apps. 1904); cf. Straus v. Notaseme Hosiery Co., 240 U.S. 179 (1916) (rejecting damages claim in trademark suit asserting that mark under which Macy's sold house brand hosiery infringed competitor's mark); Hatfield v. Straus, 82 N.E. 172 (N.Y. 1907).

15. Tosdal, "Price Maintenance in the Book Trade," 32n13.

16. *Bobbs-Merrill,* 210 U.S.

17. *Straus,* 177 N.Y.

18. *Bobbs-Merrill,* 139 F. at 172.

19. See 210 U.S. at 350. Technically, in addition to holding that a copyright owner has no power to limit resale price after sale, the trial court also held that the overall net pricing system was an illegal conspiracy under the Sherman Act. It refused for that reason to grant Bobbs-Merrill an injunction against below-cost sales, under a rule of equity requiring that plaintiffs in equity must have "clean hands" to be entitled to equitable relief. 139 F. at 190. The Supreme Court did not rely on this separate ground.

   The same judge also held in a related case decided on the same day that the Strauses' conduct did not illegally interfere with the publishers' contracts with wholesalers. Regardless of the extent to which the Straus brothers caused book wholesalers to breach their contracts with the publishers, by supplying Macy's with books that they knew would be sold below net price, it was not actionable. Scribner v. Straus, 139 F. 193 (S.D.N.Y. 1905).

20. 231 U.S. 222 (1913).

21. See generally J. P. Poort et al., "Digitally Binding: Examining the Feasibility of Charging a Fixed Price for E-Books" (SEO Economic Research Report No. 2012-18, March 2012), https://pure.uva.nl/ws/files/1845442/117502_375441.pdf; Norbert Schulz, "Does the Service Argument Justify Resale Price Maintenance?," *Journal of Institutional and Theoretical Economics* 163 (2007): 236–255.

11. Content and the Digital Transition in Historical Context

1. See Ku, "Creative Destruction of Copyright," 268 (making this point with regard to music distribution).

2. For a careful study showing this to have been true for a very long time in a range of different industries, see Peter Dicola and Matthew Sag, "An Information-Gathering Approach to Copyright Policy," *Cardozo Law Review* 34 (2012): 173–248.

3. Amy Harmon, "Harry Potter and the Internet Pirates," *New York Times,* July 14, 2003; Jason Kincaid, "Harry Potter Author JK Rowling Attacks Scribd for Pirated Content," *Tech Crunch,* Mar. 30, 2009, http://techcrunch.com/2009/03/30/harry-potter-author -jk-rowling-attacks-scribd-for-pirated-content/.

4. Stone, *Everything Store,* 250.

5. David Nimmer, "On the Sony Side of the Street, Symposium: Sony v. Universal: the Betamax Decision Twenty Years Hence," *Southwestern University Law Review* 34 (2004): 205–230 (discussing the broader reception of the *"Betamax* case"—Sony Corp. of Am. v. Universal City Studios, Inc., 464 U.S. 417 (1984)—which held that home recording of television programs on VCRs was fair use); D. Dunas, "Oct. 1, 1982: Portable Music Enters the Spin Zone," *Wired,* Sept. 30, 2009 (rise of CDs and consumer technology).

6. Isaacson, *Steve Jobs;* Sheryl Garratt, "Jonathan Ive: Inventor of the Decade," *Guardian,* Nov. 28, 2009; Apple Corporation, Press Release: iTunes Downloads Top 275,000 in First Week (Jan. 16, 2001); Cabel Sasser, "The True Story of Audion," *Panic Extras,* https://panic.com/extras/audionstory/.

7. See Justin Oppelaar, "MTVi, RioPort, Big 5 Pact for Downloads," *Variety,* Apr. 5, 2001.

8. See generally Isaacson, *Steve Jobs,* 308–309, 338–339, 378–393.

9. Ibid., 394–410.

10. See In re BMG, 2000 WL 689347, No. 971–0070 (F.T.C. 2000) (complaint and consent decrees).

11. See generally Chris O'Malley, "A New Spin," *Time,* Aug. 24, 1998, 60.

12. On home recording technology, see Audio Home Recording Act of 1992, Pub. L. No 102–563, 106 Stat. 4237 (1992), now codified at 17 USCA §§ 1001–10. The act had origins in the conflict over tape recordings, as well as concerns about emerging digital technology. See S. Rep. No. 102–294, 102nd Cong., 2nd Sess. (1992). On MP3 player technology, see R.I.A.A. v. Diamond Multimedia Systems Inc., 180 F.3d 1072 (9th Cir. 1999).

13. See Randal C. Picker, "Mistrust-Based Digital Rights Management," *Journal of Telecommunications and High Technology Law* 5 (2006): 47–72, 55–62.

14. Ibid., 52.

15. Unbundled sales might threaten the industry if there are supracompetitive profits to be made from bundled sales. There may be theoretical doubt that tying or bundling of this kind is profitable, but the industry itself perceived individual song sales as a threat, and it aggressively opposed it for years. It seems they relented and agreed to unbundled sales through iTunes only because digital piracy had already resulted in massive unbundling. See Isaacson, *Steve Jobs,* at 397.

16. MGM Studios, Inc. v. Grokster, Ltd., 545 U.S. 913 (2005).

17. See Eliot Van Buskirk, "RIAA to Stop Suing Music Fans, Cut Them Off Instead," *Wired,* Dec. 19, 2008; Electronic Frontier Foundation, "RIAA v. The People: Five Years Later" (EFF white paper, Oct. 1, 2008), https://www.eff.org/files/eff-riaa -whitepaper.pdf.

18. On industry consolidation and reorganization, see generally Federal Trade Commission, "Statement of Bureau of Competition Director Richard A. Feinstein In the Matter of Vivendi, S.A. and EMI Recorded Music," Sept. 21, 2012 (explaining approval of merger creating a worldwide three-firm oligopoly); Ben Sisario, "Universal Closes on EMI Deal, Becoming, by Far, Biggest of Remaining Big Three," *New York Times: Media Decoder,* Sept. 28, 2012. On litigation, see in re Pandora Media, Inc., 2013 WL5211927 (S.D.N.Y. Sept. 17, 2013).

19. See Picker, "Mistrust-Based Digital Rights."

20. Ingrid Lunden, "Google Bought Waze for $1.1B, Giving a Social Data Boost to Its Mapping Business," *TechCrunch,* June 11, 2013, https://techcrunch.com/2013/06/11/its -official-google-buys-waze-giving-a-social-data-boost-to-its-location-and-mapping -business/.

21. Williams & Wilkins Co. v. U. S., 487 F.2d 1345 (Ct. Cl. 1973), aff'd by equally divided Court, 420 U.S. 376 (1975).

22. See White-Smith Music Pub'g Co. v. Apollo Co., 209 U.S. 1 (1908) (finding that creating player-piano rolls of copyrighted musical compositions was not infringement).

23. See Steven Pearlstein, "How Avis Will Ruin Zipcar," *Washington Post,* Jan. 2, 2013, http://www.washingtonpost.com/blogs/wonkblog/wp/2013/01/02/how-avis-will-ruin -zipcar/ (making this argument).

24. See Litman, *Digital Copyright,* 35–69 (canvassing the long history of copyright lobbying and reform); ibid., 25, 37 ("Negotiated copyright statutes have tended, throughout the century, to be kind to the entrenched status quo, and hostile to upstart new industries. . . . The process leading to the 1998 enactment of the Digital Millennium Copyright Act extended the familiar, multilateral, interindustry negotiation to the point of self-parody"); Dicola and Sag, "Information-Gathering Approach."

25. See Peter J. Alexander, "Peer-to-Peer File Sharing: The Case of the Music Recording Industry," *Review of Industrial Organization* 20 (2002): 151–161; Diane Leenheer Zimmerman, "Modern Technology, Leaky Copyrights, and Claims of Harm: Insights from the Curious History of Photocopying" (NYU Law and Economics Research Paper No. 12-22, Aug. 14, 2012), http://papers.ssrn.com/sol3/papers.cfm?abstract_id= 2129458.

26. See Alexander, "Peer-to-Peer File Sharing," 154.

27. Ibid., 159.

12. The Promise and Threat of Electronic Books

1. Stephen J. Dubner, "What Is Stephen King Trying to Prove?," *New York Times Magazine,* Aug. 13, 2000.

2. Antonio García Martínez, "What Microsoft's Antitrust Case Teaches Us about Silicon Valley," *Wired,* Feb. 11, 2018.

3. See, e.g., Auletta, "Impossible Business," 50, 60.

4. Jeffrey Toobin, "Google's Moon Shot: The Quest for the Universal Library," *New Yorker,* Feb. 5, 2007.

5. On the dot-com economy, see, e.g., William A. Sahlman, "The New Economy Is Stronger Than You Think," *Harvard Business Review* 77, no. 6 (Nov./Dec. 1999): 99. On the stability of mortgages, etc., see generally Fitzpatrick and Sagers, "Faith-Based Financial Regulation," 557–610.

6. Alexandra Alter, "Audiobooks Turn More Readers into Listeners as E-Books Slip," *New York Times,* Sept. 23, 2016.

7. John Updike, "The End of Authorship," *New York Times Sunday Book Review,* June 25, 2006.

8. Elizabeth L. Eisenstein, *The Printing Revolution in Early Modern Europe,* 2nd ed. (Cambridge: Cambridge University Press, 2005), xvi.

9. See, e.g., Kevin Kelly, "Scan That Book!," *New York Times Magazine,* May 14, 2006.

10. Stone, *Everything Store.*

11. Oya Y. Rieger, "Preservation in the Age of Large-Scale Digitization: A White Paper" (Council on Library and Information Resources Publication No. 141, February 2008), https://core.ac.uk/download/pdf/30687940.pdf.

12. See, e.g., Kelly, "Scan That Book!"

13. See generally Paul Stephen Dempsey, "Transportation: A Legal History," *Transportation Law Journal* 30 (2003): 235–366; Arthur Donovan, "Intermodal Transportation in Historical Perspective," *Transportation Law Journal* 27 (2000): 317–344; Sagers, "Demise of Regulation," 786–804.

14. See, e.g., Nicholas Carr, "Words in Stone and on the Wind," *Rough Type,* Feb. 3, 2012, http://www.roughtype.com/?p=1576; Adrian Johns, "The Book in, and as, American History," *New England Quarterly* 84 (2011): 496–411 (reviewing the series *A History of the Book in America,* edited by David D. Hall).

15. Kevin Kelly, *The Inevitable: Understanding the 12 Technological Forces That Will Shape Our Future* (New York: Penguin Books, 2016).

16. These points were all made in the brilliantly perceptive Carr, "Words in Stone."

17. This is nicely elaborated in Nicholas Carr, "Books That Are Never Done Being Written," *Wall Street Journal,* Dec. 31, 2011.

18. See generally Kelly, *Inevitable.*

19. See generally Rieger, "Preservation"; Paul Conway, "Preservation in the Age of Google: Digitization, Digital Preservation, and Dilemmas," *Library Quarterly: Information, Community, Policy* 80 (2010): 61–79.

13. How Electronic Books Came to Be, and What It Would Mean for the *Apple* Case

1. Strictly speaking, bound collections of sheets or tablets had existed for some centuries before then, but only in crude and not very useful forms, and they were apparently uncommon. Examples include bound clay tablets from Mesopotamia and bound wooden boards from Rome. See Alberto Manguel, *A History of Reading* (New York: Penguin Books, 1996), 125; Craig Kallendorf, "The Ancient Book," in *The Oxford Companion to the Book,* ed. Michael Suarez et al. (Oxford: Oxford University Press, 2010).

2. The story was recorded by Pliny the Elder in 79 AD and is widely recounted in histories of books. See Manguel, *History of Reading*, 126, 126n2 (quoting Pliny the Elder, *Naturalis Historia*, vol. 13, ed. W. H. S. Jones [Cambridge, MA: Harvard University Press, 1968], 11). Some of its details are disputed, most importantly the claim that under Eumenes the Pergamonese invented parchment. Parchment documents are known to have existed at least a century earlier, and writing materials made of animal skins (including parchment) are much more ancient than that (126).

3. See generally Manguel, *History of Reading*, 125–129; Kallendorf, "Ancient Book."

4. Craig Saper, *The Amazing Adventures of Bob Brown: A Real-Life Zelig Who Wrote His Way through the 20th Century* (New York: Empire State Editions, 2016); Jennifer Schuessler, "The Godfather of the E-Reader," *New York Times*, Apr. 8, 2010; "The History of eBooks from 1930's 'Readies' to Today's GPO eBook Services," *Government Book Talk*, Mar. 10, 2014 https://govbooktalk.gpo.gov/2014/03/10/the-history-of-ebooks-from-1930s-readies-to-todays-gpo-ebook-services/.

5. Bob Brown, *The Readies* (New York: Roving Eye Press, 1930), 40.

6. Ibid., 27–28.

7. Ibid. 38.

8. Readies web site, http://readies.org.

9. Brown, *Readies*, 41–51.

10. Virginia Heffernan, *Magic and Loss: The Internet as Art* (New York: Simon & Schuster, 2016).

11. "Ángela Ruiz Robles: Google rinde homenaje a la precursora del 'eBook,'" *El País*, March 28, 2016; "Ángela Ruiz Robles: Así funcionaba el precursor del 'ebook' inventado por una maestra española," *El Mundo*, March 28, 2016; "Ángela Ruiz Robles," *Unlearned Lessons*, http://www.unless-women.eu/biography-details/items/ruiz-robles .html. For assistance with translating these sources, I thank Paola Raska.

12. Bush, "As We May Think."

13. As of this writing, Nelson is still active and has begun generating working prototypes. For explanation of current goals and some current prototype applications, see the Project Xanadu homepage, http://xanadu.com.

14. Ted Nelson, *Literary Machines* (Sausalito, CA: Mindful Press, 1981); Ted Nelson, *Computer Lib/Dream Machines* (Chicago: Author, 1974).

15. Steven Levy, *Hackers: Heroes of the Computer Revolution* (New York: Doubleday, 2010), 143–144.

16. See, e.g., T. H. Nelson, "Complex Information Processing: A File Structure for The Complex, the Changing, and the Indeterminate," *ACM '65: Proceedings of the 20th National Conference* (New York: Association for Computing Machinery, 1965), 84.

17. See Ibid., 87–88.

18. This may be captured best in Nelson's live appearances, as in a short segment in Werner Herzog's 2016 documentary *Lo and Behold, Reveries of the Connected World*. https://www.youtube.com/watch?v=Bqx6li5dbEY.

19. Gary Wolf, "The Curse of Xanadu," *Wired*, June 1, 1995.

20. Douglas C. Engelbart, "Augmenting Human Intellect: A Conceptual Framework" (SRI Summary Report AFOSR-3223, October 1962), http://www.dougengelbart.org/pubs /augment-3906.html.

21. Although Kay initially conceived of it in his 1968 dissertation at the University of Utah, he described it most famously in his visionary article, Alan C. Kay, "A Personal Computer for Children of All Ages" (Xerox Palo Alto Research Center, 1972), http://www.vpri.org/pdf/hc_pers_comp_for_children. pdf.

22. Kay wrote his 1972 paper while resident at Xerox's fabled PARC laboratory in Palo Alto, best known for pioneering the computer mouse, the graphical user interface, and the desktop metaphor. Many of the Dynabook's principles were captured in a groundbreaking personal computer prototype known as "the Alto." Developed at PARC and first produced in 1973, the Alto would become central to Silicon Valley lore. In 1979 Steve Jobs and Apple engineers visited PARC to examine the Alto. They licensed some of its technology as part of a joint venture arrangement between Apple and Xerox, and then Apple developed that technology—some say stole it—for its Lisa and McIntosh computers. See Thomas A. Wadlow, "The Xerox Alto Computer," *Byte,* Sept. 1981, 58–68. See also Stone, *The Everything Store,* 19. Kay's work influenced Jobs personally in the development of the iPad, as Kay himself has acknowledged in interviews. See Wolfgang Gruener, "Did Steve Jobs Steal the iPad? Genius Inventor Alan Kay Reveals All," *Tom's Hardware,* Apr. 17, 2010, http://www.tomshardware.com/news/alan-kay-steve-jobs-ipad-iphone,10209.html.

23. Glyn Moody, "Gutenberg 2.0: The Birth of Open Content," *LWN.Net,* Mar. 29, 2006, http://lwn.net/Articles/177602/; quote from Marie Lebert, "A Short History of eBooks" (Project Gutenberg, 2009), http://www.etudes-francaises.net/dossiers/ebookEN.pdf.

24. Glyn Moody, "Michael Hart (1947–2011): Prophet of Abundance," *ComputerWorldUK,* Sept. 8, 2011 (quoting an email from Hart).

25. 537 U.S. 186 (2003).

26. Pub. L. 105–298, §§ 102(b) and (d), 112 Stat. 2827–2828 (amending 17 U.S.C. §§ 302, 304).

27. U.S. Const., Art. I, §8, cl. 8.

28. Moody, *Michael Hart.*

29. Lebert, "Short History," 5.

30. Ibid..

31. Defense Advanced Research Projects Agency, "A History of the ARPANET: The First Decade" (DARPA Report No. 4799, Apr. 1, 1981), https://apps.dtic.mil/dtic/tr/fulltext/u2/a115440.pdf.

32. Lebert, "Short History," 7–8.

33. Leonid Taycher, "Books of the World, Stand Up and Be counted! All 129,864,880 of You," *Google Book Search Blog,* Aug. 5, 2010, http://booksearch.blogspot.com/2010/08/books-of-world-stand-up-and-be-counted.html.

34. Jonathan Band, "The Long and Winding Road to the Google Books Settlement," *John Marshall Review of Intellectual Property* 9 (2009): 227–329, 229.

35. Specifically, the 1976 Act made copyright effective immediately on the creation of a work, without any need for registration or other formalities, and extended the copyright term from a fixed period of years to a floating period based on the author's lifetime. See U.S. Copyright Office, "Report on Orphan Works" (Jan. 2006), https://www.copyright.gov/orphan/orphan-report.pdf.

36. On the number of books in copyright and in print, see Einer Elhauge, "Why the Google Books Settlement Is Procompetitive," *Journal of Legal Analysis* 2 (2010): 1–68, 10; Toobin, "Google's Moon Shot."

37. Jonathan Band, "The Google Library Project: Both Sides of the Story," *Plagiary: Cross-Disciplinary Studies in Plagiarism, Fabrication, and Falsification* 1 (2006): 6, 14, https://quod.lib.umich.edu/cgi/p/pod/dod-idx/google-library-project-both-sides-of -the-story.pdf?c=plag;idno=5240451.0001.002;format=pdf; Pamela Samuelson, "The Dead Souls of the Google Book Search Settlement," *Communications of the ACM,* July 2009, 28.

38. See generally U.S. Copyright Office, "Orphan Works and Mass Digitization" (June 2015), https://www.copyright.gov/orphan/reports/orphan-works2015.pdf; U.S. Copyright Office, "Report on Orphan Works."

39. Nate Hoffelder, "Internet Archive Now Hosts 4.4 Million eBooks, Sees 15 Million eBooks Downloaded Each Month," *Digital Reader,* July 9, 2013, https://the-digital -reader.com/2013/07/09/internet-archive-now-hosts-4-4-million-ebooks-sees-15 -million-ebooks-downloaded-each-month/; Gary Wolf, "The Great Library of Amazonia," *Wired,* Dec. 1, 2003.

40. Wolf, "Great Library of Amazonia."

41. HathiTrust, "Press Release: Launch of HathiTrust—October 13, 2008," Oct. 13, 2008, https://www.hathitrust.org/press_10-13-2008.

42. Angelina Zaytsev, "14 Million Books and 6 Million Visitors: HathiTrust Growth and Usage in 2016" (HathiTrust, Feb. 2017), https://www.hathitrust.org/files/14MillionB ooksand6MillionVisitors_1.pdf.

43. Digital Public Library of America, "Strategic Plan 2015–2017" (2014), https://dpla .wpengine.com/wp-content/uploads/2018/01/DPLA-StrategicPlan_2015-2017-Jan7 .pdf. An extensive range of the DPLA's historical and founding documents is available at https://dp.la/info/about/history/materials/.

44. See Hathi Trust, "Copyright Review Program," https://www.hathitrust.org/copyright -review; Zaytsev, "14 Million Books," 1.

45. The provision in question is 17 U.S.C. § 108(h). Section 108(h) was added by the Sonny Bono Act. See generally Brewster Kahle, "Books from 1923 to 1941 Now Liberated!," *Internet Archive Blog,* Oct. 10, 2017, http://blog.archive.org/2017/10/10/books-from-1923 -to-1941-now-liberated/.

14. Google Books

1. Digitization projects have been undertaken by a few other for-profit firms, including Yahoo's Open Content Alliance and Microsoft's short-lived Live Book Search project. They remained much smaller, and they digitized only works in the public domain or for which they had received explicit permission. They were to some degree reactive commercial responses to Google Books. See generally Katie Hafner, "In Challenge to Google, Yahoo Will Scan Books," *New York Times,* Oct. 3, 2005; "Book Search Winding Down," *BingBlogs,* May 23, 2008, https://blogs.bing.com/search/2008/05/23 /book-search-winding-down.

2. Toobin, "Google's Moon Shot."

3. Wolf, "Great Library of Amazonia."

4. Stone, *Everything Store,* 207–208.

5. Initially named "Google Editions," the project was unveiled in December 2010 as "Google eBookstore" to substantial fanfare, and it still sells eBooks through the Google Play content platform. It has remained small as a commercial endeavor because its selection of books for purchase consists mostly of the public domain works it had scanned, which are mostly old and esoteric. There also have been problems with the quality of many of the scans and (ironically) the store's search functionality. Laura Miller, "Is Google Leading an E-Book Revolution?," *Salon,* Dec. 7, 2010, http://www.salon.com /2010/12/08/google_ebookstore/. In Google's original model it did not take a cut of sales made through its book site. That seems likely to have been meant to lure publishers into sharing in-copyright material. See Toobin, "Google's Moon Shot."

6. Toobin, "Google's Moon Shot."

7. Ibid.

8. Rieger, "Preservation"; "Google Books Library Project: Library Partners," Google Books, http://books. google.com/googlebooks/partners.html.

9. Wolf, "Great Library of Amazonia."

10. First, a user could view only three snippets from any one work, even if the search term appeared many times in the work. Second, no snippets would be displayed for reference works such as dictionaries or encyclopedias, because that might be the entirety of what the user wanted to see. Band, "Google Library Project."

11. The publishers' suit was not a class action; it was brought by five major publishing firms in their individual capacities.

12. The publishers then settled separately, and because their action was not a class action, it did not require court approval and has not been made fully public. The settlement preserves the publishers' right to opt out of Google digitization, and provides that for out-of-print works to which they consent to digitization, Google will supply them with digital copies. See Claire Cain Miller, "Google Deal Gives Publishers a Choice: Digitize or Not," *New York Times,* Oct. 5, 2012.

13. Compare, e.g., Elhauge, "Google Books Settlement," with James Grimmelmann, "The Google Book Search Settlement: Ends, Means, and the Future of Books," *Advance: The Journal of the ACS Issue Groups* 3 (2009): 15–29.

14. See Band, "Long and Winding Road," 231n38.

15. See, e.g., Statement of Interest of the United States of America Regarding Proposed Class Settlement, Authors Guild, Inc. v. Google, Inc., No. CV 8136-DC (S.D.N.Y. Sept. 18, 2009); James Grimmelmann, "The Elephantine Google Books Settlement," *Journal of the Copyright Society of the U.S.A.* 58 (2010): 497–520, 520; Samuelson, "Dead Souls," 28.

15. The Kindle

1. Nate Hoffelder, "Blast from the Past: Sony Data Discman DD-S35," *Digital Reader,* Oct. 9, 2011, http://the-digital-reader.com/2011/10/09/blast-from-the-past-sony-data -discman-dd-s35/.

2. Stone, *Everything Store,* 225.

3. Andrew Richard Albanese, *The Battle of $9.99: How Apple, Amazon, and the Big Six Publishers Changed the E-Book Business Overnight* (New York: Publisher's Weekly, 2013), 204.

4. Dubner, "What Is Stephen King Trying to Prove?" For King's open letter to readers, see http://stephenking.com/library/other_project/plant_zenith_rising_the.html.

5. Stone, *Everything Store,* 232.

6. Epstein, *Book Business.* See also Dinitia Smith, "A Vision for Books That Exults in Happenstance," *New York Times,* Jan. 13, 2001.

7. See William C. Dougherty, "Print on Demand: What Librarians Should Know," *Journal of Academic Librarianship* 35 (2009): 184–186, 185.

8. Stone, *Everything Store,* 224–226.

9. Robert LaFranco, "The Patent Terrorist," *Forbes,* May 17,1999; Richard Siklos, "Math Whiz vs. the Media Moguls in a Battle for Millions," *New York Times,* Apr. 3, 2006.

10. Steven Donohue, "Fugitive Gemstar Founder Henry Yuen Wins 100th Patent," *Donohue Report,* Apr. 19, 2016, http://www.donohuereport.com/fugitive-gemstar -founder-henry-yuen-wins-100th-patent/; Jane Spencer and Kara Scannell, "As Fraud Case Unravels, Executive Is at Large," *Wall Street Journal,* Apr. 25, 2007; "Gemstar-TV Guide Ex-Chairman Is 'a Fugitive' after Indictment," *San Jose Mercury News,* May 16, 2008.

11. Stone, *Everything Store,* 230–231.

12. Ibid., 231–233.

13. Ibid.

14. An online product-review comment quoted in Nicholson Baker, "A New Page: Can the Kindle Really Improve on the Book?," *New Yorker,* Aug. 3, 2009.

15. Ibid.

16. Stone, *Everything Store;* Baker, "New Page."

17. Baker, "New Page"; Auletta, "Publish or Perish."

18. Gary Wolf, "Great Library of Amazonia."

19. Stone, *Everything Store.*

20. Ibid., 250–251.

21. Carr, "NSFW: Hey, 1997."

22. Albanese, *Battle of $9.99.*

23. Thompson, *Merchants of Culture,* 317–321.

16. The eBooks Conspiracy

1. Auletta, "Publish or Perish." The publishers themselves broadly acknowledged that windowing was counterproductive. See *Apple,* 952 F. Supp. 2d at 653.

2. Harmon, "Harry Potter and the Internet Pirates."

3. *Apple,* 952 F Supp. 2d at 657.

4. *Apple,* 952 F. Supp. 2d at 657 n.15 (quoting a Feb. 2009 email from Eddy Cue to Steve Jobs). See also ibid. ("Some months earlier, Apple had considered acting as 'an ebook reseller exclusive to Amazon and Amazon becom[ing] an audio/video iTunes reseller exclusive to Apple'").

5. See generally Alex Lux, "Yesterday's Tomorrows: The Origins of the Tablet," Computer History Museum, Dec. 17, 2014, http://www.computerhistory.org/atchm/yesterdays-tomorrows-the-origins-of-the-tablet/; Charles McLellan, "The History of Tablet Computers: A Timeline," *ZDnet,* Mar. 3, 2014, http://www.zdnet.com/article/the-history-of-tablet-computers-a-timeline/.

6. See Kay, "Personal Computer for Children."

7. *Apple,* 952 F. Supp. 2d at 654.

8. *Apple,* 952 F. Supp. 2d at 647, 654.

9. *Apple,* 952 F. Supp. 2d at 654.

10. *Apple,* 952 F. Supp. 2d at 677.

11. *Apple,* 952 F. Supp. 2d at 657.

12. Quoted in Andrew Albanese, "Albanese on the Apple E-books Case: Apple's Anticlimactic Appeal," *Truth on the Market,* Feb. 15, 2016, https://truthonthemarket.com/2016/02/15/albanese-on-the-apple-e-books-case-apples-anticlimactic-appeal/.

13. See, e.g., Thomas Catan and Nathan Koppel, "Regulators Eye Apple Anew; Enforcers Interested in Whether Digital-Subscription Rules Stifle Competition," *Wall Street Journal,* Feb. 18, 2011 (noting MFNs in new Apple rules governing apps for delivery of subscription content).

14. See, e.g., Walt Mossberg, "First Impressions of the New Apple iPad," *All Things D,* Jan. 27, 2010, http://allthingsd.com/20100127/apple-ipad-impressions/. This review by a leading technology reporter observed that on its launch date the iPad boasted "a new e-book reader app with built-in online book store that, visually at least, blew away the Amazon (AMZN) Kindle, even if it seemed to lack all of the Kindle's features and may have a smaller catalog."

15. Jeffrey A. Trachtenberg, "Publisher in Talks with Apple over Tablet," *Wall Street Journal,* Jan. 18, 2010; Sarah Weinman, "Publishers Try to Protect E-Book Prices from Apple, Amazon," *AOL Finance,* Jan. 20, 2010, https://www.aol.com/2010/01/20/publishers-try-to-protect-e-book-prices-from-apple-amazon/.

16. "BoomTown's Apple iPad Day, Starring Walt Mossberg (Plus a Steve Jobs Cameo!)," *All Things D,* Jan. 28, 2009, http://allthingsd.com/20100128/boomtowns-apple-ipad-day-starring-walt-mossberg-plus-a-steve-jobs-cameo/. The video has been widely shared on the internet, and can be viewed in many places, including the Swisher post just cited and https://www.youtube.com/watch?v=czyEr_0YH8E.

17. Pls. Ex. 607 (email from Elisa Rivlin, General Counsel, Simon & Schuster, to Carolyn Reidy, CEO, Simon & Schuster, Jan. 29, 2009); Albanese, *Battle of $9.99.*

18. See, e.g., Motoko Rich and Brad Stone, "Publisher Wins Fight with Amazon over E-Books," *New York Times,* Jan. 31, 2010 (noting that Macmillan CEO John Sargent had only days before demanded that Amazon permit agency pricing and accept the same prices the five defendants had just agreed with Apple).

19. See, e.g., Carr, "NSFW: Hey, 1997."

20. Ibid.

21. State government investigations were underway as early as June 2, when the Texas attorney general confirmed the first state inquiry. Jeffrey A. Trachtenberg and Yukai Iwatani Kane, "Texas Questions E-Book Publishers," *Wall Street Journal,* June 2,

2010, B4. Connecticut opened a second investigation in August, and other states soon joined. Anonymous sources confirmed that federal investigation was underway at least that early. Jeffrey A. Trachtenberg and Chad Bray, "E-Book Pricing Draws More Antitrust Scrutiny," *Wall Street Journal,* Aug. 3, 2010, B1.

22. As is fairly customary, the Justice Department did not publicly confirm the investigation until much later, at a congressional oversight hearing on December 7, 2011. Catan, "Justice Department Confirms," B5.

23. On Google and Barnes & Noble, see *Apple,* 791 F.3d at 309 n.12; on Kobo, see W. Michael G. Osborne, "The Ebooks Saga: Kobo's Challenge Explained," *Litigator,* Apr. 30, 2014, http://www.thelitigator.ca/2014/04/the-ebooks-saga-kobos-challenge-explained/.

24. Each of the publisher defendants settled with DOJ well before trial and agreed to a set of conduct remedies ending the "agency" pricing scheme with Apple, Amazon, and other eBook retailers. See Leslie Kaufman, "Macmillan Will Settle a Lawsuit on E-Books," *New York Times,* Feb. 9, 2013, B9; *Apple,* Civil Action No. 12-CV-2826 (DLC) (Aug. 12, 2013) (final judgment as to defendants Verlagsgruppe Georg Von Holtzbrinck Gmbh & Holtzbrinck Publishers, LLC, d/b/a Macmillan).

Each of the defendants, including Apple, also settled a parallel EC action, imposing similar injunctive prohibitions. See Laura Hazard Owen, "European Commission and Penguin Finally Wrap Things Up in Apple Ebook Pricing Case," *Gigaom,* July 25, 2013, http://gigaom.com/2013/07/25/european-commission-and-penguin-finally-wrap-things-up-in-apple-ebook-pricing-case/. And the publisher defendants each settled private follow-on actions, agreeing to money damages of about $162 million. See Laura Hazard Owen, "Heads Up, Ebook Buyers: Here's How Much You're Likely to Get in The Apple Ebook Settlement," *Gigaom,* Aug. 30, 2013, http://gigaom.com/2013/08/30/heads-up-ebook-buyers-heres-how-much-youre-likely-to-get-in-the-apple-ebook-settlement/.

25. See letter from Lawrence E. Buterman, U.S. Dep't of Justice, to Hon. Denise L. Cote (Oct. 15, 2012) (1:12-cv-02826-DLC-MHD (S.D.N.Y. 2012), Dock. Entry No. 140) (the contract's "illegitimacy results from the fact that [they] . . . were entered into as part of a larger price-fixing conspiracy [and not] . . . specific characteristics of the distribution relationship between Apple" and the individual publishers); letter from Joel M. Mitnick, Sidley & Austin, Counsel to Macmillan, to Hon. Denise L. Cote (Oct. 17, 2012) (1:12-cv-02826-DLC-MHD (S.D.N.Y. 2012), Dock. Entry No. 142) ("[We] understand the Department of Justice's letter to state that the Department of Justice will not challenge the genuineness of the agency agreements . . . , and that those contracts may be unlawful only if formed through collusion"); letter from Daniel Floyd, Gibson Dunn & Crutcher, Counsel to Apple, to Hon. Denise L. Cote (Oct. 17, 2012) (1:12-cv-02826-DLC-MHD (S.D.N.Y. 2012), Dock. Entry No. 141) ("Apple understands that the DOJ contends the agency agreements are unlawful" if they were horizontally collusive, "but does not dispute that they are genuine contracts of agency in form and substance.")

26. *Apple,* 952 F. Supp. 2d at 650.

27. See, e.g., *Apple,* 952 F. Supp. 2d at 650 (Penguin executive report to Penguin directors under the heading "Competition and Collaboration," that it "will not be possible for any individual publisher to mount an effective response" to Amazon "because of

both the resources necessary and the risk of retribution, so the industry needs to develop a common strategy"); ibid. at 651 (email from Simon & Schuster CEO Carolyn Reidy, stating, "We've always known that unless other publishers follow us, there's no chance of success in getting Amazon to change its pricing practices. Clearly, we need to gather more troops and ammunition first. . . . And of course you were right that without a critical mass behind us Amazon won't 'negotiate,' so we need to be more confident of how our fellow publishers will react if we make a move"); ibid. at 652 (noting publishers' view that "windowing" would require group action).

28. For example, as early as December 2008, Stefan von Holtzbrinck of Macmillan and Arnaud Nourry of Hachette agreed "to exchange information and cooperate very tightly on all issues around e-books and the Kindle," with a goal "less to compete with Amazon than to force it to accept a price level higher than 9.99." *Apple,* 952 F. Supp. 2d at 650–51.

29. *Apple,* 952 F. Supp. 2d at 709.

30. For example, the publishers tightly coordinated the windowing strategies, with three of them initiating the program and following up with communications and efforts to pressure the others to join. A Hachette executive told his CEO Arnaud Nourry in late fall 2009, "Completely confidentially, Carolyn [Reidy] has told me that they [Simon & Schuster] are delaying the new Stephen King, with his full support, but will not be announcing this until after Labor Day." That executive added that "it would be prudent for you to double delete this from your email files when you return to your office." When HarperCollins soon followed with its own windowing announcement, Hachette's Nourry congratulated a HarperCollins executive on his decision: "Well done . . . and welcome to the Club!" Later, Simon & Schuster CEO Carolyn Reidy advised Macmillan that it would "love" for Macmillan "to join" Hachette, HarperCollins, and S&S in windowing, and "fel[t] if one more publisher comes aboard, everyone else will follow suit." *Apple,* 952 F. Supp. 2d at 652–53.

31. See, e.g., *Apple,* 952 F. Supp. 2d at 661 (quoting emails that Cue sent to the publishers to summarize his individual negotiations, in which he wrote, "After talking to all the other publishers and seeing the overall book environment, here is what I think is the best approach for e-books").

32. *Apple,* 791 F.3d at 301; *Apple,* 952 F. Supp. 2d at 654 & n.12.

33. *Apple,* 791 F.3d at 306.

34. 15 U.S.C. § 1 (emphasis added).

35. Interstate Circuit v. United States, 306 U.S. 208 (1939); Toys R Us v. FTC, 221 F.3d 928 (7th Cir. 2000). See also Leegin Creative Leather Prods., Inc. v. PSKS, Inc., 551 U.S. 877, 893–94 (2007) (citing *Toys R Us* with approval). Substantial other authority is to similar effect, as the government nicely explained in its appellate briefing. See Apple, Inc. v. United States, No. 15-565 (U.S. Dec. 2015) (brief of United States opposing certiorari), at 15–19.

36. The majority pointedly noted in the beginning that Judge Cote had also found the conspiracy illegal under the rule of reason. *Apple,* 791 F.3d at 297 (citing 952 F. Supp. 2d at 694).

37. On the criminal cases, see, e.g., United States v. Wilson, 610 F.3d 168 (2d Cir. 2010) (vacating death sentence for improper statements by prosecutor); Tippins v. Walker,

77 F.3d 682 (2d Cir. 1996) (finding constitutionally ineffective assistance of counsel). On same-sex marriage, see Windsor v. United States, 699 F.3d 199 (2d Cir. 2012), aff'd 133 S. Ct. 2675 (2013).

38. "Dennis Jacobs," http://www.ca2.uscourts.gov/Judges/bios/dj.html.

39. In re Aluminum Warehousing Antitrust Litig., 833 F.3d 151 (2d Cir. 2016); Elec. Trading Group, LLC v. Banc of Am. Securities LLC, 588 F.3d 128 (2d Cir. 2009); Apotex Inc. v. Acorda Therapeutics, Inc., 823 F.3d 51 (2d Cir. 2016); In re Payment Card Interchange Fee and Merchant Discount Antitrust Litig., 827 F.3d 223 (2d Cir. 2016), cert. denied sub nom. Photos Etc. Corp. v. Home Depot U.S.A., Inc., 137 S. Ct. 1374 (2017); In re Air Cargo Ship. Services Antitrust Litig., 697 F.3d 154 (2d Cir. 2012). For what it's worth, his one opinion finding for a plaintiff was decided after the Supreme Court had reversed a Second Circuit procedural ruling, requiring the Second Circuit to hear the case. See Gelboim v. Bank of Am. Corp., 823 F.3d 759 (2d Cir. 2016), cert. denied, 137 S. Ct. 814 (2017).

40. For example, Judge Jacobs wrote the opinion undoing the largest settlement of private antitrust claims in history, in In re Payment Card Interchange Fee and Merchant Discount Antitrust Litig., 827 F.3d 223 (2d Cir. 2016), cert. denied sub nom. Photos Etc. Corp. v. Home Depot U.S.A., Inc., 137 S. Ct. 1374 (2017). Likewise, after the Supreme Court ruled that antitrust could be "implicitly repealed" by the federal securities laws, in Credit Suisse Securities (USA) LLC v. Billing, 551 U.S. 264 (2007), many predicted it would open the gates for courts to hold defendants exempt from antitrust in all kinds of circumstances, because they were also subject to some other federal statute. But Judge Jacobs's opinion in Elec. Trading Group, LLC v. Banc of Am. Securities LLC, 588 F.3d 128 (2d Cir. 2009), remains one of the very few lower court decisions to apply *Credit Suisse* to find a defendant exempt.

41. On the ACLU lawsuit, see Amnesty Intern. USA v. Clapper, 667 F.3d 163, 203–04 (2d Cir. 2011) (Jacobs, C.J., dissenting from denial of rehearing en banc) ("This lawsuit is litigation for its own sake" and "bears similarity to a pro se plaintiff's allegation that the CIA is controlling him through a radio embedded in his molar"). For criticism, see Scott Horton, "Injudicious Judge," *Harper's Magazine: Browsings,* Sept. 23, 2011, https://harpers.org/blog/2011/09/injudicious-judge/. On the speech see, Dennis G. Jacobs, "Pro Bono for Fun and Profit" (speech before the Rochester, NY, Lawyers Chapter of the Federalist Society, Oct. 6, 2008), https://fedsoc.org/commentary/publications/speech-by-judge-dennis-g-jacobs. See also Erwin Chemerinsky, "Not a Self-Serving Activity," *National Law Journal,* Oct. 27, 2008 (critical of that speech).

42. Dennis Jacobs, "The Secret Life of Judges," *Fordham Law Review* 75 (2007): 2855–2864.

43. See Richard J. Gilbert, PhD, Direct Testimony in *Apple,* Apr. 25, 2013, at 50–52, http://www.justice.gov/atr/cases/apple/exhibits/px-1105.pdf.

44. Laura Hazard Owen, "Free Is Not the Magic Number: New Trends in eBook Pricing," *PaidContent,* May 30, 2013, http://paidcontent.org/2013/05/30/free-is-not-the-magic-number-new-trends-in-ebook-pricing/#comments.

45. *Apple,* 952 F. Supp. 2d at 685.

46. Technically, Judge Cote's opinion resolved two separate lawsuits—both the Justice Department's claims and claims separately filed by thirty-three states and US territories under their own state antitrust laws. See 952 F. Supp. 2d at 645 n.1.

47. Texas, et al. v. Hachette Book Group, Inc., et al., 12 Civ. 6625 (DLC) (parens patriae); In re: Electronic Books Antitrust Litigation, 11 MD 2296 (DLC) (S.D.N.Y. 2011) (consumers).

48. See Andrew Albanese, "Publishers Have Paid $166 Million to Settle E-book Claims," *Publishers Weekly*, Jul. 24, 2013.

49. Isaacson, *Steve Jobs*.

50. See, e.g., United States v. Microsoft Corp., 97 F. Supp. 2d 59, 62 (D.D.C. 2000), appeal denied, cause remanded, 530 U.S. 1301 (2000), and vacated, 253 F.3d 34 (D.C. Cir. 2001) (entering drastic order of divestiture, after finding Sherman Act § 2 monopolization violation, because "Microsoft as it is presently organized and led is unwilling to accept the notion that it broke the law or accede to an order amending its conduct").

51. See United States v. Apple Inc., 787 F.3d 131 (2d Cir. 2015) (affirming Judge Cote's denial of motion to stay monitoring order). See United States v. Apple Inc., 992 F. Supp. 2d 263 (S.D.N.Y. 2014) (denying motion to stay monitoring order; emphasizing Apple's intransigence and reaffirming need for aggressive monitoring); Colin Lecher, "How Apple's Court-Appointed Monitor Became Cupertino's Most Wanted," *The Verge*, May 22, 2015, https://www.theverge.com/2015/5/22/8639999/apple-court -monitor-michael-bromwich-ebook-trial.

52. Apple, Inc. v. United States, 136 S. Ct. 1376 (Mar. 7, 2016) (Mem.).

53. Assume, conservatively, that Apple—one of the world's most profitable businesses— would keep the $500 million at work at an annual return of 5 percent. Delaying payment for the eight months it took the Supreme Court to reject the case would be worth nearly $17 million.

54. Jim Milliot, "As E-book Sales Decline, Digital Fatigue Grows," *Publishers Weekly*, June 17, 2016.

55. On increases in e-readers and eBooks, see Kathryn Zickuhr and Lee Rainie, "E-Reading Rises as Device Ownership Jumps," Pew Research Center, Jan. 16, 2014, http://www.pewinternet.org/2014/01/16/e-reading-rises-as-device-ownership-jumps/.

56. Poort et al., "Digitally Binding," 42. See also Hailiang Chen, Yu Jeffrey Hu, and Michael D. Smith, "The Impact of Ebook Distribution on Print Sales: Analysis of a Natural Experiment" (2013), https://papers.ssrn.com/sol3/papers.cfm?abstract_id=1966115 (finding that delayed eBook introductions caused only small and statistically insignificant increases in hardcopy new-release sales, but substantially depressed eBook sales for the same title).

57. Milliot, "As E-book Sales Decline."

58. Gessen, "War of the Words."

17. The Long Agony of Antitrust

1. See William Letwin, *Law and Economic Policy in America* (Chicago: University of Chicago Press, 1959), 76–77; Clark, *Federal Trust Policy*, 78–108 (exhaustive analysis of views of professional economists of late 19th century, finding uniform opposition to government-enforced competition; finding that no American economist explicitly supported theory underlying Sherman Act until 1903); Richard Hofstadter, "What Happened to the Antitrust Movement?," in *The Paranoid Style in American Politics and*

Other Essays (New York: Alfred A. Knopf, 1964), 188, 190 (so describing the "conventional history").

2. See, e.g., John Kenneth Galbraith, *The New Industrial State,* 3rd ed. (1967; Princeton, NJ: Princeton University Press, 1978), 195-196 (antitrust is a "fig leaf by which power is kept out of sight"); Thurman W. Arnold, *The Folklore of Capitalism* (Garden City, NJ: Blue Ribbon Books, 1937), 212, 217 ("The actual result of the antitrust laws was to promote the growth of great industrial organizations by deflecting the attack on them into purely moral and ceremonial channels. . . . By virtue of the very crusade against them, the great corporations grew bigger and bigger, and more and more respectable"). Kreps, "Symposium," 701 ("The most palatable course [for federal enforcers] is . . . a maximum appearance of enforcement with minimum actual alteration in highly profitable practices"); cf. Walter Lippman, *Drift and Mastery: An Attempt to Diagnose the Current Unrest* (New York: Mitchell Kennerly, 1914), 121-148 (characterizing the antitrust movement as a "nation of villagers" attempting to stop inexorable social change).

3. For one archetypal statement that antitrust should be limited to the narrowest circumstances, see Frank H. Easterbrook, "The Limits of Antitrust," *Texas Law Review* 63 (1984): 1-40. On rejection, see, e.g., Dominick Armentano, *Antitrust and Monopoly: Anatomy of a Policy Failure,* 2nd ed. (Oakland, CA: Independent Institute, 1996), xiii, 3 ("All of the antitrust laws ought to be promptly repealed" because "our formal antimonopoly policies have been a fraud, and . . . public attention concerning the monopoly problem in America has been totally misdirected"); Edwin S. Rockefeller, *The Antitrust Religion* (Washington, DC: Cato Institute, 2007), 1 ("There is no such thing as antitrust law. Antitrust is a religion. Antitrust enforcement is arbitrary, political regulation of commercial activity, not enforcement of a coherent set of rules adopted by Congress").

4. On institutional reasons, see, e.g., Frederick M. Rowe, "The Decline of Antitrust and the Delusions of Models: The Faustian Pact of Law and Economics," *Georgetown Law Journal* 72 (1984): 1511-1570 (arguing that litigation moves so slowly that markets often change before remedies take effect); Kovacic, "Failed Expectations" (arguing that periods of agitation for more aggressive enforcement self-defeatingly generate periods of political reaction). See also Eugene V. Rostow, *National Policy for the Oil Industry* (New Haven, CT: Yale University Press, 1948), which argues that antitrust remedies in the oil industry were evaded when firms devised other means to the same ends. Regarding unintended consequences, for example, it has been suggested many times that the Sherman Act's ban on collusion caused the Great Merger Wave of 1890 to 1910, and that strict limits on horizontal mergers observed by the Warren Court drove the conglomerate merger wave of the 1960s. See, e.g., Bittlingmayer, "Did Antitrust Policy Cause the Great Merger Wave?," 33-34; Samuel R. Reid, "Antitrust and the 'Merger Wave' Phenomenon: A Failure of Public Policy," *Antitrust Law and Economics Review* 3 (1969): 25-42, 28; Rowe, "Decline of Antitrust," 1527.

5. See, e.g., Robert D. Novak, "Vendetta against Microsoft," *Washington Post,* Sept. 23, 1999 (claiming the Clinton administration sued Microsoft because it was "too big and too successful for liberal sensibilities"); cf. David B. Kopel and Joseph Bast, "Antitrust's Greatest Hits: The Foolish Precedents behind the Microsoft Case," *Reason,* Nov. 2001, 29. Microsoft, of course, stressed that it had merely succeeded through hard work and creativity. See Microsoft, Inc., "Setting the Record Straight: Microsoft Statement

on Government Lawsuit" (press release, Oct. 1998), http://www.ulb.ac.be/cours/soco /sish/droit-techinfo/microreb.htm ("Microsoft has focused on a single goal since it was formed in 1975: making the best possible products, and offering them at the most competitive prices, to benefit consumers. The DOJ has chosen to ignore the choices made by consumers in an incredibly innovative and competitive free market; the importance of technology to the economy; and the many powerful facts supporting Microsoft's case").

6. For educated disagreement, see, e.g., William H. Page and John E. Lopatka, *The Microsoft Case: Antitrust, High Technology, and Consumer Welfare* (Chicago: University of Chicago Press, 2007), 243–248 (analysis by two distinguished antitrust scholars raising doubts about the desirability of the *Microsoft* enforcement action).

7. 253 F.3d 34 (D.C. Cir. 2001) (en banc). While *Microsoft* was an unsigned per curiam opinion, it is widely assumed to have been written by Judge Douglas Ginsburg. See, e.g., Jennifer Frey, "Introducing Douglas H. Ginsburg," *NYU Law Magazine,* 2011, http://blogs.law.nyu.edu/magazine/2011/introducing-douglas-h-ginsburg/. Judge Ginsburg was a professor of antitrust law at Harvard Law School and later, during the Reagan administration, assistant attorney general for the Justice Department's Antitrust Division.

8. See Andrew I. Gavil and Harry First, *The Microsoft Antitrust Cases: Competition Policy for the Twenty-First Century* (Cambridge, MA: MIT Press2014), 158–165, 181–184; Richard Blumenthal and Tim Wu, "What the Microsoft Antitrust Case Taught Us," *New York Times,* May 18, 2018; Brian Feldman, "U.S. v. Microsoft Proved That Antitrust Can Keep Tech Power in Check," *New York Magazine,* Dec. 12, 2017.

9. See Richard A. Posner, *Economic Analysis of Law,* 8th ed. (New York: Wolters Kluwer Law and Business, 2010).

10. Some dispute that commonly made claim. See, e.g., Daniel A. Crane, "The Paradox of Predatory Pricing," *Cornell Law Review* 91 (2005): 1–66, 4, 4n12, 15–16. But even on their numbers, predation plaintiffs win even limited legal success in only a tiny fraction of 1% of cases filed. See Sagers, "#LOLNothingMatters," 22n84.

11. 15 U.S.C. §§ 13–13c.

12. See Pac. Bell Tel. Co. v. Linkline Commc'ns, Inc., 555 U.S. 438, 448 (2009), citing United States v. Colgate & Co., 250 U.S. 300, 307 (1919) ("As a general rule, businesses are free to choose the parties with whom they will deal, as well as the prices, terms, and conditions of that dealing"). The exception is that a monopolist may violate the law by refusing to deal where the effect is to exclude competition in order to acquire or maintain the firm's monopoly power, but the Supreme Court describes this rule as a "limited exception" it recognizes only "very cautious[ly]." Verizon Commc'ns, Inc. v. Law Offs. of Curtis V. Trinko, 540 U.S. 398, 408–09 (2004).

There are surprisingly few clear statements on the rule that charging high prices is legal, but it is strongly implicit in the principle that mere size is not illegal. In the absence of predation or discrimination, courts will not inquire into actual prices charged. See United States v. Aluminum Co. of Am., 148 F.2d 416, 429–30 (2d Cir. 1945).

13. See William E. Kovacic, "The Intellectual DNA of Modern U.S. Competition Law for Dominant Firm Conduct: The Chicago / Harvard Double Helix," *Columbia Business*

Law Review 2007 (2007): 1–82, 36–37 (discussing the contemporary concern with "institutional" limitations, and the calls often made for caution in government antitrust interference).

14. United States v. Alum. Co. of Am., 148 F.2d 416, 429–30 (2d Cir. 1945).

15. 220 U.S. 373, 404 (1911), rev'd Leegin Creative Leather Prods., Inc. v. PSKS, Inc., 551 U.S. 877 (2007).

16. United States v. Colgate & Co., 250 U.S. 300 (1919).

17. 250 U.S. at 307 (emphasis added).

18. See, e.g., *Linkline*, 555 U.S. at 448 (reaffirming *Colgate*); *Trinko*, 540 U.S. at 408 (same).

19. Compare *Trinko*, 540 U.S. at 408 (quoting *Colgate*, 250 U.S. at 307) ("the Sherman Act 'does not restrict the long recognized right of [a] trader or manufacturer engaged in an entirely private business, freely to exercise his own independent discretion as to parties with whom he will deal'"), with *Colgate*, 250 U.S. at 307 ("*In the absence of any purpose to create or maintain a monopoly*, the [Sherman] act does not restrict") (emphasis added).

20. See S. Rep. No. 94-466 (1975) (Senate committee report favorably reporting Miller-Tydings repealer bill and reporting these data).

21. See Thompson, *Merchants of Culture;* Jim Milliot, "E-Book Sales Bolster Publishers' Bottom Lines," *Publishers Weekly,* Mar. 29, 2013.

22. See Richard A. Posner, "The Social Costs of Monopoly and Regulation," *Journal of Political Economy* 83 (1975): 807–828; Harvey Leibenstein, "Allocative Efficiency vs. 'X-Efficiency,'" *American Economic Review* 56 (1966): 392–415.

18. So Are Books, After All, Special? Is Anything?

Epigraph: Hal Varian, "Markets for Information Goods" (paper prepared for Bank of Japan conference, June 18–19, 1998), http://people.ischool.berkeley.edu/~hal/Papers /japan/.

1. A problem first elaborated in Phillip Nelson, "Information and Consumer Behavior," *Journal of Political Economy* 78 (1970): 311–329.

2. See "About Search Inside the Book," Amazon, https://www.amazon.com/gp/help /customer/display.html?nodeId=10197041.

3. Richard E. Caves, *Creative Industries: Contracts between Art and Commerce* (Cambridge, MA: Harvard University Press, 2002).

4. Canoy, van Ours, and van der Ploeg, "Economics of Books," 721, 734–735.

5. Madison, *Book Publishing in America,* viii, quoting, without citation, G. H. P and J. B. P., *Authors and Publishers: A Manual of Suggestions for Beginners in Literature,* 7th ed. (New York: G. P. Putnam's Sons, 1897), 188.

6. Carl Shapiro and Hal Varian, *Information Rules: A Strategic Guide to the Network Economy* (Cambridge, MA: Harvard Business Review Press, 1998).

7. See Joost Poort and Nico van Eijk, "Digital Fixation: The Law and Economics of a Fixed E-Book Price," *International Journal of Cultural Policy* 23 (2017): 464–481, 471.

8. See generally Pittman, "Who Are You Calling Irrational?" See also Shapiro and Varian, *Information Rules.*

9. See, e.g., Vidar Ringstad, "On the Cultural Blessings of Fixed Book Prices," *International Journal of Cultural Policy* 10 (2004): 351–365, 353–354.

10. See generally Canoy, van Ours, and van der Ploeg, "Economics of Books," 734–743.

11. Stephen Breyer, "The Uneasy Case for Copyright: A Study of Copyright in Books, Photocopies, and Computer Programs," *Harvard Law Review* 84 (1970): 281–351; Ku, "Creative Destruction of Copyright."

19. The Virtues of Vertical and Entry for Its Own Sake

1. Poort et al., "Digitally Binding."

2. See, e.g., Canoy, van Ours, and van der Ploeg, "Economics of Books," 721, 744–48.

3. In fact, one study found that suspension of RPM in the UK in 1995 did not affect the publication of new titles. James Dearnley and John Feather, "The UK Bookselling Trade without Resale Price Maintenance—An Overview of Change 1995–2001," *Publishing Research Quarterly,* Winter 2002, 16–31.

4. Poort et al., "Digitally Binding," an academic study commissioned by the Dutch authorities, found that a Dutch RPM law probably did help preserve independent bookstores but had little other effect. Likewise, Dearnley and Feather, "UK Bookselling Trade," analyzing the effect of suspension of the UK Net Book Agreement in 1995, found that while it appeared to cause the exit of about 6 percent of independent book stores in Britain over the course of some years, the predictions of harm it would do were exaggerated.

5. Alexander MacKay and David Aron Smith, "The Empirical Effects of Minimum Resale Price Maintenance" (Nielsen Dataset Paper Series 2-006, 2014), https://papers.ssrn .com/sol3/papers.cfm?abstract_id=2513533 (first study broadly measuring effects of RPM across a range of products, finding substantial price increases and output reduction, implying lack of any social benefit).

6. Yamey, "Retail Price Competition," 32–34.

7. See Dearnley and Feather, "UK Bookselling Trade," 18–19.

8. See Poort and van Eijk, "Digital Fixation," 473.

9. See, e.g., Peter Kafka, "Apple Fires Back at Feds, Amazon," *All Things D,* Apr. 12, 2012, http://allthingsd.com/20120412/apple-fires-back-at-the-feds-amazon/ (quoting Apple spokesperson Tom Neumayr, arguing that "the launch of the iBookstore in 2010" had to be good, because it "br[oke] Amazon's monopolistic grip on the publishing industry"); U.S. v. Apple, No. 13-3741(L), at 1 (2d Cir. Feb. 25, 2014) (Apple's opening brief on appeal, which states, "Apple's entry as an e-book retailer marked the *beginning,* not the end, of competition" (emphasis in original)); Geoff Manne, "How Apple Can Defeat the DOJ's E-Book Antitrust Suit," *Forbes,* Apr. 12, 2012, https://www.forbes .com/sites/beltway/2012/04/12/how-apple-can-defeat-the-dojs-e-book-antitrust-suit /#7f7d7e003c7f (arguing that agency pricing with most-favored-nations clauses protect fixed costs of entry).

10. See Leegin Creative Leather Products, Inc. v. PSKS, Inc., 551 U.S. 877, 891 (2007); Marvel and McCafferty, "Resale Price Maintenance" (arguing that manufacturers offer RPM to secure distribution with high-quality retailers, who thereby certify their products' quality).

11. For a statement of this traditional idea, and its prevalence in antitrust case law, see Einer R. Elhauge, "Why Above-Cost Price Cuts to Drive Out Entrants Are Not Predatory—and the Implications for Defining Costs and Market Power," *Yale Law Journal* 112 (2003): 681–828, 699, 699n56 (citing Brooke Grp., Ltd. v. Brown & Williamson Tobacco Corp., 509 U.S. 209, 223 (1993)).

12. United States v. Socony-Vacuum Oil Co., 310 U.S. 150, 224 n. 59 (1940).

13. Apple argued that it brought technological improvements, but in each case they either violated "cross-market efficiencies" rule or predated Apple's entry altogether. See United States v. Phila. Nat'l Bank v. 374 U.S. 321, 371 (1963).

14. A point nicely made in Albanese, "Albanese on the Apple E-books Case."

15. See Stone, *Everything Store,* recounting the history of Amazon's development of the Kindle.

16. For the classic formulation of the two-sided market model, see William F. Baxter, "Bank Interchange of Transactional Paper: Legal and Economic Perspectives," *Journal of Law and Economics* 26 (1983): 541–588. For a recent summary of the massive literature that followed Baxter's original paper, see David S. Evans and Michael Noel, "Defining Antitrust Markets When Firms Operate Two-Sided Platforms," *Columbia Business Law Review* 2005 (2005): 667–701.

17. 253 F.3d 34 (2d Cir. 2001).

18. See, e.g., George L. Priest, "Apple Should Win Its E-Book Appeal," *Wall Street Journal,* Dec. 14, 2014.

19. On the newspaper problem, see American Bar Association, *Federal Statutory Exemptions from Antitrust Law* (Washington, DC: ABA Book Publishing, 2007). For the Supreme Court's recent decision, see Ohio v. Am. Express Co., 138 S. Ct. 2274 (2018).

20. The Second Circuit case was United States v. American Express, 838 F.3d 179 (2d Cir. 2016), aff'd, 138 S. Ct. 2274 (2018). Defendants have attempted to apply two-sided theory to other industries including college sports, hospitals and health insurance, and airlines. In re Natl. Collegiate Athletic Assn. Athletic Grant-In-Aid Cap Antitrust Litig., 14-MD-02541 CW, 2018 WL 4241981, at *3 (N.D. Cal. Sept. 3, 2018); United States v. Charlotte-Mecklenburg Hosp. Auth., 248 F. Supp. 3d 720, 731 (W.D.N.C. 2017); US Airways, Inc. v. Sabre Holdings Corp., 11 CIV. 2725 (LGS), 2017 WL 1064709, at *2 (S.D.N.Y. Mar. 21, 2017).

20. Amazon

Epigraph: John Stuart Mill, *Collected Works of John Stuart Mill,* vol. 26, *Journals and Debating Speeches,* ed. John Robson (Toronto: University of Toronto Press, 1988), 429.

1. See United States v. Apple Inc., 952 F. Supp. 2d 638, 681 (S.D.N.Y. 2013), aff'd, 791 F.3d 290 (2d Cir. 2015) (noting that federal government learned of the conspiracy from a letter sent by Amazon to the Federal Trade Commission).

2. John S. McGee, "Predatory Price Cutting: The Standard Oil (N.J.) Case," *Journal of Law and Economics* 1 (1958): 137–169.

3. *Apple,* 952 F. Supp. 25 at 650.

4. *Apple,* 952 F. Supp. 2d at 648–49 (noting that Kindle was the first commercially successful eBook reader).

5. *Apple,* Plaintiff's exhibit PX-0835.
6. Stone, *Everything Store,* 110–111.
7. Ibid.
8. In fairness, Apple might have failed to put on hard evidence of predation because it lost some discovery skirmishes against nonparty Amazon. But Amazon's retail prices are public and the wholesale prices it paid were in the defendant publishers' possession. Sales at an overall loss should not have been too hard to prove it if it were true, and defendants did nothing to prove it. Perhaps they didn't produce that evidence because it would not be legally relevant in defense of price fixing. but they did raise a number of other arguments, mainly efficiency arguments, that also were technically irrelevant.
9. The Court has frequently restated its view that "predatory pricing schemes are rarely tried, and even more rarely successful." Weyerhaeuser Co. v. Ross Simmons Hardwood Lumber Co., Inc., 549 U.S. 312, 313 (2007); Brooke Grp., Ltd. v. Brown & Williamson Tobacco Corp., 509 U.S. at 209, 226 (1993); 324 Liquor Corp. v. Duffy, 479 U.S. 335, 343 n.5 (1987); Cargill, Inc. v. Monfort of Colo., Inc., 479 U.S. 104, 121 n.17 (1986); Matsushita Elec. Indus. Co., Ltd. v. Zenith Radio Corp., 475 U.S. 574, 589 (1986).
10. 509 U.S. 209 (1993).
11. See Sagers, "#LOLNothingMatters," 22, 22n84.
12. See United States v. AMR Corp., 335 F.3d 1109 (10th Cir. 2003).
13. 335 F.3d at 1116–21.
14. See generally Blair and Harrison, *Monopsony in Law and Economics,* ch. 3.
15. See generally ibid., ch. 2.
16. See *Apple* Complaint, at ¶¶ 34, 49.
17. The music and video industries have made the same arguments during various squabbles. DiCola and Sag, "Information-Gathering Approach."
18. Auletta, "Publish or Perish."
19. Kelly, *Inevitable.*
20. See, e.g., Shapiro and Varian, *Information Rules.*
21. See Heffernan, *Magic and Loss.*
22. Stone, *Everything Store,* 41.
23. Ibid., 51.
24. Ibid., 134.
25. Ibid.
26. Gessen, "War of the Words"; Claire Cain Miller, "Need Advice on What to Read? Ask the Internet," *New York Times Bits,* Mar. 10, 2011.
27. Gessen, "War of the Words"; Miller, "Need Advice."
28. Thompson, *Merchants of Culture.*
29. See, e.g., "A Call to Investigate Amazon," Authors Guild, July 13, 2015, https://www .authorsguild.org/industry-advocacy/a-call-to-investigate-amazon/.
30. See generally Selwyn Duke, "Antitrust Should Be Used to Break Up Partisan Tech Giants Like Facebook, Google," *The Hill,* Dec. 27, 2016, http://thehill.com/blogs /pundits-blog/media/311886-antitrust-should-be-used-to-break-up-partisan-tech -giants-like.

31. Michael Nunez, "Former Facebook Workers: We Routinely Suppressed Conservative News," *Gizmodo,* May 9, 2016, https://gizmodo.com/former-facebook-workers-we -routinely-suppressed-conser-1775461006.

32. See Jessica Guynn, "Twitter Accused of Political Bias in Right-Wing Crackdown," *USA Today,* Nov. 18, 2016; Gab Ai, Inc. v. Google, LLC, Civ. No. 17-4115 (E.D. Va. Sept. 14, 2017) (complaint).

33. See, e.g., "Call to Investigate Amazon"; Duke, "Antitrust Should Be Used."

34. As early as 1938, the Commission refused to issue a license on editorial diversity grounds, and in the early 1940s it established a set of ownership and cross-ownership rules. See Genesee Radio Corp., 5 F.C.C. 183, 186–87 (1938); Nat'l Broad. Co. v. United States, 319 U.S. 190, 206–08, 224–27 (1943) (upholding the rule). At the same time, the Commission prohibited common ownership of stations within the same broadcast service (AM radio, FM radio, and television) in the same community. See Rules Governing Standard and High Frequency Broadcast Stations, 5 Fed. Reg. 2382, 2384 (June 26, 1940) (FM radio); Rules Governing Standard and High Frequency Broadcast Stations, 6 Fed. Reg. 2282, 2284–85 (May 6, 1941) (television); Rules Governing Standard and High Frequency Broadcast Stations, 8 Fed. Reg. 16065 (Nov. 27, 1943) (AM radio).

35. The pressure to deregulate came initially from the Telecommunications Act of 1996, Pub. L. No. 104–104, 110 Stat. 56 (1996), codified at various sections of 47 U.S.C. The Act specifically repealed or modified some of the Commission's ownership rules and required periodic, ongoing review to consider further deregulation. The Reagan-era FCC also undertook significant deregulatory steps of its own, eventually encountering serious opposition from the courts. Prometheus Radio Project v. FCC, 373 F.3d 372 (3d Cir. 2004); Prometheus Radio Project v. FCC, 652 F.3d 431 (3d Cir. 2011).

Certain rules are still in place, though the statutorily required reviews continue, and so the agency could take further deregulatory steps. As the rules now stand, no person may own a collection of TV stations reaching more than 39 percent of US households. Second, no person may own more than two TV stations in the same metropolitan area, and may not own two if their service areas overlap. Third, no person may own more than one of the four traditional broadcast television networks (ABC, CBS, Fox, and NBC). Likewise, the rules limit ownership of radio stations in any given city, on a sliding scale based on the number of stations in that city; the maximum allowed is eight stations in the largest cities. Lastly, the rules preserve two cross-ownership limits. They prohibit common ownership of a daily newspaper and a full-power broadcast station (AM, FM, or TV) if the station's coverage encompasses the newspaper's city of publication, and they prohibit some cross-ownership of TV and radio stations in the same city, under a complex rule that depends on the number of stations in that city.

36. Any such rule would be vigorously opposed; booksellers would claim it violates their own First Amendment rights, among other things. Yet, Congress has in various ways imposed competition-oriented rules in speech industries, and the Supreme Court has explicitly held that subjecting speech industries to competition policy *serves* First Amendment values of diverse opinion. See Associated Press v. United States, 326 U.S. 1, 19–20 (1945).

21. The Threat to Writers and the Threat to Cultural Values

1. See, e.g., "Letter from Scott Turow: Grim News," Authors Guild, Mar. 9, 2012, http://www.authorsguild.org/advocacy/letter-from-scott-turow-grim-news/.
2. See Breyer, "Uneasy Case for Copyright." See also Ku, "Creative Destruction of Copyright," making a related argument with regard to music.
3. Breyer, "Uneasy Case for Copyright," noting that foreign published books had no copyright protection in the United States until late in the nineteenth century, but were published here successfully and without deterrence to their authors.
4. See, e.g., Julie E. Cohen, "Lochner in Cyberspace: The New Economic Orthodoxy of 'Rights Management,'" *Michigan Law Review* 97 (1998): 462–563, 505, 303n160 (summarizing this argument and discussing evidence supporting it); Lloyd L. Weinrib, "Copyright for Functional Expression," *Harvard Law Review* 111 (1998): 1149–1254, 1232 ("The vast majority of authors, artists, and composers, professional as well as nonprofessional, do not earn a living from their works").
5. Books vary in price elasticity, depending on their audience and the volume of their production, but general interest trade books are quite elastic. George Bittlingmayer, "The Elasticity of Demand for Books, Resale Price Maintenance and the Lerner Index," *Journal of Institutional and Theoretical Economics* 148 (1992): 588–606. An outlier is Thomas J. Webster, "Retail Consolidation and the Price Elasticity of Demand for Books," *International Business & Economics Research Journal* 1, no. 12 (2011): 27–33, 30, which found trade books to be fairly inelastic, but "paperbound" books quite elastic. A weakness of this study is its failure to explain how books were categorized into these groupings.
6. James T. Farrell, "The Fate of Writing in America," *Western Socialist,* Apr. 1947, https://www.marxists.org/history/etol/writers/farrell/1947/publishing.htm.
7. Edwin McDowell, "Statement on the Continuing Trend to Concentration of Power in the Book Publishing Industry," *Authors Guild Bulletin,* 1979.
8. "Barry Eisler's 'Detachment' from 'Legacy' Publishing," *NPR: Morning Edition,* Oct. 7, 2011.
9. See, e.g., Jason Pinter, "Barry Eisler Explains Self-Publishing Decision," *Daily Beast,* Mar. 24, 2011, https://www.thedailybeast.com/barry-eisler-explains-self-publishing-decision.
10. Band, "Google Library Project."

22. The Creeping Profusion of Externalities

Epigraph: Archie Green, *Torching the Fink Books and Other Essays on Vernacular Culture* (Chapel Hill: University of North Carolina Press, 2001), 211.
1. LaVecchia and Mitchell, "Amazon's Stranglehold," 53.
2. See Nicholas Carr, "Don't Burn Your Books—Print Is Here to Stay," *Wall Street Journal,* Jan. 25, 2013, noting the general expectation that paper books will soon no longer exist, but suggesting reasons to doubt it.
3. See Woeste, *Farmers Benevolent Trust.*
4. Those changes included a dramatic increase late in the century in world trade, an end to protectionist legislation in Britain, and the opening of the Suez canal in 1869.

Charles K. Hawley, "The Shift from Sailing Ships to Steamships, 1850–1890: A Study in Technological Change and Diffusion," in *Essays on a Mature Economy: Britain after 1840*, ed. Donald N. McCloskey (Princeton, NJ: Princeton University Press, 1971), 215, 223–224.

5. See Gerald S. Graham, "The Ascendancy of the Sailing Ship, 1850–85," *Economic History Review* 9 (1956): 74–88, 77, 83–87.

6. See generally Directorate of Science, Technology and Industry, OECD, *Competition Policy in Liner Shipping: Final Report* (Paris: OECD, 2002), 18; Graham, "Ascendancy of the Sailing Ship"; Douglass North, "Ocean Freight Rates and Economic Development 1750–1913," *Journal of Economic History* 18 (1958): 537–555, 542–543; Hawley, "Shift from Sailing Ships," 221–222; Sarah Palmer, "'The Most Indefatigable Activity': The General Steam Navigation Company, 1824–50," *Journal of Transport History* 3 (1982): 1–22.

7. North, "Ocean Freight Rates," 537.

8. Carl J. Ryant, "The South and the Movement against Chain Stores," *Journal of Southern History* 39 (1973): 207–222, 208.

9. Levinson, *Great A&P*, 67–69; Walter S. Haywood and Percival White, *Chain Stores: Their Management and Operation* (New York: McGraw Hill Book Co., 1922), 18.

10. Louis D. Brandeis, "Cutthroat Prices: Competition That Kills," *Harper's Weekly*, Nov. 15, 1913, 10, 12; Levinson, *Great A&P*, 67–69.

11. See Scroop, "Anti-Chain Store Movement," 943.

12. Ch. 592, §§ 2 to 4, 49 Stat. 1526 (1936).

13. Marc Levinson, "A History of Chain Stores, and Their Enemies: Echoes," *Bloomberg View*, Nov. 25, 2011.

14. Daniel Boorstin, *The Americans: The Democratic Experience* (New York: Vintage, 1974), 111. For critique of that view, see Scroop, "Anti-Chain Store Movement."

15. See Americans for Tax Fairness, "Walmart on Tax Day" (Apr. 2014), https:// americansfortaxfairness.org/files/Walmart-on-Tax-Day-Americans-for-Tax-Fairness -11.pdf; Van Buren, "Walmart Wages Are the Main Reason People Depend on Food Stamps," *The Nation*, Feb. 16, 2016.

16. See Levinson, *Great A&P*.

17. Ibid.; Ryant, "The South," 209.

18. See Scroop, "Anti-Chain Store Movement," collecting those views.

19. See generally Lizabeth Cohen, *A Consumers' Republic: The Politics of Mass Consumption in Postwar America* (New York: Vintage Books, 2003); Meg Jacobs, "State of the Field: The Politics of Consumption," *Reviews in American History* 39 (2011): 561–573, 568–69; cf. Richard Hofstadter, *The Age of Reform* (New York: Vintage, 1955), 172–173, noting a shift from a popular concern with producer interests "to an equal concern with consumption as a sphere of life," which "gave mass appeal and political force to many Progressive issues and provided the Progressive leaders with a broad avenue of access to the public."

Acknowledgments

The Oxford legal scholar Patrick Atiyah, a great lawyer indeed, recognized the problem of lawyers who write books with ambitions like this one. I owe the same apology with which he began his monumental *Rise and Fall of Freedom of Contract*:

> This book is primarily a study in the history of ideas although it also attempts to explore the interrelationship between social and economic conditions and those ideas. . . . Nobody could hope to be equally proficient in all the disciplines encompassed in a work of this kind. Ideally, this book should have been written by someone qualified not only as a lawyer, but also as an economist, a social and economic historian, and a student of political theory and philosophy. I need not say that I make no claim to these qualifications, and I am acutely aware of the dangers of venturing into this work without them. (1979, vii)

I would like to thank a number of people in connection with this book. Among the many reasons to appreciate an editor like Thomas LeBien is that he is willing to give his name at fancy restaurants as *le-be-YAHhhhnnn,* instead of *le-BEAN,* to get us a better table. He also rescued this book at a point when I thought it would not come to be. He waited patiently in many different respects, including waiting for me to realize the ways he understood the book better than I did. His ideas are evident throughout.

I learned about the *Apple* case and the publishing industry from many conversations with Andrew Albanese of *Publishers Weekly* and from a cordial and unexpected correspondence with a great student of the publishing industry, John Thompson of Cambridge University. Ariel Katz of the University of Toronto was the first person outside the book industry, as far as I am aware, to notice that the *Apple* conspiracy was just like book cartels that started in Britain and the United States early in the twentieth century ("History Repeats: Publishers, Retailers and Antitrust," 2012). To book industry people, I suppose, it was obvious right away.

Two anonymous peer reviewers read the entire manuscript and wrote meticulous, extremely useful advice, and in one case said things that made my heart sing.

The book benefitted from discussions with many other people, including Jonathan Baker of American University, Diane Bartz of Thomson Reuters, Brian Bix of the University of Minnesota, Peter Carstensen of the University of Wisconsin, Miriam Cherry of St. Louis University, Mickey Davis and Doron Kalir of Cleveland-Marshall College of Law, Justin Elliot of ProPublica, Eric Fink of Elon University, Harry First of New York University, Warren Grimes of Southwestern Law School, Bert Foer of the American Antitrust Institute, Allen Grunes of the Konkurrenz Group, Tom Horton of the University of South Dakota, Ankur Kapur of Constantine Cannon, Brent Kendall of the *Wall Street Journal*, Jack Kirkwood of Seattle University, Elizabeth Knoll, then of Harvard University Press, Stacy Mitchell of the Institute for Local Self-Reliance, Barry Lynn, then of the New America Foundation, Geoff Manne of the International Center for Law and Economics, Frank Pasquale of the University of Maryland, Mark Patterson of Fordham University, Aaron Perzanowski of Case Western Reserve University, Russ Pittman and Anant Raut of the US Justice Department, Barak Richman of Duke University, Matthew Sag of Loyola University of Chicago, my great former student Joe Shininger, Keith Sipe of Carolina Academic Press, and Maurice Stucke of the Konkurrenz Group and the University of Tennessee. I was fortunate to present on the subject before the Loyola Chicago Consumer Antitrust Colloquium, and for this and other kindnesses—including a meticulous read of the entire first draft—I thank Spencer Weber Waller. I also presented the book before the Antitrust Sections of the American and New York State Bar Associations and the law faculties of American, Case Western

Reserve, Elon, New Hampshire, Pittsburgh, Villanova, West Virginia, and Cleveland State Universities.

Several people read the manuscript in its entirety and for that I am very grateful. They were Barak Orbach of the University of Arizona, Don Resnikoff of the DC Consumer Rights Coalition (and formerly the DC Attorney General's Office), Guy Rub of Ohio State, Spencer Waller of Loyola Chicago, and Abe Wickelgren of the University of Texas.

The book was supported with sabbatical leave from Cleveland State and the generosity of the James A. Thomas Chair in Law.

I first gave the *Apple* case serious thought when I spoke about it at the In re Books conference at New York Law School in fall 2012, hosted by Professor James Grimmelmann, who now teaches at Cornell. One of the things I learned from the crowd there, which contained many representatives from the city's large publishing community, was how open-minded most of them are about the industry they so obviously love. They received me with conscientious tolerance, even though not many of them were thrilled to hear an outsider say that their industry's dilemmas aren't really so special. A very few of them wouldn't hear of it, including an executive who stood to report that her own boss was among the chief participants in the *Apple* conspiracy. As the room noticeably hushed, she made clear how appalled she was that the dealings of such persons could be called a "cartel" or a "conspiracy." I don't doubt the sincerity of her surprise or judge her for her reaction, and they were important to me. I kept to myself the fact that for what her boss had done, he was lucky not to have gone to prison.

Thanks finally to the Holland-America Line, and to a carved, teak chaise longue on the aft navigation deck of the *M/S Amsterdam,* the kind of setting to which persons of my station are unaccustomed. Mechanized, ocean-going passenger carriage surely first arose in the 1880s (see Chapter 22) so that writers could write.

Index

Actavis, Inc., FTC v., 71
Addyston Pipe & Steel Co., United States v., 22–24, 51
Agricultural cooperative, 73
Alfred A. Knopf (publishing firm), 84, 88, 91
Alienation, restraints on, 32–33
Allocational efficiency, 8–9, 46, 208
Amazon: and authors, 247–252, 263; as censor, 244–246; early digitization project, 164–166; and eBook business, 77, 95, 128, 130–131, 140–142, 144, 147, 162, 171–179, 223; and eBooks conspiracy, 105, 180–193, 195–196, 199; and economics of books, 213–214, 224; history, 97, 99–104, 165–166; and innovation, 103–104; and intermediation, 238–244, 251; and monopsony, 235–238; and platform theory, 225–226; and potential monopoly liability, 8, 13, 41, 235–238, 264; and predatory pricing, 228–235; as the real danger, 2, 4–8, 10, 12, 18, 27, 97, 104, 198–199, 210, 222, 228–246; and vertical relationships, 64, 78, 88, 105, 108, 112–113, 222–223
Amazon marketplace, 225
America COMPETES Act, 39
American Economic Association, 54, 262
American Economic Review, 54
American Law Institute, 58
Antitrust Paradox, The, 206
Apple: and the digital revolution, 132–139, 175–176, 183–184; history, 133, 134–135; and music, 133–135; and tablet computing, 184–185; vis-à-vis Amazon, 141, 165–166, 174, 175–179
Apple, Inc., United States v., 3–5; on appeal, 197–199, 200–201; and authors, 250–252; the conspiracy, 178, 181–190; and cultural values, 96, 97, 253–259; and digital distribution, 128, 133; effects of the conspiracy, 7–8, 104, 139, 169–170, 179, 183, 199, 201–202, 213, 230; factual evidence, 3, 181–192, 195–196; government action, 193–196, 228–235; and the history of book cartels, 106; and independent bookstores, 104; and innovation, 140–142; and the legal problem of generalization, 17–27, 30–31; and monopoly law, 12–13; and no-fault monopoly, 235–238; popular reception, 3–6, 9–11, 30–31, 37, 45–47, 63–64, 78, 81, 187–191, 205–206, 210–219, 253–254; and predatory pricing, 229–235; and vertical restraints, 64–65, 107–114, 120, 121, 220–227; and vested interests, 169–170; vis-à-vis Amazon, 12–13, 97, 228–246
App Store, 185, 190–191
Aquinas, Thomas, 31, 154
Arnold, Thurman, 12, 261
ARPANET, 8, 160
Associationalism, 55–62, 84
Associative indexing, 155, 157
Atlantic Monthly, 87

Backlist, 94–95, 102, 169, 173, 214, 240
Banking regulation, 39, 60
Barnes & Noble, 78, 96, 99–102, 104,
174–175, 193
B. Dalton Booksellers, 78, 99, 104, 251
Behavioral economics, 54
Berle, Adoph, 54
Bertelsmann, 88, 91
Betamax, 293n5
Bezos, Jeff: and creation of Kindle, 135,
141, 144, 157, 164–165, 171–178; and
innovation, 103–104, 157, 164–165, 171,
176–178, 242; personal history, 102–103;
vis-à-vis Apple, 141, 164; vis-à-vis the
publishers, 176–178, 202
Bilateral monopoly, 13, 21, 250, 263
Black, Hugo, 38
Bobbs-Merrill, 91, 125
Bobbs-Merrill Co. v. Straus, 113, 125–126
Boni, Albert, 84–85
Boni & Liveright, 84
Bookland. *See* Books-a-Million
Books.com. *See* Book Stacks
Books-a-Million, 99
Bookseller: Amazon as, 102–104, 244–246;
and business losses, 5, 99, 104, 254; as
censor, 244–246; cultural significance,
18, 97–98, 221, 243, 254; and govern-
ment protection, 126, 221; history, 79,
97–102; and vertical restraints, 100–101,
119, 121–127, 221; vis-à-vis publishers,
105–109, 121–124, 188, 221, 243
Book Stacks, 103, 172
Book store. *See* Bookseller
Borders, 78, 96, 99–102, 104
Bork, Robert, 5, 206, 290n9
Brand, 66–67, 91, 241
Brandeis, Louis, 5, 198
Brentano's, 99
Bromwich, Michael, 200
Brown, Bob, 8, 152–155, 156, 170
Busa, Roberto, 154
Bush, Vannevar, 154–157

Camus, Albert, 87
Carey, Henry, 57, 60, 87
Carey, Matthew, 57
Carey & Lea, 57, 87

Cartel. *See* Price fixing
Castaway, The, 125
Caves, Richard, 214, 239
CBS, 136, 284n28, 312n35
Censorship, 87, 156, 244–246
Cerf, Bennett, 77, 85, 87, 94
Chain store, 115, 129, 257–259; booksellers,
96, 99–101, 128; populist opposition, 117,
125, 258–259
Chain store tax, 117–118, 259
Chicago School, 68, 113–114, 229
Christianson, Clayton, 269n16
Circumstantial evidence, 194–196
Civil war, 29, 38, 43, 44, 57, 79, 82–83,
98–99, 115, 255
Classical liberalism. *See* Liberalism
Clay, Henry, 57
Clayton Act, 58, 119; §3, 288n2; §7,
41–42
Coase, Ronald, 68
Codex, 150–152, 154, 155
Common law, 19, 32–33, 56
Commons, John, 54
Conglomerate, 1, 78, 89, 90–95, 246,
284n28
Consensus history, 28–31, 34, 62
Conspiracy: as defense against a monopolist, 2, 4, 108, 179, 222, 234–235, 248; as
distinguished from procompetitive
conduct, 20–22; horizontal, 194–195;
hub-and-spoke, 107–108, 195–197; proof
of, 180–181, 193–194; vertical, 107–108,
194–196
Continental T.V. v. GTE Sylvania, 114,
280n12
Copyright: and capture by industry,
138–139; and competition, 72, 138; and
digital revolution, 136–137; first sale
doctrine, 126; as frustrating digital
distribution, 160–163, 165–170; history,
80, 82–83, 122; orphan works, 161–162;
and piracy, 218–219; and sufficiency of
authors' incentives, 218–219, 247–248,
252; term extensions, 159, 161; and
vertical restraints, 113, 125–126
Corporate liberalism. *See* Liberalism
Cote, Denise, 2–3, 8, 184–185, 194–201
Credit rating agency, 39
Credit Rating Agency Reform Act, 274n29

Credit Suisse Secs. (USA), LLC v. Billing, 72–73
Criminal antitrust, 20–21, 74
Cue, Eddy, 185

Decreasing marginal utility of money, 52–53
Degler, Carl, 32
Department of Agriculture, 73
Department of Justice, 1, 200–201, 234
Department of Transportation, 73
Deregulation, 70, 119, 245, 280n5
Destructive competition, 23–24, 27, 45, 47, 51, 55–64, 131, 205, 215, 227
de Tocqueville, Alexis, 56, 62
Diamond Multimedia, 133, 134
Differentiation, 36, 116, 211
Digital Public Library of America, 163
Digital rights management, 136–137, 161, 172
Digitization, 7, 128–139, 141–152, 157–163, 164–170, 213–214, 247, 252
Direct evidence, 194–196
Disintermediation, 238–244
Disruption, 10, 128–129, 137–139, 144–145, 200, 249, 251
Distribution (of goods), 34, 239–240; and antitrust law, 112–114, 117–120; of books, 4, 79–81, 97–104, 140–142, 157–163, 171–179, 182, 188–190; digital, 7–8, 10, 72, 128–139, 239–241, 249; economics of, 106–112, 124; history, 114–127, 257–259; jobber, 98, 115–117, 257; wholesale, 65, 67, 100–102, 110–112, 115–118, 124, 188–190
Distribution (of wealth). *See* Inequality
Dodd–Frank Wall Street Reform and Consumer Protection Act, 73
Dr. Miles Medical Co. v. John D. Park & Sons Co., 113–117, 119, 120, 122, 126, 209
Dynabook, 157, 185

eBay, 179, 225
Economic cost, 232
Economic profit, 36, 273n24
Economics of books, 213–219
Eddy, Arthur Jerome, 60–61

E-Ink, 173–174, 242
Eisenstein, Elizabeth, 143
Eldred v. Ashcroft, 159
Empty core theory, 63–64, 227
Englebart, Douglas, 156–157
Enlightenment, the, 44, 53
Entry: by Amazon, 104; by Apple, 4, 132–133, 184, 190; and destructive competition, 59; as an economic phenomenon, 35–36, 39, 208; for its own sake, 221–227; and price predation, 230, 239
Entry barrier, 35–36, 223, 230
Exemption, statutory antitrust, 22, 70, 73
Externality, 216–217, 221, 223–227, 253–254, 263

Federal Communications Commission, 39, 245
Federal Maritime Commission, 73
Federal Trade Commission, 60–61, 100–101, 125, 135, 193, 238
Federal Trade Commission Act, 58
FireWire, 133
First amendment, 37–38, 312n36
Fixed cost, 45, 55, 58–59, 215, 231–232, 248
Ford, Gerald, 114
Franklin, Benjamin, 57, 79–80
Freedom of contract, 38
Free riding, 65–67, 114, 221
FTC v. Actavis, Inc., 71
Fuller, Lon, 19
Fungibility, 35–36, 116

Galambos, Louis, 275n9
Gemstar, 175
Generalization: in antitrust, 9, 20–27; as a problem in law, 17–27, 256; as a problem in social science, 44, 50–54, 256
German historical school. *See* Historical school of economics
Gerstle, Gary, 45–46, 62
Google: as book distributor, 193, 213–214, 239; books project, 144, 163, 164–170; as censor, 244; and the digital revolution, 141, 174, 178, 239; as monopolist, 22
Gordon v. New York Stock Exchange, 73

Great Atlantic & Pacific Tea Company, 257–259
Great depression (America), 38, 41–42, 61, 100, 101, 258, 261
Great depression (Europe), 44
Great merger movement, 44
Grocery, 116, 118, 259
Grove Press, 84, 87
Gutenberg press, 143, 151, 157, 158, 205

Hachette, Louis, 82
Hachette Books, 82, 88, 107, 190, 244, 285n28
Harper & Brothers, 81–83, 86, 87, 98
Harper's, 87, 98
Hart, H.L.A., 19–20
Hart, Michael, 8, 157–160, 162, 170
Hart, Philip, 119
Hart-Scott-Rodino Act, 119
Heffernan, Virginia, 153
Historical school of economics, 53
Holmes, Oliver Wendell, 17, 37–38
Holtzbrinck, 285n28
Hoover, Herbert, 60–61
Hovenkamp, Herbert, 30, 109, 267n3
Hub-and-spoke conspiracy. *See* Conspiracy

Individualism, 28, 30–31, 43, 45–46, 56, 62, 207–208
Industrial revolution (American), 23, 43, 45, 51, 55, 58, 69, 256
Industrial revolution (British), 44
Inequality, 38, 53, 144, 158, 254, 258, 263
Information: cultural value, 8, 38, 142–144, 147–148, 150, 153–160; in economics generally, 35–36, 240–244, 263; as a good, 213–219, 263; in vertical restraints economics, 66
Ingram, 173
Institutional economics, 44, 54
Internet Archive, 162–163, 169
Interstate Commerce Commission, 73
Invisible hand, 35
iPad, 102, 176, 181–182, 184, 186–187, 191–193, 222–223, 231
iPod, 133, 175–178

Iron cage, 8
iTunes, 133–136, 175–178, 185, 190–191

Jackson, Andrew, 28, 259
Jackson, Thomas Penfield, 200
Jacksonian politics, 56, 259
Jacobs, Dennis, 197–198
Jesus tablet, 102
Jobber. *See* Distribution (of goods)
Jobs, Steve: and *Apple* conspiracy, 1, 181, 185–186, 187, 189–192, 196; and the digital revolution, 133–135, 141, 175, 184; and innovation, 103, 157; personal history, 134–135, 185, 200
Johnson, Hugh, 275n8
Just price, theory of, 31

Kahle, Brewster, 162, 169
Kay, Alan, 157, 170, 185, 297nn21–22
Kelly, Kevin, 145, 241
Kindle, 77, 95, 97, 128, 130, 161, 164, 180; history, 150, 171–179, 242; and predatory price, 231; significance, 140, 147, 171–177; vis-à-vis printed books, 201–202; vis-à-vis the iPad, 176, 191; vis-à-vis the publishers, 141, 177–179, 186–187
Kmart, 100, 104
Knopf, Alfred (individual), 86, 95–96
Kobo, 173, 193
Korda, Michael, 78, 95, 247

Labor: antitrust labor exemption, 21; as a concern in competition policy, 5, 210, 254–259; history, 44, 46, 58–59
Lady Chatterly's Lover, 87
Lagardère, 285n28
Legal realism, 54
Letwin, William, 32
Liberalism: classical, 28–30, 32, 45–46; corporate, 45–46
Liberty, 56, 69, 209
LIBRIé, 173
Lincoln, Abraham, 57, 87
Lippmann, Walter, 70
Liveright, Horace, 84–85, 87
Lochnerism, 38

Macmillan (UK), 81, 123, 192
Macmillan (US), 88, 105, 107, 192, 252
Macmillian, Frederick, 105, 123, 192
Manber, Udi, 164–165, 167
Marginal cost, 58–59, 215–216, 231, 233, 288n5
Marginalism, 44–54, 55–58, 123
Marginal utility, 48–50, 52–53
Marketplace of ideas, 37
Market power, 36, 41, 110–112, 117, 208, 249
Marshall, Alfred, 123
Means, Gardiner, 54
Mercantilism, 30, 33
Merger, 42, 44, 64, 71, 78, 84, 88–91, 95, 119, 210, 248, 264
Methodenstreit, 53–54
MFN. *See* Most-favored-nation
Microsoft, 172, 206–207, 224–225
Microsoft, United States v., 200, 224–225
Miller-Tydings Act, 117–119, 120, 125, 210
Mitchell, Wesley, 54
MIT Media Lab, 173, 242
Moerer, Keith, 185
Monitor remedy, 200
Monopolization. *See* Sherman Act: section 2
Most-favored-nation, 63, 189–191, 193, 222
Murdoch, James, 187, 189, 191
Murdoch, Rupert, 92–93, 187, 285n28
Music, 128, 130, 132–137, 139, 140–141, 168, 175–176, 183–184, 190, 200, 222

Nader, Ralph, 9, 238
National Association of Securities Dealers, United States v., 73
National Conference of Commissioners on Uniform State Laws, 58
National Industrial Recovery Act, 30, 46, 60–62, 117–118, 261
National Recovery Administration, 61, 117
Neal, Phil, 42
Neal Commission, 42
Nelson, Theodore, 155–157, 170
Neoclassical economics. *See* Marginalism
Network effects, 223–225
New Deal, 59, 61, 70, 119, 261–262

New Press, 87
News Corp, 187, 285n28
Newspaper, 39, 80, 99, 226, 245
Newspaper Preservation Act, 270n14
New York Times, 4
Nixon, Richard, 114, 119
"Nobody knows" problem, 214, 239
No-fault monopoly, 41–42, 238, 245
Nourry, Arnaud, 190
Numerosity, 33–34, 38–39
NuvoMedia, 171, 174

Ocean shipping, 12, 56, 73, 254–256
Open price association, 61
Optical character recognition, 165
Optical scanning, 163
Optical writing, 153
Organizational synthesis, 46
Orphan works, 161–162
Overdrive, 172–173

Palo Alto Research Center, 173, 297n22
Pantheon Books, 84, 88, 91, 94
Papyrus, 150–152
Paradox of water and diamonds, 32, 48–49, 272n12
PARC. *See* Palo Alto Research Center
Parchment, 150–152, 296n2
Pearson, 88, 285n28
Penguin, 88, 91, 286n48
Penguin Random House, 88, 285n28
Per se rule, 20–23, 64–65, 71, 108, 113, 120, 126, 182–184, 194–197, 234
Platform economics, 224–227
Player piano, 12, 138–139
Populism, 5, 198, 259
Predatory pricing, 228–235
Price fixing, 2, 13, 20–23, 56, 74; in agriculture, 73; in books, 78, 82, 92, 105–106, 121–127; horizontal, 187; in securities, 72; vertical, 64–68, 112–118
Progressive era, 30, 59, 62, 70, 119, 198
Progressive politics, 6, 13, 254, 264
Project Gutenberg, 157–162, 164
Project Xanadu, 155–156
Property, 28, 32, 37, 207–208
Public Utility Holding Company Act, 42

Quality-adjusted price, 34, 131, 222–223

Rakuten, 173
Random House, 77, 84, 85–88, 91, 94, 96,
    171–173, 180, 186, 193, 285n28, 286n48
Rationality, 54, 66, 208, 230, 240
Readies, The, 152–153
RealNetworks, 134
Redstone, Sumner, 285n28
Reidy, Carolyn, 192
Resale price maintenance. *See* Price fixing:
    vertical
Retail. *See* Distribution (of goods)
Rio music player, 133
RioPort, 134
Rives, Hallie Erminie, 125
Robinson-Patman Act, 100–101, 117–118,
    208, 258
Rocketbook, 171, 174–175
Romanticism, 44, 53
Roosevelt, Franklin, 61, 125, 261–262
Roosevelt, Theodore, 138
Ross, Dorothy, 32
Rosset, Barney, 87
Ruinous competition. *See* Destructive
    competition

Saper, Craig, 153
Sargent, John, 192
Satyricon, 87
Saul, Kevin, 185, 188–189
Schiffrin André, 87, 94
Schumer, Charles, 267n6
Schuster, Max, 85
Scottish Enlightenment, 33
Sea of doubt, 23
Securities and Exchange Commission,
    39, 72
Securities regulation, 60, 72, 304n40
Sensenbrenner, James, 69–70
Shain, Barry Alan, 56
Sheet music, 138
Shenefield report, 70
Sherman Act, 22–24, 29, 32, 37, 40, 205,
    209, 257; section 1, 41, 74, 193, 197,
    235–236; section 2, 12, 41, 193–194
Simon, Herbert, 54

Simon, Richard, 85
Simon & Schuster, 78, 84–86, 88, 91, 101,
    107, 171–172, 192, 284n28, 286n48
Smith, Adam, 33
Socialism, 28, 46, 62
Social science, 17–18, 32, 46, 51, 77, 96, 211
SoftBook, 171, 175
Sonny Bono Copyright Term Extension
    Act, 159, 163
Stack, Charles, 103
Stacked, 93
Standard setting, 46, 58, 62
Steam power, 12, 255–256
Stevens, John Paul, 24, 26
Stone, Brad, 174
Substantive due process, 38
Surface Transportation Board, 73

Tablet, 102, 157, 184–185, 222, 224
Taft, William Howard, 22–24, 51
Taraporevala, Russi Jal, 121
Taylor, Frederick, 8, 46
Taylorism. *See* Frederick Taylor
Telser, Lester, 65–67, 114, 227
Ticknor & Fields, 81, 86–87
Times book war, 92
Trade courtesy, 57, 82–83, 182
Trademark, 115, 116, 240, 244
Transaction cost, 35
Tropic of Cancer, 87
Two-sided markets. *See* Platform
    economics

Ulysses, 87
United States v. Addyston Pipe & Steel Co.,
    22–24, 51
United States v. Microsoft, 200, 224–225
*United States v. National Association of
    Securities Dealers,* 73
Utilitarianism, 48, 53
Utility, 48–52
Utility regulation, 30, 60, 62, 70, 119

VCR. *See* Video cassette recorder
Veblen, Thorstein, 54
VHS. *See* Video cassette recorder

Video, 128, 130, 137, 140–141, 180, 200, 224
Video cassette recorder, 224

Waldenbooks, 78, 99, 104, 251
Wall Street Journal, 4, 192
Walmart, 100, 104, 106, 258–259
Wealth of Nations, The, 33, 56
Weber, Max, 8
Welfare (economic concept), 48, 207–208,
   239
Welfare (public assistance), 62, 259

Wholesale. *See* Distribution (of goods)
Willingness to pay, 50, 254
World War I, 257
World War II, 29, 72, 154, 262
World wide web, 103, 147, 155, 157

Xerox, 173

Yamey, Basil, 121
Yuen, Henry, 175